Plunder, Profit, and Paroles

Plunder, Profit, and Paroles

*A Social History
of the War of 1812
in Upper Canada*

GEORGE SHEPPARD

McGill-Queen's University Press
Montreal & Kingston • London • Buffalo

© McGill-Queen's University Press 1994
ISBN 0-7735-1137-7

Legal deposit first quarter 1994
Bibliothèque nationale du Québec

Printed in Canada on acid-free paper

This book has been published with the help of a
grant from the Social Science Federation of Canada,
using funds provided by the Social Sciences and
Humanities Research Council of Canada.

Canadian Cataloguing in Publication Data

Sheppard, George Christopher, 1959–
  Plunder, profit, and paroles: a social history of the
  War of 1812 in Upper Canada
  Includes bibliographical references and index.
  ISBN 0-7735-1137-7
  1. Canada – History – War of 1812 – Social aspects.
  2. Canada – Social conditions – 1763–1867. I. Title.
  FC442.S54 1994   971.03'4   C93-090479-6
  E359.85.S54 1994

Typeset in Baskerville 10/12 by
Caractéra production graphique inc., Quebec City.

For Elalie, Kim, and Maude

Contents

Tables, Maps, and Figures

Acknowledgments

The staff at the National Archives in Ottawa and the Archives of Ontario in Toronto have been very helpful. So too were employees at the Baldwin Room in the Metropolitan Toronto Library and in the interlibrary loan department at McMaster University. Thanks also to Margaret Houghton at the Hamilton Public Library's Special Collections, to Bill Yeager from the Norfolk Historical Society's Eva Brook Donly Museum, to Carl Benn and Aldona Sendzikas at Fort York, and to David Cook and Carol Mazur in the government documents section of McMaster's Mills Library.

The last few years of research were made possible by a doctoral fellowship from the Social Sciences and Humanities Research Council of Canada and by scholarships from McMaster University and the Ontario government. And, as my spouse is fond of noting, none of this would have been possible without Kim Sheppard's having gone to nursing school so we didn't starve while I conducted research and scraped together cash from various contract teaching positions.

Peter Blaney, the acquisitions editor at McGill-Queen's University Press, proved to be a reliable source of information and wise counsel when it was most needed. John Knox helped with the computer programming, René Roy gave up a weekend to scrutinize some of the calculations involved, and Donald Graves took the time to read the original dissertation and then did his best to explain concepts of military history to a social historian.

Over the last four years, this manuscript has been read, in whole or in part, by about a dozen other people who offered advice and criticism. C.M. Johnson, Richard Rempel, David Russo, T.R. Hobbs, G.R. Purdy, and George Rawlyck all mulled over, and occasionally mauled, some of the book's weaker points. Above all, thanks go to John Weaver, who suggested the area of inquiry and then offered guidance and support throughout the process of research and writing. Finally, the three anonymous readers for the Social Science Federation of Canada offered painstaking appraisals of the manuscript's strengths and deficiencies.

It seems customary at this point to say that all the good parts of the work are a result of my critics' efforts and that any mistakes that remain are my fault. I really want to break with tradition on this matter and note that if these various experts failed to point out the errors, then they should accept some of the blame. But I can't do that, because I made only those changes that appeared to me to be fair and reasonable, and rejected a few I thought were off the mark. So a "nineties version" of the old standard will have to do. This book is a much better product because of the efforts of my readers. I blame my parents for any shortcomings.

Plunder, Profit, and Paroles

1 Introduction

This book is about the War of 1812 in Upper Canada. It differs from other accounts of this period in that it focuses on how the conflict affected the people in the colony. It shows that the population was deeply divided before the war and explains why so many Upper Canadians wanted nothing to do with the fighting. It illustrates how the majority of men in the province avoided serving in the struggle and discusses why labour and food had to be coerced from the population. This book also shows how the fighting affected various regions in very different ways and reveals how the legacy of the war complicated colonial politics. Finally, it deals with how the conflict contributed to the maturation of the colony and to the development of Canadian nationalism. While these topics have sometimes been addressed by other historians, the treatment has often been superficial. Most accounts of the War of 1812 consist of detailed reports of military campaigning, and the impact of the fighting is rarely addressed. In general, most writers have been reluctant to admit that the war was in any way injurious to the colony. Typically, the conflict is seen as a boon to the economy, a stamp that impressed a British character on the province, and a "crucial step in the emergence of an undefended border."[1]

Many of these ideas date back to the nineteenth century, when writers were especially fond of claiming that colonists had been responsible for the successful defence of the province.[2] Egerton Ryerson, the "father of the Ontario school system," believed that the fighting had created a united populace. In 1880 he wrote that it had forced colonists of various backgrounds to forget "former distinctions and jealousies" so they might fight "as one man in defence of the country." In Ryerson's works the exploits of the Upper Canadians, like those of the warriors of ancient Greece, assumed epic proportions: "The Spartan bands of Canadian Loyalist volunteers, aided by a few hundred English soldiers and civilized Indians, repelled the Persian thousands of democratic American invaders, and maintained the virgin soil of Canada unpolluted by the foot of the plundering invader."[3] One of the descendants of those "Loyalist volunteers," Matilda Ridout Edgar, also believed every Canadian should be aware of the role played by the militia. She suggested that anyone seeking a sense of national pride look no farther than the actions of the "brave little band of heroes" who had "saved the land in its hour of need."[4]

Most of these nineteenth-century writers relied on the public pronouncements of wartime officials for information about the conflict without being aware that such statements were part of a propaganda campaign designed to distort the truth.[5] Many of these early chroniclers were also of Loyalist background, and at its most basic level the maintenance of the legend that citizen-soldiers "saved" Upper Canada was a form of ancestor worship.[6] By asserting that it was the colonists who threw back the American invaders, these writers proclaimed their forefathers' heroism. On one level, the facts seemed to speak for themselves. In 1812 large American armies had invaded a province defended by fewer than 2000 regular troops. In almost every battle the militia played some role, and its contributions were regularly praised by British commanders. In the end, the American armies fell back, having failed in their attempt to conquer the colony. By noting only those obvious skeletal points, writers such as Jennie McConnell, a member of the Women's Canadian Historical Society of Ottawa, could announce that the militia "came out of the war covered with glory."[7]

Less exaggerated accounts of the role of the militia have been written in more recent years. In 1958 military historian C.P. Stacey bluntly told a meeting of the Ontario Historical Society that "the chief credit for the saving of Canada in 1812 is due to British soldiers."[8] Five years later, G.F.G. Stanley, the deputy director of the Canadian Army's Historical Section, provided further proof that the successful defence of the province was due to trained regular soldiers. At the same time, however, both historians argued that the actions of the citizen-soldiers should not be considered less valuable. Stanley, for instance, said that the militia played an important part in the contest by transporting provisions, constructing fortifications, and providing fighting men, especially during the first year of war. Unfortunately, like their predecessors, Stanley and Stacey also failed to note that those who took an active part in the war were not typical Upper Canadians. By continuing to focus only on those who did serve during the struggle, Canadian historians have missed the point that voluntary service was aberrant behaviour. Stanley and others who have discussed the role of the militia have also maintained the fiction that the defeat of the American invasions "proves both the activity and efficiency of the aid rendered."[9] A closer examination of wartime events suggests otherwise. Most Upper Canadian males, although obligated to fight, did not do so. The squads of volunteers and those forced to do their duty, while sometimes useful, could rarely be relied upon for more than a few days at a time. Many inhabitants exhibited little enthusiasm to shoulder arms and, as we shall see, they employed an amazing array of excuses and tricks to evade military service.

Discussions of the financial effects of the war have also suffered from partisan examination. In 1900, for instance, McConnell spoke only of the disastrous impact the fighting had on the economy of the United States. With a note of satisfaction, she observed that American foreign trade had been ruined and that their merchant marine was destroyed by the British navy.[10] In 1913 Adam Shortt offered the first assessment of the economic effect of the struggle on Canada. One of the earliest Canadian historians to employ empirical methods, Shortt observed that the war years represented the "greatest era of prosperity" ever enjoyed by Upper Canada until the 1860s. He did acknowledge that there were certain drawbacks to this exceptional period and he felt that some people were unequipped to deal with their new-found wealth, so "drunkenness and other forms of vice flourished." All the same, he said that the use of army bills during the conflict served only to benefit the province. This "efficient and reliable" currency made people accustomed to cash transactions. Thus, according to Shortt, when the war ended the inhabitants were in a "proper frame of mind for the establishment of banks."[11]

The army bills have been described by other writers as a "financial triumph," since they "cracked the psychological barrier" that the inhabitants had put up against paper money.[12] In general, later historians have followed Shortt's view of the economic impact of the war, but have been even more prone to gloss over any harmful effects. While some might refer to the dislocation of business in certain areas, all agree that heavy British expenditures more than compensated for such isolated occurrences.[13] Bray Hammond, in a 1967 monograph on banking in Canada before Confederation, wrote that the gains to the provincial economy were "immediate and unqualified." The only exception to this rule was along the New York border, where "the housewives suffered some loss of teaspoons ... to the ungentlemanly invader."[14] Most researchers suggest that the benefits of wartime spending continued to be felt long after the nuisance of silverware raids had ended, and the economy is usually depicted as remaining bouyant until 1819. At that point, historians say the province began to feel the first effects of a worldwide depression.[15] On the whole, however, the conflict has been depicted as a "virtual godsend," and A.R.M. Lower went so far as to say that the economy of "all of Canada benefited from the War of 1812."[16]

These assessments of the financial effects of the war are simply inaccurate, and some writers have relied exclusively on versions of the war written by officials and merchants stationed at York or Kingston.[17] These accounts, however, do not present a complete picture of the conflict, and colonists in other regions that were the site of pitched battles saw no "immediate and unqualified" benefits. Eventually, more than two thousand war sufferers would submit claims for losses incurred during the fighting, and for many of them the long delays in payment spelled financial ruin. In economic terms, the colony was in no way prepared to deal with the legacy of war; the Upper Canadian government simply did not have the means to assist the victims of the fighting. Widows and orphans, the disabled and homeless, saw no benefit from the expenditure of funds on military projects, and the money borrowed to pay pensions and compensation for victims of the conflict eventually contributed to the complete bankruptcy of the colony.[18] Nor was it destruction of some mysterious psychological barrier that led to the widespread use of banknotes in the postwar period.[19] The recession that followed in the wake of the departing British troopships was so severe that the colony was forced to send all its hard currency out of the province to pay debts. Reduced government spending, as well as wartime losses and a declining population, brought the threat of a major economic collapse in 1817.[20] Because of that insolvency, Upper Canadians had no choice but to create a new medium of exchange.

The conflict also changed the political atmosphere of the province. As early as 1880, Ryerson noted that "elements of discord" had begun to appear after the cessation of hostilities. He attributed this strife to the numerous appointments of discharged British officers to positions formerly occupied by Loyalists.[21] That oversimplified explanation of postwar discontent has not been greatly expanded on by other writers. Over one hundred years later, for instance, Stanley would point to issues that arose out of the war, but he offered no explanation on how these "seeds of political discontent" served to complicate provincial affairs.[22] Still other writers have commented on the emergence of a permanent opposition in the Legislative Assembly by 1818, without explaining why this development occurred.[23] If the topic of postwar politics is raised, the tendency has been to focus on the alien question, which proved to be one of the most explosive political issues to emerge out of the conflict. But this concentration on the dispute over the rights of American residents in the 1820s has meant that discussions about war claims, pensions, and other grievances related to the conflict are difficult to find even in works devoted to postwar politics.[24] Only Ernest Cruikshank and W.R. Riddell ever attempted to link postwar discontent to political issues, and they restricted their writing to articles.[25]

The war spawned many controversies, but the role of those issues in making colonial politics more complex after 1815 has yet to be fully recognized. J.K. Johnson, for example, has recently declared that the war's "ripple effect" produced an "anti-democratic, pro-establishment" reaction in the Assembly which did not begin to subside until 1824.[26] Yet in the immediate postwar period, long before the alien question became a topic for popular discussion, disputes emerged over militia pay, pensions, land grants, and medals, and particularly over immigration restrictions and compensation for property losses. The first concrete expression of widespread dissatisfaction was evident as early as 1817, when the elected Assembly denounced the administration's mishandling of colonial affairs. The postwar "pro-establishment" attitude of legislators had ended by 1817, and British appointees were forced to prorogue the Assembly in order to stifle criticism. With official efforts to address grievances suppressed, hundreds of colonists who harboured serious concerns about the future of the province turned to another champion – Robert Gourlay.[27] Although this Scottish immigrant has sometimes been portrayed as a mere "gadfly" who arrived in the province and then stirred up trouble, that is too simplistic an appraisal.[28] Many settlers in postwar Upper Canada had real cause for complaint, and Gourlay harnessed this popular discontent. An analysis of the membership of his movement shows that only a minority of his supporters were war sufferers; the claims for losses, however, formed a central part of Gourlay's plans for reforming the colonial administration. The "Banished Briton's" agitation, with his use of a popular convention and his attacks on the structure of government, also represented a real departure in Upper Canadian politics.

Gourlay's expulsion from the colony in 1819, and the simultaneous repression of many of his followers, led directly to the election of nine "Gourlayite" reformers the next year. These members of the eighth parliament (1820–4), along with other oppositionists such as Robert Nichol, often argued with the administration over the handling of pensions, land grants, and other war-related items. Assemblymen who were elected to subsequent parliaments faced one war issue – the claims for damages – that seemed nearly impossible to resolve. In 1823 the British government declared it would pay only a portion of the value of the claims, and it pressed the province to make its own contribution. From then on, the losses ceased to be a "reform" issue, and disputes over the claims transcended nascent party boundaries.[29] Although representatives struggled with the problem quite often, members of the Assembly could not even agree on who was really responsible for the damages. Some radical reformers argued that the colony had too few means to pay for old damages as well as new improvements, and they felt the British should reimburse the sufferers. Others, including moderate reformers and most conservatives, believed the province was obliged to pay part of the compensation. Because of the difficulties associated with this issue, William Lyon Mackenzie was driven to say that it was the "most puzzling question" ever to emerge in colonial politics. Full restitution was not made until 1837. The decision to repay the sufferers in that year contributed to the bankruptcy of the colony. The financial embarrassment of the provincial treasury was one of the reasons why Upper Canada accepted a union with Lower Canada in 1840.

Despite the political unrest that was spawned by the fighting, most writers have claimed that the War of 1812 brought a new sense of unity to British North America. Just after the Union Act of 1840, for example, war veteran John Richardson announced that the conflict had really "knit together" the French and English races. Later, Ryerson claimed that within the colony the war had served to "cement the people together" so that all "classes were Loyalists."[30] Many others have asserted that the fighting led to a wave of anti-American sentiment throughout the province.[31] That attitude led to the turning back of immigrants from the United States and prompted a renewed sense of loyalty to the British tie which enabled the so-called Family Compact to rule over the province for more than a generation.[32]

There is evidence which suggests these views are unsound. Far from uniting British North Americans, the war actually created new divisions. Some Upper Canadians, for instance, argued that they had been left to fight the "arduous and unequal contest" by themselves, while Lower Canadians "hardly felt the pressure of war."[33] That same sense of resentment was sometimes directed towards fellow Upper Canadians, particularly against residents of York and Kingston, who had managed to stay home and profit by the war. Likewise, the idea that the fighting automatically intensified anti-American feeling among all segments of the population has already been called into question by Jane Errington. As she has pointed out, most early Upper Canadians were actually "Americans"; it seems likely that a simple hatred of all things related to the United States was a sentiment primarily restricted to members of the ruling clique at York.[34] An investigation of the war claims may help explain why the fighting actually did little to increase anti-American sentiment. Almost half of all wartime plundering incidents were blamed on British troops or their Indian allies. For hundreds of ordinary colonists, members of the imperial forces, not soldiers of the invading army, were the real enemies in this war.

As to the turning back of Americans, most elected representatives of the Upper Canadian population favoured an "open-door" immigration policy because many pioneers were counting on land sales to recoup losses suffered during three years of fighting. The failure of British officials to heed this advice contributed to the postwar economic depression; the vacuum created was not immediately filled by immigrants from Britain and the provincial population actually began to decline in 1817. Hundreds of well-to-do farmers who might have moved to the province in that year, when it really needed settlers, were forced to go to the Ohio region instead. As well, the decision to exclude Americans in the immediate postwar period did not automatically make Upper Canada more "loyal," since thousands of Americans entered the colony anyway in the 1820s and 1830s.[35] By that time, the province had missed a crucial opportunity and the area that later British newcomers settled in was far less prosperous and stable than it might have been.[36] The 1815 decision to exclude immigrants from the United States certainly did not make colonial politics any less acrimonious. Within two years the immigration issue led to serious divisions between appointive and elective elements in the government, and it was the main reason why the Assembly was prorogued in 1817. Finally, it should be remembered that in the ranks of the newcomers from Britain were volatile individuals like Gourlay and Mackenzie.

The war eventually contributed to the "knitting together" of Canadians, but that did not occur until the 1840s when the detrimental aspects of the conflict were less apparent. As old veterans passed away, the first-hand knowledge of hardship, jealousy, and disaffection was replaced by a new appreciation of the war. Colonists who had entered the conflict with no conception of a shared nationality discovered years later that the war offered all inhabitants a past that was worth remembering. The cult of Brock worship and the militia myth had little to do with the reality of the war, but they did lead to the flowering of Upper Canadian nationalism. Ironically, that development may have been hastened because some real heroes of the war, men who had fought for years in flank companies and in the Incorporated Militia, were deprived of the recognition they deserved. Left without suitable heroes to worship, many Upper Canadians were willing to believe that all had done their duty and that every inhabitant had stood shoulder to shoulder with Isaac Brock.

As noted above, those developments have never been adequately examined because most twentieth-century works dealing with the War of 1812 have been restricted to discussions of various campaigns. Over the last half-century, military history has been studied in dramatically different ways. Prior to the 1950s, most military historians produced simple "battle pieces" that focused on the strategy of generals or on the successful tactics behind decisive encounters.[37] Most popular histories of war are still "drum and trumpet" chronologies of various battles, and most of the recent Canadian writing on the War of 1812 follows that path.[38] After the Second World War, however, an increasing number of American and British researchers abandoned those conventions and started to examine war in a different way. These new military historians did not discuss operations or tactics but instead wrote social accounts of armies, organizational and institutional histories, and even psychohistories of participants. Some of these works never dealt with campaigns at all, and a few researchers were accused of having almost written "combat out of military history."[39] But those sorts of inquiries eventually spawned other studies. Practitioners of this newer brand of history have attempted to bridge the gap between the two other versions by considering not only how wars are waged and how battles are fought, but also by examining armies and campaigns in terms of their impact on social and economic structures. Rather than dealing only with tactics and operations, these historians have analysed diet and health, wounds and their treatment, the taking of prisoners, provisioning and plundering, and the importance of logistical considerations. In many cases these researchers attempt to document the lives of ordinary men in combat as well as the way civilians are affected by war.[40]

This study has been influenced by those recent shifts in historical research. While mention is made of generals and strategy, this book also examines how the War of 1812 influenced the social and economic structures of Upper Canada. The chapters that follow deal with enlistment and the taking of prisoners, desertion and casualty rates, conflicts between civilians and the military, treason and sedition, profiteering, and the financial and political repercussions of the fighting. In addition to printed collections of primary and secondary sources, I have utilized garrison records, muster rolls, diaries, and pension lists. The records of the various war-claims commissions have been consulted for an examination of plundering and provisioning. A computer-based analysis of the data from the final 1823–6 committee of revision, using the Statistical Package for the Social Sciences (SPSS[x]), has revealed who took what from whom, and it indicates how and when the losses occurred.[41] For the postwar period, I have relied on Assembly debates, newspapers, and the correspondence between colonial officials and their superiors in Britain.

Chapter 2 deals with prewar Upper Canada. Emphasis is placed on the divided, self-absorbed nature of colonial society. The next two chapters discuss militia participation and reveal that the fragmented and pre-modern character of early Upper Canada was reflected in an apathetic response to militia mobilization. As a result, participation on either side remained the preserve of a small number of colonists. Next, chapter 5 deals with provisioning, plundering, and a consideration of military diets and the conduct of combatants. Requisitioning, looting, and the punitive destruction of property were engaged in by both friendly and enemy forces, but the majority of losses were sustained by residents in the Niagara area and the western regions of the province. The response of civilians in the colony to the perils and possibilities offered by the war form the subject of chapter 6. As was the case with militia service, Upper Canadians were reluctant to assist the military by supplying inexpensive goods to the commissariat; eventually, martial law had to be imposed to ensure that the British army did not starve. Merchants in the villages of Kingston and York appear to have benefited most from military expenditures, but inhabitants throughout the province sought to better their economic circumstances through both legal and illegal activities.

Chapter 7 chronicles the events of the immediate postwar period and shows that many of the political and economic crises of that time can be directly related to events that took place during the conflict. The development of an opposition group within the Assembly, and the severe depression that gripped the colony for almost a decade, were both spurred on by the destruction and dislocation of trade and industry which occurred between 1812 and 1815. Chapter 8 traces the quest for war-losses compensation, which lasted until 1837, and shows how the legacy of war contributed to the economic downturn of that year. Finally, chapter 9 deals with the changing perceptions of the war. The view that the conflict was a "blessing in disguise" originated with a select group of colonial officials and merchants, but, by the middle of the nineteenth century, it became the accepted version of wartime events. By ignoring the truth, the descendants of the early pioneers created a past that promoted unity and a sense of common purpose. This provincial patriotism, in turn, served as a fertile field for the growth of a variety of Canadian nationalism that was cultivated by writers such as Egerton Ryerson and Jennie McConnell. Their works often owed little to the real events of the war, but their writings proved attractive to generations of readers.

For the colonists who lived through the war, the fighting presented opportunities as well as dangers. Admittedly, good profits could be secured from supplying the military garrisons, but all those gains might be wiped out in a moment if their property fell prey to marauding bands of troops from either side. Militia service offered enthusiasts a chance to feel they were participating in events of great importance. Of course, it also carried with it the possibility of crippling injuries or premature death. The memories of those days remained fresh in the minds of the inhabitants for years to come. According to John Howison, a British writer who visited the province after the conflict, Upper Canadians referred to every event as having "happened before or after the war."[42] Even without embellishment, the story of how the colonists responded to invasion remains exciting. One finds real people with recognizable fears and dreams attempting to make the best of very trying times.

2 "A Motley Population": Prewar Upper Canada

In the fall of 1811 Isaac Brock was a troubled British officer and part of his anxiety stemmed from concern over his career. In October he had been appointed administrator of Upper Canada, but, as a professional soldier, his real desire was to be stationed elsewhere. While men half his age were serving with Lord Wellington on European battlefields, the forty-two-year-old officer felt he had been "placed high on a shelf" in a distant corner of the empire.[1] Still, the posting had potential for some excitement. Just after Brock had been installed as administrator, a "great comet" had streaked across the northern sky and a number of observers in the colony were sure it portended some sort of "harm" for the province.[2] A few nervous colonists even thought the celestial occurrence was proof they would soon face invasion from the south. President James Madison had recently recommended an increase in the army and in military matériel, and other signs pointed to an imminent invasion as part of the larger quarrel between Britain and the United States. As commander of the military forces of Upper Canada, Brock was charged with the responsibility of turning any intruders back. If he succeeded he might acquire the recognition he so earnestly desired.

Defeating an American invasion, however, would not be an easy task. Brock had fewer than 2000 regular troops to defend a frontier over 1200 miles long. On the British side of the border a tiny population of some 80,000 was spread over a territory amounting to nearly ten million acres.[3] Worse yet, few of those inhabitants seemed to share their leader's determination to engage the Americans in

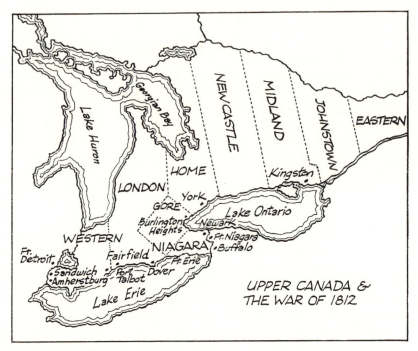

Map 1   Upper Canada and the War of 1812
Drawing by Cy Morris

battle. It was not that the majority of colonists were disloyal, just uninterested. On taking over the administration of Upper Canada in October 1811, Brock found himself commanding a province that in many respects appeared more American than British. A majority of the inhabitants had only recently arrived from the United States, a fact that had led some American politicians to argue that the conquest of Upper Canada would be a "matter perfectly easy." Only three years earlier, a British spy had reported that Washington strategists were counting "much on the disposition of the Canadians as friendly to them. They reckon also, on a ready welcome from a number of Americans who have of late years become Settlers in Upper Canada."[4]

For a number of reasons, however, the conquest of Canada would not be "a mere matter of marching."[5] First, Upper Canada was defended by well-trained redcoats, while the United States army, for the most part, was undisciplined and poorly led. Second, in Isaac Brock, the province had a brilliant strategist who knew precisely what actions would best prevent a successful takeover. Brock recognized that most inhabitants were determined to avoid military service and, if possible, stay out of any conflict altogether. So, in order to "animate the Loyal and controul the disaffected," he decided to strike at the enemy as soon as possible.[6] Finally, even more than American unpreparedness or Brock's competent leadership, the ambivalence of the Upper Canadian population would help to defeat the enemy. Although most colonists had little regard for Britain, it did not follow that they would actively support an invasion of their territory. Upper Canada was home to a very pragmatic populace. For most, their first concern was self-preservation, not necessarily allegiance to king or president. Their next desire was to protect their property. Francis Gore, Brock's predecessor, had recognized those truths some four years before war began. In 1808 Gore wrote to Sir James Craig that in the event of a protracted conflict, British forces would have to surrender the province and retreat to Quebec. He urged that this plan should be "carefully concealed from Persons of almost every description in this colony," for if the inhabitants suspected that Britain was prepared to abandon Upper Canada, no militiaman would serve. Most colonists would fight only if their lives and property were at risk. As Gore noted: "There are few people here that would act with Energy, were it not for the purpose of defending the lands they actually possess."[7]

Upper Canada in 1811 bore little resemblance to the well-ordered, self-sufficient, British community envisioned by its first lieutenant-governor. Twenty years earlier, John Graves Simcoe, a veteran soldier and member of parliament, had arrived in the colony after a "blustery passage" aboard the HMS *Triton*.[8] He was determined to build a province that would be the "perfect Image and Transcript" of Britain, and his ideal society was to be made up of happy yeoman united by their common loyalty to the crown. These subjects would follow the dictates of their clergymen, shoulder arms when required, and elect only those representatives who could work harmoniously with the provincial administration. By the time Simcoe made his appearance in Upper Canada, however, some 20,000 settlers were already established in the province and, while many were British subjects, they were not "British" in the sense that Simcoe would have preferred.[9] The greater part of them were Americans, and very few of these settlers were communicants of the Church of England. Some of them exhibited that non-deferential attitude towards authority for which Americans were famous; of those who expressed an interest in politics, the majority appeared to desire the familiar, more democratic systems of their pre-revolutionary American homes. Simcoe was aware of these facts, but he remained convinced that such individuals could be moulded into the proper material. Under his guiding hand,

Simcoe thought that the inhabitants of Upper Canada would eventually learn "British Customs, Manners & Principles."[10] In short, he
believed the foundation would adapt itself to the structure imposed
upon it.

Tucked away in Simcoe's battered baggage was a document which
contained the rough outline of that edifice. The Constitutional Act
of 1791 was intended to provide Upper Canadians with the same
"Peace, Welfare, and Good Government" supposedly enjoyed by
Britons at home. The framework for this new administration involved
both appointive and democratic elements, and the document had
been drafted by British officials who were determined to avoid the
mistakes of the past. It was believed that the American Revolution
had occurred, in large measure, because the democratic arms of the
colonial legislatures had grown too powerful.[11] There would be no
repetition of that error in Upper Canada. The architects of the act
hoped that the stabilizing influence of appointed officials and an
established church would prevent another rebellion from occurring.
Under the Constitutional Act, the lieutenant-governor, as the representative of the crown, was empowered to appoint no fewer than
seven "discreet and proper Persons" to an upper or Legislative
Council. These councillors were expected to help the lieutenant-
governor, or administrator of the province, initiate and pass legislation. Provision had also been made for an Executive Council, which
eventually became a very important body. Members of this select
group took on the role of advisers to the lieutenant-governor and,
in private sessions, they helped formulate administrative policy.
Under these two councils was to be a Legislative Assembly composed
of sixteen members elected by their fellow subjects. The power of
this body was quite limited; it could only block measures introduced
by the upper house by refusing to vote money required for implementation or by amending bills so they bore little resemblance to the
original proposals. At the same time, however, legislation that originated in the Assembly could be vetoed by either the Legislative
Council or the lieutenant-governor. Like most British officials who
had first-hand knowledge of the American Revolution, John Graves
Simcoe believed that such restrictions were necessary. The "checking
of the Elective Principle," either through the use of appointments or
executive power, would help ensure their continued control of the
province.[12]

The Constitutional Act also empowered the lieutenant-governor to
set aside lands for the "Support and Maintenance of a Protestant
Clergy" in the province, but the exact intent of that provision was
unclear. Simcoe and most British officials supposed that the reserves

were for the sole use of the colonial Church of England and that "Protestant" did not include Presbyterians or any other sect. The next year Simcoe was also authorized to set aside a further share of the colony's land as a source of revenue for the government. These clergy and crown reserves, as they became known, accounted for two-sevenths of the land in each township. With one-seventh of the surveyed land in the province reserved for Protestant clergy, it was hoped that the Church of England would thrive. Similarly, the crown lands were expected to eliminate the need for burdensome taxes since parcels could be sold whenever extra income was required by the government. Revenue from the sale or lease of these reserves was also considered a form of insurance. With the money raised from that land, the British administrators of the colony were expected to be freed from any reliance on the Assembly. If assemblymen chose to block an unpopular piece of legislation by refusing to vote funds, the administration could use the proceeds from the crown reserves to implement the measure without the Assembly's approval.[13]

Simcoe and other officials believed the Constitutional Act would prompt newcomers to become loyal subjects of the crown, but such expectations were to prove exceedingly naïve. One of the few mechanisms for assimilation available to colonial authorities – the oath of allegiance – could be mumbled through or avoided altogether, if the settler so desired. For most immigrants it was a trivial formality that was performed in order to acquire property. In 1799 Richard Cartwright said that many of his neighbours in eastern Upper Canada had little affection for the British empire. This did not surprise him, since he had never believed that an oath of allegiance could "check the bias of the mind."[14] Several years later a British visitor reported meeting a settler from Norfolk who was on his way to purchase a parcel of land in New York State. When asked how he could reconcile making a declaration of obligation to two governments, the Upper Canadian replied "that the oath to each only applied while resident within their territories – he could never take an oath to be otherwise understood."[15] It seems, therefore, that the oath of allegiance did little to foster loyalty or national pride among newcomers. Of course, nationalism, as it is understood today, was a relatively new phenomenon when Upper Canada was created. Prior to the 1700s, people might have been patriotic about their city, locality, or ruler, but the fusion of patriotism with the consciousness of nationality, which produces genuine nationalism, had not occurred in the colony by the time Brock became administrator.[16] Instead of the cohesive, model society envisioned by Simcoe a generation earlier, Upper Canada began and remained a multicultural colony that was divided along ethnic, racial, religious, political, class, and linguistic lines. As one colonist noted, the province had a "motley population."[17]

The oath of allegiance proved to be a poor mechanism for assimilation. Other instruments of nationalist indoctrination, such as a reverence for national symbols, a successful state church, a thriving indigenous press, or a state-supported and directed school system for all citizens, did not exist in antebellum Upper Canada.[18] Because of its short existence, the province had no war memorials, monuments, or other symbols that might have fostered a sense of nationalism. Likewise, the Constitutional Act of 1791 established the Church of England as the official religion of the province, but by 1812 there were only six Anglican clergymen in the colony, and their field of influence was restricted to the larger villages and towns. Also, on the eve of war, only the Kingston, York, and Niagara regions supported newspapers, and most of the space in these publications was devoted to advertisements or to reports of Old World affairs. The vast majority of inhabitants would rarely have seen either an Anglican priest or a colonial newspaper, and throughout the province there was no "uniformity of manners, sentiment, and characters." Some colonists believed that the establishment of a common school system might compensate for these deficiencies. In 1810 one subscriber to the *Kingston Gazette* suggested that public schools would mould the descendants of the colonists "into one congenial people," but no immediate steps were taken to institute such a system. Before the war, therefore, the colonial population was still "composed of persons born in different states and nations, under various governments and laws, and speaking several languages."[19]

The largest section of this fragmented community was made up of American-born individuals. One visitor estimated that in 1812 some 60 per cent of the population had been born in the United States or were of American descent. Yet even this group was not homogeneous in composition.[20] The original Loyalist settlers, who numbered about 6000 in 1784, had fled the neighbouring states before the conclusion of the American War of Independence. Few of these individuals had left the republic only for reasons of sentiment or loyalty. The decision to support the British side during the revolution, often made when it appeared that royal forces had the upper hand, left thousands in an unenviable position when the British army suffered reverses. Those who could moved to areas in the republic where their wartime activities were unknown. Others who faced physical reprisals or the loss of businesses and positions chose to live in other areas in the British Empire rather than face the bleak social and economic opportunities offered at home. In contrast to conditions in the neighbouring republic, Upper Canada presented a fertile field to prospective settlers. Loyalists were promised land grants and assistance from the British government in the form of implements and foodstuffs – in short, a chance to begin anew. The Royal Instructions of 1783 offered heads of Loyalist families one hundred acres of land while their offspring received fifty acres. Discharged soldiers received grants according to rank. Privates were given one hundred acres, but field officers could acquire up to five thousand acres. Such generous terms meant Loyalists could maintain or better their economic situation by living in Upper Canada. Land hunger, rather than loyalty, was the factor that motivated most of these first settlers.[21]

There were also individuals who were neither economic nor political refugees. These people merely sought free land, and Upper Canada was the only area where that was available. After the revolution, public lands in the United States were sold for cash in parcels no smaller than 640 acres. In Upper Canada, in contrast, newcomers merely had to take the oath of allegiance and assert they had not served in the rebel forces to acquire a free grant of land.[22] Simcoe had made it clear that such settlers would be welcomed. His proclamation of 7 February 1792 outlined this generous system of land grants and was directed at anyone who was "desirous to settle on the Lands of the Crown." Many of those who accepted this offer had not originally intended to reside in the province. The easiest route to the Ohio frontier was by means of British-held territory. New Englanders on their way west were "funnelled through" Upper Canada, and many decided to go no further once they discovered the colony had free land and few native problems.[23] Anxious to increase the population, Simcoe later permitted even those who had fought against Britain to settle in the colony. New regulations issued in 1794 allowed any individual who professed to be a Christian and was capable of manual labour to be admitted into the province. The attractions of Upper Canada and the gradual abolition of strictures against American immigrants eventually induced thousands to move. Between 1791 and 1811 the population of the province increased about three-fold.[24]

Loyalists and later settlers, therefore, were motivated primarily by economic concerns and in some cases by naked self-preservation. That is not to say that these groups were united in other ways. The original settlers considered themselves refugees who had been as much "pushed" out of their old homes as they had been "pulled" by attractive opportunities under the familiar Union Jack. The same could not be said for those who came after them, and there was some opposition to the easing of settlement requirements. One visitor noted that more recent arrivals, the so-called Late Loyalists, were often viewed "with an eye of suspicion" by older inhabitants. Isaac Weld said some pioneer residents thought the Late Loyalists would not remain on their lots and would soon return to the United States. Weld disagreed with that prediction; he noted it was the prospect of acquiring land on advantageous terms that had prompted them to settle in Upper Canada and, so long as self-interest continued to operate, they would remain where land was cheapest.[25] One pioneer, Richard Cartwright, agreed with Weld that Late Loyalists had emigrated north not for "hostile or treacherous" reasons, but only because they sought to "better their circumstances, by acquiring land on easy terms." Although Cartwright was sure they had no traitorous intentions, he was equally convinced that many of his neighbours retained that "affectation for equality" so common among Americans in the United States.[26] Regional rivalries may have contributed to these antipathetic feelings. While most early immigrants had been from New York, New Jersey, and Pennsylvania, later colonists included people from Vermont, Massachusetts, and from as far away as the Carolinas.[27]

The American element of the population was also divided by race, since there were hundreds of African-Americans, both free and slave, and thousands of native Americans throughout Upper Canada.[28] The province was originally peopled by Algonkian Indians, and it has been estimated that in 1768 nearly five thousand aboriginal people occupied the region north of Lake Erie and Lake Ontario. A further five thousand resided north and east of Lake Superior.[29] These groups were known by various names – Chippewa, Ojibwa, or Mississauga – but they preferred to call themselves Anishinabe. In 1781 a group of Anishinabe ceded an area of land west of the Niagara River to the British government. It was on this land that Colonel John Butler's Rangers established farms for the purpose of supplying the garrison at Niagara with food. That sale was quickly followed by others. In October 1783 land between Cataraqui and the Trent River was purchased, and in 1784 a group of Anishinabe also alienated over half a million acres on either side of the Grand River.[30] This strip of land was purchased as a reserve for Iroquois people who had remained loyal to the crown during the revolutionary war. Under the leadership of Joseph Brant, some sixteen hundred members of the Six Nations (Mohawk, Cayuga, Oneida, Onondaga, Seneca, and Tuscarora) and a handful of other aboriginal people moved onto land originally occupied by Anishinabe.[31]

The Anishinabe and the Six Nations had rarely had amicable relations in the past, and the two groups remained hostile to each other in Upper Canada. However, this traditional animosity was also encouraged by government policy designed to prevent the native groups from forming a unified threat to British rule.[32] Internal disputes also arose among members of the Six Nations confederacy; many grew out of the long-running feud between Joseph Brant and the British authorities. Essentially, Brant wished for greater control over the lands his people occupied. It was his belief that the Six Nations should be allowed to sell or lease lands to non-natives without British permission. Official government policy discouraged such private transactions because they often resulted in later disputes, but in 1796 Brant threatened to attack York unless his wishes were granted. Before the revolt occurred, however, a compromise was reached and deeds were given to the individual buyers. No further lands were to be sold. Despite that ruling, the Six Nations' territory was rapidly reduced in size through both sanctioned and unofficial sales. Of the approximately 570,000 acres granted to the confederacy in 1784, some 350,000 had fallen into non-native hands by 1798.[33]

There were also other Amerindians in Upper Canada. A small settlement of Delaware had been established at Fairfield on the Thames River in 1792. The settlement was also known as "Moravian-town," because there were a number of Moravian missionaries on the site. Further west, members of the "Western Nations," the native confederacies of the upper Great Lakes, could sometimes be found at Amherstburg conferring with merchants and government officials over the state of the fur trade. The western warriors had served with the royal forces during the revolution, and they considered the Six Nations to be their guardians or "uncles."[34] After hostilities had ceased, the western groups had retreated to the upper lakes area, where they continued to resist American encroachment. In their relationships with these peoples the British authorities were forced to steer a difficult course. They tried to discourage open warfare, but they also sought to maintain the Indians' friendship and fur trade. On 7 November 1811, however, a bloody engagement occurred between Shawnee warriors and an American force at the Battle of Tippecanoe. Tecumseh, one of the leaders of the Western Nations, fled to Upper Canada after the battle, and that action reinforced American suspicions that the British were inciting the Indians. That was untrue, but the Upper Canadian authorities did regard Tecumseh and his followers as a force that could be called upon in the event of invasion.[35]

While native people were viewed as potential allies by British officials, other colonists often had little good to say about their Indian counterparts. Part of the problem stemmed from the fact that most settlers were from the United States, and Americans were taught "from nursery tales and fireside legends" to fear and hate all Indians.[36] As a result, relations between the two races were often strained and the allegiance of the aboriginal peoples was at times questioned, especially after Brant threatened to attack York. The Six Nations, however, no less than other Loyalists, had moved north for practical reasons. Those who chose to leave the United States for new lands in Upper Canada had done so because they believed that the survival of their way of life could more readily be assured under the British flag. Like most other inhabitants of the colony, Upper Canadian Amerindians were pragmatically prepared to adopt a stance of neutrality should the British prove themselves unwilling or unable to repel an invasion from the United States. As historian Carl Benn has noted, because of their small numbers, the Iroquois feared that heavy casualties in battle would destroy their society.[37] If forced, the Six Nations would reluctantly come to an understanding with the detested American "Big Knives" rather than risk annihilation.

After the Americans, the second largest segment of the population was of British origin. In the eastern end of the province, Roman Catholics from the Scottish Highlands were settled in the Glengarry region; in addition, a small colony named "Baldoon" had developed near the junction of Lake St Clair and the Detroit River in western Upper Canada by Lord Selkirk, Thomas Douglas, in 1804.[38] Scottish Presbyterians with connections to British mercantile firms had early on established themselves as the leading merchants in the colonial towns. Irish immigrants, both Protestant and Roman Catholic, arrived as individuals or as part of colonization schemes. English immigrants, who were willing to forsake comfort for guaranteed salaries, took positions in the colonial administration and provided Church of England clergymen with small but loyal congregations. Although divided along ethnic and religious lines, the British colonists shared in the spirit of acquisitiveness that characterized life in early Upper Canada. Most of them also had a healthy dislike for their American counterparts.

One of the most important of these British immigrants was John Strachan. Faced with little chance for advancement in his native Aberdeen, the twenty-one-year-old Scot accepted a teaching post offered to him by the Kingston merchant Richard Cartwright. Strachan arrived in the colony in 1799, but within two years he was considering a move to the United States in search of more lucrative employment.[39] Before leaving, however, Strachan decided to apply for a vacant Church of England post that guaranteed an annual income of £180. Strachan had been a lifelong Presbyterian until his application for the pastorship of the Scottish Presbyterian Church on St Gabriel Street in Montreal was refused. Drawing on Cartwright's connections, he then applied for the Anglican pulpit. This time Strachan's entreaties were successful and he was offered the job in December 1802. The next spring he received Holy Communion, for the first time in any church, and later took up his duties at Cornwall. A year later he applied for, and received, a grant of 1200 acres of land.[40] In 1807 Strachan improved his situation further through marriage to the widow of Andrew McGill, a member of the rich fur-trading family. He wrote to an old acquaintance that he found himself "happy in this connexion. My wife has an annuity of three hundred a year during her life."[41] To make certain that this windfall did not disappear through the untimely demise of Mrs Strachan, he immediately insured his wife's annuity with a British firm. It would be wrong to suggest that a guaranteed lifetime income was Strachan's sole motive for getting married, but the union nonetheless cemented Strachan's connections to the Montreal fur-trading elite. By 1807 the young Scot had acquired both influence and a measure of affluence. Like other arrivals he was "on the make," although his quick success was certainly extraordinary.

What was not unusual about Strachan was his view of the American colonists in Upper Canada. In common with other British immigrants, he had a low opinion of most of the settlers from the United States. Strachan noted that the original Loyalists, under the assumption that they would receive substantial compensation for their losses during the revolutionary war, had negotiated loans and credit from local merchants. When the payments failed to cover the obligations, Strachan said that the Loyalists resorted to "telling lies" until nothing "but the shadow of virtue" remained among the whole lot of them. In regard to the newer American arrivals, Strachan was even less impressed: "Plenty of them have now acquired property, but in point of information they are brutes. They have frequently got no education at all, or so little, that it cannot be known in conversation. And yet like all the ignorant, they know everything."[42] Clearly, there was some friction between the two communities. Other British immigrants complained that the American settlers, Loyalist and non-Loyalist alike, spoke with a peculiar "Yanky" twang and rarely gave a straight answer to any query. Instead, they "swore, vowed and guessed" until the frustrated questioner moved on. Upper Canadians were also accused of perpetuating those "sharp" business practices so common south of the border. British immigrants considered the American settlers to be exceptionally shrewd when it came to money matters. "If there be a single error in a bill or account," Strachan remarked, "they are sure to discover and profit by it. For this reason they bind each other by contracts in the smallest matters, and they are continually going to law."[43] Apparently even a tightfisted Scot could find himself at the mercy of a "calculatin' and reckonin'" American.

Strachan's dislike of his fellow colonists was based on more than contempt for their business dealings. As an ordained Anglican priest he also had a real aversion to the religious preferences of his neighbours. Apparently, many Upper Canadians had little interest in religion. In 1803 Strachan said that most "people have little or no religion," and that view was shared by others who visited the colony. In 1798, for example, a Moravian missionary dismissed the old belief that New Englanders generally took a minister with them to new settlements. According to Benjamin Mortimer, the common saying in Upper Canada was that "New Englanders, when they leave their country, leave their religion behind."[44] Some of that lack of interest might be attributable to the poor roads and long distances between houses of worship. T.G. Anderson, who at the age of twenty spent the winter of 1799 in Brockville, later reminisced that "churches were scarce in those days, and as the sleighing was not good yet we kept in doors, romping with the girls." But William Case, a Methodist minister who rode the ciruit near Ancaster in 1808, thought the fault rested with the low moral and spiritual nature of Upper Canadians. On his route there were "some bad houses kept by tavern keepers," and, Case said, on "Sundays, evenings, & other times large companies of neighbours & others convene for the purposes of drinking, dancing etc., which has already been the ruin of many."[45]

Colonists fond of more pious activities could join a bewildering array of organized religions. Concentrations of Roman Catholics were to be found in the eastern area of the province among the Glengarry Highlanders and in the extreme western portion of the province among French-Canadian settlers. There were also Lutherans, Presbyterians, and a variety of Anabaptist sects. The largest of these groups, the Mennonites, had followed acquaintances and relatives from New Jersey and Pennsylvania into Upper Canada. There were also hundreds of Tunkers or "Dunkards," who were also of German origin but who practised three immersions rather than just one adult baptism. Like most Americans in the province, the Mennonites and Tunkers were not "Loyalists," since participation on any side during a war would have led to disownment. They, along with other pacifists such as members of the Society of Friends, settled in the Niagara region and along the Grand River.[46] These groups were often admired by certain government officials for being "peaceable and industrious." They, in turn, found Upper Canada to be an attractive destination because the administration permitted the men to avoid militia duties through the payment of small fines. However, these pacifists were sometimes harassed or beaten by soldiers and other settlers. When John Melish discovered one of these "poor good Dutch" who had been insulted by a number of British officers, the settler admitted that the "soldiers were a little rude sometimes, but it was a good government for all that."[47]

The only contact with religious teaching that most Upper Canadians experienced was through Methodist circuit riders. These itinerant preachers made great progress among the population after the turn of the century. In 1803 Strachan wrote that in the Cornwall region there were only a few Methodists, but three years later he noted that the circuit riders were achieving great success in spreading their "deplorable fanatacism." The Methodist services provided backwoodsmen with relief from the monotony of frontier life. "They will bawl twenty of them at once," Strachan observed, "[then] tumble on the ground, laugh, sing, jump and stamp, and this they call the working of the spirit." Concern over the spread of Methodism involved more than a dislike for their exuberant style of worship. Brock believed that these American-based preachers held political principles that were "highly prejudicial to the peace of Society."[48] Among government officials, therefore, there was a fear that the circuit riders were promoting republican values while dispensing religious lessons.

American settlers sometimes complained about the attitudes of their British counterparts. A number of Americans in the province were annoyed by the haughtiness of British officials, and some resented that they were constantly suspected of dark designs. Melish, who visited the province before the war began, spoke to a man from New Hampshire who had little good to say about Upper Canada. He complained that there was no freedom of the press or of speech and that the "pride and insolence of the ruling powers were excessive."[49] Those sorts of sentiments prompted Francis Gore to dismiss most American settlers as "mere adventurers" who had brought with them the "very worst principles of their constitution."[50] Of particular concern to officials like Gore was their feeling that most colonists favoured more democratic forms of government. David Smith, an Englishman and member of the first provincial Assembly, observed that his fellow legislators had been raised with ideas quite foreign to him. He said most of the assemblymen had "violent levelling principles," and he was concerned that the "Neighbouring States" were too often "brought in as patterns & models." His comments were prompted by the actions of other legislators who wanted representatives elected at town meetings rather than appointed officials to control local government. Smith opposed the measure because he believed that such democratic functions led only to "Riot & Confusion" and had contributed to the "late unhappy Rebellion."[51]

In some respects a system of appointed officials was well suited to Upper Canadian conditions. With a small and generally uneducated population, those with schooling or suitable qualifications could be placed in positions that required those attributes. Originally, the appointees provided a relatively economical and efficient system of administration. The greatest number of appointments involved the local justices of the peace who presided over courts of quarter sessions and were empowered, in the absence of Anglican clergymen, to solemnize marriages.[52] Only a half-dozen or so of the positions available in the province were worth more than £100 sterling a year in the 1790s. By 1812, however, both the number of posts and the scale of pay had increased dramatically.[53] The tendency of one individual to hold several of these positions at one time naturally led to resentment on the part of those who felt their talents were being ignored. As the colony grew in size, increasing numbers of suitable candidates found themselves excluded from positions they felt qualified to fill.

A system whereby appointed officials could ignore complaints by elected representatives was also prone to abuses of various kinds; Melish reported that affairs at York consisted of "a great deal of underhanded management and intrigue."[54] Certainly favouritism existed and, under the administration of Peter Russell, for example, legislative councillors were granted no fewer than six thousand acres of land each as compensation for moving expenses when the capital was changed from Newark to York. Those grants were thirty times the size of parcels given to ordinary settlers, who received only two hundred acres. Such lavish gifts must have appeared grossly unfair, but even more absurd acts of officially sanctioned patronage occurred. With the assistance of Simcoe, for example, Thomas Talbot acquired a grant of five thousand acres in western Upper Canada on the understanding that he was to attract settlers to the region. Confusion over the exact terms of the agreement meant the "benevolent despot" of western Upper Canada was eventually able to acquire more than fifty thousand acres of land.[55] While appointed officials and their friends acquired huge blocks of property, other less influential settlers often had legitimate grievances that were ignored. These types of abuses prompted one observer to warn prospective British immigrants not to expect the "same security of rights or freedom from oppression" they enjoyed in England.[56] The power and privileges enjoyed by colonial officials, compounded by the distance from the Mother Country, meant that the government of Upper Canada could operate in a manner that was sure to foster opposition.

In general, however, few Upper Canadians were affected by affairs in the capital of the colony. Strachan remarked in 1801 that politics in the province were "hardly worth notice" and that members of the Assembly squabbled among themselves or argued with legislative councillors. Appointed officials, in contrast, dismissed any opposition to government decisions as the work of "damned Democrats". Nor was there agreement among the servants of the crown. Frederick H. Armstrong, a researcher who is familiar with the nature of colonial affairs, has attributed much of this bickering to the number of "fractious misfits" who decided to make the province their home during the prewar period.[57] As a frontier society, Upper Canada attracted its share of extremely aggressive pioneers who were determined to better their economic circumstances by any means available. In this tiny community, therefore, personalities and interests were often in conflict, and usually the frustration of private ambition was at the heart of such contests. Paul Romney, another scholar familiar with colonial affairs during this period, has suggested that most political issues in early Upper Canada arose out of "non-ideological sectional and personal rivalries."[58] Usually these early opponents of the colonial administration were driven by selfish motives and, in general, they were men who had been denied a promotion or refused a grant of land. But not every individual who opposed government was driven by personal interest at all times, since favouritism and petty corruption did affect others. One supporter of the colonial administration admitted in 1814: "However specious the pretences of such demagogues may be, self-interest generally be at the bottom of all they do or say; [nonetheless] ... some grievances may and must exist."[59]

The actions of one of these early critics, Judge Robert Thorpe, illustrates how a personal dispute with the provincial administration could be tied to issues of real importance to other Upper Canadians. Thorpe had arrived in Upper Canada in 1805 to serve as a puisne judge of the Court of King's Bench, but he had his sights set on a more lofty appointment. When the coveted post of chief justice went to Attorney-General Thomas Scott instead, Thorpe was indignant. That such a "contemptible creature" could be promoted over himself only confirmed Thorpe's suspicions that something was seriously wrong with the provincial administration.[60] The judge immediately began to notice other irregularities, including the treatment afforded some Loyalists. Prior to Thorpe's arrival, it had become evident that a number of impostors had managed to have their names added to the lists of United Empire Loyalists. Those registered as Loyalists, and their children, were entitled to land grants. It was advantageous for unscrupulous newcomers to claim that during the revolutionary war they had taken an active part in the struggle, since they could then acquire free land. In order to minimize these abuses, a review of the lists was eventually undertaken. Only those Loyalists who arrived prior to 1783 were to be considered for inclusion on the register, with all others being struck off the list. The process resulted in a real paring down of the lists and, between May 1802 and November 1804, more than nine hundred individuals lost their "UE" designation and the benefits it conferred.[61] Naturally, those affected by that process were displeased with this policy. Even those who maintained their free grants were upset because they could not acquire full title to their allotments. Under General Peter Hunter, who assumed the post of provincial administrator in August 1799, Loyalist and military claimants found themselves placed last in line for surveys and patents. Since these individuals paid no fees for those services, the various officials found the work unprofitable. Their incomes were increased only when fees were paid. Wealthy new-comers from the United States found their needs attended to promptly.[62]

Settlers affected by such measures found they had a champion in Thorpe. He began writing letters to influential friends in London which detailed the abuses he had observed. According to Thorpe, officials in the provincial government were driven only by greed; their motto appeared to be, "Get as many dollars as you can." Large grants were given to the "Scotch peddlars," who, in turn, would sell them to Americans. Thus only the "Shopkeeper Aristocracy" and the appointed officials who received fees gained any benefit from land transactions. Thorpe was particularly concerned that the development of Upper Canada was suffering as a consequence of this cor-ruption. While a select few got rich, the rest of the province was left with "no roads, bad water communications, no Post, no Religion, no Morals, no Education, no Trade, no Agriculture, no Industry attended to."[63] There may have been an element of truth to what Thorpe was saying, but one can only wonder what his view of the situation would have been had he managed to acquire the post of chief justice.

Under the all-encompassing banner "The King, The People, The Law, Thorpe & the Constitution," the judge sought and won a seat in the Assembly for the east riding of York. In 1807 he served as a vocal opponent of the policies of the new lieutenant-governor. Francis

Gore's first act on taking control of the government, however, had been to reopen the United Empire Loyalists lists.[64] That proclamation was welcome news to many individuals affected by Hunter's policies, and the judge lost some support as a result. Characteristically, Thorpe was unimpressed with the conduct of the new administration and he found Gore to be "imperious, self-indulgent and ignorant."[65] It was not long before the lieutenant-governor took steps to remove this irritant. By the summer of 1807 Thorpe found himself suspended from the bench and, seeing no future for himself in Upper Canada, he left the province later that year. His departure, of course, did not eliminate any of the legitimate grievances that existed in the colony. In 1811, almost two hundred of Thorpe's former constituents in the York region signed a petition condemning the provincial administration for its "Partiality and Corruption." Four years after the judge had left, things had changed little. A few Loyalists, "unable to obtain those just Rewards" they felt entitled to, decried the "mal adminis-tration" under which they were forced to live.[66]

Joseph Willcocks, who arrived in the colony in 1799, perhaps best represents the type of individual whose personal ambition dictated his political actions. Born in 1773 near Dublin, he came to Upper Canada at the age of twenty-six to join relatives already in the prov-ince. He soon made friends among the political elite of the colony and acquired positions under Peter Russell and Chief Justice Henry Allcock, eventually becoming sheriff of the Home District. Willcocks was pleased with his success and he noted that, although the "officers of the Government disagree very much, I have the good fortune to be always on the strongest side."[67] Only a few months later, Willcocks's world began to collapse around him. At the end of 1804 his bene-factor Allcock was transferred to Lower Canada, and Willcocks's fortunes took a turn for the worse. The next year the young Irishman struck up an unfortunate relationship with Judge Robert Thorpe. That friendship was to cost Willcocks his position as sheriff and it ended any possibility of advancement in the inner circle of appointed officials. No longer on the "strongest side," Willcocks then took the next logical step and became a leading critic of the provincial admin-istration. He did this first through the pages of his newspaper, *The Upper Canadian Guardian or Freeman's Journal*, which was published at Newark. In 1808 Willcocks was elected to the Assembly, where he continued to criticize the provincial administration.[68] Over the next four years, Willcocks was able to exert an increasing influence over the affairs of the Assembly. He discovered that other representatives, who wanted changes to the School Act of 1807 or to land-granting regulations, could be relied on to provide support for his amendments.

Most of these legislators represented ridings in the Niagara District or in western Upper Canada, where the majority of recent American arrivals had settled, but Peter Howard, who sat for Leeds, also often sided with Willcocks on a majority of parliamentary votes. This opposition group was not a political party in the modern sense of the term. Willcocks had no "whip" to enforce discipline, and members voted independently on all issues. Nonetheless, by early 1812, Willcocks was sometimes able to marshall enough support to block or amend legislation. The young Irishman had placed himself in a position of considerable strength, and he took great pleasure in abusing members of the "tyrannical" Scottish "Shopkeeper Aristocracy."[69]

Realizing that Willcocks's actions stemmed from frustration at having been ignored by government officials, Brock went out of his way to placate him. In 1812 Willcocks was invited to dine with the major-general at Government House, where he found Brock to be deeply interested in winning him over to the side of the administration. Willcocks accepted Brock's offer of a militia position, but his loyalty could only be guaranteed if the British succeeded in throwing back the Americans. When, in 1813, that appeared doubtful, Willcocks joined the American side. One historian has succinctly described Willcocks as an "opportunist whose major concern was his own personal career."[70] In many respects, however, Willcocks differed from his fellow Upper Canadians only in the degree of his opportunism and in that, early on, he had been denied access to government favours. Had Willcocks not been "cast out" of the colonial inner circle in 1807, his actions during the war might have resembled those of other colonial leaders whose fortunes were more closely tied to the maintenance of the royal connection.

In antebellum Upper Canada, therefore, there were individuals who disagreed with the manner in which the province was ruled, but there was not an organized opposition party.[71] Before the War of 1812, as historian David Mills has noted, the critics of the colonial government remained a collection of individuals rather than a formal movement; political opposition in the colony was "highly personal and of a limited nature."[72] It is true that many of these oppositionists drew upon old notions of constitutional propriety to bolster their arguments. Graeme Patterson has shown that most influential prewar opponents of the administration actually adhered to Whig views of politics. Like their seventeenth-century counterparts in England, they usually emphasized the dangers inherent in the arbitrary use of power by a corrupt executive. Of course, many prewar oppositionists had personal reasons for feeling that way and, as Patterson notes, their well-developed rhetoric often masked private ambition.[73]

What is too often overlooked by historians, however, is that prewar oppositionists acted in a very conservative manner. For instance, they restricted their activities to entering elections, publishing personal attacks in pamphlet form, and writing letters of complaint to officials in London. Antebellum critics never ventured so far as to call for township meetings or popular conventions to discuss grievances and, if they had, it is likely the results would have disappointed the organizers. Before the War of 1812, most colonists had few dealings with government officials, and the Upper Canadian administration must have appeared quite unobstrusive to the majority of inhabitants. Without widespread support, these early oppositionists also failed to formulate a real critique of the basic form of government. For example, they never suggested that the whole system of appointed officials, or the reservation of decisions for British approval, was at fault. Only *certain* appointees or decisions were a problem. Prior to the war, dissatisfaction with the government was restricted to relatively small numbers of people, and the attacks that did develop were aimed at addressing only minor grievances. Calls for the radical restructuring of the colonial administration would not arise until the postwar period when both the the number of problems, and those affected by them, increased exponentially.

Like provincial politics, the Upper Canadian economy was also in a formative stage before the War of 1812. Specie, for example, was in constant demand in the province and almost any form of money was considered acceptable. The colony, having no currency of its own, made do with American dollars, English shillings, and even Spanish "half-joes." To complicate matters further, individual merchants printed their own paper money for amounts under £5.[74] This bewildering array of tender made business transactions somewhat complex and, according to at least one contemporary observer, this haphazard system of credit and currency contributed to a high rate of bankruptcy.[75] Because of the dangers associated with uncertain credit, successful merchants in Upper Canada were those with the closest connections to British firms. Merchants with friends or relatives overseas could weather difficult times through lenient extensions of due dates. Probably the most successful of these colonial shopkeepers was Robert Hamilton. A native of Dumfries, Hamilton established a shop and forwarding business near the falls at Niagara. From that advantageous position he transshipped goods going east or west and made handsome profits supplying the nearby post at Fort

George. Between 1784 and 1791 Hamilton brought over four of his relatives to extend the operations of the firm. Robert, William, and Thomas Dickson and Thomas Clark established shops throughout the Niagara region.[76] Along with Richard Cartwright's concerns, the Hamilton firm was considered an institution of the "greatest weight" in the early colonial economy.[77]

The career of one of Hamilton's relatives, Robert Nichol, gives some indication of how family connections and associations with colonial officials could be financially rewarding. Nichol, a native of Dumfries, followed his cousins the Dicksons to Upper Canada in 1792. Although only eighteen years old, he was soon given a responsible position in the Hamilton firm. Nichol eventually entered into a partnership with Thomas Clark and he used his profits to establish a mill at Port Dover. His most important customers were the British garrisons at Fort Erie and Fort George and, between 1805 and 1811, he sold the commissariat more than £2800 worth of meat and flour. Nichol was appointed a militia captain in 1803, and later a justice of the peace and a road commissioner. Eventually he was elected to the Assembly in 1812, where he proved to be one of the most able defenders of government policies. Those activities earned Nichol the emnity of Willcocks, who sought to have the "squinty eyed" Scot imprisoned for embezzling government money.[78] While it is true that Nichol "thought it absurd for an individual to give his time to the Public gratuitously," it seems unlikely that he had consciously misappropriated funds.[79] Despite continued questions about his bookkeeping practices, Brock considered Nichol to be a man of "strict probity" and "ardent loyalty."[80]

Whether scrupulously honest or not, successful merchants were powerful individuals in Upper Canada; in conjunction with appointed British officials, they constituted an elite class. They were appointed as justices of the peace, granted militia commissions, and sometimes offered posts in the Executive or Legislative councils. Members of this "Shopkeeper Aristocracy" were also the largest landowners in the province. By 1805 Hamilton had accumulated at least 40,000 acres, Joseph Forsyth had nearly 10,000, while William Dickson had managed to acquire 5300 acres.[81] When Cartwright died in 1815, his widow and children inherited more than 27,000 acres of land located throughout the province.[82] Some of this land was granted by government, but much was taken from debtors who were forced to relinquish their titles or face jail sentences. These actions sometimes earned merchants a great deal of ill will among the general population, but in Upper Canada shopkeepers were indispensible and powerful individuals.

Upper Canadians, therefore, were also separated by class concerns. E.A. Talbot, a visitor of the colony, said: "In Upper Canada, there are only two classes of society. The First is composed of professional men, merchants, civil and military officers, and the members of the Provincial Parliament: The Second, of farmers, mechanics and labourers, who associate together on all occasions without any distinction." Needless to say, class differences and national origins were closely associated. Loyalists and British immigrants made up the bulk of the "first" class in Upper Canadian society. The lower orders were comprised primarily of American settlers who had arrived after 1791, and most of them were unimpressed with the pretensions of the professional class. Talbot remarked that every American considered himself "quite as good as his neighbour, though the latter be loaded with distinctions."[83]

But differences between the classes did exist, and children of the Upper Canadian establishment were usually the only youngsters who were educated in the province. They attended private schools and, until suitable colonial institutions were created, they were often sent to the United States or Britain to complete their education. The School Act of 1807 provided £100 per year for the establishment of grammar schools in each of the eight districts of the province, but only those youngsters who already had the benefit of several years of private elementary education were admitted.[84] The grammar schools were not designed to be instruments of nationalist indoctrination and no British curriculum was specified, but the students who attended usually needed little prompting in the patriotism department. The Hamilton children and their relatives in the province were exposed quite early to notions of chivalry and duty to country. The students who might have been influenced most by this type of education were, for all practical purposes, excluded from the grammar school system.[85] Each district acquired only one institution, and for the children of most ordinary settlers a daily trip to the main village was simply not feasible.[86]

As might be expected, educated members of the Uppper Canadian establishment sometimes differed from their neighbours in regard to dress, manners, and ethics. Before the war, for instance, a number of the colonial elite wore buckles, lace, and seventeenth-century style powdered wigs as they went about their business. Similarly, fox hunts and duels appear to have been the preserve of the Upper Canadian gentry. In the case of the York elite, winter hunts sometimes involved crossing the ice of the local harbour.[87] The first recorded duel took place in Kingston in 1793 between a British officer and Peter Clark, chief clerk of the Legislative Council. Every similar engagement in

Upper Canada occurred between members of the colony's "first" class; ordinary settlers appear to have cared little about avenging perceived insults. Young members of the provincial establishment were taught that chivalrous gentlemen had a duty to uphold the honour of their families. This concept of "glory got by courage of manhood" extended back to the Old World and was widely accepted during the Middle Ages.[88] In early nineteenth-century Upper Canada, however, the idea was apparently restricted to members of the colonial elite.

The culture and lifestyles of the majority of colonists would have resembled those found in other pre-modern, rural societies. Many Upper Canadians were superstitious, and interest in witchcraft seems to have been widespread.[89] Apparently, a few colonists also dabbled in the occult arts. Those who fell sick, for instance, might suspect that their illness was a result of being bewitched. If so, the solution was obvious. A silver coin could be melted into a musketball and fired at an image of the suspected witch. If done at sunset, the spell was sure to be broken and good health would soon follow.[90] Even inhabitants who were educated might still believe that physical phenomenon were supernatural events. On 15 November 1801, for example, the afternoon sky above Cornwall darkened to such a degree that students in the local school could not see to read. Strachan, who considered himself a rational product of the Scottish enlightenment, thought the darkness was a sure sign of God's displeasure. The belief that eclipses or comets were "signs" of future "harms," such as wars or earthquakes, probably stretched back to Neolithic times. Those who believed that God was angry over some matter might resort to fasting in an attempt to appease the diety and prevent the actual occurrence of the "harm."[91]

In addition to culture and lifestyle, Upper Canadians were also divided by language. Strachan said that the "motley population" was "chiefly capable of speaking English," but not all members of the community were able to boast of that ability.[92] In the east, many of the Glengarry Highlanders spoke only Gaelic, and German was often the only language spoken among the numerous Anabaptist sects. To the west, the French Canadians were also separated from their fellow colonists by this language barrier. The first European settlers in the province had established themselves near Detroit in 1701, and a sizeable French-Canadian population still existed in the area before the War of 1812.[93] An inhabitant from near Amherstburg, Joseph Bartheaume, would later recall that the "usual way of giving publicity to anything interesting to the Canadian population was by giving notice thereof at the French service after divine service." Most other citizens in this pre-modern community would also have been forced to rely on word of mouth for news of important events since, even as late as 1812, the three newspapers in the province had only limited circulation.[94]

Rather than be concerned with news from other regions, people in the countryside devoted attention to their two-hundred-acre land grants. In 1798 an Irish visitor remarked that settlers in Upper Canada seemed less worldly than their counterparts in the United States. Benjamin Mortimer said Upper Canadians were "more humble in their views" and were "chiefly concerned to manage, in the best manner, the farms which have been given them by government." A number of years later, a surgeon who served with the British forces during the War of 1812 was also struck by the self-absorbed nature of colonial Upper Canadian society. John Douglas remarked: "The settlers thus enclosed by thick woods, are occupied chiefly in the labourious concerns of husbandry ... They love their homes, because they are the abode of peace and independence. Those events which are related to their own state of life, seem alone worthy of their notice."[95] This life of "hardship and labour," which most Upper Canadians shared, also served to divide neighbour from neighbour. One observer noted before the war that life for Upper Canadians was "uninterrupted by Religious or National holidays. They have no Fairs, no habits of Public Amusements, few of Public Works or any cure from the daily routine of their domestic life."[96] Occasionally neighbours would band together to raise a barn, providing that the owner offered compensation in the form of free liquor, but these were relatively rare events. The only activity in which a large proportion of the inhabitants were expected to participate was the annual militia muster. All able-bodied males between the ages of sixteen and sixty were required to attend, but no actual training occurred. Like the "bees" and barn-raisings, the musters also tended to end "in excess."[97]

Life in the villages of the colony was only somewhat more advanced. Less than 5 per cent of the colony's population was to be found in the three "urban" centres of Upper Canada. Kingston was the largest village, with about 150 houses and one thousand inhabitants. The British garrison was the economic base on which the town thrived, and local merchants like Cartwright made a good living through provisioning the army.[98] Further west stood York, which was also a garrison town. On the eve of war the population of "muddy York" amounted to about six hundred souls housed in sixty modest frame homes. The site had none of the majesty usually associated with a capital; Dr William Dunlop described it as "a dirty straggling

village." As late as 1812 the legislature was housed in a nondescript
wooden building, and the clerk of the peace was forced to remind
"owners of Swine" not to allow their pigs to run at large.[99] Far more
pleasing to the eye was the village of Newark, also known as Niagara,
which served as the supply depot for the garrison at nearby Fort
George. With a population just under that of Kingston's, Newark
had a number of fine buildings, including a gaol, a court house, and
the old legislature. As early as the 1790s the town supported both a
Masonic lodge and an agricultural society. Prior to the war the
Niagara District, of which Newark was the centre, was the most
improved region of the province, with neat farms and well-built
homes.[100]

From the outset, therefore, Upper Canada was a pre-modern,
multicultural society that was divided along numerous lines. Racial
and cultural differences, as well as class and distance, divided neighbour from neighbour. Simcoe's goal of replacing "indifference" with
a "zealous attachment" to the British empire had not been achieved
by the time Brock became administrator. One of the few things the
inhabitants seemed to share was a concern that war with the United
States would affect them financially.[101] Hostilities would bring a halt
to both British and American immigration. Successful colonial merchants, who were often also land speculators, knew they would lose
prospective customers. Appointed officials, who derived much of
their income from land surveys and patents, would be similarly
affected. Those settlers who had managed to clear their land and
produce a surplus were aware that any conflict would endanger their
property and disrupt the export of their produce. While Upper
Canadians knew that British government expenditures would
increase dramatically, they also knew that their province would most
likely be the battleground in any contest with the United States.
Individuals might lose their property and maybe even their lives.
The editor of the *Kingston Gazette* was certainly troubled by such
thoughts, and he cautioned Upper Canadians about the possibility
of an American invasion in 1810. "Besides the destruction of lives,
the burning of houses, the plunder of cattle, and all other species of
moveable property," he warned, "it would throw back the state of
business and improvement for many years."[102] For those reasons, some
Upper Canadians wished the whole issue would just go away. If
fighting between Britain and the United States was inevitable, many
desired that it take place elsewhere. One correspondent to a colonial
newspaper offered a solution that must have been popular with other
Upper Canadians. "If your quarrel is with Britain," he told Americans, "go and revenge yourselves on her own shores."[103]

The colonists were firm in their belief that they were not responsible for the deteriorating relationship between Britain and the United States. The reasons cited by American politicians for the necessity of war did not directly involve actions on the part of their neighbours to the north. The impressment of American seaman, which had almost led to war in 1807, was done by the British navy. The contraction of American trade caused by hostilities in Europe was surely not the fault of the upper province. Nor were the Indian troubles of the Ohio region. Upper Canadians had no quarrel with their neighbours and, even among some Loyalists, the United States was scarcely seen as a foreign country. A few, like Samuel Street, Sr, owned land in both places, and many had relatives they often visited.[104] In a number of respects the border between the two regions was ignored. Upper Canadians crossed it freely, sometimes to trade, to return home, or even to find a suitable partner for marriage. Now this "community of interests" was threatened because of incidents in far-off places that they neither comprehended nor wished to understand.[105] One British visitor recorded that when he tried to explain these world events to the average colonist, his explanations were greeted with "few emotions of interest."[106] This attitude has prompted one historian to conclude that, in general, Upper Canadians "did not invite the war, did not care about the issues, and did not want to fight."[107]

Of course, not all Upper Canadians viewed the approaching conflict in this dispassionate manner. A few vocal patriots existed here and there and they sometimes took to the pages of colonial newspapers to arouse some enthusiasm for the expected contest. Men like Cartwright and Strachan, who wrote under the pen-names "Falkland" and "Loyalist," respectively, had much to lose if the province fell to the Americans. Their arguments, however, were not based on simple loyalty but were directed to the practical side of the populace. Recent arrivals were warned by Strachan in February 1812 that the invaders would not be respectable yeoman like themselves but landless ruffians from American cities. This "horrid banditti" would plunder their homes, pausing only to rape their women, and then drive them from their farms. Loyalists were reminded that these invaders would be Democratic thugs who would take special care to torment their old enemies. Strachan asked all his "fellow countrymen" to "rally round the Government" and show "brother Jonathan" that Upper Canadians were willing to "brave the impending storm like men." He also informed the American government that the colonists were not "a parcel of Quakers," and he warned that for "every Canadian Cabin you burn or destroy, the British will retaliate upon you tenfold."[108] Cartwright avoided such bravado, but he too felt that an invasion would lead to savage attacks and reprisals. In a letter to the *Kingston Gazette* he said that Upper Canadians did not desire war, but that if they were attacked the colonists would be "anxious to avenge themselves." Cartwright also offered a pragmatic appraisal of what the future would hold if the territory was conquered. "One immediate consequence," he predicted, "would be heavy taxes compensated for to us by no adequate advantages."[109] Apparently, no appeal to the loyalties of Upper Canadians was complete without some reference to the effect defeat would have on the pocketbooks of the colonists.

Another correspondent noted that it was a common belief that the Americans would immediately overwhelm the province with an immense army. He pointed out to his fellow residents that the British navy and army would be there to greet them. He was also sure that all inhabitants would rise up and defend those things most dear to them. As "John Bull" warned: "Our wives, our children, our property our all is at stake, and shall we then tamely submit and see ourselves plundered of our well earned property, of property for which we have fought and bled?"[110] This writer, and others like him, tried to appeal to the pragmatic as well as the patriotic instincts of the settlers. Because of the fragmented nature of antebellum Upper Canadian society, an appeal to rally around the king or flag was insufficient. As Gore noted in 1808, the inhabitants had to believe that their own lives and estates were in jeopardy. It seems that a love of private property and a desire for self-preservation were the only things that all members of Upper Canada's "motley population" shared, and it was this concern that Brock addressed on the opening of the first session of the fifth parliament on 5 February 1812. He told the House of Assembly that the province owed its prosperity to its ties to Britain and he warned that if those connections were severed, the colony would "inevitably sink into comparative poverty and insignificance." Although Brock assured the legislators that this was not meant as a threat and was not designed to spur them into taking appropriate actions, the tone of the speech suggested otherwise. The assemblymen responded to Brock's blunt message by stating that they required no such "incitements" to animate their patriotism. They also noted that the "commercial advantages" of the imperial ties were felt in Britain as well as in Upper Canada.[111]

In newspapers, in sermons, and from public platforms, the colonists were advised that their property and lives were in danger and, on 19 June 1812, some inhabitants sprang into action. One day after Congress had voted to declare war on Britain, but before the news had reached the province, Upper Canadians gathered to observe a "Day of PUBLIC FASTING and HUMILIATION before GOD" to ward off the peril of war.[112] When hostilities actually began, however, the invaders assured residents that no measures would be taken against those who remained neutral. Brigadier-General William Hull crossed the Detroit River and entered western Upper Canada with some 2500 men on 11 July 1812. The next day he issued a proclamation directing the colonists to remain at home and suggesting that they continue to follow their "peaceful and customary avocations." Hull warned against taking up arms and he asked that his "Army of friends" be given a cordial welcome.[113] Many colonists were more than happy to oblige. John Askin, a prominent western merchant, wrote to a colleague that Hull had proved a man of his word and that the American soldiers would not dare "take a Cherry" for fear of punishment from their superiors. Askin, a man who only a few days before had wondered how any British subject could change his allegiance, now felt quite prepared to do just that. Perhaps it was Upper Canada's destiny to become part of the United States. If so, the merchant could not think of a better man to supervise the transition than Hull. According to Askin, he was a man who would "not only respect my property, but that of my friends."[114] Predictions of raping and pillaging had proved false. So too, apparently, had the speculation that invasion would require the colonists to fight. Hull offered the inhabitants what they desired most – an opportunity to ignore the war and get on with their lives. In doing so, he had uncovered the collective Achilles heel of the "Spartan bands" of Upper Canadian defenders.

3 "Cool Calculators": Brock's Militia

Despite the increased tempo of military preparations during 1812, most colonists still believed that war would somehow be avoided. Prideaux Selby, the receiver-general of the province, wrote to a friend in April 1812 that the British forces were acting "as if war was expected, but my own opinion is that all Jonathan's blustering will end in nothing of that sort."[1] It would seem that years of incessant rumours of impending conflict had made the inhabitants of Upper Canada somewhat complacent. A correspondent to the *St David's Spectator* would later recall that although "relations with our neighbours were very gloomy," most Upper Canadians were simply "not apprehensive of war" and the commencement of hostilities was a "totally unexpected ... subject of wonder."[2] Thus, when the news reached York on 27 June that the long-dreaded event actually had occurred, the villagers appeared to be in a state of shock. Eli Playter, a farmer who lived north of the capital, rushed to the garrison and "found all York in alarm, everyone's countenance wore the mark of surprise."[3]

Isaac Brock was not startled by the news. Since April increasing numbers of "armed men in coloured clothes" had gathered on the opposite shore, and early in May he received a secret dispatch from Sir George Prevost advising that he "consider war as inevitable." The message went on to warn that hostilities would commence by July at the latest.[4] This information confirmed Brock's belief that the course of military preparations he had embarked upon the previous autumn had been the right one. At that time he had arranged to improve the fortifications at the various garrisons and had made plans to place his militia forces in a state of readiness. Brock considered those plans to be of prime importance since, in his opinion, the "active and efficient aid" of at least a portion of the population would be necessary if the colony was to be defended successfully.[5]

The Militia acts of Upper and Lower Canada dated from June 1793, when fears that the United States was intent on attacking the British colonies prompted the governments in those provinces to pass legislation allowing for the creation of official local defence forces.[6] In Upper Canada, John Graves Simcoe was the author of the colony's first Militia Act, and its governing principle was near-universal liability for service. All able-bodied men between the ages of sixteen and fifty were required to attend authorized militia parades or pay fines ranging from two to eight dollars an offence. The first muster in 1793, however, only produced an enrolment of 4213 men. Alarmed by the small turnout, the authorities amended the Militia Act the next year so that men up to the age of sixty were liable for service. From 1794 until 1812 the Militia Act of Upper Canada remained relatively unchanged.[7] The basic militia unit was the company, and each was to consist of between twenty and fifty privates and three officers (a captain, a lieutenant, and an ensign). Regiments consisted of eight to ten companies, in other words 160 to 500 privates, commanded by one colonel, one lieutenant-colonel, one major, one adjutant, and one quartermaster. Officers and men were expected to bring to every muster their own firearms and at least six rounds of ammunition. Quakers, Mennonites, and Tunkers were excused from service but were required to pay twenty shillings a year in peacetime, and £5 a year in wartime, for that privilege.[8]

Brock was concerned that the annual musters had failed to prepare men for actual combat. The parades, usually held on 4 June every year, were looked upon by the men as an opportunity to socialize and by the authorities as a chance to engage in military census-taking. Brock's concern about the utility of the Militia Act was grounded in fact. By 1805, for instance, only 200 of the province's 8600 militiamen had received any genuine training.[9] To remedy this situation, Brock wanted to revamp the old law so that at least a portion of the militia had proper instruction in military matters. He also thought new regulations dealing with discipline and training were required. Though there were "many wise and salutory provisions" in the old act, Brock felt there were too few means of enforcing them.[10] When he addressed the provincial legislature in February 1812 he requested that the House of Assembly add an oath of abjuration to the Militia Act. He felt that the number of Americans in the province who openly professed that they would never fight against their former country made this amendment necessary. Under the proposed legislation, each militiaman would be required not only to pledge allegiance to the king but also to take an oath abjuring every foreign power. Yet many representatives, especially those born in the United States, refused to support the bill. Aware that an oath of abjuration would eliminate any pretext for claiming neutrality, they voted against the measure and managed to have it laid aside. According to Michael Smith, an American Baptist preacher in Upper Canada at that time, the assemblymen were only following the wishes of their constituents. Smith also believed that passage of the bill would have led to a rebellion by American settlers.[11]

Brock's request for legislation to suspend Habeas Corpus for a period of eighteen months met a similar fate. Had he been granted that power, Brock could have arrested and detained without trial anyone he felt was endangering the public peace. A majority of assemblymen, however, believed that the measure was unnecessary. They reasoned that hostilities would probably be avoided and that in any case the province had managed to survive over two decades without such radical legislation. In addition to this "dread of arming Government" with extraordinary powers, the American element in the Assembly was cognizant that Brock sought the change in order to "keep the numerous body of Americans in a proper state of subordination."[12]

Brock had better luck with the amendments to the Militia Act that dealt with organization, training, and discipline. The new legislation increased the size of militia companies from fifty to one hundred men. The old regulation, which stipulated that companies could not exceed fifty men, had offered a means for some settlers to escape attendance at musters. Apparently a number of Upper Canadians had approached the wording of the Militia Act as they would any contract, and their "sharp" business sense had uncovered a loophole. When their officers attempted to force them out, they replied that their company's fifty-man limit had already been met. Ralfe Clench complained that these absentees even managed to avoid paying any fines because local magistrates agreed with this strict interpretation of the law.[13]

The new regulations also called for the creation of two "flank companies" from every battalion. These forces were to be deployed on the sides, or "flanks," of a body of regular troops and each company was to consist of up to one hundred volunteers willing to undergo training as often as six times a month. Should the number of enlisted men fall short of one hundred, a ballot system would be employed to draft the remainder from those men under forty years of age who had failed to volunteer. To ensure that balloting was kept to a minimum, various inducements were offered to those men willing to enlist of their own free will. Flank volunteers were exempt from both statute labour and jury duty, and from personal arrest on any civil process. Widows and children of flank members killed on active duty were promised annual pensions of five pounds provincial currency, while disabled veterans would receive nine pounds a year.[14]

The amendments meant that a larger proportion of the nearly 13,000 militiamen in the province would be better prepared for war.[15] Under it, one-third of the eligible men under forty, totalling some 1800 recruits, would at least have a smattering of proper training. Over time that number would increase, since provisions had been made for new recruits to replace one-third of the flank members at regular intervals. The remaining men under forty, and those up to sixty years of age, would continue in "sedentary battalions" and were only to be called upon if absolutely necessary. With 1800 partially trained militiamen, and about 11,000 more or less untrained, Brock believed a successful defence of the province might be possible. Moreover, to ensure greater compliance with military decisions, all militiamen were now required to take an oath of allegiance if asked to do so. Members of both flank companies and the sedentary battalions were also subject to trial by court martial for misbehaviour. A new scale of fines and jail sentences was created so that a refusal to follow lawful orders would now prove costly.[16] Although pleased with these changes to the Militia Act, Brock was less than satisfied that the Assembly had limited the duration of these amendments to the end of the current parliamentary session. Having failed to acquire either the oath of abjuration or the suspension of Habeas Corpus, he was forced to accept this limitation rather than come away from the session empty-handed.

While Brock issued orders directing the various districts to establish flank companies, Joseph Willcocks did his best to discredit the new system. In the pages of his Niagara newspaper, Willcocks announced that all members of the provincial militia would be forced to train at least six days a month. The *Kingston Gazette*, in contrast, pointed out that only flank volunteers were liable to train so often and that it was highly unlikely this would be necessary. The editor expressed surprise that a member of the provincial legislature could be "so base, so wicked" as to spread lies that would only lead to increased disaffection.[17] To counter Willcocks's campaign, Brock released circulars to the various colonial newspapers which explained why flank companies were needed and which stressed the benefits of volunteering. These bands of "Loyal, Brave and Respectable Young Men" would serve only as a supplementary force to the British army.[18] Should an emergency arise, the authorities would have at their disposal a group of men able to assist regular troops, who were expected to do most of the fighting. Such explanations seemed to work. After a tour of the Niagara region in early May, Brock reported that an "almost unanimous disposition to serve is daily manifested." He felt that all the flank companies could be completed shortly if arms and accoutrements were sent from Montreal.[19]

What Brock failed to appreciate was that the eagerness to enlist in the flank companies was not proof that Upper Canadians were anxious to fight. Since most inhabitants thought war was unlikely, the volunteers looked upon enlistment quite differently from Brock. For most, enlistment meant only that they acquired exemptions from statute labour, jury duty, and personal arrest for small debts. There was, however, another incentive to peacetime service in the militia. In a new colony, where marks of distinction were rare, service in the elite flank units of the militia could enhance one's status. A few serious social climbers even went so far as to purchase their own swords to brandish over the heads of their subordinates.[20]

In addition to the militia forces, Brock also had a group of volunteers gathered primarily from the eastern portion of the province. A proposal to raise a corps of volunteers from among the Scots of the Glengarry region had first been made after the *Chesapeake* incident in 1807 when a confrontation between a British warship and an American frigate nearly led to a full-scale conflict. Although not considered feasible at that time, the same proposal was understandably greeted with greater interest by Brock in 1811. He petitioned the British government to offer land grants and cash bounties to those volunteers willing to join the Glengarry Light Infantry Fencible Corps, led by Captain "Red George" Macdonell.[21] By May 1812 some four hundred "fine, young men," said to be "chiefly Scotch" in origin, were training at a camp near Three Rivers. The regiment was not made up solely of Upper Canadians, however, and recruiting parties went as far afield as Prince Edward Island in search of volunteers. Sir George Prevost believed that the recruiting had proved successful because of the "zeal of the Officers," who also received bounties for each private enlisted, and because the promised land grants had proven to be "a powerful Auxillary."[22]

After the declaration of war, the regulations dealing with those "auxillaries" underwent a change. From then on, privates who joined only for the duration of the American conflict were given four guineas bounty but were not entitled to land grants. Individuals willing to guarantee their services for three years, or until a general peace was declared in Europe, received slightly more money and were promised a one-hundred-acre farm. The change, therefore, meant that in order to acquire a land grant, volunteers also had to be willing to serve overseas. But these more demanding terms did not seem to hamper recruitment, and over 700 men eventually enlisted in 1812. Unfortunately for "Red George," some signed up only to receive the cash bounty and then disappeared. Thomas Armstrong, for instance, enlisted early in May at Kingston but was still missing in June. Apparently he was one of thirty-six men who had deserted after being awarded a bounty, and another thirty left after they reached headquarters. It was later discovered that five of those deserters were already wanted for similar incidents with other regular units.[23] A soldier who served with the British army in Upper Canada later recalled that once enrolled in the ranks, the "military ardor of the young Glengarrians had evaporated like the morning dew." Donald McLeod also noted that the high rate of desertions forced future recruiting parties to be far less selective. Eventually the Fencible companies "were soon filled up with runaway sailors, English, Irish, Dutch, Americans, Canadians, and a sprinkling of Africans, with a considerable portion of broken-down raftsmen." [24]

There were also problems meeting the quotas established for the militia flank companies. Recruitment of volunteers had been limited by shortages of rations and weapons, and only in the Niagara and Home districts were the flank companies well established. At the end of April some 700 men had been embodied but, with the arrival of the confidential dispatch in May warning that war was imminent, Brock decided to call out the 1800 men which the new Militia Act permitted. On 15 May he ordered the flank companies to begin training as often as the law allowed.[25] Brock then approached the Executive Council to supplement the incentives offered to flank-company volunteers. Four days after calling out the companies, he suggested that the Council request from the prince regent that militiamen be granted "UE" status if killed or wounded on active service. Following Brock's advice that "immediate disclosure" of this request was necessary, the adjutant-general of the militia, Eneas Shaw, announced a few days later that the government was seeking a "portion of the Waste lands of the Crown" for such individuals.[26]

In addition to recruitment difficulties, the militia suffered from problems dealing with training and discipline. Militiamen were expected to bring their own arms to training sessions, but some were too poor to afford weapons and others claimed to have lost those supplied by the government. Between 1795 and 1812 several thousand muskets were given to the militiamen of the province, but when Brock attempted to account for those weapons he found most were "lost to the service."[27] Since such a valuable item was not likely to be accidentally misplaced, it was probable that many inhabitants had sold the weapons for a profit. To prevent the "disappearances of guns so common in the past," Brock directed that all government-supplied arms were to be stored in depots after each day's training.[28] Although this procedure might have reduced the number of incidents, it did not prevent all weapons from going astray. In June 1812 Abraham Nelles, a captain of one of the Fourth Lincoln flank companies, reported that seven of his men had still managed to misplace their muskets.[29]

The policy of storing guns nightly also had been prompted by the uncertain loyalties of the Upper Canadian populace. Earlier in the year Brock had noticed that some of the "most dubious characters" in the province had expressed a desire to acquire arms from the government.[30] It was probably for that reason that Brock had also decided to create the flank companies. Not only would flank members be better trained than their fellow militiamen, but it was expected that the majority would be volunteers who, unlike unwilling conscripts, could be relied on to act properly. Sir George Prevost was convinced that only about a third of the militia in Upper Canada was loyal enough to be entrusted with arms.[31] The new militia system, which limited access to the king's stores, was a reflection of the suspicions and doubts that plagued the fragmented society of Upper Canada.

Meanwhile, the mistrust that existed between British and American Upper Canadians caused problems for Robert Nichol. Brock had appointed Nichol to the command of one of the Norfolk flank regiments, but on taking up his post, the men refused to follow Nichol's orders. Apparently his junior officers, because of some personal animosity, had spread rumours about him; among others, it was alleged that he believed no American should ever be trusted. Try as he might, Nichol could not erase the impression created by such gossip. After printing and distributing handbills denying the charge, he still found that the men refused to recognize his authority. "My wish is to *command* a regiment," complained Nichol to a superior, "and *not to be* the *leader* of a mob."[32] Problems between the officers and men of the Norfolk militia undoubtedly played a part in Nichol's being offered the full-time post of quartermaster general of the militia. The Scottish merchant, concerned as always about the effect such public duty would have on his private interests, at first refused the offer. But Brock persisted and eventually the "clever little

Scotsman" was persuaded. His decision to undergo such "a great personal sacrifice" was made easier when Brock reminded him that the "British government was never backward in rewarding faithful and meritorious service."[33]

On the eve of war, therefore, Brock's situation had improved only slightly. The new militia system was well suited to provincial conditions and would eventually provide a portion of the male population with the skills needed for military operations. All the same, shortages of both money and recruits had hampered the complete implementation of the plan, and the province was still far from secure against invasion. Moreover, no assurances could be given about the loyalties of the large American element in the population. Worse still, even members of the British and Loyalist communities appeared to need added inducements to ensure their support. Members of the Six Nations also appeared to be indifferent. As a result, one could not blame Brock for having "no great confidence in the majority" of the provincial population.[34] Despite that realistic assessment, even he was surprised by how passively the inhabitants responded to the invasion of their province.

News of the outbreak of hostilities between the United States and Great Britain first reached General Brock on 24 June, but he decided against immediately informing the population of this development.[35] He reasoned that the information would eventually spread throughout Upper Canada anyway, and he was determined to use the interim period to his best advantage. He quickly ordered both the British regulars and the militia flank companies in the Niagara region to assemble and march to Fort George. Members of the flank companies were told only that muskets were to be acquired at the garrison and they were then to be sent home. According to Michael Smith, the volunteers "obeyed with cheerfulness," having no idea that war had already been declared.[36] This little act of deception served its purpose. Before they realized what was happening, some nine hundred militiamen reported for duty and found themselves distributed among the four posts along the Niagara frontier. Not surprisingly, when the real situation was made apparent to the men there were many expressions of dissatisfaction. Brock attempted to molify the militia by announcing on 2 July that they would be entitled to the same pay and provisions as regular troops, but few seemed impressed by this offer. The next day Brock admitted to Prevost that the original cheerful disposition of the Upper Canadians had been replaced by "a spirit of impatience."[37]

Though his trick had brought the militia out, Brock's actions also meant that the volunteers had not been given the opportunity to bring blankets and other necessary equipment. Since the men were expected to supply their own kits, they demanded pay to buy the required items. When this was not given, the men began to desert. On 4 July 1812 Brock warned that if this behaviour continued, the enemy would soon "destroy and lay waste to the province."[38] That stern message appeared to have little effect, however, since the number of desertions continued to mount. To reduce the number of absentees, Brock announced on 10 July that half the men could return to their homes, but only if they left their muskets behind.[39] Of those who remained on duty, Brock was sure most would leave anyway once the harvest began in spite of the £20 fine for desertion. That possibility worried Brock immensely. Although many of the militiamen appeared willing to defend their own property, Brock felt that the majority were "either indifferent to what is passing, or so completely American as to rejoice in a change of government." Had he had a greater number of regulars at his disposal, Brock believed the population would offer its support more readily. As things stood, however, most were content to wait out events. Trying to put the best light on the situation, Brock reminded Prevost that such "cool calculators" were numerous in every society.[40]

The British were no more successful in acquiring Indian support. The New York Six Nations had adopted a position of neutrality at a council held at Buffalo on 6 July. Emissaries were then sent to their Canadian counterparts urging them to follow the same course. Previously, Brock had called on the Grand River settlements to send all their warriors to Fort George. To Brock's disgust only one hundred men of "that fickle race" appeared, and these only for a few days. Brock thought he might yet win their support, but he was sure that the crown would have to "sacrifice some money to gain them over."[41] For that purpose Joseph Willcocks, who was known to the Six Nations, was approached to serve as intermediary and he eventually achieved a good deal of success on this mission. In the meantime, the Canadian Six Nations returned the answer to the deputation from their American brothers: "We know not your disputes ... We do not want to fight ... but if you come to take our land, we are determined to defend ourselves."[42] Those were sentiments with which Upper Canadians of every background appeared to agree.

Meanwhile, without the support of the Six Nations and with half his trained Niagara militia on leave, Brock received word that Brigadier-General William Hull had entered western Upper Canada on 11 July. After arriving in the province, the American commander issued his proclamation asking the inhabitants to exchange British tyranny for "Civil and Religious Liberty and their necessary result –

individual and general prosperity." He went on to request that the men remain at home, and he warned that any white man found fighting at the side of an Indian would be put to death. That last provision was designed to discourage the use of native warriors by the British. Tales of horrible atrocities had left many Americans, including Hull, with a considerable fear of the Indian style of fighting. News of the proclamation soon spread throughout the province, but the effect of this warning, while impressive, was not exactly what Hull had intended. A number of American settlers in Upper Canada were offended by the tone of the offer and upset by its terms. According to Smith, few of the inhabitants of the province considered themselves subjects of a tyrannical government. If they had, they would have crossed back over the border. Nonetheless, they did not wish to fight for either side in the contest; Smith said that originally many had decided they would run to the American lines and surrender when battles occurred. The threat of giving no quarter to anyone found fighting beside an Indian, however, would have made that ploy suicidal. Smith explained that the Upper Canadians were angry because they "were well assured that Hull knew every man in Canada to be under the controul of government, and that they were obliged to bear arms ... and that they could not prevent the Indians from marching with them." As to Hull's "friendly advice" about staying home and remaining neutral, most would have done so if circumstances had permitted. "This proposal they would willingly have acceded to," Smith believed, "for they dreaded the war with their whole souls."[43]

The decision to remain at home was made easier if no strong British garrison was nearby. In the western regions, where there were few regulars, the proclamation "operated very powerfully on our Militia," reported Colonel Matthew Elliot of the First Essex. Nor should it be forgotten that the American offer promised greater prosperity and guaranteed the protection of private property if citizens remained neutral. For a people dedicated to improving their economic circumstances, these were powerful incentives to obey Hull's directions. Some months later an American spy reported to Major-General Van Rensselaer that the proclamation worked primarily because there was "a security for private property contained in it."[44]

In an attempt to limit the effect of Hull's proclamation, Brock countered with one of his own only ten days later. To those who thought that the economic prospects of the colony would improve under American control, Brock explained that the "unequalled prosperity" already enjoyed by the province was a product of government expenditure and access to British markets. Brock also warned the American element in the province that the United States actually intended to give Canada back to France after the war was over. Instead of enjoying American liberty, Upper Canadians would find themselves "slaves to the Despot" Napoleon. Finally, Brock reminded all inhabitants, including those who had never taken the oath of allegiance, to resist any American appeal for assistance. As "Canadian Freeholders," every citizen owed allegiance to Britain. Those who failed to heed this advice did so at their own peril, Brock warned, since Britain would eventually win the war.[45]

A recent occurrence added an air of plausibility to that statement. In the early hours of 17 July, a small British force from St Joseph Island captured the American post at Michilimackinac. The victory was bloodless, as the American forces surrendered after being caught completely by surprise. Having never been informed by their own forces that war had been declared, the Americans at Michilimackinac were not prepared to fight when Captain Charles Roberts and his redcoats appeared at the gates. The capture of this small post proved to be of monumental significance to the British war effort. For the western Indians, such as the Miami, Shawnee, Ottawa, and Delaware, it was proof that their old ally Britain was determined to defeat the Americans. As a result, hundreds of western warriors were now committed to the British cause.[46]

Encouraged by the success at Michilimackinac, Brock began preparations to regain control of the territory occupied by Hull's forces. On 22 July he ordered all militia furloughs cancelled. Colonel Thomas Talbot was directed to assemble the two hundred members of the flank companies of the Oxford, Norfolk, and Middlesex regiments at Moraviantown. Brock assumed that the one thousand Western militiamen, many of whom were French Canadian and not recent American arrivals, could offer a spirited defence until Talbot's London militia joined them. In combination with a force of Indian volunteers expected to number at least 150, and with the regular troops from that region, Brock thought he could force Hull to retreat. In this expectation, however, he was to be sorely disappointed.[47]

Those militiamen directly in Hull's path had originally assembled at Sandwich "with as much promptitude as could be expected."[48] On hearing of Hull's generous offer of protection for the property of neutrals, however, the majority of Essex and Kent militiamen left their posts and returned to their homes. The remainder retreated to Fort Amherstburg with some three hundred regulars of the 41st Regiment on 10 July 1812.[49] Three days later Lieutenant-Colonel T.B. St George reported to Brock that the retreat to Amherstburg had been prompted by the militia, which was "in such a state as to be totally inefficient in the field." Even after leaving Sandwich the local men continued to desert, and St George noted they were "going off in such numbers" that half the men had left in only a few days. The desertion of more than five hundred Western militiamen meant that Brock's front-line defences were too weak to offer resistance to the invaders.[50]

At that point Brock turned to the men of the London Distict, but here he had even less luck. Colonel Talbot had managed to assemble the militia from the Long Point region and they set out for Moravian-town, but along the way the whole force, except for a handful of officers, mutinied and turned back.[51] The number of other volunteers from the London District was described as "very small," and Charles Askin said on 21 July 1812 that only fifty Grand River Indians appeared willing to fight the invaders.[52] Brock reported that the other four hundred warriors, after hearing from emissaries sent by General Hull, had determined to "sit quietly in the midst of war." He also noted that the refusal of the Six Nations to follow the British standard had produced a "domino effect" among their white neighbours. Some militiamen claimed they could not leave their families and property so long as the "fickle" natives remained behind.[53]

Not only had most western Upper Canadians refused to follow orders, but one group had even decided to aid the invaders. The most prominent members of that disloyal body, Ebenezer Allan, Andrew Westbrook, and Simon Zelotes Watson, had crossed over to the American camp and offered to form a cavalry unit to help distribute copies of Hull's proclamation. Allan had served as a spy for the British during the revolutionary war, but in 1783 he had been imprisoned for ten months by his superiors who suspected that he was acting as a double agent. Nonetheless, after the war he moved to Upper Canada and in 1798 he received 2000 acres as a reduced officer. Allan proved to be a particularly "fractious misfit" and, after numerous disputes with neighbours, he was again arrested in 1806. This second jail term may have soured Allan's views towards the British government. One of his biographers has noted that his "allegiance to higher authority was never strong" anyway and that he was "primarily motivated by self-interest."[54]

Watson and Westbrook had both quarrelled with Thomas Talbot over business matters. Apparently Watson had sought to enter into a partnership with the colonel to settle immigrants, but the deal was never formalized and the two men had nearly come to blows over this misunderstanding. Brock remarked that Watson had paraded as far as Westminister Township in the London District distributing news of Hull's offer while at the same time vowing "bitter vengeance against the first characters of the province."[55] For his part, it seems Westbrook had quarrelled with Talbot about a number of issues in the past and he may have harboured a grievance over not being appointed an officer in the local militia.[56] His decision to support Hull in 1812, however, was probably related to more immediate concerns over property losses. A successful blacksmith, Westbrook was described as a "large, red-haired, rough featured man" who had managed to acquire land in four townships. According to Captain Daniel Springer, Westbrook had publicly declared he would not take up arms against Hull's force because "he had too much at stake."[57] Whatever Watson and Westbrook's motivations were for their actions, they could at least take some pride in knowing that they had succeeded in acquiring more followers than their old enemy. While Talbot's men deserted to their farms, Brock noted that Watson and Westbrook managed to gather about fifty individuals to assist in spreading word of the American offer.[58]

Reports of these events unnerved Brock. Though aware that most inhabitants desired to avoid war at all costs, the numerous desertions and evidence of widespread treasonous activity surprised him. "The population, although I had no great confidence in the majority," he informed Prevost on 28 July, "is worse than I expected to find it." Such an opinion is understandable. The Essex and Kent militia had done nothing to impede Hull's progress. The London area militia appeared equally unreliable, although Brock had previously placed great store in the loyalty of the settlers in that region. To prevent the "impending ruin of the country," he had determined two days earlier to go west himself and drive the enemy from the province.[59] Before embarking on such an expedition, however, Brock required a greater degree of control over the militia forces and population of the province. To acquire that power, he gathered together the members of the new sixth parliament for an emergency session on 28 July 1812.

During his speech at the Assembly's introductory session, Brock found himself offering contradictory messages about the state of the province. He claimed that the number of disaffected was few and that the militia had responded to the recent American invasion with conduct "worthy of the King whom they serve."[60] Yet his renewed request that Habeus Corpus be suspended and that more rigorous laws be enacted to deal with militia desertions revealed that the province was as threatened from within as it was from without. Aware that his speech would be published in colonial newspapers, Brock tried to put the best light on the situation, although that meant distorting the truth. Only a few days later, for example, he would admit to the Executive Council in a private session that the militia was in a "perfect state of insubordination." His purpose in addressing the Assembly had been to acquire a partial suspension of the Habeas Corpus Act. Once that was accomplished, Brock intended to begin wholesale prosecutions and he hoped the arrests would "restrain the general population from treasonable adherence to the enemy."[61] By lying to the Assembly, however, Brock had undercut his case for wider powers. Although most members of the legislature had surely heard rumours about the situation in western Upper Canada, Brock's speech offered them a way out of a difficult situation.

It seems that almost all of the assemblymen were convinced that the province would soon become part of the United States. In what they perceived to be the waning moments of British power in the colony, none wished to offend prospective American masters by offering Brock everything he wanted. Therefore, instead of authorizing a declaration of martial law, the assemblymen agreed only to amend certain aspects of the Militia Act. They spent the next eight days discussing the repeal of the 1807 School Act. In Brock's opinion those men had abandoned the "honest fulfillment of their duty" to avoid "incurring the indignation of the Enemy." Knowing that little further would be gained from the session, he prorogued the Assembly on 5 August 1812 after it had voted £10,000 for the militia.[62] For their part, the assemblymen were angered by Brock's actions and on 5 August they issued an address to the people of Upper Canada explaining the legislation adopted during the last session. They noted that "owing to the loyalty of the great body of the people," there was no need for a declaration of martial law. They also observed that the changes to the Militia Act permitted the use of very strict discipline. New regulations made it a crime to sell or barter arms and equipment, to counsel others not to appear for duty, and even to use disrepectful language against the royal family. Moreover, court martials were now empowered to deliver death sentences for desertion to the enemy and for fomenting mutiny or desertion.[63]

Of course, Brock had sought more than changes to the Militia Act, and this experience with the Assembly marked the lowest point in his career as leader of Upper Canada. The day after the Assembly began proceedings, Brock informed a fellow officer, Edward Baynes, that his situation was "most critical, not from anything the enemy can do, but from the disposition of the people – the population, believe me, is essentially bad – a full belief possess them all that this Province must inevitably succumb – this prepossession is fatal to every exertion. Legislators, magistrates, militia officers, all have imbibed this idea ... Most of the people have lost all confidence. I however,

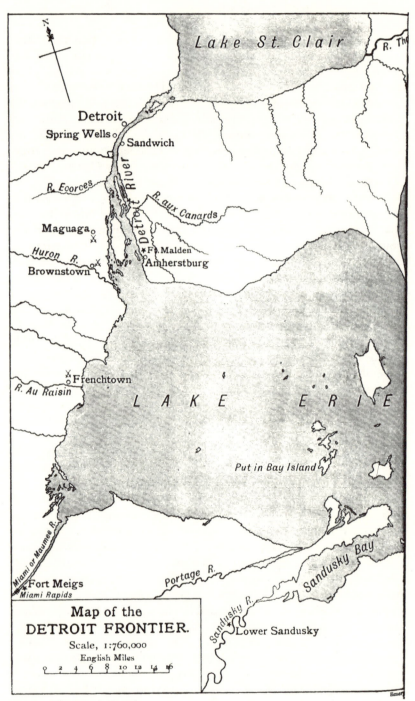

Map of the
DETROIT FRONTIER.

Scale, 1:760,000
English Miles

Map 2   The Detroit Frontier

speak loud and look big." But that bravado had turned to desperation as the session dragged on without any movement on the question of wider powers for the executive. Eventually, as he later admitted to Prevost, Brock considered declaring martial law on his own authority but was warned that, if he did so, the whole of the provincial militia would disperse.[64]

After deciding to prorogue the legislature, however, Brock appeared reinvigorated. W.D. Powell remarked that after taking that step, Brock immediately "proceeded to the Barracks and harrangued the militia." Apparently this tirade impressed a number of the York militiamen. Several hundred volunteered that same day for service in any part of the province, and Brock selected 100 men and ordered them to march to Long Point. A further 150 militiamen from the Home and Niagara districts eventually followed that first group of volunteers. In this manner over the next two weeks, Brock managed to assemble a motley force for the relief of Amherstburg. He detached just over 300 regulars from the Niagara frontier and eventually acquired 600 native allies, including a handful of Six Nations warriors. He also managed to assemble 400 militiamen, including 150 from the London and Western districts; altogether, the British relief force totalled just over 1300 men.[65]

On 13 August Brock's force reached Amherstburg, only to find that the Americans, after surviving food shortages and outbreaks of disease, had retreated to their own shore. Although outnumbered two to one by the Americans, Brock decided to cross the Detroit River in pursuit of Hull's army. To fool the enemy into believing that the British force was much stronger than it actually was, the militia were supplied with the red jackets usually worn by regular soldiers. Before launching this audacious attack, Brock warned the Americans that the Amerindian warriors attached to his force would "be beyond control the moment the contest commences."[66] This announcement must have been chilling to Detroit's defenders since even British soldiers who served with the native volunteers were frightened by their appearance. Thomas Verchères recalled that the warriors afforded an "extraordinary spectacle," with bodies covered in red or blue clay, or tatooed black and white from head to foot. He described the scene as "horrifying beyond expression," and said watching the assembly of warriors made him feel as if he were "standing at the entrance to hell."[67] Hull, who was also deathly afraid of the Amerindians, heeded the British warning and surrendered Fort Detroit without firing a shot. Brock's gamble had paid off and, when later accused of being reckless, he countered by arguing "that the State of the Province admitted of nothing but desperate remedies." Yet he also denied that the unconditional surrender of the numerically superior enemy had been a matter of luck, preferring instead to see it as a product of the "cool calculation of the *pours* and *contres*."[68]

The 400 volunteers who followed Brock to Detroit, however, constituted only about 7 per cent of the 5850 militiamen eligible for service in the Home, Niagara, London, and Western districts. If the 500 men who remained on duty on the Niagara frontier are added to that number, about 85 per cent of the militiamen from those areas are still not accounted for, although the authorities had called out both the flank companies and the sedentary battalions in those districts. Where had the rest of the "Spartan Band" gone? Almost all, it seems, had returned quietly to their farms or had never left them in the first place.[69]

Most of the militia in the London and Western districts had simply returned home after Hull issued his proclamation, and many of their officers had quickly followed suit. On his arrival at Amherstburg, Brock had issued a general order expressing his discontent over the numerous desertions that had taken place during the last few weeks. Instead of fining deserters, however, Brock only asked commanding officers to transmit the names of those few militiamen who had remained faithful so "that immediate measures may be taken to discharge their arrears of pay."[70] A court of enquiry, appointed by Brock after the capture of Detroit, recommended that ten officers of the Essex and Kent militias be removed from their positions. But the court also announced that there were many others "to whom no share of blame can justly attach."[71] With no realistic means of punishing the hundreds of deserters in that region, it seems the British authorities were forced to settle for the token chastisement of a few of the most prominent offenders.

In the Niagara District, those who had been granted leave to attend to their farms early in July had refused, almost to a man, to return to their posts when called for by Brock. That left only 500 members of the Lincoln flank companies on duty, and many of them served very reluctantly. Colonel Christopher Myers, in charge of the district after Brock's departure for Amherstburg on 5 August, reported that "desertion to their homes is rather prevalent among them."[72] It seems likely that had no regular forces been present in central and eastern Upper Canada, militiamen in those areas, like the citizen-soldiers in the Western District, would have dispersed completely. For instance, a muster roll for Lieutenant Eli Playter's militia company during the month of August reveals that the men of the Home District were quite anxious to avoid service. Although by law the company could contain up to one hundred men fit for duty, the corps never reached half that total in August. Apparently one of the men had only recently discovered that he was near-sighted and therefore ineligible for duty. Beside another man's name was the notation "delirious," while others were simply classified as "deserters." Interestingly, Playter seems to have differentiated between those men who had left the ranks and two men who were listed as "gone to the States."[73] This would seem to imply that, at least for Playter, deserters were those who had returned to their farms and might yet be forced back on duty. Whether that was true or not, the muster roll for Playter's company illustrates how a fighting unit could quickly become a "paper force."

In the Niagara and Home districts, however, refusal to attend a militia summons could lead to arrest and imprisonment at the hands of British regulars. For that reason many individuals evidently decided to follow the path chosen by Playter's two men. The *Buffalo Gazette* and other American newspapers carried regular articles detailing the "escapes" made by "native born citizens of the United States."[74] Donald McLeod, a British soldier who served in the colony during the war, remarked that hundreds of people "escaped to the United States to avoid being drafted in the militia" at this time. It seems that most of those who chose to cross over were young tradesmen with little stake in Upper Canada. Those Americans with large holdings were more inclined to remain and guard their property, although the fear of military service induced a number of them to leave as well. An official list of landowners in the province who abandoned their farms during the war to flee south contains 336 names.[75]

In view of the behaviour of most Upper Canadians, it is scarcely surprising that Brock considered the men actually willing to do their duty to be particularly deserving of praise. After his western expedition he wrote to the earl of Liverpool in August 1812 about the exploits of his "little Band" of regulars, Indians, and militia. Brock claimed that he had never "witnessed greater cheerfulness and constancy" among any other troops. That attitude apparently proved infectious. Later, Brock told his brothers that other inhabitants had been inspired with confidence by the recent successes, and he noted that the whole situation of the province was "of late much improved."[76] Because of that change he now felt sure he could repeat the experience in the eastern region of the province. Within days of his victory at Detroit, Brock was making plans to attack the American posts along the Niagara River.

But on his arrival at Fort George on 22 August he discovered that Sir George Prevost had negotiated a temporary armistice five days before.[77] Since the militia were anxious to deal with their crops, Brock announced on 26 August that four-fifths of the flank members would be granted indefinite furloughs. Before being sent home, the men were warned that they should be prepared to return at a moment's notice. He then directed that general inspections of the Home, Niagara, and London militias take place weekly. At these drills the officers were expected to call upon the men to take the oath of allegiance and to note the names of those who refused. Some officials apparently went beyond these instructions and jailed men who declined to repeat the pledge. "Many took the oath," observed Smith, "rather than suffer this."[78] Of course, not all officers acted this way, and those who ordered colonists disarmed and jailed without proper recourse to the law were described by McLeod as "insolent, cruel, and oppressive" men.[79]

Brock was in a position to grant furloughs, not only because of Prevost's armistice, but also because he had finally acquired the support of the Grand River Six Nations. The warriors had originally stood back because they feared that the contest might lead to a fratricidal struggle. The Iroquois were afraid they might end up fighting members of the New York Six Nations and most, therefore, simply chose to ignore Brock's first appeals. Apparently the recent British victories, and the offer of "good wages to engage in the war," had led the Indians to reconsider their position of neutrality.[80] By 7 September some three hundred warriors had arrived in the Niagara District. Aside from frightening the American soldiers, however, Brock feared he would get "no essential service from this degenerate race." At the same time, he noted that the warriors appeared "ashamed of themselves" and had promised "to whipe away the disgrace into which they have fallen by their late conduct."[81]

Unfortunately for Brock, those flank members who remained on active duty seemed to share none of the determination now evinced by the Six Nations warriors. Although only 20 per cent of the militia were required to remain on duty, their officers were hard pressed to keep even that small number. On 21 September deserters were informed that Brock was willing to overlook their offence if they returned voluntarily. As the problem increased, however, Brock realized that the indifference of the majority of the inhabitants made a successful defence of the province increasingly unlikely. "I am quite anxious for this state of warfare to end," he wrote his brothers on 18 September, "I scarcely can think the people will suffer it to continue."[82]

On 13 October the war between Britain and the United States came to an end for Major-General Isaac Brock. At Queenston, on the Upper Canadian side of the Niagara River, he lost his life attempting to halt the second invasion of the colony by American troops. The next day his successor, Sir Roger Hale Sheaffe, managed to drive back the invaders, but not without loss of life on both sides. British dead, aside from twelve regulars, included two York militiamen and five Six Nations warriors. A further thirty-one York and Lincoln militiamen were wounded. Compared with casualty rates for battles in Europe, however, the losses at Queenston Heights were modest. A little over one month before, for example, Napoleon's army of 130,000 soldiers engaged a Russian force at the Battle of Borodino where casualties on both sides totalled over 70,000.[83]

Historians have sometimes said that the Battle of Queenston Heights was a turning point for Upper Canadian morale. C.P. Stacey, for instance, saw it as a "victory which further raised the spirits of the people of Upper Canada."[84] Yet an examination of the subsequent actions of the provincial militia reveals that the mood and behaviour of the inhabitants remained fundamentally unchanged. Immediately after the battle, Sheaffe called out both the flank companies and the sedentary battalions in the London, Niagara, and Home districts. This action, designed to bring together a force of 5000 men, was considered necessary in the face of further American invasions.[85] A majority of the inhabitants, however, were unwilling to answer that call. A British soldier who served in the colony during the war said that at this time hundreds of colonists "absoutely declined doing any kind of duty, civil or military, under the colonial authorities."[86] If caught, of course, shirkers could be jailed, and some chose to avoid punishment by leaving their homes. In Whitchurch Township, north of York, some seventy men chose to hide out in the woods rather than serve in their units. By December 1812, when Smith passed through the region, more than three hundred rebels had banded together. At that time Smith spotted a fifty-man contingent walking brazenly "on the main road, with Fife and drum beating for volunteers, crying Huzza for Madison."[87]

The republican sympathies of the Whitchurch rebels, and their determination to endure life away from their farms, certainly set them apart from other Upper Canadians. Most men in the province who managed to avoid service never abandoned their cozy farms for caves in the countryside. The experiences of Eli Playter with his militia company were probably typical. His diary describes the situation after the Third York regiment was once again called into service: "17th [October] I waited for the Men's coming till late the P.M. not more than ½ the company appeared ... 18th went early to some of the peoples Houses but they kept out of the way – I was much vexed at their conduct." Eventually Playter managed to gather about twenty men together. They set out for York, where two-thirds were excused and seven were balloted for service at the Niagara front.[88]

In addition to running off to the bush, or just lying low until their commanding officers had given up in frustration, Upper Canadians also avoided militia service through other means. Owing to recent amendments to the Militia Act, those with enough money could employ substitutes. Previously, the militia regulations had required draftees to appear for service whenever a partial call of the militia occurred. As of 5 August 1812, however, a draftee was permitted to send an able-bodied man in his place.[89] For a number of reasons, the use of substitutions, although a time-honoured and acceptable practice in most armed forces, was not as common in Upper Canada as one might expect. Since substitution was never permitted during a general call of the militia, the original draftee was still liable for service in the unlikely event that the whole regiment was called out. Also, it seems that it was exceedingly difficult to entice anyone to take the job. Those lucky enough to find a willing candidate were forced to barter away valuable items – such as a yoke of steer or as much as £50 cash -in exchange for a year's service.[90] For some Upper Canadian confidence artists, these transactions proved to be both profitable and relatively risk free. Philip Philips, for instance, deserted from the Third York militia only days after he took the place of William Shaw.[91]

As a traditional and respectable means of avoiding service, substitution was obviously a preferred method of steering clear of the fighting, but other legal means were also available. Amendments to the Militia Act passed by the Assembly in August had created a host of newly exempt occupations. According to the revised regulations, the following people now joined religious groups such as Tunkers, Quakers, and Mennonites in being excused from duty: "The Judges of the court of Kings bench, the Clergy, the Members of the Legislative and Executive Councils and their respective Officers ... His Majestys Attorney General, Solicitor General, the Secretary of the Province ... as well as all Magistrates, Sheriffs, Coroners, Halfpay Officers, Physicians, Surgeons, the Masters of Schools, ferrymen and one miller to every Grist Mill." Of course, the assemblymen thought it wise to include exemptions for themselves, at least "for the time being."[92]

If by some misfortune a well-to-do colonist did not qualify for an exemption or was unable to find a substitute, he could choose to remove himself from danger by simply ignoring the call and paying any fine that was levied. It has been estimated that in peacetime a farmer with thirty to forty acres cleared could expect a gross annual income of at least £110. During the war, however, inflationary pressures meant farmers' gross incomes doubled, and this prospective prosperity was a tremendous incentive to avoid militia duty. Since calls for service often came at harvest time and the largest fine that could be levied against a militia deserter in 1812 was only £20, risking punishment was often worthwhile.[93] Job Lodor, from the London District, admitted after the war that he "always procured a substitute when his tour of duty came" except when a general call for the militia was made. When that occurred, he would merely "go home & secure his many goods & property" and then await a fine. Of course, those who wished to avoid paying fines could also leave the province. That was the course chosen by Samuel Sherwood, who departed for Lower Canada as soon as war was declared. Sherwood, the son of a prominent Loyalist and a former member of the Assembly for Grenville, was apparently anxious about remaining in a region where the militia was "liable to be called out en masse." He therefore decided to go east to a safer area until hostilities had ceased.[94]

Some militia officers shielded their friends and relatives from serving by sending ineligible replacements in their stead. One such case involved Philip Lang, a private in the First York militia, who was described as being "lame an[d] sick better than two years." Nonetheless, Lang was balloted and sent to the garrison at the capital as part of the quota of men from the First York militia. His commanding officer, Captain James Mustard, was told by a superior: "Do not for the future have any man or men drafted for Actual Service that you know is sick or anyway not fit." Lieutenant-Colonel Graham went on to explain that such deception was "great trouble to me and a disappointment to the Public Service."[95] It also seems that a good number of settlers avoided militia service by simply announcing that they were Americans and, therefore, could not be forced to fight against their fellow countrymen. Brock had sought an oath of abjuration in February precisely because he foresaw that some inhabitants would take this position, but the refusal of the Assembly to pass the measure meant that the issue remained unresolved throughout the summer and it was not until 9 November that steps were finally taken to eliminate the practice. On that date, Sheaffe issued a proclamation directing the "divers Persons" claiming exemptions because of American citizenship to appear before boards that had been established in every district. Those who could prove they were Americans were to be given passports and escorted to the border. Any American who failed to appear before such a board by 1 January 1813 was warned that he would be considered an "enemy Alien" and was therefore "liable to be treated as a Prisoner of War, or a Spy."[96]

Declaring oneself an American, and therefore a noncombatant, sometimes proved risky even before Sheaffe announced his program of deportation. Some of those who had refused to take the oath of allegiance in August had been arrested and jailed for that refusal. Donald McLeod recalled that after hostilities had broken out, those Americans suspected of being disloyal were disarmed "and strictly watched."[97] Others were harassed by militiamen or British regulars who "thought it hard and unreasonable that they must bear all the burden and danger of war." Some Indian warriors, if they came across a "Yankee" who refused to serve, would threaten to kill him. According to Smith, the Indians sometimes made good on their threats.[98] In the end, however, a number of Americans who continued to refuse to fight were permitted to remain in the country even after reporting to the alien boards. Despite all Sheaffe's tough talk, it quickly became apparent that some well-established gentlemen who had purchased land and had never taken the oath of allegiance would be ruined by this order. For that reason, Sheaffe allowed such men to remain in the province under a "modified allegiance, or security of good conduct."[99] Other Americans, who it was felt knew too much about the defences of Upper Canada to be sent back to the United States, were also granted permission to remain in the colony.[100]

Whether they remained at home through legal or illegal means, or left their farms for Lower Canada, the United States, or the backwoods, the majority of Upper Canadians managed to avoid service in the militia. After the Battle of Queenston Heights on 13 October, Sheaffe had summoned 5000 colonists to duty on the front lines, but on 24 October the paymaster recorded the presence of only 846 militia officers and privates in the Niagara peninsula.[101] Instead of increasing as time passed, the number of men on duty actually declined and, as another Canadian winter set in, the British authorities knew they would be faced with the difficult task of trying to keep even that small contingent on duty.

In addition to worsening weather, the British forces were experiencing problems with logistics. Although Sheaffe had ordered out 5000 men, he had neither the rations nor the equipment to feed and house additional soldiers. On 3 November he informed Prevost that the militia on the frontier was "in a very destitute state with respect to clothing, and in all regards bedding and barrack comforts in general." Not surprisingly, Sheaffe also went on to report that such conditions were prompting desertions. Ten days later he announced that the "many absentees" would not be punished if they returned voluntarily. The next day he sweetened the offer by promising to supply trousers, shoes, and jackets to flank members free of charge. Even men absent without leave could receive these items providing they returned "voluntarily and without delay."[102]

Other steps were also taken to reduce the number of absentees and to entice men back to duty. To help in uncovering desertions, officers commanding militia units were ordered to institute three roll calls a day. They were also instructed to establish squads comprising "a trusty sergeant and a file of men" to search for and apprehend any deserters.[103] Finally, a local resident, Samuel Street, Sr, was appointed as paymaster to the militia forces. It seems that the official formerly employed by the regular forces had often ignored the calls of the militia for pay and this, in turn, caused much dissatisfaction.[104] Several weeks after implementing this program, Sheaffe was able to report that the combined policy of bribes, strict discipline, coercion, and prompt payment had worked. On 23 November he informed Prevost that the number of militia in the field had increased recently and he was pleased to report that the men "continue generally, to evince the best disposition."[105]

Sheaffe's appraisal of the morale of the militia was optimistic. It was clear that miserable camp conditions were taking an enormous toll. The combination of inadequate hygiene and the lack of basic camp equipment, such as tents, blankets, and kettles, made disease the principal killer of Upper Canadians in the first year of the war. James Mann, a surgeon who served on the American side of the lines, reported that soldiers in nearby New York were struck by waves of different diseases. From July to September most men suffered from dysentery, diarrhoea, and fevers but, once winter arrived, there were also outbreaks of measles and severe pneumonia. The same sort of conditions existed on the British side, with predictable results. Pension lists record the deaths of only three members of the provincial militia during battles at Queenston and Fort Erie in late 1812. Disease, however, accounted for at least forty-six casualties among men on duty. As winter progressed, so too did the number of deaths from disease. The two men who died in September were followed by five the next month, and by eleven in November. Finally, in December, a minimum of twenty-eight militiamen died from diseases contracted while on duty.[106]

The large concentration of untrained men and dangerous weapons also ensured that accidents were commonplace. On 27 September 1812 Brock was forced to issue a general order reminding Upper Canadians to guard against "careless negligence" in the handling of weapons. He informed the militiamen that no greater military

Table 1
Lincoln Militia Service, 1812

	30 Nov.	4 Dec.	11 Dec.
	Captain Crook's Lincoln Flank Company		
Active	32	23	15
Ill	18	14	15
AWOL	31	44	51
Total	81	81	81
	Captain Macklem's Lincoln Flank Company		
Active	40	27	15
Ill	6	7	7
AWOL	8	20	32
Total	54	54	54

Source: AO, Abraham Nelles Papers, Field Reports, 1812–14. These designations are a simplified version of the various systems of notation used at that time. "Active" includes "Present and Fit" or "Present under Arms," those on leave or on duty elsewhere. "Ill" includes sick at home, in hospital, or in barracks. The "AWOL," or absent without leave, designation was at times noted explicitly, but sometimes had to be determined by eliminating other designations from the original total.

offence could be committed than the reckless use of firearms or the "willful waste" of ammunition. Nonetheless, at his own headquarters four days later, Brock was forced to specifically forbid the "practice of individuals firing in the swamp or any other place within the neighbourhood" of Fort George. Such activities had predictable results. Pension lists record four militia casualties from accidents between September and December 1812. It would appear that at this point in the war colonists were more likely to be wounded by their comrades than by the enemy.[107]

Hungry, cold, fearful of becoming sick or injured, and worried about their families, it is hardly surprising that Upper Canadians simply walked away from the war. After all, most considered it none of their affair in the first place. Surviving muster rolls of two flank companies from the fall campaign of 1812 reveal the course of action adopted by most militiamen (see table 1). In less than two weeks, Crook and Macklem found themselves with more men absent without leave than on duty. The situation seems to have prevailed throughout the district. Captain Applegarth's flank company of the Second York militia had only three men present and fit for duty on 11 December.[108]

In their anxiety to return home, a number of deserters may have unwittingly spread the diseases ravaging the men at the front. Militia officer William Hamilton Merritt wrote to his fiancée in the United States on 8 December 1812: "You cannot conceive the state our frontier is in. Not a woman to be seen and you, I hope, hardly know that war exists. I am sorry to say that we have had a very sickly season, many young men have died through fatigue, and fifty people from the 10 and 12 Mile Creek with a fever which is equal to a plague."[109] Apparently even some Upper Canadians who managed to remain at home found they could not escape the wider effects of the war.

The muster rolls represented in table 1 suggest that most men seemed unconcerned about the possibility of court martial, and it appears that the desire to get away from careless and diseased comrades was greater than the fear of potential punishment. The leniency with which both Brock and Sheaffe had dealt with previous instances of mass desertion no doubt helped foster that attitude. Thus, when permission to leave was not forthcoming, the men took matters into their own hands. For Sheaffe this action represented a threat to his authority as commander of the forces in Upper Canada. Faced with the complete collapse of the militia defence system, Sheaffe was forced into action. On 11 December he dismissed almost all the militia, and five days later he allowed most of the remaining flank members to return home.[110]

The expedient of letting the men return home when it appeared they were all going to go anyway had been resorted to already by Brock in July. When Sheaffe confronted the same problem he was wise enough to perceive that nothing could be done to halt the numerous desertions. These militiamen were not hardened regular soldiers but settlers with families to care for and farms to tend. Dragging the men back to the field would only have made the British army unpopular; besides, the effort was not likely to work for long. There was also another benefit to the granting of a general leave. By adding official sanction to what had occurred, Sheaffe saved face since he at least maintained the appearance of being in control of the situation.

Sheaffe could consider himself lucky in one respect. On the opposite shore, General Alexander Smith was experiencing even greater difficulty with the New York militiamen. Their refusal to cross the Niagara River had led to the American defeat at the Battle of Queenston Heights. After that loss, the men began to desert in great numbers. The New York *Evening Post* reported on 11 November 1812 that the militia companies along the Niagara River were "dwindling to mere skeletons."[111] By the end of November the remaining men had mutinied and then "disembodied themselves." According to one witness, later taken prisoner by the British, the militiamen responsible for this mutiny declared that the Upper Canadians "were brothers and sisters, with whom they had always been at peace." Determined to keep matters that way, the American mutineers posted a $200 reward for Smith's head and then left for their farms.[112]

On the British side of the border there was also little enthusiasm for the war. Robert Nichol believed that the situation of the province had changed for the worse since Brock's death. "Confidence seems to have vanished from the land," he informed Colonel Talbot, "and a gloomy despondency has taken its place." One individual who refused to submit to the general miasma of depression was John Strachan. Reports of the frightful conditions at the front already had alarmed some members of the colonial elite and, on 22 November 1812, they met at York for the purpose of raising funds to buy supplies for the militiamen still on duty. Strachan chaired the meeting and told those in attendance that it was their duty "to comfort those who are fighting our battles."[113] By the end of the evening the Loyal and Patriotic Society of Upper Canada had been formed. A proposal to restrict voting rights in the organization to those who had paid a £10 fee was rejected and that privilege was instead automatically granted to members of the Executive and Legislative councils and, not surprisingly, to clergymen of the Church of England. Apparently, a good deal of resentment still existed over the Assembly's refusal to assist Brock, and only the speaker of the House was granted voting rights.[114]

Rather than simply assist active militiamen, the new society agreed to fund a number of projects. Families in distress because of the war were to be offered relief, and disabled militiamen were also considered fit objects for the society's bounty. The group even decided to award medals to those men who had distinquished themselves while on service. Aware that desertion was rampant at the front, the directors announced they would withhold medals from any "militiaman or soldier who has been or shall be convicted of desertion or absenting himself from duty." Of course, few of the directors themselves were on active service, chiefly because they had been lucky enough to have acquired exemptions. Chief Justice Thomas Scott was too old for militia service, but most of the other directors were under sixty years of age. Thomas Ridout was fifty-eight, William Powell had just celebrated his fifty-seventh birthday, and Alexander Wood was only forty. John Strachan, who was thirty-four years of age when he founded the society, later remarked that everywhere in the province "inhabitants rejoiced" to see those "who were exempted from their age or situation" coming forward to "comfort those who were called out." Although ostensibly designed to assist war sufferers, the society also served another purpose. It allowed Strachan and the other members of the colonial establishment to claim later that they had taken an "active part in the war" even though most of them never left the comfort of their homes.[115]

Avoidance of militia duty was the norm for Upper Canadian males throughout the struggle. Despite the high number of desertions during the first part of the war, participation in the militia actually reached a peak before Brock's death in October 1812. One researcher who has examined the postwar "cult of Brock worship" thinks that Upper Canadians idolized the British officer because they thought he was "merely a striking specimen of the men he led."[116] Yet Isaac Brock died less than four months after hostilities had commenced, and the war would rage for more than two years after his death. The victory at Michilimakinac had been gained without his direct participation, and the capture of Detroit was as much a product of Hull's cowardice as it was a result of careful planning on Brock's part. Why, then, was he chosen as an object for praise and raised to near demigod status by Upper Canadians? To answer that question one need only examine the conduct of the colonists after 1812. While the level of militia participation was certainly low before Brock's death, it dwindled even further in the months that followed. In contrast to this pitiful record, the dismal display of the first four months of the war appeared postively remarkable. Years later, writers would focus on Brock and the first few weeks of the conflict because there was at least a grain of truth to the claim that large numbers of Upper Canadians had responded with "unwearied exertions" when called to arms by their "immortal" leader.[117]

4 "A Parcel of Quakers?"
Militia Service, 1813–15

As dawn broke on the morning of 20 February 1813, John Strachan took pen in hand and settled in for a long day of writing at his new home in York. The ambitious young priest had moved to the capital from Cornwall less than a year before, after his request for the rectorate of the Kingston church had been denied. Although he had refused at first the alternate offer of a position at York, Strachan later changed his mind when Isaac Brock informed him that an extra £150 per annum could be acquired if he agreed to serve as chaplain for the troops.[1] Since that time, the new chaplain had established the Loyal and Patriotic Society and had become a director and the chief fundraiser for the group. It was in the latter capacity that Strachan had spent the last few days composing requests for donations. His latest effort, "An Appeal to the British Public," offered a selective view of recent events in the province and, according to Strachan, the people of Upper Canada deserved greater support from England because of the heroic actions of the colonists in 1812. He claimed that the patriotism of the Loyalists "had burst forth in all its ancient splendour" the moment war had been declared. Strachan also said that this enthusiasm still "burned with unabated vigour," and he even went so far as to declare that this "spirit of patriotism" had also spread among the recent American arrivals, making them "efficient soldiers" as well.[2]

While Strachan was composing this highly imaginative account, the British military authorities in the colony were engaged in a desperate search for a cure to the problems that afflicted the provincial

John Strachan, circa 1820
Archives of Ontario

militia. Contrary to Strachan's rosy opinions, and those of more recent writers such as G.F.G. Stanley, it was clear that when given a chance to "prove their worth," the flank companies had failed miserably.[3] To the men responsible for the military defence of the colony, the experiences of the previous few months had shown that the provincial militia system was next to useless. It could not be relied on to provide the number of militiamen that were needed, and it proved incapable of holding onto the few men who did offer their services.

As the architect of the flank and sedentary organizations, the late General Brock was blamed for some of the failures of 1812. While all agreed that he had been a brilliant strategist, some also thought he had shown himself to be an incompetent administrator. His tendency to overlook details while making grandiose plans had meant that the Upper Canadian militia forces were often left without sufficient clothing, food, or shelter. "Poor General Brock's high spirit," Major Thomas Evans wrote early in the new year, "would never descend to particulars." Evans also observed that what Brock considered "trifles" had eventually proven to be "essentials." Nor was Evans alone in his criticism. Sir George Prevost warned Sheaffe to pay greater attention to the proper feeding, clothing, and payment of the militia forces. He remarked that on his last visit to the province in 1812 "these essentials appeared to me not sufficiently attended to, and the cause of serious complaint."[4]

Other observers believed that the problems of the provincial militia could be solved if the men were treated more like regular troops. The amendments to the Militia Act passed by the Legislative Assembly in March 1813 were based on that assumption and seem to have developed from a proposal made earlier in the year by an officer stationed in the eastern region of the province. Concerned about what he called the "inefficient state of the militia," Lieutenant-Colonel Thomas Pearson wrote to Eneas Shaw about his plan for a new corps of volunteers to replace the old flank companies. In a letter dated 19 January 1813, Pearson explained that these battalions of volunteers should consist only of men willing to serve full-time until the end of the war. While these soldiers would receive the same pay as flank members had been given, Pearson thought they should also be supplied with bounties and uniforms. He even suggested that these new militia volunteers be offered land grants like those promised to members of the Glengarry Light Infantry Fencible Corps. Finally, Pearson proposed that each battalion of five hundred volunteers be led by competent militia lieutenant-colonels and that the whole regiment be commanded by a senior officer from the regular army who was well versed in discipline and training.[5]

Pearson's plan formed the basis of the legislation proposed by Roger Sheaffe on 13 March 1813 and passed by the Assembly later in the week.[6] The new provincial statute allowed for the creation of one or more regiments, each consisting of several battalions, to be styled Regiments of Incorporated Militia. Various privileges and exemptions, "as well as pecuniary encouragement," were offered to men willing to tender their service.[7] Volunteers were guaranteed freedom from arrest for any debt under £50, protection against their property being seized for debts, and exemption from tax rates and statute labour.[8] In addition, the Assembly offered a small reward to every recruit who offered his services. Sheaffe originally had asked for a twenty-dollar bounty, but the assemblymen feared that such an enormous sum would bankrupt the province. Sheaffe planned on enrolling as many as 3000 recruits, and the bounties could have amounted to as much as $60,000, or £15,000. Rather than vote a sum greater than the annual prewar provincial revenue, the Assembly agreed to give each recruit eight dollars.[9] Determined to see that the volunteers received all they deserved, Sheaffe petitioned his superior, Sir George Prevost, for the additional money. Before he received a response, however, Sheaffe announced that an extra bounty of ten dollars would be given to all recruits.[10]

Several factors prompted Sheaffe to announce the granting of an increased bounty before he had received the proper approval. First, he feared that the eight-dollar bounty was too small to "operate as an inducement" for full-time, indefinite service. That was especially true since the men were expected to supply their own uniforms from this money. Second, Sheaffe had been informed by Sir George Prevost that no regular reinforcements would be sent from Europe in 1813. In light of this news, he later wrote that a "most urgent necessity existed for forming without delay a force more efficient than the ordinary Militia of the Province."[11]

A recruiting campaign, designed to fill the several Incorporated Militia battalions, began almost as soon as the legislation was passed by the Assembly. Circulars announcing the creation of the force were published in the colony's newspapers, and all "strong and healthy" men between the ages of sixteen and forty-five were invited to enrol. To allow for speedy recruiting, each officer who was appointed to the Incorporated Militia was given a quota of men. Captains of companies, for instance, were to recruit twenty men, lieutenants were responsible for ten more, while ensigns had to enlist five. As an incentive to ensure that the limit of fifty men per company was reached, officers were not paid until they completed their quotas. Each private was to receive eight dollars as a cash bounty; the other ten dollars was to go to the commanding officer of the company to pay for the arms and clothing required by the volunteer. Potential recruits were promised the same pay as regular soldiers and were told that Sheaffe had applied for land grants, but the men were warned not to expect a position above private.[12]

That last restriction was designed to prevent the creation of an excessively large officer class. Experience with regular companies had shown that recruiters often exaggerated the number of lucrative officer positions that were available in order to induce men to enlist. Later the military authorities would be forced to accept these unwanted officers rather than risk the great discontent that would arise from wholesale demotions. In Upper Canada, moreover, the militia system was already burdened with an officer class that far exceeded its needs. The problem had existed before the war and was even used by John Strachan as an excuse for his acquisition of an honorary doctoral degree in 1808. As he explained at the time: "Altho there are no distinctions of rank in this country, no people are so fond of them. If a fellow gets a commission in the Militia however low he will not speak to you under the title of a Captain. Squires and Colonels we have without number – the same rage pervades persons of sense ... so that I have no doubt, but that a degree might in some measure increase my influence." A militia return for that year reveals that there was some truth to what Strachan was saying. In 1808 more than 650 officers, and over 500 sergeants, held appointments in the provincial militia. At the same time, there were only 7821 privates in the force. In other words, there was a commissioned or non-commissioned officer for about every seven rank-and-file members of the force. A number of these officers were given appointments, even though no vacant position existed. For example, at least eleven of the 198 lieutenants in the militia in 1808 were holding commissions contrary to regulations.[13]

Places in the militia officer corps were sought after, not only because they offered a position of recognized importance, but also because they paid well. While privates earned only six pence a day when on duty, commissioned officers received about ten times that amount, or five shillings a day.[14] As one writer has observed, the difference in pay scales might help explain why officers appeared more willing to remain on duty while their men deserted.[15] It also reveals why the British military authorities constantly complained about the bloated state of the militia officer corps, and illustrates why they attempted to put a halt to the granting of superfluous commissions.

One of the chief inflators of the officer ranks was Colonel Thomas Talbot. His Middlesex regiment was organized in 1812 and, according to the March amendments to the Militia Act of that year, Talbot should have appointed only two captains, two lieutenants, and two ensigns to lead his 187 privates. Instead, anxious to reward his many favourites, Talbot decided to place five men in each of those positions. Those nine additional officers constituted yet another unnecessary demand on an already strained military chest, and the colonel was rebuked strongly for this infraction by Brock. One of Talbot's biographers excused this wrongdoing by claiming that the colonel was merely exercising "a wise, if possibly somewhat paternal discretion in placing officers on duty."[16]

The use of appointments to fill militia officer positions, while of little consequence during peacetime, had led to innumerable difficulties once war had been declared. Most of the appointees were untrained and many were unaccustomed to dealing with large groups of men. Under the best of conditions, it was unlikely that such individuals would be able to inspire confidence in their subordinates. The special circumstances of Upper Canada, moreover, made that outcome even more improbable. The American settlers, with their notions of equality, were not inclined to accept orders unhesitatingly, especially if the officer in charge was one of the younger members of the local "Shopkeeper Aristocracy." Robert Nichol, who had first-hand experience with that type of situation, warned other officers "that in a Militia, composed as ours is of independent yeomanry, it would be both impolitic and useless to attempt to introduce the strict discipline of the line. They must in great measure be governed by opinion."[17] Pearson reported that many of the desertions that had occurred in 1812 could be traced to a lack of rapport among the various ranks. He placed most of the blame on the "officers who have been for the most part selected from family connection without respect to *capacity* or *respectability*." Instead of benefiting the militia by their zeal, these officers had "irreparably injured the service by their imbecility."[18]

Not all British officers agreed with Pearson, and some thought the reliance on wealthier colonists was natural and proper. Lieutenant-Colonel John Harvey, the deputy adjutant-general of the forces, believed that rich shopkeepers and other colonists of "princely possessions" had a greater interest in the continuation of British rule because they owed much of their wealth to government connections. Since such people "must stand or fall with the country," Harvey believed these wealthier inhabitants should be placed in positions where they could display their gratitude for favours received.[19] Colonel Edward Baynes felt that members of the colonial establishment could lead sedentary companies, but he suggested that no "Gentlemen of Influence in the Province" be appointed for service in the Incorporated Militia. Baynes, who was the adjutant-general of the forces, believed that their lack of knowledge about military matters, "combined with the strong ties and prejudices which their Colonial Interests and connections cannot fail of producing," made them unsuitable candidates for such jobs.[20]

Despite such objections, the old system of appointing favourite "imbeciles" to militia positions continued throughout the war. With the announcement of the formation of the Incorporated Militia, Sheaffe was deluged with applications for the top posts. For example, John Strachan forwarded the name of Neil McLean, the father of one of his former students, whom he described as "a Gentlemen of the very first respectability – highly worthy of the protection of

Government."[21] Other men were apparently so eager to acquire the coveted posts that they began forming companies before receiving the required authorization, and some made unwarranted promises about whole families being placed on rations. Sheaffe was forced to remind such enthusiasts that he did not have a "battalion or place of profit for every one who may be desirous of one or the other."[22]

Problems soon arose when it was realized that the quotas set for the Incorporated Militia were hopelessly unrealistic and as General Sheaffe found himself with dozens of extra militia officers. The original plans called for the creation of several five-hundred-man battalions of volunteers which were to be organized into one or more regiments. Altogether it was thought that as many as 2500 or 3000 men would join the corps and, to ensure that would be the case, Sheaffe announced in July that land grants of fifty acres would be given to those willing to serve.[23] Of course, that excited little interest since ordinary settlers before the war had received two-hundred-acre grants and few Upper Canadians were willing to risk their necks for one-quarter of that amount. A correspondent to the *St David's Spectator* later said that when "the promise of a crown reserve at the end of the war was undermined," the recruiting officers "were disgusted and became less active." By the end of 1813 the "want of ardour" among Upper Canadians, as well as broken promises about bounties, rations, and land grants, had combined to limit Incorporated Militia enrolment to about three hundred volunteers.[24]

That disappointing turnout indicates how little support existed for the war effort; it shows too that this indifference was not restricted to the recent arrivals from the United States.[25] Faced with a community that refused to assist wholeheartedly in the defence of British territory, Sheaffe was forced to order all three hundred volunteers into one understrength battalion. The five or six lieutenant-colonels, and the dozens of other appointed officers, apparently spent the summer "in vain exertions" to fill their quotas.[26] William Drummer Powell later sarcastically remarked that the Incorporated battalions "were never filled but with officers," and some of those men tried to reach their required totals by signing up men who were too old or too infirm for active service.[27] In April 1813 the Loyal and Patriotic Society was forced to offer relief to four volunteers who had arrived at York only to be "discharged from age and debility."[28] Unsure of the future of the corps, Sheaffe directed that the rank-and-file members build fortifications and serve on the boats on the lakes.[29] Like the flank system which had preceded it, the Incorporated Militia proved to be less than a roaring success.

It is clear that none of the British military planners had understood the real reasons for the failure of the flank system in 1812. Evans had thought that the blame rested with Brock for his neglect of material resources. Those deficiencies may have contributed to the high rates of desertion in 1812, but they cannot be blamed for the failure of most men to appear for duty in the first place. Similarly, both Pearson's proposal and Sheaffe's legislation dealing with the Incorporated Militia were intended to remove obstacles supposedly holding back otherwise eager Upper Canadians. By encouraging enlistment for the duration of the war, for instance, it was assumed that the volunteers would remain on duty during harvest times. Other amendments in the new Militia Act were designed to reassure those who feared that the neglect of their farms or businesses would lead to seizure by creditors. Finally, Sheaffe must have reasoned that a promise of a land grant, no matter how small, would increase the number of young, unpropertied volunteers. All these plans, there-fore, were based on the naïve assumption that Upper Canadians wanted to serve in the militia.

From the outset, however, most inhabitants had displayed an aver-sion to military service, and by this time it should have been clear to British authorities that few colonists were eager to fight for their king. If anything, sentiment may have been swinging to the Amer-ican side early in 1813. According to Michael Smith, the Upper Canadians he contacted believed the province "ought now to be conquered for the good of inhabitants on both sides." Hundreds of citizens who had fled the province stood to lose everything if Britain emerged victorious. Of greater importance, thousands of other col-onists feared that they had left themselves open to charges of dis-loyalty and possible punishment. Some had joined the enemy, others had spoken against the king or government, and almost all inhabi-tants had failed to appear for militia duty or were guilty of desertion at some point during the previous year.[30] These were hardly the sort of people likely to volunteer their services for an indefinite period simply because the Assembly had temporarily guaranteed their prop-erty against seizure by creditors. Not all Upper Canadians were attempting to avoid service, however, and some young enthusiasts actually jumped at the chance to join the military. John Richardson, a cousin of the Hamiltons and a grandson of John Askin, "rejoiced" at the outbreak of war because it signalled "the 'break-up' of the school." Although only fifteen years old, Richardson immediately volunteered for service and he later claimed that he "felt disposed to bless the Americans" because their declaration of war had freed him "from the hated shackles of scholastic life."[31] Allan Napier MacNab, who was the son of a retired British officer, also found military life too appealing to resist and he joined up at the tender age of fourteen. He saw action at Fort Erie and Fort Niagara and, by the time he was sixteen, he had been promoted to ensign. For certain young members of Upper Canada's "first" class, the war offered an exciting opportunity to give full rein to their chivalrous instincts.[32]

Other youthful enthusiasts, like William Hamilton Merritt, were especially anxious to lead provincial units. In 1812 he had served in a local company of dragoons, but the next year Sheaffe authorized the creation of official cavalry and artillery regiments. Merritt, who was only nineteen years old but whose father was a Niagara merchant, was promised the command of the "Provincial Light Dragoons." Men accepted for service in the Dragoons were required to provide their own horses, received only a small bounty, and were paid fifteen pence a day, or two-and-a-half times what a private in the regular militia received.[33] Despite these limited incentives, it seems that the romance and prestige associated with service in a cavalry corps were enough to persuade some Upper Canadians to join the force. Only a few weeks before, for example, Merritt had announced that he would never again serve in the militia, but once approached by Sheaffe to lead a cavalry unit he found the offer too attractive to refuse. According to one historian who has dealt with the ambitious cavalry officer's postwar career, Merritt's dominant goal in life was to "rise in the social scale, to become a person of some consequence." Instead of slogging about in the mud with ordinary militiamen on foot patrols, Merritt pictured himself and his companions galloping "together and having an opportunity of distinguishing themselves." The same idea must have presented itself to other young Upper Canadians, since Merritt completed his quota of fifty men in only a few days. Once formed, though, the corps was immediately divided up and the gallant youths were forced to serve as "post boys and Orderlies" for regular troops who treated the dragoons with a good deal of contempt.[34]

The Incorporated Militia, unlike the Provincial Light Dragoons, never fired the imagination of young Upper Canadians, and its inability to attract more than a fraction of the men expected meant that the province was forced to rely on the sedentary battalions instead. The well-known inadequacy of these forces was graphically displayed in the spring of 1813. Early in the morning of 27 April, sixteen American ships were sighted sailing for the provincial capital. The regular forces at York consisted of only three hundred soldiers, although an additional three hundred militiamen and a number of Indians were also on hand. Along with Colonel William Chewett, Major William Allan was placed in charge of the main body of militiamen stationed in the village at the head of Toronto Bay. A company of regulars from the king's regiment was also stationed in the capital, and both units were expected to defend the village if the enemy force landed there. Sheaffe had directed a group of about forty Mississauga warriors, under Major James Givins of the Indian Department, to the shoreline west of the town where it was also thought a landing might be made. The rest of the British force was kept in reserve at the garrison in between these two points because Sheaffe was still unsure where the main assault would take place.[35]

By the time the Indians arrived at the shore they discovered that several hundred Americans were already disembarking. Sheaffe had ordered a contingent of Glengarry Fencibles to assist the Mississauga warriors but, unfortunately for Givins and his men, the reinforcements were intercepted on the way to the shore by Eneas Shaw, adjutant-general of the Upper Canadian militia. Although he had had extensive regular army experience during the American Revolution, Shaw acted more like a typical militia officer. He immediately countermanded Sheaffe's order and directed that the Glengarries remain with his company instead. Sheaffe had previously ordered Shaw to watch the rear of the main British force, but it seems that the adjutant-general was more concerned about protecting his own rear. Shaw's action delayed the Glengarry reinforcements and assured the success of the American landing.[36]

The invasion might still have been repulsed if Chewett and Allan had followed their orders. When the landing began, Sheaffe directed all men, including those in the town, to march to the garrison. While the company of regulars managed to rush to Sheaffe's side and played a part in the day's fighting, Allan's and Chewett's men did not. Isaac Wilson, who was there at the time, said he and other militiamen were "paraded early in the morning," but their officers did not instruct them to follow the regulars until much later. Supposedly because they were still "waiting for orders," the majority of York militiamen never engaged the Americans. This "hesitancy about doing battle," as historian Charles Humphries described it, helped ensure an American victory, since Wilson and his companions were still a mile from the scene of the landing area when fighting erupted. A few days later, Chewett and Allan would join with other York notables in a vindictive campaign to end Sheaffe's military career. One researcher, Carl Benn, has suggested that this was done in order "to cover up their own incompetence" during the battle.[37]

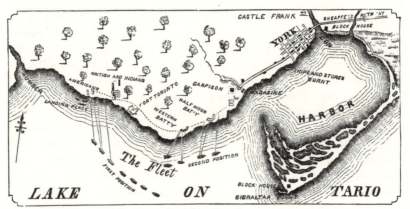

Map 3   Invasion of York, Upper Canada, 1813
Lossing, *Pictorial Field-Book of the War of 1812*

Without all his reinforcements, and facing a force of at least 1600 men, Sheaffe ordered the troops to fall back towards York, but the premature demolition of an ammunition dump brought an end to the orderly retreat. An eyewitness described what he saw after the magazine exploded: "The terrible appearance of the killed and wounded, being all black and scorched dispirited the troops ... The militia began now visibly to melt away, there was no person to animate them nor to tell them where to make a stand, their officers knew nothing of what was to be done."[38] In the midst of the confusion, Sheaffe decided to gather his regular troops and retreat to Kingston. He directed Colonel Chewett and Major Allan to negotiate with the Americans over the terms of surrender. After consulting with John Strachan and John Beverly Robinson, Chewett and Allan, true Upper Canadians that they were, agreed to an immediate capitulation with only one stipulation -that private property be respected.[39]

Strachan had spent most of the morning several miles away from the fighting. He had remained in the town "to look after the Ladies," but after the explosion of the magazine he rushed home to Ann and then sent "her to a Friend's a little out of town." Later, he carefully made his way to the garrison, where he found "the Militia scattering," and he offered his services to help draft the terms of capitulation. Before the document was ratified, however, Allan was arrested by the Americans and held overnight. The next morning Strachan flew into action. If the capitulation agreement was left unratified, Allan and the other militiamen could be held indefinitely and the article respecting the protection of private property was worthless.[40] Before landing, General Henry Dearborn had warned his men that private property "must be held sacred" and that any soldier convicted of plundering the inhabitants would be punished with death. To reduce temptation, he later ordered the American troops to remain in the garrison overnight, and, to prevent looting, he stationed a rifle company in the town.[41] Strachan was sure that this move was merely a "pretence" and that the American refusal to receive the articles of capitulation was only designed "to give the riflemen time to plunder." He confronted the commander of the invasion flotilla, Commodore Isaac Chauncey, and warned that if the document was not immediately signed the Upper Canadians would withdraw the offer. He suspected that the enemy would first rob the town, "then perhaps sign the capitulation, and tell us they respected private property; but we were determined that this should not be the case, & that they should not have it in their power to say, that they had respected private property after it had been robbed." That evening, perhaps weary of Strachan's badgering, Dearborn ratified the agreement and the militiamen were released.[42]

Of the three hundred militiamen on duty during the invasion, only two died from wounds received in battle. After the explosion of the magazine, 241 citizen-soldiers had surrendered their arms and had spent the night imprisoned in the block house at the garrison. The next day all were given papers that the Upper Canadians, somewhat imprecisely, called "paroles."[43] The military parole system was a practical and traditional solution to the problems associated with large groups of prisoners of war. Rather than be responsible for the care and feeding of captured enemies, warring nations had long before developed a system whereby prisoners could be given partial or conditional freedom. In return, the captive offered his *parole d'honneur*, or "word of honour," that he would not bear arms against his captors. Over the years the meaning had changed somewhat and, by the time war had been declared between the United States and Great Britain, prisoners usually spoke of acquiring a "parole" from their captors rather than of giving their "*parole* of honour" to the victorious enemy.

Under the terms of the treaty dealing with this subject that was signed on 12 November 1812, both the British and American forces agreed to keep accurate lists of any men who had been captured and granted parole. If both sides consented, an exchange of lists could take place and men on parole would, once again, be free to serve their country. In keeping with the stratified nature of the military, not all persons were considered equal. The Americans, for example, agreed to release two privates for every sergeant returned to them, three privates for every colonel, and thirty privates for a

Parole issued to Noah Fairchild, 9 November 1814.
Eva Brook Donly Museum, Simcoe; photograph by Steve Wigmore

brigadier-general. The American and British representatives also pledged that they would prevent their paroled subjects from taking up arms unless such official exchanges took place.[44] Considering the attitude of most Upper Canadians towards the war, it was unlikely that this provision would be violated often.

Clutching the papers that excused them from military service, the York militiamen returned to their customary pursuits. One can only imagine their surprise at this good fortune. According to Isaac Wilson, who was stationed at the York garrison, most of the men had planned on deserting at the end of the month after they had received their pay. Instead, the Americans arrived and "they were set at liberty in a way they little expected."[45] News of this action spread like wildfire through the district, and apparently the residents nearly tripped over themselves in the rush to acquire the documents that everyone called paroles. Although only 241 of the papers were given to militiamen immediately after the battle, many more were drawn up over the next few days. Dr William Beaumont, a surgeon with the Sixth United States Infantry Corps at York, noted in his diary: "30th April [1813] – Dressed the wounded, most of them doing well ... The Militia and people giving themselves up to paroled, nearly 1,700 since the 27th."[46] If Beaumont's figure is correct, and additional evidence suggests it was, then more than 1400 other Upper Canadians must have applied for paroles. Since York had a population of only about six hundred, including women and children, many of the other men paroled came from distant settlements.[47] An Upper Canadian official involved in the certification process, Stephen Jarvis, later said that even "old men of seventy and boys of twelve years of age" took advantage of the American offer. "To the everlasting disgrace of the country," Jarvis ruefully recalled, "they were hourly coming in and giving themselves to Major-General Dearborn as Prisoners."[48] In fact, it appears that in only three days almost all the eligible militiamen in the Home District had journeyed to York to offer their *parole d'honneur* that they would never take up arms again.[49]

The rush to acquire these documents is understandable, and for most Upper Canadians the offer must have seemed too good to be true. By merely appearing before a tribunal of American soldiers, and by promising not to "bear arms or act in any military capacity against the United States during the present war," a settler obtained an official document that excused him from further service in the militia.[50] Just as important, the paper also permitted the parolee to remain at home and protect his property. For that reason even active and loyal militiamen eventually sought paroles. Eli Playter, for example, was one of the men who had "melted away" after the magazine explosion and he continued to refuse to surrender, preferring instead to remain in hiding, until 29 April. On that day he returned home to find a group of American soldiers looting a farmhouse they considered abandoned. Outnumbered by the burglars, and in no position to protest anyway because of his unparoled status, Playter was forced to watch from a distance as they "broke the Door and took many things away." The next day Playter accepted Major William Allan's advice and acquired a parole and a pass to return home.[51] Playter's stubborn refusal to follow the course eagerly adopted by hundreds of his neighbours may have been prompted by loyalty to the British cause or by a fondness for his salary as a militia officer, or both. Whatever his motivation, his hesitancy certainly set him apart from the rest of his countrymen.

By the time Sheaffe's force reached Kingston, the Americans had abandoned York for their own shore. On 8 May the invasion fleet

Table 2
Lincoln Militia Service, 1813

	17 May	18 May
	Captain Nelles's 4th Lincoln Company	
Present	52	44
Leave	18	21
AWOL	32	31
Sick	6	12
Total	108	108

Source: AO, Robert Nelles Papers, Series B-6

arrived at Fort Niagara, where the Americans planned to launch another attack upon Upper Canada.[52] In expectation of this event, Brigadier-General John Vincent, the British commander at Fort George, had already called on the nearby sedentary companies for support. A few days after the capture of York, Vincent issued a Militia General Order which directed 1700 militiamen to assemble for service on the Niagara frontier.[53]

At the best of times Upper Canadians had shown themselves to be unwilling participants in this war, and Vincent's latest call to arms, coming as it did after the fall of York and during planting season, was to prove particularly unsuccessful. A militia officer from the London District, Mahlon Burwell, likened the task of taking the men from their farms at this time to "drawing their eye teeth" out.[54] Furthermore, even those colonists who appeared for duty did not stay long and, as usual, most resorted to desertion. For instance, in Captain William Nelles's company of Fourth Lincoln militia, the number of men absent from the front lines was soon greater than the number of men on duty. Muster rolls reveal how serious the problem had become by mid May (see table 2). Nelles's company was not unique in having large numbers of absentees, since scores of militiamen left their posts without permission all along the Niagara peninsula. On 19 May Vincent reported to the commander of the forces, George Prevost, that desertion "beyond all conception continues to mark their indifference to the important cause in which we are now engaged."[55]

Because of the high number of militia absentees, Prevost was forced to reconsider his decision not to send reinforcements to the upper province. In a letter to Lord Bathurst, the British secretary of state for war and the colonies, Prevost explained that the zeal of the inhabitants was almost exhausted and he noted that even loyal settlers had recently resorted to desertion in order to plant their crops. Prevost added that, as a result of the "growing discontent and undissembled dissatisfaction of the mass of the people of Upper Canada," he had been compelled to send regulars from Quebec to the Niagara and Detroit frontiers.[56]

While Prevost was in the process of writing this report, the Americans busily engaged in an invasion of the Niagara peninsula. On the morning of 26 May, troops under the command of General Henry Dearborn attacked and overwhelmed the British force at Fort George. Vincent, who a week earlier had complained that militia desertions were placing his position at risk, was forced to abandon Fort George and retreat towards Burlington Heights. Those militiamen who had remained on duty were told they were at liberty to return home. When some insisted on following the regulars on their retreat, Vincent suggested they reconsider since it was possible that the British "would not stop, until they arrived at Kingston." The implications of this statement were not lost on the local inhabitants. William Hamilton Merritt came to the conclusion that Upper Canada was going to be abandoned by the British army, and he reported that this "opinion was entertained by most people."[57] Convinced that the Americans would soon be in total control of the province, and still anxious to avoid service should that not prove to be the case, Niagara area males engaged in a "parole-rush" as feverish as that which had occurred at York a month earlier. Although only 507 militiamen had been captured during the actual assault on Fort George, American military records reveal that almost 1200 individuals received paroles on 27 May.[58]

Dearborn attributed the demand for paroles to the fact that most Upper Canadians were "friendly to the United States and fixed in their hatred of Great Britain." A British officer, in contrast, reported in the pages of the *Kingston Gazette* that the recent conduct of the inhabitants of the Niagara District revealed "that if there are some bad subjects among us, that there is still a preponderating majority of men zealously devoted to their country's service."[59] Both of these men, of course, were wrong and the actions of most colonists over the past year had shown that Upper Canadians had no strong attachment to either the United States or Great Britain. The stampede to acquire paroles was not evidence that the inhabitants preferred republican political principles, but it was proof that the colonists desperately wished to evade militia service. Dearborn's documents, since they made that avoidance possible, became higly prized items.

It seems that the Americans did their best to ensure that every inhabitant who wanted a parole was able to acquire one. William

Hamilton Merritt remarked that the Americans preferred to parole "all from 14 to 100 years of age" even though militia service was restricted to those between the ages of sixteen and sixty. Merritt believed that the Americans did this so they would not be responsible for feeding prisoners, but since no elderly inhabitants could have been participating in the fighting, the Americans would not have captured them in the first place.[60] It seems likely that rather than take a chance on the odd colonist lying about his age so as to remain unparoled and able to assist the British, the Americans simply paroled all post-pubescent males however old or young they may have looked. Elderly inhabitants may have been pleased by this process since it suggested they were still fit enough to be considered a threat. More importantly, they received a document which insured that they would not be harassed by troops from either side.

At Fort Erie the inhabitants began pressuring the Americans for paroles as soon as the wagons carrying the British troops retreated. To reassure the anxious residents, James Preston, an officer in the United States army, publicly declared that all Upper Canadians who wanted "special protections" would be given them. Preston explained that colonists who enrolled their names with him would have "their property and persons secured to them inviolate." Always quick to recognize a good deal, five hundred Upper Canadians from the area between Port Abino and Chippawa immediately appeared before the Fort Erie tribunal and acquired what they considered to be legitimate paroles.[61]

Other colonists were also anxious to receive the documents, and some of the parolees even came from areas that were still in British hands. Apparently some residents from settlements on the Grand River, over one hundred miles from Fort George, believed that the benefits of a parole outweighed the risks of a long journey during wartime.[62] It is likely that the settlers travelled by water, and at night, since British sentries had been posted all along the front lines with orders to prevent any Upper Canadian from getting "between the Army and the Enemy."[63] The increasing popularity of this type of action so exasperated Sir George Prevost that he eventually was forced to remind Upper Canadians that their first loyalty was supposed to be to Britain. In a proclamation issued on 14 June, Prevost explained that citizens who were "not under the immediate controul or within the power of the Enemy" were still obligated to assist in "repelling the Foe."[64]

A recent reversal had reduced the amount of American-controlled territory just before Prevost issued his proclamation. A successful night attack on an American encampment at Stoney Creek on 6 June

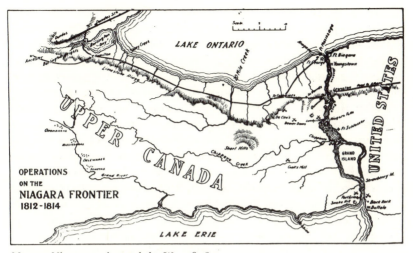

Map 4   Niagara region and the War of 1812
Lossing, *Pictorial Field-Book of the War of 1812*

had severely shaken the morale of the invaders. British regulars from the 49th and 8th regiments, with a small group of loyal militiamen and Glengarry Fencibles in reserve, had managed to surprise and capture a good part of the enemy's army. Dispirited and disorganized by the encounter, the main American force returned to Fort George while smaller posts at Fort Erie, Chippawa, and Queenston were abandoned. For the next five months the Niagara District was the scene of an uneasy stalemate as neither side was able to overwhelm the other.[65]

The sudden change in the fortunes of the American army left some Upper Canadians in a perilous position. While most had been content to accept a parole and return to their private pursuits, a small number had thrown in their lot with the invaders. Now, however, it seemed that the British were not simply going to give up and leave. The annexation of the province appeared much less certain. Those who had offered aid or encouragement to the enemy were afraid they would be charged with treason if the British regained control of the region. Faced with that possibility, some inhabitants decided to join the United States army to ensure that the victories of May were made permanent.

On 10 July, Joseph Willcocks visited Dearborn's headquarters and offered to organize and lead a corps of volunteers to fight alongside the American forces.[66] Willcocks never issued a manifesto or declaration of his political principles and he seems to have undertaken this course of action because he thought it might lead to an important position in the new government of the State of Upper Canada. One scholar who has studied the actions of this transplanted Irishman has declared that Willcocks "held loyalty to no country and nothing else but himself." Donald Graves believes that Willcocks's career involved a continual search for more powerful patrons. Beginning first with Peter Russell, Henry Allcock, and Robert Thorpe, and even later with Brock, Willcocks sought the assistance of influential men in his attempts to gain power and wealth. At certain times he was guilty of poor selections, as in his decision to back what would eventually prove to be an unsuccessful invasion, but his choices were always based on a "cool calculation" of the possible risks and benefits. Graves even believes that Willcocks did not view his decision to form a volunteer corps as an act of treason. Rather, the ambitious Irishman was simply "leaving one patron and taking up with another."[67]

Dearborn accepted Willcocks's offer and a corps known as the "Canadian Volunteers," made up entirely of residents of the upper province, was soon ready for deployment. By September the recruits numbered a respectable 130.[68] Men who enlisted were promised land grants, and this apparently proved to be a powerful incentive since almost all the volunteers owned no property in the province. Dearborn was so impressed by the success of the recruiting campaign that he came to believe that the force would eventually number between 600 and 800 men. Like the estimates for the Incorporated Militia, however, that prediction proved wildly optimistic and it revealed that Dearborn's insight into the Upper Canadian character was no better than that of his British counterparts. Only 164 men actually served in the corps during the unit's existence.[69]

Yet, considering that Willcocks's area for recruitment was largely limited to regions controlled by the American army, 164 volunteers is a sizeable number. Even with a much larger base to draw upon, and with far more attractive inducements, the Incorporated Militia managed to acquire fewer than twice that number of recruits in 1813. Both bodies of men, moreover, represented only a tiny fraction of the adult male population, and voluntary service for either side during the war remained the preserve of a small group of colonists. Upper Canadians, indifferent as always, proved to be as unwilling to fight for their American cousins as they had been to fight against them.

Throughout the summer the British attempted to reassemble their militia companies in the central portion of the province. But Vincent's curt dismissal of the men who had accompanied his army after the fall of Fort George seems to have discouraged formerly active militiamen. Only sixty-five of 1620 troops stationed at Burlington Bay on 3 June 1813 were listed as members of the provincial militia.[70] The plethora of paroles produced by the tribunals added to the difficulties of British authorities. More than three thousand of the documents had been distributed over the course of a few days after the American victories at York and Fort George; at least a quarter and perhaps as many as a half of all the members of the provincial militia considered themselves exempt from service. It is clear, however, that the British authorities would have had difficulty drumming up support even if the colonists had not been paroled. William Macewen, an officer who was stationed on the Niagara frontier in the autumn of 1813, described the inhabitants as being "indifferent [as to] who gains the day. They are determined to do nothing themselves."[71]

Almost all the colonists in the Niagara and Home districts appear to have had paroles during 1813. Those York residents who had failed to acquire the documents in April or May were given another opportunity at the end of July when, for the second time, an American force captured and occupied the capital for several days. On 29 July 1813, 240 American soldiers entered the town unopposed when the British regulars under Lieutenant-Colonel Francis Battersby fled at the first sight of the enemy fleet. The only British presence left to greet the invaders was the group of curious villagers and former militiamen who gathered to watch the American rowboats pull in to shore.[72]

Unparoled residents from outlying areas of the Home District may have responded to news of invasion in much the same manner that Michael Corts did. This farmer, who lived a day's journey north of the capital, hitched his wagon, collected his son, and immediately set out for York in search of the parole tribunal. It seems that Corts was concerned his son might miss a chance to acquire an exemption from militia service.[73] These actions reveal that Corts, like most of his neighbours, was somewhat confused about the exact nature of the military parole system.

Traditionally, paroles were granted only to prisoners who were captured during battle. Unarmed spectators, and men who were nowhere near the actual fighting, were not expected to surrender to the enemy and forswear further military service. In the confusion that surrounded the invasions of York and the fall of Fort George, however, that distinction seems to have been ignored. The Americans, who wished to prevent as many men as possible from serving again, made no effort to point out that most colonists were acquiring the documents against established conventions. Upper Canadians, while undoubtedly unaware of the finer points of the parole tradition, also did not appear anxious to question the propriety of the American practices. Since most viewed the war as an unwelcome intrusion into their lives anyway, they must have reasoned it was best to accept the documents and not inquire into why they had received an exemption from militia service. For farmers such as Corts, who needed all the hands they could get at harvest time, a chance to apply for a parole was an opportunity not to be missed.

A few individuals from the Home District who were eligible for paroles did not immediately receive them because of their unfamiliarity with the practice. In the confusion that surrounded the first American invasion of York, many Upper Canadians seemed to be under the impression that an American victory meant that all militiamen in the region automatically acquired paroles. After the explosion of the magazine in April, for instance, Elijah Bentley testified that he saw "Twelve to Twenty armed men pass his House with bandages on their arms, at which he was alarmed and went after them having heard that they were parolled (sic) and asked them if they were really parolled – they said no. He likewise asked them if they knew the meaning of a parole – to this question he does not recollect that they gave him any answer." These men, apparently part of the group that had "melted away" after the explosion, were eligible for paroles, but do not seem to have been aware that they had to surrender their arms and enrol their names before they received an official document. Bentley, a Baptist preacher who was later accused of being an American sympathizer, suggested that the soldiers discuss their situation with Major William Allan.[74] If they did, it is possible that they spent the next few days standing in line outside the office of the parole tribunal at York, since Allan was aware that these men qualified for legitimate paroles.

Of much greater concern to the British military authorities were the thousands of residents who had obtained paroles under dubious circumstances and who continued to insist they were exempt from service even after the true nature of military paroles was explained to them. Men like Corts refused to perform the smallest task for the British because they claimed it might lead to brutal reprisals at the hands of the enemy. Strachan noted in early September that public works in the Home District were at a standstill. He went on to observe that it was widely believed throughout the region that all males had been legally paroled.[75] This belief may have been encouraged by the Americans during the first invasion of York, since Bentley later reported that even General Dearborn considered the entire district to be "parolled" because of his victory.[76]

As a result of the confusion, Sir George Prevost was forced to issue a proclamation in September 1813 dealing with the subject of paroles. Since most inhabitants had not been captured "with arms in their hands," Prevost explained they should never have been listed as prisoners in the first place. He denounced the American practice of imprisoning unarmed citizens as a "novel and unjustifiable principle." He went on to explain that, under such circumstances, individuals who had offered their word never to serve in the British forces again were not bound to these promises. Even the men who had acquired paroles in the traditional manner, however, were still liable to perform roadwork and other duties so long as the acts did not include armed military service. While Prevost was sure that many Upper Canadians were not aware of these facts, the commander of the forces also declared that "he has strong reason to believe that in several instances the paroles thus taken have been sought for by the persons, giving them as the means of evading the performance of their Militia and other duties." Prevost warned "such useless and disaffected characters" that if they continued to refuse to do their duty he would have no choice but to send them "out of the Country to the Enemy, to whom they consider themselves as belonging."[77]

The great parole rush of 1813 was not prompted by mere cowardice, since even in regions where service was unlikely to result in injury or death Upper Canadians displayed a similar attitude towards militia duty. To some militiamen in the eastern districts of the province, for example, musters and patrols were viewed as inconveniences best to be avoided. Like their counterparts in the Home and Niagara regions, many militiamen from the east continued to place personal concerns, such as tending to farm matters, ahead of military duty.[78] Two scholars who have investigated militia participation in several eastern Upper Canadian companies have declared that desertion was a common occurrence. Donald Akenson's study of three companies in Joel Stone's regiment of Leeds militia from east of Kingston has uncovered an average desertion rate of 24.8 per cent throughout the war. Shirley Campbell Spragge noted that the regiment of Grenville militia experienced a nearly identical rate of absenteeism. In both cases, moreover, some of the missing men were sons of United Empire Loyalists, and it is easy to understand why, in June 1813, Stone complained about "so many desertions and vile elopements" having taken place.[79]

Both Akenson and Spragge, however, failed to indicate that deserters often far outnumbered men on duty. Before the war, the Grenville militia held 644 men, but Spragge has observed that after January 1814 the regimental musters attracted as few as 185 men.

At times, therefore, the desertion rate for the Grenville militia was in the region of 70 per cent. That figure was actually surpassed by the men in Stone's regiment. When mustered in 1811, the rank and file of the Second Leeds militia amounted to 484. By October 1813, however, Stone was able to assemble only seventy or so privates. Outraged by the absence of about 85 per cent of his men, Stone instituted an investigation and ordered a court martial to convene. Many of the absentees, who had "promised to make good soldiers" at the start of the war, had lost their enthusiasm for the service, and Stone thought their elders had advised them to remain at home where their labour was needed. Stone wrote that "Fathers, Mothers and other Heads of Familys had, (by their example and bad counsel), poisoned the minds of the youth." He ordered his junior officers to levy heavy fines, but the absentees began "clamouring aloud and threatening to prosecute them for extortion."[80]

Older colonists, who needed their sons' labour and who were perhaps familiar with the realities of fighting, may well have been much less enthusiastic about the war, and there was probably a good deal of truth to Stone's statements. At the same time, parental influence could not have been responsible for all the desertions; the special circumstances of the region must also be considered. At seven court martials held between 8 March 1813 and 16 January 1815, all but one of the sedentary militiamen convicted of desertion came from regiments in the Midland, Johnston, and Eastern districts. That is not surprising; the Americans never mounted a successful invasion of the eastern area of the province, and militiamen from that region were not given the opportunity to offer their *parole d'honneur*. Those men denied permission to tend to their crops or to visit their wives and families were left with no choice but to skulk away from their posts. In the western regions of the colony, individuals who wanted no part in the war merely sought out the nearest parole tribunal. Easterners who felt that way, however, had to desert. For example, Isaac Simpson, a private in Stone's regiment of Leeds militia, was listed as being absent from duty three times. He was said to have deserted his company on 20 December 1812, 6 January 1813, and 12 May 1814. Early the next year the authorities managed to catch up with Simpson and he was ordered detained to await trial. Ever the resourceful fellow, Simpson had charges filed against him a few days later for "escaping from the guard ordered to apprehend him for the above desertions."

Most absentees had little fear of being punished since harsh treatment for desertion was rare. In 1812 most deserters were offered amnesty if they returned to duty, but the vast majority simply ignored those warnings until the whole militia was released from service. Although the 5 August 1812 amendments to the Militia Act permitted court martials to sentence deserters to death, Brock and Sheaffe avoided using that provision. Even officers guilty of desertion usually received only mild reprimands. On 20 January 1813, for example, Sheaffe cashiered three Lincoln officers for having absented themselves without leave. He warned other officers that this lenient sentence would be the last and any future deserters would be subjected to the full extent of the law. Two days later, however, the Court of Inquiry assembled to investigate the activities of the Essex militia in 1812 announced that ten officers guilty of desertion would be superseded by other men of their regiment who had remained faithful.

It was not until the spring of 1813 that British authorities resorted to court martials, and only a handful of offenders were ever brought up on charges. The trials seem to have been reserved for incorrigible recidivists, officers who were expected to be above such actions, and men who had deserted to the enemy and then had the misfortune to be captured by British forces. Still, most of those who were found guilty received very light sentences. An examination of general orders issued between 1813 and 1815 reveals that twelve sedentary militiamen were judged to be guilty of desertion. Of these, one was given a public reprimand, two were fined, three were given jail sentences ranging from six to twelve months, four were sentenced to be transported as felons for periods ranging from three years to life, and only two were sentenced to be shot. However, the punishments meted out by the courts were often amended by military commanders. One six-month jail sentence was remitted, two men ordered transported were instead released and sent back on duty, and at least one of the men scheduled for capital punishment had his sentence commuted to seven years' transportation as a felon. As befit their status as "near-regulars," members of the Incorporated Militia received harsher sentences. Of the three members of that battalion convicted of desertion, two were sentenced to seven years' transportation, although one was later granted a full pardon and one unlucky man was actually shot by a firing squad on 20 December 1813.[81]

Despite the potential for harsh punishment, most of the Upper Canadians who had appeared for service in 1812 were never again involved in military manoeuvres after the summer of 1813. Try as they might, the British military authorities had little success in drawing men out. One colonel on the Niagara frontier became so frustrated with the situation that he threatened that the homes of absentees would be given to the western Indians. The continued refusal of Niagara area residents to give up their paroles of dubious legality and return to duty also unnerved the usually composed Vincent. Apparently he eventually "threatened to burn the houses over the heads of militiamen who did not obey his calls," but the few men who took such warnings seriously did not stay for long. On 1 October 1813 Vincent reluctantly informed his commanding officer that he was dismissing Eneas Shaw because the adjutant-general had "no militia to act on having almost all deserted home."[82]

With only a few militia volunteers at his disposal, Vincent was unable to send any regulars to the assistance of Colonel Henry Procter at Detroit. The British right division was experiencing food shortages and the American naval victory on 10 September at Put-in-Bay left Procter in a desperate situation. On 27 September he abandoned Detroit and began a slow retreat eastward in an attempt to ease his supply problems. At the Battle of Moraviantown on 5 October 1813 the American army that followed Procter into Canada caught up to his force and overwhelmed the smaller group of British regulars and western Indians.[83] No citizen-soldiers were present that day because Procter had some months earlier decided that militiamen were more trouble than they were worth and he had confiscated all their government-issued firearms in June 1813. After the Battle of Moraviantown, the Americans claimed to be in control of the Michigan territory and the Western and London districts of Upper Canada. In fact, however, the region was controlled effectively by no one; the inhabitants were subjected to predatory incursions carried out by American troops, who were guided by renegade Canadians such as Andrew Westbrook and Benejah Mallory.[84]

American raiding parties, which directed their attacks mainly against private property, eventually succeeded in rousing some Upper Canadians into action – a response that British officers since Brock had been unable to elicit. After the disaster at Moraviantown, Colonel Thomas Talbot fled to Burlington, but he left behind instructions for the militia officers of the London District to call out their companies in his absence.[85] With no stomach for further fighting, the officers seized the opportunity to return to their farms, and the official militia of the London District ceased to exist. It quickly became apparent, however, that some sort of defence force was needed if the Upper Canadians expected to keep their personal possessions out of American hands. Enemy patrols, led by Upper Canadian scouts, had proven to be as interested in gathering loot and kidnapping militia officers as they were in obtaining intelligence on British positions. Early in November a number of these officers and other citizens of Dover attended a meeting called to discuss the problems posed by the marauders. The principal inhabitants of the village were afraid they would be left penniless if the attacks continued. In addition, since many of these gentlemen held appointments in the militia, there was also a good chance they would be arrested and taken to the United States during a future raid. One of the leaders of the Dover meeting later explained that the residents were given no choice but to form a vigilante force; it was the only way they could secure their "persons and property from such lawless banditti."[86]

Some of the raiders were former neighbours of the Dover residents, and it seems that prewar conflicts between individuals prompted much of the plundering. Some who joined the American side also claimed that their original purpose was to put an end to all militia service in the London District. Pinkey Mabee, who along with his brother was caught stealing horses from Robert Nichol's barn, said that he and Simon joined the Americans because they believed the object of the raids was to "take away the officers that the militia may be at peace and that they might go to work."[87] Since the militia system was already in complete disarray, and in view of their subsequent actions, it would be safe to say that the Mabee brothers and others like them were more interested in settling old scores and enriching themselves in the process than they were in avoiding militia service. Had that been their real aim they could simply have remained at home, as they had done in July 1812 when Brock summoned them for duty at Detroit.

To Upper Canadians, joining the enemy was one thing, but carrying off private property was a different matter altogether. On 11 November the Dover vigilantes bolted into action. Under the command of Colonel Henry Bostwick, a small force of angry Upper Canadian civilians and former militiamen killed five raiders and captured a further sixteen at Nanticoke Creek. For their efforts, the Dover men were hailed as heroes and received a portion of the proceeds of all goods seized from the Americans and later sold at auction. A militia general order issued not long after instructed other inhabitants to "observe how quickly the energetic conduct of 45 individuals has succeeded in freeing the inhabitants of an extensive district from a numerous and well-armed banditti, who would soon have left them neither liberty nor prosperity." Bostwick's success encouraged others, and a few weeks later a second attack was carried out on a marauder outpost near Chatham. Henry Medcalf and thirty-three followers managed to kill several raiders and capture a number of others.[88]

The incidents at Nanticoke Creek and Chatham proved that the colonists, when properly motivated, were more than willing to fight.

In 1812 the inhabitants of this same area had refused, almost to a man, to march to Detroit to meet Hull's advance. Later, when their property was in danger, they sprang into action. Residents in the Niagara region, when faced with similar threats, also reacted this way. Starting in the summer of 1813 they found themselves at the mercy of a group of volunteers from Buffalo led by Dr Cyrenius Chapin. This group of New Yorkers quickly acquired the nickname of "Dr Chapin and the Forty Thieves," and only the intervention of the regular American army put a stop to their "rapine and pillage."[89] These minor instances of looting were soon followed by gross violations of the American promise of protection for private property. Eventually whole villages, such as Niagara and St Davids, were put to the torch by groups of American militiamen and by renegades like Joseph Willcocks.

As in the London area, Upper Canadians in the Niagara District responded to the violation of private property rights by fighting back. "The whole population is against us," Major Daniel MacFarland of the 23rd United States Infantry informed his wife in July 1814, "not a foraging party but is fired on, and not infrequently returns with missing numbers." While this letter is sometimes cited as proof that all Upper Canadians were solidly behind the British, and therefore actively serving in militia units, it is nothing of the sort. It only shows that by 1814 residents in the Niagara District were willing to shoot troops caught *foraging* for food in Upper Canadian fields. "This state was to have been anticipated," MacFarland went on to explain, "the militia and Indians have plundered and burnt everything."[90]

During the final year of the conflict the colonists remained only lukewarm in their support for the war effort. The actual level of indifference among the general population came as a shock to Lieutenant-General Gordon Drummond, who took over command of the province in December 1813. Within two months, Drummond had come up with a plan to turn the militia into a "tolerably efficient force." Only three hundred men had joined Sheaffe's Incorporated Militia the year before, and Drummond was convinced that conscription was necessary. He planned to draft three-fourteenths of all adult Upper Canadian males under the age of forty-five. The 1500 draftees, along with the three hundred volunteers from 1813, were to be subjected to the same training and discipline as regular soldiers and were to receive the same pay. The regiment was to be composed of three six-hundred-man battalions, and the conscripts would be forced to serve for one year. Drummond requested that Prevost forward "2,000 suits of scarlet clothing" so that the Incorporated militiamen would more closely resemble British regulars.[91]

Drummond presented his plan to the Assembly on 14 February 1814, but the members felt that the 1500 man limit was too high.[92] They believed that an additional one-fourteenth, or five hundred men, was all the colony could spare "from the necessary pursuit of agriculture."[93] Drummond was so angered by this amendment that he told Earl Bathurst he had given some thought to dispensing with the militia altogether, and only the small size of his regular force prevented such a drastic step. He then thought he could skirt the restriction by conscripting other men for three-month periods. Drummond consulted the provincial attorney-general, John Beverley Robinson, about the legality of this proposal, but he was told he could not conscript extra men without calling out the whole militia.[94]

In the end, though, the British authorities did not even manage to raise the number of men permitted by the Assembly. The pool of available manpower in Upper Canada had been greatly reduced by desertions to the United States, and the few young men interested in military service had long since found places in the Glengarries or Dragoons, or even in units of the regular army. Balloting did not prove to be a solution to the slow pace of enlistment because the British had no control over large areas of the province and they were unable to organize a system of conscription. In the regions where a militia system still existed, some inhabitants continued to insist they were paroled and could not serve. Even after the Americans and British exchanged parole lists on 18 April 1814, Drummond was unable to round up the required number of conscripts.[95] Sheaffe's Incorporated battalion had held three hundred men, and by 27 April 1814 those veterans had been joined by only one hundred draftees. By June the Incorporated Militia amounted to only 406 men, or less than half the number Drummond had expected to have under the Assembly's revised legislation.[96]

Although the number of Upper Canadians who took an active part in hostilities in 1814 was smaller than it was in previous years, the men who were still in arms when peace was declared on 24 December were dedicated and reasonably well-trained soldiers. The handful of residents who chose not to hide behind bogus paroles were also more determined to stand their ground in the face of enemy attacks. The changing circumstances of militia service during the war can be determined through an examination of pension lists. Widows and orphans of militiamen who were killed on duty were granted pensions after the war was over, and the pension lists published in the colony's newspapers offered information on the cause of death. Pensions were provided to the families of 157 militiamen, but only twenty-six of those citizen-soldiers had been killed in action.

The 131 other militia fatalities were a product of miserable camp conditions, primitive medical practices, and simple mishaps. Figure 1 compares the number of men who died through accident or disease with the number who died in battle.

While over 83 per cent of these militiamen died from disease or by accident during the war, most of those deaths occurred during the first twelve months of the conflict when thousands of colonists were forced to participate in the struggle despite shortages of food and supplies. Ninety-five men perished from disease or accidents during that time and only twelve died from wounds received in battle. The sharp decline in participation that began in 1813 and continued throughout the war was a result of American paroles and the loss of British control over certain key areas. That more restricted level of militia activity led to an equally dramatic reduction in the number of deaths from all causes. The few dedicated colonists who continued to serve in 1814, however, paid a high price for that commitment and, during the last six months of 1814, battle casualties among Upper Canadian servicemen outnumbered deaths by disease or accident for the first time in the war. Nearly one-third of all the militiamen whose deaths during battle are recorded on the pension lists died at one engagement at Chippawa on 5 July 1814.[97]

To keep matters in perspective, though, it should also be noted that these eight militiamen were only a small fraction of the 148 British deaths at that battle.[98] That is not to suggest, however, that the sacrifices made by the colonists were unimportant. On the contrary, when one considers how unusual this type of commitment was among Upper Canadians, the activity of men from the Lincoln militia companies and the Incorporated battalion assumes an even greater significance. At the 25 July 1814 Battle of Lundy's Lane, for example, the sedentary militia, made up primarily of men from the Niagara Lincoln regiments, had one member killed and nineteen wounded. The Incoporated batallion suffered much more, with seven killed, fifty wounded, and almost ninety taken prisoner or missing in action.[99] During the summer of 1814, the Incorporated Militia experienced a casualty rate of over 40 per cent, and at least 166 of 406 members were either killed or wounded.[100] The fighting that summer, which was the fiercest of the war, seems to have eventually discouraged many Lincoln militiamen. A resident later admitted that the sedentary regiments were "harassed ... by continual duty and ... almost worn out" by events in 1814.[101] In September only 150 of the 1774 militiamen in the Niagara District answered Drummond's summons.[102] Throughout the fall of 1814 most sedentary militiamen

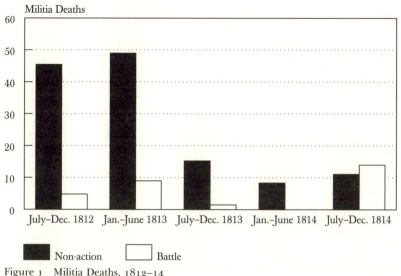

Figure 1   Militia Deaths, 1812–14
Source: Niagara Spectator, 11 December 1817

refused to appear when called for and Drummond was eventually forced to express "his dissatisfaction at the[ir] tardiness." At the same time, he offered sincere thanks to those colonists who consistently responded with "loyalty and Zeal."[103] Thus, while thousands of their neighbours stayed away, a few rare individuals chose to remain at the side of the British army and risk their lives in military service.

The Battle of Chippawa on 5 July 1814 also marked the end of Six Nations' participation in the war effort. Over the course of the previous two years the Six Nations had been of some assistance to the British at certain times, particularly at Queenston Heights and at the Battle of Beaver Dams in June 1813. But by July of the next year their enthusiasm for the war was gone. At Chippawa, moreover, the two hundred Grand River Iroquois who fought on the British side found themselves fighting against Six Nations warriors from New York. Amerindian losses at this battle, estimated to be in the neighbourhood of one hundred killed, forced both factions to reconsider their participation in the conflict. The Grand River Iroquois were also concerned about the defence of their homes, since Procter's defeat had left their territory open to attack by American patrols. Tired of a conflict they had never wanted and they had always feared might lead to fratricidal battles such as Chippawa, the majority of the Six Nations warriors left the Niagara frontier after July 1814.

Three months later, following the practice established to deal with mass desertion by other militia forces, Drummond issued a proclamation which allowed the Iroquois to return to their homes.[104]

It would be wrong to conclude that the inhabitants of Upper Canada played a dominant, or even an "important and essential role" in the fighting of the War of 1812. G.F.G. Stanley has argued that Upper Canadians undertook the "necessary and important tasks" of supplying food to the garrisons and transporting military supplies. None of these activities, however, was done out of a sense of duty. The inhabitants expected to be paid handsomely for these goods and services and, like Robert Nichol, most would have considered it absurd for an "individual to give his time to the Public gratuitously."[105]

While a few colonists assisted the British forces, the majority resorted to desertion or paroles to avoid serving. Strachan pointed with pride to the fact that half the colonists served in the militia in 1812, and at least one-third offered their services the next year. When one considers that the British authorities had summoned all members of the provincial militia for duty, those figures appear less impressive. More precise data on the total number of Upper Canadians who served in the militia is difficult to find. A study undertaken by the federal government in 1876 reported that 5455 militiamen of all ranks served in the province between 1812 and 1815. If correct, that figure represents less than half the number of eligible men, since there were nearly 13,000 Upper Canadians in the militia in 1811. Even if Strachan's estimate is right, it seems only 50 per cent of the men who were called in 1812 chose to answer the summons, and the proportion was even smaller the next year. The military authorities, moreover, never knew how long those men would remain on duty, and at times these soldiers proved to be more of a handicap than a blessing to the British forces. The continued failure of the Incorporated Militia recruitment campaign shows that most colonists had no interest in fighting except when their own property was in danger.[106]

Upper Canadians, of course, viewed events quite differently. While the colonists had not started this war, many soon found that they could not avoid being adversely affected by it and they understandably resented any suggestions that they were not doing enough for the war effort. When Drummond presented his proposal for the second Incorporated Militia to the Assembly in February 1814, for instance, he told the legislature that without conscription the "militia cannot be relied on as an efficient force." The Assembly angrily reacted against what Drummond was implying, that the force had not yet proven to be of any use, by saying that they themselves had "witnessed the brave, zealous and meritorious exertions" of the province's citizen-soldiers over the past two years.[107] This protest did not stop at the doors of the legislature and, one month later, the assemblymen, assisted by the able pen of John Strachan, composed an address to the prince regent on the subject. The politicians wanted to ensure that the biased reports posted by British officers did not remain unchallenged. In their petition the assemblymen said that they had reason to think that the prince regent did not know of the "zealous services" rendered by colonists in the various battles fought. The members went on to argue that the simple fact that the province had not been conquered was proof enough of the value of the militia. After having endured the most "severe privation and distress," the colonial representatives wanted the consolation of knowing that these facts would be laid before the prince regent, "whose favourable Notice they looked forward as their greatest reward."[108]

Strachan considered himself a victim of the same "severe privation and distress" although, in common with most of his fellow colonists, he had never served a day in the militia. This did not prevent him from boasting to a friend near the end of the war that his own actions had been of "singular use in promoting the defense of the Province."[109] Aside from soliciting donations for the Loyal and Patriotic Society, and badgering Americans who dared to touch private property during the invasions of York, Strachan had also assisted in the composition of the address to the prince regent and he had written two sermons about the conflict. All these actions, Strachan said, helped "to preserve and increase the Spirit of Loyalty which principally saved the Province during the first two years of the war." While Strachan believed that he had played a crucial part in the struggle, even he was willing to admit he had not won the war singlehandedly. "All would have been lost," he reminded Dugald Stewart, "but for the astonishing exertions of the Militia."[110]

5 "A Grand Attack on the Onions":
Provisions and Plundering

On 4 September 1813 Thomas Gibbs Ridout reported to his father, Surveyor-General Thomas Ridout, that he had recently met with "rather an ungracious reception" at the home of a prominent Niagara District farmer. While senior officers of the commissary department had been invited to dine at the main house and were offered accommodation there, Ridout and two other junior officers had been directed towards an old abandoned shack at the rear of the property which appeared to them to have been last occupied "at an early period of the world." At first, the commissary assistants were forced to rely on army field rations, since the farmer refused to provide the men with any provisions except milk, which he measured very carefully. Nonetheless, over the next few weeks Ridout, his friend Gee, and a French dragoon ate extremely well, and they managed to exact a revenge of sorts on their parsimonious host by carrying out "an extensive robbing of peas, apples, onions, corn, carrots" and other items. Out of sight at the rear of the property, the soldiers dismantled the farmer's rail fences for use as firewood and developed a daily routine of petty plundering that left them quite content. As Ridout reported on 21 September 1813: "Tonight our dragoon is to make a grand attack on the onions. The nests are kept very nice and clean from eggs. The dragoon has just come in with a fine musk melon and a peck of onions. We feed a turkey at the door, which is doomed for our Sunday dinner." During the painstaking process of luring the unsuspecting bird to their table, the soldiers had even surmounted the problem of a stingy milk supply. By late September,

Ridout was pleased to inform his father that "sometimes a cow happens to get milked over night."[1]

In spite of general orders from both American and British commanders which stipulated that looters would be punished, Ridout's wartime adventures would have been familiar to soldiers throughout Upper Canada. Private plundering, as opposed to the lawful taking of booty, provided much work for the members of the four compensation boards that examined war losses.[2] The third committee, appointed in 1815, eventually received 2884 claims from districts all across the province. Those submissions amounted to about one-quarter of the adult male wartime population, and it would be safe to assume that almost all families had experienced a loss of property or knew of someone who had.[3] The sheer variety of damages sustained by the inhabitants forced the commissioners to divide and then further subdivide the different claims. "Class One" submissions, for instance, were for losses attributed to British forces. This classification included damage done by British troops, losses caused by Indians associated with the army, and claims submitted for the loss of oxen or other property while in the service of His Majesty's military departments. "Class Two" submissions dealt with damages caused by enemy forces. These were subdivided into the districts where the loss occurred and included a separate category for damages sustained by "Domiciliated and Friendly Indians" during enemy attacks. Altogether the inhabitants had estimated that their losses amounted to £390,152 12s 6d.[4] To place that figure in proper perspective, one need only note that from 1808 to 1811 the average annual revenue of the province was less than £8000 a year.[5]

Very little of that property damage occurred during the first six months of the war. A few of the residents of the Niagara District, where most of the early action had taken place, reported losses, but most of these amounted to mere inconveniences. An inhabitant of Queenston, for example, informed William Drummer Powell in December 1812 that during their short stay in Upper Canada the Americans had overturned his sleeping quarters to such an extent that his bed "was scarcely to be discovered." But his actual losses were minimal and were limited to some epaulettes removed from one of his coats.[6]

Beginning in 1813, however, the war began to be fought in an increasingly vicious manner. During the capture of York in April, for instance, any homes found abandoned were considered fair game by American looters. Later, on their second visit to the capital at the end of July, American soldiers entered storehouses owned by York merchants and removed flour and other provisions. Ever vigilant when it came to private property, John Strachan immediately stepped forward to protest against this looting, but he was informed that provisions were considered "lawful prise, because they were the subsistence of armies."[7] York was also the scene of the first implementation of what one Upper Canadian, Thomas Clark, called the "burning system of the Americans." On 30 April 1813 the townspeople discovered that the church had been robbed and that the government buildings were on fire. At a meeting of the chief residents of the capital later that day a letter of complaint was composed and submitted to General Henry Dearborn. Strachan remarked that Dearborn expressed regret over the destruction of the provincial parliament and added that the American commander was also "greatly embarrassed" about the whole affair.[8]

Events in the Niagara District in the autumn of that year easily eclipsed those at York both in terms of the amount of damage done and the savagery involved. During the summer of 1813 the Americans had gained control of much of the frontier, but their advance was halted at Stoney Creek on 6 June 1813. A little over two weeks later the Americans suffered another crushing defeat at the hands of a combined force of Caughnawaga and Six Nations warriors at the battle of Beaver Dams on 24 June 1813. As the British forces pushed eastward and recaptured parts of the Niagara frontier they had lost over the summer, General George McClure, who commanded the American army at Fort George, decided it would be prudent to abandon that position and return to Fort Niagara in New York State. He hoped thereby to avoid a direct confrontation with the British forces under Colonel John Murray, which had advanced to within twelve miles of the town of Niagara. Murray had decided to move forward with all possible speed to prevent McClure from "carrying off the loyal part of the inhabitants" and to prevent the destruction of Fort George.[9]

Several months before Murray began his advance, John Armstrong, the secretary of state for war in the United States, had suggested to McClure that a successful defence of Fort George might require the destruction of the town of Niagara. If McClure thought that move was necessary, Armstrong directed that he apprise its inhabitants of these plans, giving them ample time to remove themselves and their belongings to a place of safety.[10] Contrary to Armstrong's directions that the destruction take place only if necessary for the defence of Fort George, McClure decided on 10 December to abandon his position but still set fire to the town. Joseph Willcocks was placed in charge of the operation, and the four hundred remaining inhabitants were given only half an hour to gather their

Warehouses set aflame by British raiders.
Lossing, *Pictorial Field-Book of the War of 1812*

possessions before the former capital was put to the torch. Within minutes of starting this work, three hundred homes worth an estimated £37,625 were reduced to ashes.[11] An eyewitness later remarked that the "once beautiful town of Newark" had been turned into "a ruin, nothing to be seen but brick chimneys standing."[12]

The next month George Prevost issued a proclamation concerning the American "burning system." Prevost thought that future generations would scarcely believe "that in the enlightened era of the 19th century, and in the inclemency of a Canadian Winter, the troops of a nation calling itself civilized and christian ... forced 400 helpless women and children ... to be the mournful spectators of the conflagration and the total destruction of all that belonged to them."[13] For all his apparent horror at the burning of Niagara, Prevost did not hesitate a few weeks later to commend the work of British troops who had undertaken retaliatory raids on the villages of Lewiston, Black Rock, and Buffalo in western New York. On the American side of the Niagara River a total of 334 buildings, including houses, barns, sheds, and stores worth an estimated $350,000, were completely "enlightened" by British torches.[14]

At the opening of the February 1814 session of the Legislative Assembly of Upper Canada, the members took the opportunity to express their displeasure with the recent deviations from the gentle-manly standards of warfare which had prevailed during the first part of the conflict. While lamenting the loss and destruction visited on both sides of the border, the assemblymen placed much of the blame on the "too credulous inhabitants of the Town of Niagara." The members felt that the recent burnings should serve as a warning against accepting "delusive promises" of protection for private prop-erty from enemy commanders. Lulled into inactivity by such pledges, the townspeople had been the authors of their own misfortune, but the assemblymen now hoped that Niagara residents would "unite more firmly in defence of the just cause" with other loyal Upper Canadians.[15] For many of the inhabitants of that district, such warn-ings were unnecessary. Hard lessons had been learned the moment Willcocks had struck his flint in December, and the next spring British forces along the frontier were pleased to discover that an increased number of Upper Canadians seemed determined to fight back.

On 3 July 1814 the first units of yet another American invasion force crossed the Niagara River into Upper Canada. Over the next few weeks these soldiers simply took what provisions they desired, and to one onlooker it appeared as if they were "plundering every house they could get at." William Hamilton Merritt also characterized the conduct of the Americans as "infamous in the Extreme" and he believed they were determined to rob the Upper Canadians of "every-thing they had."[16] That was a belief shared by other inhabitants, and the plundering eventually prompted many residents to dust off their muskets and take to the field.

Yet this new sense of duty did not guarantee that Upper Canadian property would be preserved; indeed, in the case of the village of St Davids it actually ensured its destruction. On 18 July 1814 a party of American foragers led by Isaac Stone was attacked by a group of Lincoln militiamen. According to Major Daniel MacFarland of the 23rd United States infantry, Stone's men had been sent to "scour the country" and it was presumed that this activity might meet with resistance. What the Americans had not expected, however, was fighting so fierce that Stone and his men would barely escape with their lives.[17] The next day the entire village of St Davids was set on fire in retaliation for the attack on the foraging party. Altogether the flames consumed fourteen homes, two shops, and one mill, worth a total of £5731.[18] As was the case after the destruction of Niagara, the loss of property infuriated the inhabitants, who were more eager than ever to strike a blow against the American marauders. On 19 July 1814 the commander of the British forces in the district,

Sir Phineas Riall, excitedly informed his superior "that almost the whole body of Militia is in Arms & seem actuated with the most determined Spirit of hostility to the Enemy."[19]

The London and Western districts were also the scene of a good deal of deliberate destruction. The first indication of what was in store for western Upper Canadians came only hours after General Procter's defeat at the Battle of Moraviantown on 5 October 1813. That night the victorious American army descended on the town of Fairfield and the inhabitants who remained were forced to bake bread for it while the soldiers requisitioned valuable possessions and stripped gardens of produce. The Indian residents had fled before the Americans had arrived and the Moravian missionaries soon followed their example. Fearing a massacre, and left without "a morsel of food" for the coming winter, the missionaries gathered their remaining effects and abandoned their homes to the invaders. From a hillside outside the town, the refugees watched flames erupt from the houses and, by the next day, the site was a smoking ruin. When the Upper Canadians reached the nearby village of Chatham they discovered that the retreating British troops had burnt the two grist mills at that settlement to prevent the grain inside from falling into the hands of the enemy. What property or food the British troops had not requisitioned or destroyed had been taken by their Indian allies, who entered the town some time later. For the residents of Chatham and Fairfield, the winter of 1813 would be the most difficult in memory.[20]

Similar events occurred throughout the region over the next few months as American raiders, sometimes assisted by disgruntled British subjects out to settle old scores, began plundering farms and destroying mills. A resident of York informed his brother in England that the origins of the looting could be traced to the fact that Upper Canadians were a "very much divided" people. "Many of them are friendly to the States and wish the country to fall into their hands," Isaac Wilson observed, "and where the Americans conquer they have no mercy on the property of the other party."[21] Those merciless attacks eventually prompted the organization of vigilante forces under men such as Henry Bostwick and Henry Medcalf. In November and December 1813 these gangs had some success against groups of marauders who had gone so far as to kidnap prominent Upper Canadians and steal their possessions. Despite these successful forays, the new year witnessed even greater levels of looting and destruction.

On 31 January 1814 a party led by Colonel Thomas Talbot's old enemy, Andrew Westbrook, raided the village of Delaware and captured Daniel Springer and Colonel Francis Baby. Both of these men were militia officers and friends of Talbot and were, therefore, prime targets for Westbrook's vengeance. In April he again led an attack, this one directed against the village of Oxford, where he managed to capture another old rival, Sikes Tousley.[22] Westbrook also launched three successive raids on Port Talbot in the months of May, July, and August 1814. In each of these attacks the real target, Talbot, made good his escape, although other less-fleet-of-foot settlers were not so lucky. During the raid on 16 August 1814, for instance, Talbot fled through the back window of his home, leaving 227 of his neighbours to discover that they were surrounded by a group of one hundred armed men disguised as ferocious Indian warriors. These raiders quickly revealed that under the war paint they were only common thieves; they set about robbing the terrorized villagers "of all their horses, and every particle of wearing apparel and household furniture, leaving the sufferers naked, and in a most wretched state."[23]

Upper Canadians who lived in the London and Western districts were also victims of fire-raids similar to those witnessed earlier in the Niagara region. On 14 May 1814 about eight hundred Americans landed at Dover, where they found that all the men had fled inland about an hour earlier, leaving only women and children behind. Talbot would later claim that this decision "to retire as far as Sovereign Mills" was made so as to give "time to the Militia to collect," but not all residents agreed with the wisdom of that measure.[24] One of the inhabitants of Dover who was left behind, Amelia Harris, said most men saw no sense in retreating to Brantford when the enemy was threatening their homesteads. Harris reported the "general wish was to try to prevent the American landing" and she recalled that most males "expressed indignation at being ordered to a safe distance from all danger."[25] Talbot's authority prevailed, however, and over the next twenty-four hours the invaders took advantage of the lack of resistance and set about burning almost everything of value. An eyewitness recalled what he saw: "A scene of destruction and plunder now ensued which beggars all description. In a short time the houses, mills and barns were all consumed, and a beautiful village, which the sun shone on in splendour that morning, was before two o'clock a heap of smoking ruin."[26] Not content with the destruction of Dover, the Americans also marched several miles along the lake and destroyed any mills or homes they found in their path. The raiders were ruthless when it came to livestock and, according to one resident, they shot any farm animals they came across and left the carcasses to "rot on the ground."[27] The damage done during this raid was extensive: Robert Nichol, for example, lost two houses, two barns, a grist mill, three stone outhouses, and a distillery. Talbot estimated the total losses from this raid to be £12,658 18s, and Nichol's share of that amount was said to be £5000.[28]

When asked by a local resident to explain his "wanton and barbarous conduct," the American commander, Colonel John Campbell, said it was done in retaliation for the British raids on Buffalo and Lewiston.[29] But Campbell was not telling the whole truth; the May 1814 American attack on Dover and the surrounding countryside was prompted by more than a desire for retribution. The property targeted – homes, barns, livestock, and mills – was chosen because its loss would demoralize the inhabitants and make defence of the region nearly impossible. Harris stated that one American officer justified his actions at Dover by saying "the Buildings were used as Barracks and the mill furnished flour for British Troops."[30] In the future, any royal force seeking to defend that part of the province would have to rely on extremely extended lines of supply.

It was this goal that also prompted the last American incursion into western Upper Canada during October and November 1814. Starting his campaign at Lord Selkirk's settlement of Baldoon, General Duncan McArthur's force eventually travelled as far east as Burford and managed to burn all but two of the grist mills in the London District.[31] For a pioneer region these were disastrous events, since mills for grinding grain represented large investments of money and were central to the economic activities of agricultural societies. Of course, the Americans justified the widespread destruction as a military necessity, but the strategic value of McArthur's march, which was designed to prevent the British from retaking the region in 1815, was nullified by the peace treaty signed a little over a month later at Ghent in Holland. Without firing a shot, the British regained complete control of western Upper Canada. However, the physical effects of the invasion and of the dozens of other predatory raids carried out in 1813 and 1814 could not be eliminated by a few strokes of a pen. The land that was returned to British control the next year was stripped of both its resources and its rudimentary infrastructure of bridges, farm buildings, and mills.

Of course, as the people of Chatham discovered in October 1813, the Americans could not be blamed for all the destruction that took place during the war. While enemy forces sought to intimidate inhabitants or hamper counter-attacks by burning and looting various districts, British soldiers and the Indians who assisted them often engaged in similar activities, although usually for different reasons. At times, His Majesty's forces destroyed valuable items to prevent them from falling into the wrong hands. More often, however, British

Retreating British troops burn a bridge over the Don River, York, Upper Canada.
National Archives of Canada, c 6147

troops and Indian warriors simply took food to supplement their
meagre diets, dismantled fences and barns to provide firewood for
warmth, or stole money and valuables to enrich themselves. Inhabitants of Upper Canada cared little about who was at fault in such
cases. Niagara mill owner Thomas Clark, for example, reported that
the "miserable state" of the country in 1814 had been produced in
equal measure "by the ravages of the Enemy and also by the Irregularities of our own troops and Indians."[32]

Any discussion of the conduct of combatants should include an
examination of the conditions in Upper Canada under which men
were expected to fight. A partial record of that lifestyle can be found
in the letters written by Lieutenant William Macewen of the First
Battalion Royal Scots during his tour of duty in the province in 1813.
Macewen first arrived in the colony on 4 June 1813, after an arduous
ten-day journey from Montreal. A veteran soldier who had served a

number of years on the continent, Macewen was unimpressed with the little village of Kingston, which he contemptuously dismissed as "poverty itself." In a letter to his pregnant wife in Montreal written two days after his arrival, the young officer complained that the British soldiers in the garrison were compelled to eat the rations supplied by the commissariat since there was nothing else "to be had for love or money." His disappointment with that situation is understandable, for Macewen suspected he would soon be sent into action on the Niagara frontier. As an experienced soldier, he was aware that extra provisions would became even more difficult to acquire once his regiment was stationed closer to the seat of war.

Three weeks later, and only twelve miles from Fort George where the Americans had established their headquarters, Macewan huddled under a lean-to built of twigs and leaves that he called an "Indian house"; the shelter hardly deserved that name since it failed to shield him from noon-day heat or late-night cold. From this humble abode he reported that, as expected, the men were forced to rely solely on government-issued food since the inhabitants refused to part with any of their produce. He could only describe the rations as "bad" and he was sure they were "too little for any man in good health."[33]

Macewen's appraisal of army food as "bad" was certainly not overly harsh. At the best of times the field ration on which British soldiers were forced to subsist when they were away from the garrison contained three basic elements. Each daily allotment was supposed to consist of one-and-a-half pounds of bread, one pound of fresh or salt beef, and half a gill of rum. If fresh or salted beef could not be procured, the soldier was supposed to receive a substitution of ten-and-a-half ounces of salt pork.[34] Macewen's lack of enthusiasm for his field rations was only partly related to their relentless monotony. The method of disbursement also produced food that was not fit for human consumption. There was rarely fresh bread in the field, because it was brought from the nearest garrison and the regulations stipulated it was only to be issued once every four days in the form of a six-pound loaf to each soldier.[35] One can only imagine the condition of that last morsel after four days of humid summer weather under a hastily constructed lean-to.

Other factors, such as the availability of grain and livestock, or transportation problems, could lead to tainted food or smaller portions. John Kilborn, a member of the Incorporated Militia, fought at Chippawa in 1814 and, after the battle, his corps was ordered to halt and enjoy a small repast. According to Kilborn, the men had "a drink of muddy sulphur water" from a creek beside the road while the officers distributed bread "that had been brought in an open wagon,

Table 3
Caloric Value of Field Rations

1½ lbs bread	1643 kilocalories
1 lb fresh beef	896 kilocalories
½ gill rum	158 kilocalories
Total	2697 kilocalories

Source: Robinson, *Normal and Therapeutic Nutrition*

and was pretty well filled with dust and gravel." Although the food was unfit for human consumption, Kilborn remembered the men "gladly eating and drinking such as could be got."[36] The eagerness of the Incorporated battalion to partake of that tainted food is understandable given that the efficiency of the commissariat department varied over time and that sometimes the soldiers received no rations at all. Since men engaged in that service suffered from the same diseases as other soldiers in Upper Canada, the department often had only one or two members capable of fulfilling its duties.[37] Even when the commissariat was functioning properly, some combatants were still deprived of the supplies to which they were entitled. It seems, as Kilborn's testimony reveals, that the half gill of liquor specified as part of the daily allotment was rarely available in Upper Canada. One doctor who served with the United States army during the war, James Mann, said British soldiers were usually in better condition than their American counterparts because of the lack of hard liquor north of the border. According to Mann, while American soldiers were forced to drink their ration all at once "in the morning before breakfast," spirits could not even "be procured in the upper province of Canada for money."[38] Those soldiers who served under larcenous or incompetent officers also sometimes found that field rations had been sold or lost after reaching their units. For example, in March 1813, Captain John Howell of the Prince Edward militia faced a court martial for "defrauding his company out of a part of their Provisions." At the trial, one of his sergeants revealed that he had "received but one Loaf of Bread from the 15th to the 24th of January." Although acquitted of the fraud charges, Howell was removed from duty for having failed to ensure that his company was fed.[39]

Even when soldiers received their field rations on time and in good condition, they often remained hungry. A close examination of the nutritional content of the standard field ration supports Macewen's opinion that these provisions were insufficient for healthy young men. In caloric terms,[40] the daily field ration was supposed to amount to a total of 2697 kilocalories (see table 3). That meal would lead to hunger in most men, since the recommended daily nutrient intake for males sixteen to eighteen years of age in Canada today is 3200 kilocalories. For males between the ages of nineteen and thirty-five the requirement drops to 3000 kilocalories. These modern standards have been formulated for individuals whose physical activity is considered "light" and whose occupation is classified as "sedentary."[41] Average nineteenth-century males, however, were agriculturalists whose physical activity was extremely heavy and whose occupation was anything but sedentary. Donald W. Engels has suggested that the ordinary daily caloric intake of nineteenth-century American males was between 6000 and 6500 kilocalories, or about double what it is today.[42] While that figure is probably too high, 2700 kilocalories certainly would have been considered an unhealthy deviation from the standards of the time. That is especially true since soldiers were often engaged in strenuous physical activities, whether erecting redoubts, digging trenches, or running for their lives.[43] Because of his lifestyle, an ordinary soldier in 1812 would probably have required a nutritional intake similar to present-day manual labourers or athletes in training. Depending on levels of exertion, athletes and manual labourers must consume between 4000 and 4800 kilocalories a day to maintain good health.[44] Clearly, grumblings about the field rations served to British soldiers were justified not only because the food was unpalatable but also because those rations were deficient in nutrient energy.[45]

Senior officers in Quebec City were well aware that field rations did not provide sufficient nutrition for active combatants. According to custom, then, soldiers were expected to supplement their diets by appropriating a part of their pay for food purchases. While that may have been possible in European campaigns, it proved impractical in sparsely populated Upper Canada. In the pioneer districts of British North America, shortages of liquor, flour, and meat were not uncommon and opportunities for replacing missing portions appear to have grown increasingly rarer as the war continued. In May 1813 one officer in the field requested that government-issued supplies be increased when men were "actually marching in situations where no provisions of any sort [can] be purchased." This request was rejected and a 13 August 1813 order warned commanding officers not to make any alterations or additions to the daily alllotments.[46]

Since all soldiers in the field were forced to subsist on the same provisions, it is easy to see why officers joined their men in complaints about the lack of adequate food. Yet the refusal of senior staff to agree to requests for larger portions is also understandable.

Increases to the daily allotments would only hasten the depletion of food resources in the province and might lead to famine. Nineteenth-century armies were expected to acquire most supplies from within their area of operations. But, because it was a frontier community, Upper Canada had only recently reached a point of self-sufficiency, and exports of flour were a relatively new phenomena. Not all regions of the colony shared in these surpluses. Residents in the sparsely populated Western and London districts, for example, could not supply their own needs, and there was no way they could feed thousands of additional men and horses. That paucity of resources made itself apparent within weeks of the start of hostilities, when General Hull's expeditionary force arrived in the province on 11 July 1812 without sufficient provisions to sustain them. One wag remarked that these "Tippecanoe boys" and "Michigan racoon catchers" had planned on filling their stomachs "out of the pockets of their enemies," but they soon discovered that this would be impossible. Even a successful raid on a large herd of sheep, who "capitulated to a force one-half their number," did not end the supply problems of the invaders.[47] Thomas Verchères, who witnessed the invasion, said most of the Americans subsisted on green apples because they lacked more "health-giving supplies."[48] After less than a month in Upper Canada, Hull was forced to abandon his outpost because the region had too few resources for an army of 2500 men.

The British contingent that regained control of the Western District was also hampered by supply problems. The disruption of the regular rhythm of agricultural pursuits occasioned by the invasion and the assembling of the militia led to a reduced harvest in 1812. Poor crop yields brought higher prices, and Henry Procter's force was prevented from buying any extra provisions because of the "very scanty and Irregular Supply of money" forwarded to his commissariat department.[49] Shortages of both currency and local resources meant that Procter's army was forced to rely on rations brought in ships from the east. That tenuous supply link was severed when the Americans gained naval superiority on Lake Erie in 1813 and, as a result, Procter was left with no choice but to abandon his position. For their part, the officials in the commissariat department were pleased by this decision since their task had become impossible. Moreover, some of the western warriors associated with the British forces had recently threatened that, if their share of the provisions did not increase, they would kidnap the men responsible and slowly starve them to death.[50]

Aiming to reduce the distance between his men and the more abundant resources of the Home and Niagara districts, Procter began a slow retreat eastward. He was overtaken near the Moravian settlement at Fairfield on 5 October 1813, where he was soundly defeated by a larger American force led by Major-General William Harrison. The remnants of Procter's army struggled on and eventually reached Burlington Heights, where they added to the supply problems that already existed around the head of the lake. In September 1813, long before Procter's force reached the shores of Lake Ontario, commissariat officials in the area reported that they had only enough food to last twenty days. A member of that department, Edward Couche, was sure there would soon be shortages, especially if Procter brought along a large number of native warriors.[51] As it turned out, Procter's force was accompanied by more than three thousand Amerindians and, over the next few months, it would become increasingly obvious that the colony's agricultural resources were simply too limited to meet the heavy demands placed on them.

In 1814 the commissariat officers in the centre of the province faced supply problems nearly as severe as those experienced the year before in western Upper Canada. The British army in the area included encampments at York, Burlington, Long Point, and at five other sites in the Niagara region. Altogether, 3939 regulars and 527 members of the militia and provincial corps were on duty at these eight posts.[52] Even if supplied with only a daily field ration, rather than the more substantial garrison fare, these 4466 soldiers would have consumed a staggering amount of food. At a baking ratio of 3:4, twelve ounces of flour were needed to produce a pound of bread. Assuming daily consumption was restricted to the one-and-a-half pounds of bread per man stipulated for field rations, the total quantity of flour needed in a thirty-day period was:

$$\frac{4466 \times 3 \times 1\frac{1}{2} \times 30}{4} = 150{,}727 \text{ lbs or } 75.4 \text{ tons.}[53]$$

In addition, the 3000 or so Indians assembled around Burlington Heights were consuming another twenty-five barrels of flour each day.[54] Every month, therefore, the soldiers and Indians of the right division consumed 297,727 pounds or about 149 tons of flour.

Commissariat officials were also expected to provide the combatants with at least a pound of beef each day. Since the warriors and their dependents required sixteen head of cattle daily, it is likely that the soldiers would have consumed at least the same number each day. Over the course of a month, the commissariat would have been expected to supply 960 head of cattle simply to feed the right division. Such an amount called for extreme resourcefulness on the part

Receipt issued to Noah Fairchild, November 1814, for goods requisitioned by
Duncan McArthur's raiders.
Eva Brook Donly Museum, Simcoe; photograph by Steve Wigmore

of commissariat officers, for it was estimated in September 1813 that
the farmers in the Burlington Heights region possessed only about
300 head of cattle.[55]

Commissariat officials were also required to find forage for the
animals that accompanied the combatants. In September 1813 the
right division of the British army used about one draught animal for
every eleven soldiers. If that ratio was the same several months later,
the soldiers and militiamen in the Home and Niagara districts would
have needed about 392 oxen and horses for their cavalry, artillery,
and baggage units.[56] Livestock require more than ten times the
amount of food needed by a man, and regulations issued in 1812
stipulated that horses and oxen were to receive twenty-eight-and-a-
half pounds of forage a day.[57] In the course of a month, therefore,
the draught animals employed at the eight encampments likely consumed about 168 tons of oats, corn, and hay. The actual total for the
right division was much higher, however, since the native warriors
also had a great number of their own ponies. The huge amounts of
food required by livestock meant that forage supplies were always
the first to be depleted and, for the British forces in the centre of
the province, that point may have been reached as early as December
1813. At that time, Isaac Wilson informed his brother that the Amerindian warriors at Burlington Heights were willing to sell their horses
at what he thought were "very cheap" prices.[58]

Over the course of the next year the forces in central Upper
Canada continued to devour food at a rate that far surpassed the
agricultural output of the region. Initially, commissariat officials

managed to acquire sufficient amounts of local produce to offset the shortages that often occurred when too little food was shipped from the east. Supplies were coaxed from reluctant inhabitants who feared that the voracious appetite of the army would leave them with nothing for their families. When these appeals to the farmers failed, however, the military employed legal devices to acquire the desired items. In August 1814 Robert Nichol, quartermaster-general of the Upper Canadian militia, was armed with special powers to acquire a quota of five to twelve bushels of wheat from each Niagara area farmer known to have such a quantity to spare.[59] In order "to prevent extortion," a scale of prices was developed through consultation with the magistrates of the area and, before requisitioning any goods, Nichol was required to submit written orders to each justice of the peace explaining what the commissariat was seeking.[60] On 5 September 1814 it was announced that inhabitants would be offered $14 for a barrel of flour and $10 for a barrel of beef.[61] Although residents at the head of the lake probably considered any amount of money as too little, at least they were promised more than their counterparts to the west. Upper Canadians in the London and Western districts were also subjected to military requisitioning, but the enemy offered only twelve dollars for each barrel of flour; those settlers holding back more than what was "absolutely necessary for domestic use" were warned they would be "severely punished."[62]

Drummond expected that the use of magistrates would solve the supply problems in central Upper Canada, but it did not. Deputy Commissary-General Peter Turquand later complained that the system devised by Drummond had proved inefficient because the military was required to work in consultation with the magistrates. Turquand noted that there were too few justices of the peace and that many were in remote regions where they were of little use to the commissariat. He also observed that many magistrates were reluctant to assist the military and he thought the majority were "unprepared to act with the stimulus and exertion" required.[63] In October 1814, three months after Nichol began requisitioning wheat, Gordon Drummond directed a letter to George Prevost which outlined why a complete collapse of the right division's supply system was imminent. A recent tour of back townships reputed to contain abundant resources had convinced his commissariat officials that no untapped stockpiles existed. For that reason, Drummond reported that "nothing but the Squadron can relieve us."[64]

Drummond placed his hopes on the importation of supplies from outside the area because the Niagara District, after more than two years of war, was a "devasted and impoverished" region. Even if large stockpiles had existed, it is unlikely the inhabitants would have sold their surpluses. In January 1815 Turquand explained that the duties of the commissariat department were made more difficult because the population of the province was made up of "inhabitants of various Dispositions, characters, & Religions." As with the militia, appeals to loyalty among this motley population had proven insufficient; he observed that most people exhibited a "preverse disposition" and a "disinclination to come forward & Serve Government." Turquand believed that the inhabitants would not give up any extra supplies unless they were physically threatened. He requested permission to take any extra forage or grain forcibly without reporting to the magistrates and asked that two companies of dragoons be attached to the commissariat to "encite" compliance.[65]

Some Upper Canadians were reluctant to provide goods to the army because they had not been paid in the past. At the beginning of 1814, Drummond noted that a number of inhabitants were demanding payment for goods taken during Brock's Detroit campaign in 1812. Other inhabitants complained that a shortage of proper change meant that commissariat officials often failed to pay the full amount owed. Farmers who sold goods worth less than $25 were sometimes not paid at all, and those who sold between $25 and $50 worth of produce were forced to settle for the lesser amount. Some residents said they had never been paid because the receipts they presented were judged to be improper.[66] One reader of the *Kingston Gazette* felt that colonists should not be held accountable for clerical errors and he suggested that the commissariat honour all vouchers whether "*in* or *out* of form."[67] Much of this confusion was the result of unauthorized requisitioning which took place without the prior approval of the commissariat department; the problem eventually became so serious that George Prevost was forced to establish a board of inquiry to determine which citizens were still owed money because of bureaucratic bungling.[68]

Clearly, conflicts betweeen the commissariat and Upper Canadians were not restricted to central or western regions, and the supply situation in the east was not much better than in the Niagara District. Lower Canada was supplied with cattle smuggled across the border from Vermont, and one eyewitness thought the droves of livestock crossing into British territory resembled "herds of buffalo."[69] The large garrisons at Quebec and Montreal consumed most of this illicit beef and, as a result, by the second year of the war troops in eastern Upper Canada sometimes faced shortages of food.[70] Considering the size of the garrisons in the east, shortages were only to be expected. The British army at Kingston, for example, had grown from 100 men of the Royal Veterans Battalion in 1812 to 3806 men by January 1815.[71] Historian Stephen Mecredy has estimated that, if sailors are factored in, there were as many as 5000 members of the British forces in Kingston as early as the fall of 1813.[72] Of course, the total quantity of flour needed for this garrison rose dramatically as the war continued. Between June 1812 and October 1813, for instance, the monthly demand on the Kingston commissariat increased from just over fifteen barrels of flour and nine barrels of pork to some 765 barrels of flour and 445 barrels of pork.[73] Although garrison meals actually involved less meat than field rations, they included generous portions of peas, butter, and rice. Not surprisingly, by March 1813 the *Kingston Gazette* featured Commissary-General advertisements for large amounts of "Flour, Pork & Pease." Contractors were required to supply as many as 1000 barrels of meat at a time, although orders of that size would have provided the commissariat with just over a two-month supply of pork.[74]

Faced with severe shortages, the Kingston commissariat sought to have martial law imposed on eastern Upper Canada as early as August 1813. Francis de Rottenburgh, however, did not actually take that step for several months. He had prohibited the distillation of rye after taking command of the province in June 1813, but only when the supply situation reached a critical point in November did he feel there was no choice but to proclaim a partial existence of martial law in the Johnstown and Eastern districts. This action meant that commissariat officers could force farmers to sell provisions whether the civilians wished to or not.[75] Although de Rottenburgh offered what were described as the "most liberal prices" possible, the inhabitants refused to part with their supplies and the attempt to requisition provisions forcibly "created much discontent."[76]

In January 1814 Gordon Drummond, who had replaced de Rottenburgh the month before, repealed the measure because he naïvely assumed that it had been only the muddy roads of autumn which had prevented the residents from bringing their supplies to market. Over the next three months the hardpacked trails witnessed no appreciable increase in traffic and Drummond was forced to declare martial law throughout the province on 12 April 1814. While he knew that measure would be unpopular, Drummond argued that it was done only as a result of the "most imperious necessity" since his troops were nearly bereft of food. At one point his stores at the Kingston garrison contained only sixteen barrels of flour, less than one day's supply of bread.[77]

Within a fortnight of declaring martial law, and after having prohibited the export or distilling of all grain, Drummond realized that even these measures would not alleviate his situation. Two weeks of investigation by experienced commissary officers had revealed that extensive reserves of flour and livestock no longer existed in eastern Upper Canada. "No effort of human exertion can supply this army for many months longer," he told George Prevost, "for the flour is not in the country." Until extra provisions could be sent to the province, Drummond believed he had no alternative but to reduce the amount of bread being distributed. Aware that this move would "excite considerable discontent" among the soldiers and Indian warriors, Drummond requested that Prevost do all he could to ease the supply difficulties before he was faced with defections or discipline problems of a more serious nature.[78]

Faced with the reality of slow starvation, British soldiers and other combatants in Upper Canada, like soldiers around the world, attempted to supplement their diets by "fair means or foul."[79] Macewen, for instance, chose the former route and he asked that his wife procure tea, sugar, peppar, mustard, and "any other thing you can think of."[80] Other soldiers without contacts in the towns but with money in their pockets could turn to the sutlers who sometimes followed the army. These civilian merchants, however, usually specialized in watered-down grog and they charged enormous sums for the little food they did sell.[81] Alternatively, combatants could supplement their diet by buying produce from local inhabitants. But as Macewen had discovered, sometimes even money would not separate Upper Canadians from their provisions. On 13 August 1813, for example, he informed his wife that the Royal Scots had abandoned their "Indian houses" for rooms in farms situated only a few miles from Fort George. It was not long before he realized that his new hosts were as reluctant to share their supplies as the residents of Kingston had been. "Where I am obliged to live," he told his wife, "the people would not sell me a fowl nor a potato, and even grumble when my men use their dishes."[82]

While one might be tempted to sypathize with the trials of men like Macewen, it would be best to remember that many Upper Canadians had a right to be distrustful. Too often, inhabitants who were imposed upon by soldiers also discovered that they had been robbed of some item or other. One settler east of York, for example, billeted a group of soldiers who were on their way to Kingston. The next morning the farmer realized that a prize hog was missing and he appealed to the commanding officer for help. A thorough search of the boats and farm was undertaken, but no trace of the animal could be found and the party embarked later that day. His curiousity aroused, the officer in charge offered pardons to the offenders if they would explain the secret of this perfect crime. Turning over one of the boats, the men revealed a hog split lengthwise and nailed like a sheath to the keel. As one commentator noted, "it would be superfluous to add that the captain had fresh pork for supper that night."[83] Thirst, as well as hunger, motivated some thieves and a number of British soldiers even managed to acquire liquor in 1814, although the province was nearly dry. On 18 February 1814, after a successful raid on the American shore, officers at the Prescott garrison commandeered a hogshead of whiskey which they ordered shipped back north. The prize never reached its destination, however, because the returning "soldiers ran up behind the sleigh, bored a hole with a bayonet, and secured in jugs the coveted fluid."[84]

The widespread theft associated with the armed forces was not simply the product of meagre rations, although they were surely an important factor. Also of some importance was the fun and excitement that could be experienced while combatants supplemented their diet, pay packet, or both. Ordinary British soldiers had acquired a reputation in other areas for seeking out "Booty and Beauty," and their activities in Upper Canada proved that at least the first prize remained a goal.[85] Like youths who raid gardens, foot soldiers considered most petty theft to be part of a simple game that had been played for centuries. Surly locals were taught who was boss, and the soldiers had a little fun at their expense. Even the language used to describe these minor incidents of looting indicated that the troops did not consider their actions to be of a serious nature. Any food or articles taken during such sport was not considered stolen but was referred to as "hooked." This expression developed from the traditional method of using a hooked stick to grab items from a merchant's counter while his back was turned.[86]

Of course the owner of a prize hog hooked by British soldiers would have found nothing sporting or humorous about these practices even though the pecuniary loss might have been relatively minor. Other inhabitants were even less forgiving, especially when the damage was substantial or when it appeared that the actions of the soldiers were entirely malicious in nature. Ebenezer Jones, who lived in Saltfleet Township in the Niagara District, witnessed a contingent of British troops shoot thirty-five of his geese and then bayonet a large sow, apparently for the sport of it. Sarah Ingersol, who operated a public house at the Credit River, was robbed a number of times by British troops seeking liquor and money.[87] Likewise, George Castor from Barton Township in the Niagara District awoke one evening to find three members of Macewen's regiment of Royal Scots in his home. They had blackened their faces to avoid being recognized and they knocked Castor to the floor when he refused to give up his savings. The intruders eventually left, but only after robbing Castor of £45 in army bills. These incidents, and hundreds like them, reinforced the negative attitudes held by most Upper Canadians about the regular foot soldier. One imagines that Castor would have heartily endorsed Dr William Dunlop's observation that the British troops sent to the province represented "the rubbish of every department in the army."[88]

Fear and hatred of Amerindians was also reinforced by incidents involving warriors associated with the British army. That was particularly true after General Procter's defeat in the autumn of 1813 when thousands of western and Six Nation warriors retreated to Burlington Heights. By January 1814 some 3000 Amerindians, at least 2000 of whom were women and children, had assembled at the western end of Lake Ontario.[89] Dispersed among numerous small encampments, the warriors and their families must have been at times overlooked by commissary officials who operated out of the garrison at the head of Burlington Bay. Faced with shortages of food for their families and with no forage for their horses, the Indians also resorted to hooking items to supply their needs.

Abel Laud, a farmer from the township of Ancaster located only a few miles from Burlington Heights, was one of many inhabitants who believed that Amerindians were stealing his property. Laud reported the loss of three hogs and, though he had not witnessed the culprits in the act, he was sure a group of natives were responsible because he had seen them chasing the animals.[90] Similarly, a neighbour of William Langs said he saw a number of warriors "turn their Horses" into Langs's field and he also testified that he "heard" the natives kill his neighbour's hog. Apparently some Upper Canadians believed that, at least when it came to a band of warriors intent on gathering provisions, discretion was the better part of valour. After all, one could always surmise what was going on outside a hiding place merely by listening for telltale sounds.[91]

The various Indian encampments in the vicinity of Burlington Heights were the staging grounds for hundreds of incidents of looting. Richard Hatt, who owned a farm and two sawmills at Dundas, estimated his losses from Indian depredations at nearly £5000. The warriors completely stripped his farm of livestock, and then cut down acres of prime timber. Manuel Overfield testified on Hatt's behalf that the Indians "were accustomed to fell trees for the sake of the nuts, branches etc. and of which he made many complaints."[92] The bold nature of many of these incidents surprised some inhabitants. Peter Swartz, who lived in Saltfleet, testified that warriors "took his horse before his face." Robert Biggar, who resided in the vicinity of Stoney Creek, reported a similar incident involving warriors from a nearby encampment. One day he stumbled upon four natives "whom he found riding away with 2 of his horses & a cart." In the "affray" that followed, Biggar claimed that he was "near losing his life" until he at last gained the upper hand.[93] On the nearby Niagara escarpment, John Rykman said that the warriors "did not hesitate to take pigs out of people's pens right before their faces." One day Ryckman's neighbour, Jacob Rymal, was working in his field when, according to one account: "His wife came running to him with the information that two Indians had stolen a couple of pigs, and had made off with the porkers. Rymal, rifle in hand was instantly in pursuit. He shot one of the Indians dead. The other returned the fire shooting his pursuer through the hand." Ryckman recalled that Rymal had not been wounded in vain since he did recover the two pigs.[94]

As Manuel Overfield testified, inhabitants could constantly complain to the authorities about damages to wood lots or farms, only to have their appeals fall on deaf ears. No British officer or Upper Canadian justice of the peace could possibly exercise control over the thousands of Indians spread around the western end of Lake Ontario, and none dared try. Confronted by the apparent impotence of constituted authority, but determined to put an end to the loss of property, Upper Canadians like Rymal were willing to resort to more primitive means of enforcement. It seems that by 1813 a number of other residents had formed posses in order to better police their territory and protect their property. This increased vigilance on the part of the farmers eventually culminated in the murder of three warriors in Saltfleet Township "as a revenge for their constant depredations upon the people." Augustus Jones, a magistrate who investigated the murders, soon realized that his neighbours were not anxious to cooperate with his inquiries. On returning home one evening, Jones found his barn ablaze and he suspected that the arsonists wished him to cease "his exertions to discover the murderer."[95]

Amerindian-white relations, which had never been good in Upper Canada before the war, reached a new low when both groups were forced to live under difficult conditions and in close proximity to each other. Many of the settlers in the province had come from the United States, and most Americans were taught from early childhood to fear and hate Indians. Now, as residents of Upper Canada, hundreds of these colonists found themselves losing property, and one supposes a good deal of sleep, because they lived near the theatre of war "about which hundreds of Indians were lurking."[96] Even recent British immigrants might be influenced by the opinions of the majority of settlers around them. Wilson, for example, told his brother that most people believed that the Indians constituted only a drain on British resources. It was commonly reported that they rarely participated in battles, but instead waited until the end of the fighting and then returned to the field to get "a good share of the plunder."[97] Some British soldiers also held low opinions of the fighting abilities of the warriors, and one officer remarked that natives attached to his force were suspected of murdering wounded British soldiers "for the sake of plunder."[98]

For their part, the "lurking and plundering" Indians no doubt resented the fact that the British soldiers under Procter had abandoned the territory to the west so vital to them without having made a final strong stand against the Americans. Those warriors who had been at the side of Tecumseh when he fell at the Battle of Moravian-town were angered to learn they were regarded as unwelcome allies by Upper Canadians who remained at home tending their farms. One suspects, therefore, that it was not mere practicality which prompted the warriors to make up for shortfalls in rations and forage by hooking provisions from settlers. Like Thomas G. Ridout, these men were probably also responding to the ungracious reception they had received on their arrrival at Burlington Heights.

Eventually the conflicts and tensions that developed between the Indian and white communities around the head of the lake led some residents to abandon their homes and seek refuge at the garrison.[99] For at least one resident of this area, however, even that option was out of the question. Richard Beasley had already been forced to abandon "the peaceable enjoyment" of his property when the British established their garrison on his farm on Burlington Heights. He complained that his family had been evicted from its home and that he was left with no choice but to support his children at "great expense in another part of the country." While he served in the militia at York, the soldiers and Indians at Burlington Heights stripped his farm of crops and livestock. He also found himself the victim of the American navy when a boat loaded with over £3000 of provisions and merchandise that Richard and his brother Henry had purchased was seized on Lake Ontario.[100] By events such as these, Beasley suffered significant losses during the war, though unlike many others his land was never subjected to enemy raids.

Exactly 2055 claims were reviewed by the 1823–6 commission appointed to investigate losses suffered by Upper Canadians during the War of 1812. An examination of these claims, which have

Table 4
Claims for Damages by District

	Claims Submitted	Percentage of Total	Estimated Damages (£)
Western	415	20.2	65,196
London	296	14.4	50,797
Niagara	678	33.0	182,169
Gore	310	15.1	44,243
Home	80	3.9	12,379
Newcastle	13	0.6	2,633
Midland	21	1.0	6,938
Johnston	63	3.1	6,007
Eastern	167	8.1	12,065
Other*	12	0.59	18,301
Total	2055	100	400,728

Source: NA, RG 19, E5 (a), Board of Claims
* There were twelve claims for damages outside the province.

survived intact, can provide us with a glimpse of what the war meant for a large sample of the population of the colony. Some of the submissions were made by individuals who had endured substantial losses, but others were of a much less serious nature. The smallest claim was for £2 worth of property, while the largest submission was for the immense sum of £9809, a figure greater than the entire province collected each year in revenue. Altogether, the claimants believed that they had sustained over £400,728 in losses, although the average claim was in the neighbourhood of only £195.[101] Yet that was a significant amount in those days considering that, with it, a settler could purchase a complete farmhouse, as well as a barn, stable, and outhouses, and still have £95 left with which to buy a team of oxen and a plough.[102]

A computer-assisted study of these 2055 claims reveals that the damages inflicted during nearly three years of fighting were not distributed evenly throughout the colony. Table 4 displays these variations and it shows the number of claims submitted from each district, that number expressed as a percentage of the 2055 claims, and the estimated losses in provincial currency. While claims were submitted from every section of the colony, clear differences between the regions are easily discernable. The four districts that were the scene of most battles and where large concentrations of troops and Indians were deployed (Western, London, Niagara, Gore) accounted for 1699 claims or over 80 per cent of all submissions. The five districts in the eastern portion of the province (Home, Newcastle,

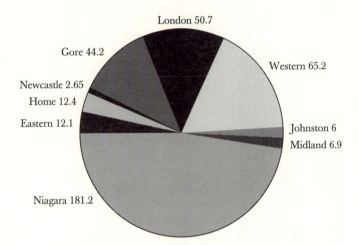

Figure 2   Estimated Losses in Each District (data in thousand of pounds currency)
Source: NA, RG 19, E5 (a), Board of Claims

Midland, Johnston, Eastern) experienced fewer incidents of damage and suffered less in terms of monetary losses. Damage claims in the four western districts amounted to £342,405 or 89.5 per cent of the total estimated losses for the whole province. Clearly, the eastern region of the colony experienced very slight damages and the claimants from that area estimated their losses at only £40,022. That figure drops significantly, moreover, if one removes the sum claimed by residents of the centrally situated Home District and considers only the £370,051 claimed by inhabitants of the eight remaining districts. The estimated losses in the four most westerly districts amounts to 92.5 per cent of that total. The £27,643 claimed by colonists from the districts furthest to the east represents about 7 per cent of the total estimated losses. Figure 2 offers a vivid image of how different the levels of losses really were.[103]

The varying levels of damage reported by inhabitants of the nine provincial districts can be related to the differing intensity of wartime activities experienced by each area. The fortunes of war dictated that the Niagara region was the scene of almost continuous action and its residents were subjected to a seemingly endless succession of invasions, raids, and counter-attacks. One day a farmer might find British troops tearing down bridges or destroying his buildings to prevent their use by enemy forces, and the next he might find himself at the mercy of one of Colonel Stone's foraging parties. In contrast, Newcastle residents lived through the war years undisturbed by enemy attacks. As a result, colonists from this district submitted fewer than

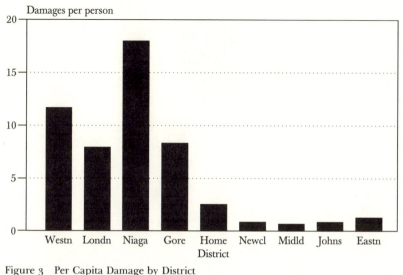

Figure 3   Per Capita Damage by District
Source: NA, RG 19, E5 (a), Board of Claims; NA, RG 5, 1814 Militia Muster

1 per cent of the claims received by the fourth and final commission between 1823 and 1826, and they amounted to less than 1 per cent of the estimated losses for the whole province. Their counterparts in Niagara, meanwhile, submitted one-third of all the claims entertained by the final commission, and these cases amounted, in value, to more than 47 per cent of the losses in the colony.[104]

Figure 3 compares per capita damages by district. A militia muster in March 1814 brought forth 11,045 men between the ages of sixteen and sixty in the colony, and the total population was likely near 63,000 at that point. The reported damages for each district can be divided by the estimated population totals for that area. While the population figures are only estimates, the results provide some insight into the differing levels of losses. The Midland District, with its large population (11,149) and low level of damages (£6938), was the least affected since the average loss amounted to just over one-half pound per person. At the opposite end of the spectrum stood the Niagara District, which endured a per capita loss of more than £18.[105]

Apparently, levels of losses also differed depending on who was inflicting the damage. The 1815–16 commission on losses reported that British forces were responsible for just over £140,000 of losses. The Americans, in contrast, had caused more than £248,000 worth of damages.[106] This difference was the result of the American fire-

Table 5
Attributed Losses

Perpetrator	Incidents	Per Cent
British Indians and others	498	33.78
British troops and others	429	29.10
Owed by His Majesty and damage	304	20.62
Upper Canadians and others	12	0.81
Enemy and others	787	54.38
American Indians and others	13	0.88

Source: NA, RG 19, E5 (a), Board of Claims

Table 6
Single-Perpetrator War Claims

Perpetrator	Incidents	Per Cent	
British Indians	226	24.5	British
British troops	117	12.7	forces
Owed by British	112	12.1	= 49.6 per cent
Upper Canadians	3	0.3	
Enemy	458	49.6	American
American Indians	7	0.8	forces = 50.4 per cent
Total	923	100	

Source: NA, RG 19, E5 (a), Board of Claims

raids that saw whole towns and villages destroyed. While the British forces may have done less damage overall, an examination of claims submitted to the 1823–26 commission suggests they were involved in almost as many incidents. By excluding the 581 cases where blame was not attached to any party, one is left with 1474 claims submitted to the 1823–26 commission that identified the individual or group responsible for the damage. Enemy forces were involved in just over one-half the total number of cases, while British Indians were involved in more than one-third. British troops were cited as having been the cause of losses in 429 cases, or over 29 per cent of all submissions. The final column of table 5 displays the number of times perpetrators were named as a percentage of 1474.

For the sake of simplicity, we can examine only those submissions where one party was at fault. An examination of these remaining 923 "single-perpetrator" claims reveals a fairly even split between British and American forces (see table 6). Although enemy forces were responsible for just over half of these single-perpetrator claims, almost one-quarter of the submissions (24.5 per cent) named friendly

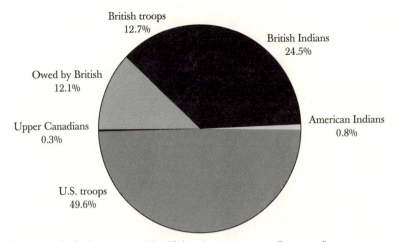

British troops
12.7%

British Indians
24.5%

Owed by British
12.1%

American Indians
0.8%

Upper Canadians
0.3%

U.S. troops
49.6%

Figure 4   Single-Perpetrator War Claims (as percentage of 923 total)
Source: NA, RG 19, E5 (a), Board of Claims

Indians as the agents responsible for the loss. An equal number
blamed British troops, either for losses from looting (12.7 per cent)
or for having lawfully requisitioned items but never followed through
with payment (12.1 per cent). Inhabitants who said they were still
owed by the British forces for oxen, horses, or other items that were
borrowed but never returned were also included in that category.
Upper Canadians, whether acting in militia units or not, were only
named as being responsible in three of these single-perpetrator
claims. Likewise, the limited role of Indians associated with American
forces during the war is reflected in their being accused of just seven
incidents of plundering. Figure 4 offers another view of the data.

The data provide support for the many eyewitness accounts of
British looting. For example, Colonel James Fitzgibbon of the 49th
Regiment, who is lauded now for having captured an American force
with the help of Laura Secord in June 1813, felt that his real notoriety
arose from other actions. Once, while making a claim for a medal
from the province, Fitzgibbon failed even to mention the Battle of
Beaver Dams. Instead, he prefaced his appeal by stating that he had
made great efforts "to protect the property of the inhabitants, as well
from the Enemy as from my own men." He said that none of the
men under his command "took even an apple" without the owner's
permission. "This was well known and was a matter of great pride
to me," the hero of Beaver Dams explained, "for I am sorry to say
that not another corps of any description was equally restrained."[107]
In light of this admission, it is easy to understand why many Upper

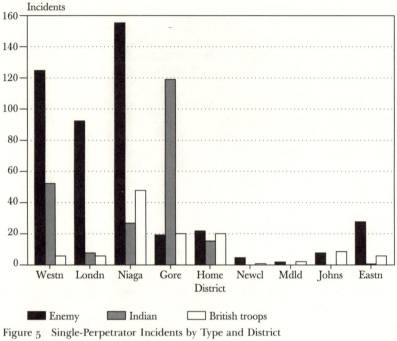

Figure 5   Single-Perpetrator Incidents by Type and District
Source: NA, RG 19, E5 (a), Board of Claims

Canadians considered the British soldier and his Indian ally to be the real menace of this war. On 5 December 1813, for example, Isaac Wilson told his brother that those residents unlucky enough to live near troop encampments suffered "very much in their property." Wilson said that foot soldiers would steal "provisions, money, and wearing apparel" while cavalrymen would "put their horses into barns and let them destroy everything they contain." Indian depredations, according to Wilson, were often of a less serious nature since they generally restricted their activities to "helping themselves to a few provisions now and then."[108]

Yet we also know that not all Upper Canadians shared Wilson's temperate opinion of Indian looting, and at least four warriors were killed as a result. Murder was resorted to, not only because many inhabitants had an irrational fear and hatred of Indians, but also because of the intensity of Amerindian looting in a few areas. Repeated incidents of plundering no doubt completely exasperated the local farmers. When one correlates single-perpetrator claims attributed to British troops, their Indian allies, and American forces with the districts in which the losses occurred, clear patterns emerge.

A quick glance at Figure 5 reveals that virtually no losses caused by British Indians, or by any other force for that matter, occurred in the four most easterly districts. In fact, only one single-perpetrator claim relating to plundering by British Indians east of the Home District was ever submitted. Residents in the Newcastle, Midland, Johnstown, or Eastern districts were, in general, far removed from hostilities and would rarely have seen native warriors. The Home District also reported relatively few incidents of plundering by friendly Indians, accounting for only fifteen cases. Residents of the Western District, where large Indian forces were stationed until Procter's retreat in the fall of 1813, were far more familiar with damages inflicted by warriors, since fifty-two claims were submitted from that area. A rapid withdrawal through the London District produced only eleven incidents of plundering in that region. The warriors reassembled in the Gore District around Burlington Heights, and this area was the scene of 118 incidents or 52.2 per cent of all single-perpetrator claims relating to British Indians. Exasperated at being the prime target for the majority of plundering done by native allies, some Gore residents fled the area, but others were driven to murder in defence of their property.[109]

The single-perpetrator claims relating to damage done by enemy forces also reflect a clear east-west split. The four most easterly districts submitted only forty-three claims relating to plundering by Americans, and most of those were either the result of two minor raids carried out on Brockville and Gananoque or were related to a single battle at Crysler's Farm in the Eastern District on 11 November 1813. Damages by Americans in the Home and Gore districts were also quite limited, totalling only forty claims. The Niagara, London, and Western districts, however, accounted for 372 submissions relating to losses by enemy forces or over 80 per cent of all such claims. Residents of the Western and London districts, the scene of predatory raids and McArthur's march, submitted 216 single-perpetrator claims relating to damages caused by Americans. The Niagara District, where armies operated throughout the conflict, accounted for just over one-third of all single-perpetrator claims submitted for losses attributed to enemy forces. The region was also hard hit by other groups, and twenty-seven similar submissions were made regarding damages done by friendly Indians and another fifty of them related to losses by His Majesty's troops. One can easily understand why Drummond was enraged by the activities of Macewen's men, whose behaviour he thought resembled "more of a plundering banditti than of British soldiers employed for the protection of the country and inhabitants."[110]

One researcher who has examined the conduct of soldiers in Wellington's army believes that theft and deliberate destruction of property were relatively rare occurrences. Anthony Brett-James noted that British troops stationed in Portugal and Spain would "sometimes burn a house for firewood or steal what few belongings the French Army had left to the inhabitants," but he suggested that these events were infrequent.[111] Theft and property destruction in Upper Canada, of course, were far from rare and the more gentlemanly conduct of soldiers in Europe might reflect the differing demands of the two campaigns. The British army in Upper Canada was forced to operate in a restricted area for more than three years. During that time, commissariat officials witnessed a steady decline in available resources and, by 1814, the supply situation reached a critical point. Soldiers who fought in Spain and Portugal, however, were often on the move, and their commissariat departments would have had access to a greater range of resources. Yet when provisions fell short, Wellington's troops acted in the same way as Upper Canadian soldiers. For example, John Harris, a private in the 95th Rifles, remembered a "dreadful march" to the Spanish coast during which commissariat wagons were left behind. As the retreat continued, the British troops finished their own supplies and then devoured "anything we could snatch from hut or cottage on our route."[112] For unlucky property owners, whether Spanish or Upper Canadian, the arrival of a famished force of battle-hardened regulars was cause for alarm.

During the War of 1812 the residents of western Upper Canada and the Niagara District were given almost nothing to replace what they had lost. The Loyal and Patriotic Society, which had been founded "in consequence of a hint in the letters of Mr. G. Ridout" to his father, failed to dispense most of the money it had collected until after the war.[113] Founded on 22 November 1812, the association spent no money during the first month of operation. In 1813 treasurer John Strachan reported that the society spent just over £275 on twenty-three individuals who received an average payment of less than £12. Of the total amount expended in 1813, fully 70 per cent was given to residents of the Home District, one of the areas that suffered the least from wartime damages. In 1814 the society dispensed another £432 15s 4d to eighteen recipients and, by the time news of the peace treaty reached Upper Canada in March 1815, only forty-seven individuals had been assisted through a total wartime expenditure of £945 7s od. Of that amount, the Niagara District, where an estimated £182,169 worth of losses had been sustained, received just over £100, or less than 11 per cent of the society's bounty.[114]

The failure of the Loyal and Patriotic Society to provide money in a timely fashion to the areas that needed it most would become one of the grievances that western Upper Canadians would harbour towards their eastern neighbours after war's end. Resentment over the activities of the Loyal and Patriotic Society, however, was only one of the many causes of postwar discontent. Upper Canada had entered the conflict as a divided society, and the fighting prompted disunity over new issues and exacerbated old divisions. Members of the regular forces were annoyed that most Upper Canadians managed to avoid taking an active part in the struggle and, after peace was declared, the tensions between the two groups sometimes led to violence. In the Amherstburg region, for example, the victorious British troops acted more like an invading force. Thomas Verchères said the soldiers treated the local merchants and ordinary inhabitants as if they had been "lazy and distrustful subjects" during the war. Eventually the attitudes of the regulars led to the beating of at least one soldier and to the shooting of another in a duel.[115] The opinions expressed by the troops at Amherstburg were similar to those held by settlers in other regions who had fought almost continually in flank companies or in the Incorporated Militia. Meanwhile, a number of colonists derided the military abilities of the British forces and many condemned the troops for their flagrant disregard of property rights.[116] One colonist later claimed in the St David's Spectator that under martial law, "shameful outrages were committed," and he attributed this to "the imbecillity of the Governor in chief, and the Generals commanding in Upper Canada."[117] The western warriors who fought during the conflict felt betrayed by the peace treaty which made no mention of their concerns and left their future unsettled. Residents of Niagara and western Upper Canada felt nothing but contempt for these "plundering" allies, and anti-native sentiment was prevalent during this period. Thus the assertion sometimes made by historians that the inhabitants of the province were "knit together" by this conflict seems more a product of wishful thinking than of a reasoned appraisal of wartime events.[118]

During the War of 1812 it was the western regions of the province that suffered the most in terms of losses and damages by both enemy and friendly forces. This area was the scene of continual campaigning, and it was also home to large garrisons of undisciplined troops and to hundreds of native warriors and their dependents. A "grand attack" on its resources by locust-like armies left many of the inhabitants of that region penniless, homeless, and without the means to start anew once peace was finally declared. From York eastward, however, the inhabitants sustained few losses, and for many of them the war represented only an opportunity to make a profit from military expenditure. American armies failed to gain a foothold in eastern Upper Canada, and there were few native warriors stationed there. As one researcher has noted, the region was "spared too close a contact with the realities of war."[119] Residents of areas east of York may have occasionally been bothered by British troops but, because little fighting took place there, the major concerns were militia service and the impressment of privately owned resources. The experiences of settlers in Augusta Township, Grenville County, may have been typical. A recent study of that region has revealed that, at least initially, a number of inhabitants reacted with some enthusiasm when war was first declared. The militia immediately set to work building fortifications even before any regulars had arrived, and some local youths apparently embarked on privateering adventures on Lake Ontario. Within a few months, however, attendence at musters began to decline and the "bucaneering enthusiasms" of 1812 gradually turned into disillusionment as the war dragged on. Over time, the settlers became increasingly frustrated as militia duties and martial law impinged on their private affairs. According to Shirley Campbell Spragge, the disillusionment among Augusta residents in 1813 turned "finally to resentment at the presence of British troops and the resulting interference in their lives."[120] Clearly, some eastern Upper Canadians faced disruptions and discomfort because of the war, but very few lives were lost and relatively little property was destroyed or impressed. For most residents of that area, the conflict proved to be an annoyance, not a disaster.

Events in Kingston, the commercial and military heart of eastern Upper Canada, resembled those in Augusta. The town was spared an enemy invasion, but Kingston did experience an influx of more than 5000 British soldiers, sailors, and labourers. For some merchants, that dramatic increase in population meant their wares were assured of a ready market. For other civilians, of course, the war years proved difficult because of high prices and chronic food shortages. On at least two occasions, in March and September 1813, there were mutinies at the dockyards, with artificers demanding better working conditions and backpay.[121] Yet, when compared with the privations and losses suffered by their neighbours to the west, those hardships amounted to mere inconveniences. One resident of Kingston believed that the most damaging effect of the conflict would be a legacy of foul-mouthed youngsters. He noted that children in the village who attended the school near the barracks had "their chaste ears every day insulted by the coarsest language."[122] In a letter dated 5 December 1813, Isaac Wilson described the wartime experiences of the majority of easterners when he wrote: "We live very quietly in this part of the country and are out of the way of the armies."[123]

6 "Enemies at Home": Treacherous Thieves

On Friday, 3 June 1814, one month before the Americans launched their final destructive invasion across the Niagara River, the residents of York gathered in their Sunday best to hear an extraordinary sermon by John Strachan. Recent "Glorious Victories" by British forces in Europe had led to the declaration of a general thanksgiving, and the inhabitants of the provincial capital took time out from their busy schedules to share in the celebrations. Although parts of the province were still under attack by enemy forces, many of the citizens of York had much to be thankful for since most of them had been paroled for over a year. During that time the capital had also been spared the worst excesses of the American burning system. Some of the inhabitants would undoubtedly have agreed with Strachan's appraisal of the war as a "most agreeable event."

Strachan, who was rumoured to be a candidate for a position on the Executive Council, said the war was the source of "many causes of joy." In a barely veiled reference to his own ostentatious tirade against American looting the year before, Strachan said that through the universal defence of the province, "we have gained a name among our fellow subjects which will be forever precious." In addition to that well-deserved notoriety, Strachan also pointed to the economic benefits of the war. He rejoiced to see "neighbours flourishing," and even believed that the raids and burnings endured by residents in western Upper Canada and in the Niagara region were blessings in disguise. After all, he noted, these events offered an opportunity for more fortunate inhabitants to assist those who were suffering.

The Loyal and Patriotic Society had already been "the dispenser of comfort and joy to so many" that its works "ought never to be forgotten."[1]

That unusual appraisal of a conflict which was responsible for the premature deaths of hundreds of colonists and which had left thousands more in distress requires an explanation. For the residents of York and the areas to the east, the war was often considered a godsend. Vast increases in military spending offered many colonists a once-in-a-lifetime opportunity to acquire huge sums of money. Isaac Wilson, for instance, informed his brother that York merchants were making "great profits" on goods brought in from Montreal. One individual he knew had purchased a shipment of merchandise for $1500 and had managed to resell within three months for $5000. Wilson himself had profited much by the war and he had recently lent money at a rate of 10 per cent for twenty days – an amount equal to 180 per cent a year. The opportunities for usury and profiteering led Wilson to conclude: "I do not think there ever was a place equal to this for making money if a person be in any kind of business or trade."[2]

Providing that residents kept out of the way of opposing armies and had needed skills or capital to invest, the war could bring benefits. William Sherman, for example, a blacksmith from Barton Township near the head of Lake Ontario, found the war years to be both enjoyable and profitable. Having lost his right eye in an accident many years before, Sherman was excused from all militia duty. Yet, since he was near the large British encampment at Burlington Heights, he was constantly employed on government works. One contract instructed Sherman to make axes for the military, and he later recalled earning a net profit of six to eight dollars a day. After the war, workingmen receiving room and board would have had to work one month to earn that amount of money. Although Sherman had been the victim of an Indian raiding party and had lost some potatoes and two large hogs as a result, he believed his losses were insignificant, especially when compared with the damages sustained by other inhabitants of his district. He explained that, as a trained blacksmith, "he was much employed during the war and might upon the whole have been a gainer than a loser by it." Sherman was one of the more fortunate residents of the region because the Americans never controlled Barton Township. In total, the blacksmith estimated that his losses during the conflict amounted to just over £43, or $172. At his average rate of net profit, therefore, in less than one month Sherman would have earned enough money to pay for all the damages he sustained during the war.[3]

Other Upper Canadians abandoned their customary trades or embarked on risky ventures to make even greater profits. John Farmer, a neighbour of Sherman's from the head of the lake, spent the early part of the war driving cattle from Niagara to Kingston. The profits made from that first leg of the trip were usually invested in groceries that he resold at Fort George on his return. Farmer would later say that he only carried on this "trade during & in consequence of the War and that he is a Taylor by trade." Similarly, the goods that were seized from Richard Beasley by the American navy were not intended for his personal use. Beasley admitted he had invested over £596 in bringing goods from Kingston to Fort George as "a merchantile speculation owing to the war."[4]

The chance to acquire previously unheard of rates of return was an opportunity few colonists could pass up, and profiteering during the conflict eventually reached enormous proportions. There was never a shortage of individuals who were willing to overcharge military purchasers or fleece civilian customers, but profiteering should not be confused with general economic well-being. Many ordinary citizens saw little real benefit from increased military spending. Farmers who received higher returns on their produce, for instance, would have found those greater profits did not compensate for the inflated prices of other goods. The item sold most often to the commissariat, a barrel of flour, more than doubled in value during the war. Between 1812 and 1815 prices for flour rose from $6 to $12 and even reached $14 a barrel in some areas. For farmers, these prices represented increases of 100 to 133 per cent, and some farm incomes were substantially augumented because of wartime demand.[5] During the conflict, according to two contemporary accounts, prices at York for mercantile goods rose by at least 300 per cent.[6] Thus, although farmers may have received record returns during the fighting, a rampant rate of inflation probably negated any increases for most Upper Canadians. Only a few dozen leading merchants in the larger villages seem to have been consistently able to acquire sufficient sums of money to offset the effects of wartime inflation.

Profiteers began their work early, even before hostilities commenced. Under General Brock the army started stockpiling flour in the spring of 1812. In April, for example, the prominent western merchant John Askin was buying as much of this item as he could from his neighbours. He paid only six dollars for each barrel since the inhabitants did not know the "secret" that "the merchants get seven & a half dollars for each barrel from Government." The use of inside knowledge and close contacts with other government suppliers placed Askin in a perfect position to profit from increased

British expenditures. He continued to hold this advantage even after the Americans invaded the Western District. Askin had resigned his militia commission in 1809 and thus Hull's invasion offered "no cause of Uneasiness" for him. That was especially true since he was a good friend of Elijah Brush, an American official at Detroit. While the mustering of the local militia had left others with no means of gathering their crops, Askin was pleased to announce that "Mr. Brush says he will send men to cut down my harvest."[7]

It must be stressed that Askin's ability to adapt quickly to the economic possibilities offered by the war was not an attribute shared by all other colonial merchants. At first, news of the outbreak of hostilities brought business to a standstill, and individuals with ready cash resorted to hoarding. In August 1812 the York merchant Alexander Wood informed a colleague that "the unsettled state of the times" had led to a shortage of money which, he said, "really seems to have forsaken this part of the country."[8] Michael Smith observed in 1812 that "no business is carried on by any person, except what is absolutely necessary." Many of the merchants on both sides of the border found that situation to be intolerable and in Buffalo an organization was started to deal with the concerns of the mercantile community. On 15 October 1812 the Friends of Liberty, Peace, and Commerce met at Buffalo for the quixotic purpose of terminating the war and returning to the friendly intercourse of the past.[9]

Some of their counterparts on the western side of the Niagara River, however, had already discovered that business could still be carried on in wartime. As early as April, Brock was faced with a shortage of specie, which was needed to buy supplies for the military. At that time he approached the leading shopkeepers of the Niagara region for help. Merchants from this district, such as Askin's cousins, the Hamilton brothers, were among the most influential and well-heeled of the province's mercantile elite. They quickly formed themselves into an alliance, the Niagara and Queenston Association, and issued several thousand pounds worth of notes guaranteed by themselves and by the government.[10] Like the provincial banks of the future, the Niagara and Queenston Association depended on the pooled financial resources of various mercantile firms for its existence. With this paper currency in his pocket, Brock was able to raise and outfit the flank companies in the Niagara and Home districts.

Upper Canadians were not, as has often been supposed, uniformly opposed to the concept of paper money. There were individuals who were adamantly against the innovation, but most colonists were simply leery of the potential for abuse. American bank notes had circulated in the province during the early part of the century but,

Army bill worth $25 issued in 1813.
Stevenson, "The Circulation of Army Bills"

because it was not illegal to issue counterfeits, the notes acquired a reputation for unworthiness.[11] Had the paper proven to be sound, it would have met with a welcome reception from many colonists. That at least was Brock's appraisal of the situation. In April 1812 he told Noah Freer of his plans to introduce a paper currency with the assistance of leading merchants. Brock believed that the issue would meet with success, especially as the colonists already had some experience with "merchant money" and American bank notes. Since they had previously been in the habit of receiving this currency, Brock thought the inhabitants "would not hesitate taking the more certain security of Government."[12]

Initially, however, the Niagara and Queenston Association notes actually exacerbated the money problems in the province. Some merchants at York and Kingston viewed the paper currency with distrust and refused to take the bills. By accepting the notes, the merchants would have had to make change in coins, and many simply refused to part with highly prized hard currency.[13] With the declaration of war came increased hoarding, and Brock felt drastic measures were needed if he was to finance a war effort. He approached the Assembly that summer and asked it to authorize the creation of a provincial paper currency.[14] Its refusal to follow through had more to do with the machinations of Willcocks and his associates than with any psychological aversion to paper money. As with Brock's requests relating to the suspension of Habeas Corpus and the imposition of martial law, his suggestion about creating a colonial currency was ignored by members fearful of "incurring the indignation of the enemy."[15]

While Brock failed in his attempt to create a provincial currency, his counterpart in Lower Canada did not. George Prevost aproached the Lower Canadian Assembly in July 1812 with a plan for the creation of £250,000 in "army bills" to compensate for the deficiency in hard currency.[16] The members agreed to the measure and the legislature granted £15,000 to pay the interest that would come due on larger notes which bore interest at the rate of four pence a day for every one hundred pounds. Army bills in denominations under twenty-five dollars were to be paid in cash or on demand.[17] These bills offered the military a means of buying produce and supplies with paper that was backed by the British government. By the time news of the Treaty of Ghent reached Upper Canada, over £1,249,000 of army bills were in circulation in the two provinces.[18]

The creation of this new currency eventually led to a resumption of business in Upper Canada. As late as October 1812 merchants in Kingston were still offering to accept payment in the form of "either cash or any kind of produce." By the next month, however, shopkeepers had dispensed with bartering and they now accepted only "Cash, Government, or Niagara Association Bills."[19] The continued existence of the Niagara Association notes was probably prompted by problems relating to the type of army bills that first reached the upper province. Too many large army bills worth $25 or more were in circulation and shopkeepers were left with no choice but to rely on these Niagara Association bills to make change. Without them a settler who had sold flour to the commissariat in return for a $25 army bill would have found the note nearly useless unless he was willing to purchase exactly $25 worth of goods from one merchant.[20]

A desire to ease this shortage of small change soon led retailers in other centres to begin endorsing their own notes. Ultimately, almost all persons doing business in the towns and villages of the province were producing paper money of their own. This practice brought problems, of course, since some individuals refused the bills of other merchants; soldiers who were given two hours' notice of a troop withdrawal found they possessed paper of no value in another part of the country. The avalanche of paper money eventually led to calls for government regulation of some sort. "When bakers, grog-shopmen, washerwomen, etc. etc., begin to issue their own trash," one critic observed, "I think it is high time for some of the higher civil authorities to interpose, and prevent an unsuspicious public from being imposed upon."[21]

Other criticisms were levelled at merchants who appeared to be taking advantage of the scarcity of small change to reap small fortunes. Jealousy arose among shopkeepers who suspected the motives of other merchants and one critic, who wrote under the name "Hawkins," questioned the value of these notes. His attack also raised anew the debate over the trustworthiness of recent American arrivals in the colony. In a letter published on 31 August 1813 in the *Kingston Gazette*, Hawkins noted that two shopkeepers in that town had each printed several thousand pounds worth of notes. While he was sure one of these men, Thomas Markland, was of "undoubted responsiblity," he was not so sure about the other, an American immigrant named Benjamin Whitney. While Markland owned large tracts of land that offered security for his notes, Whitney owned none and many considered him "almost a stranger." Hawkins suggested that Whitney's business "might in a moment be reduced to a state of insolvency" by the destruction or capture of one large shipment of goods. Of even greater concern to Hawkins was the whole concept of private money. He noted that one English statute, 15 George 3rd, chapter 17, made the issuance of personal bills worth less than twenty shillings illegal. Hawkins was joined in this attack two weeks later by "Rusticus," who argued that the laws of England relating to property and civil rights extended also to Upper Canada; the merchants, therefore, were contravening several statutes.[22]

Fearing that such attacks might lead to government intervention, the major merchants of York and Kingston decided to rid the system of its worst abuses. At a meeting held at Walker's Hotel on 28 August 1813, fourteen of Kingston's leading merchants and retailers formed themselves into an alliance known as the Kingston Association. The members agreed to deposit a sufficient amount of either specie or army bills with a treasurer to cover all the notes issued in the name of the association. They also agreed not to accept notes worth more than fifty cents from any individual outside the alliance and they immediately sanctioned the printing of one thousand pounds in dollar bills. To forestall criticism that the endeavour was motivated completely by greed, the merchants directed that the profits arising from deposits were to be sent to the treasurer of the Patriotic Society.[23] One month later, one dozen of the leading shopkeepers in the provincial capital followed suit with the creation of the York Association, which immediatedly issued three hundred pounds in one-dollar notes. The terms of incorporation were similar to those of the Kingston alliance except that the York men had directed that profits from deposits were to go to John Strachan for the "poor of the parish."[24] By the end of September 1813, therefore, at least two organizations in the province were acting as unchartered banks since they were printing notes backed by cash reserves.

The refusal of these associations to accept most of the notes of non-members meant that the paper money created by outsiders was now in jeopardy. Naturally this move to restrict the issuance of other notes angered non-members, particularly Whitney and Markland, who had thousands of pounds worth of bills outstanding. A visitor to Kingston, Abraham Lovegood, remarked that he had never seen "so much envy, malice, and revenge depicted in men's countenances" until he stumbled across a meeting of the association at Walker's Hotel on 5 September 1813. Since it was a Sunday, Lovegood at first assumed that only news of an imminent American attack could have prompted the leading figures of the village to disturb the tranquility of Kingston's sabbath. Instead he was shocked to discover that the meeting "was for the purpose of having a new bank." Apparently a vicious dispute had erupted, with Whitney and Markland on one side and the founding members of the Kingston Association on the other. The two merchants wished to join the alliance, but the other members insisted that Markland and Whitney first redeem their individual note issues. The two leading merchants objected to that requirement, fearing they would not be able to meet the demand if all their outstanding notes were returned to them at one time. The meeting adjourned without reaching a compromise and both sides resorted to the pages of the *Kingston Gazette* to air their dispute.[25]

Thomas Markland had fired the first salvo in this mercantile war by sending a letter to the local newspaper on the very day the bank was formed. Markland said that the decision to refuse most non-member notes was an "ungenerous and unwarrantable action" on the part of the Kingston Association and he believed it was intended solely to injure his credit. He went on to announce that he was prepared to redeem all his personal notes in army bills "at all times." For their part, the members of the association denounced their opponents as "selfish"; they suggested that the alliance was created simply for the benefit of the public. The town now enjoyed a more secure circulating medium and any interest earned by the Kingston Association on its reserves was to be sent to the Loyal and Patriotic Society. According to its defenders, this last measure was proof positive that the motives of the members were "of the most disinterested and public spirited [in] nature."[26]

Of course, despite assertions to the contrary, all sides in this dispute were motivated principally by self-interest. Markland and Whitney, for instance, would have joined the other merchants if their personal financial situations had permitted the move. By banding together to monopolize the traffic in small change, the majority of Kingston's merchants managed simultaneously to silence most critics and to keep money flowing into their businesses. The decision to donate profits from money lying idle in the hands of a cashier was prompted more by a desire to continue an illegal system of note-printing than by any real concern for the welfare of the poor. Sending interest payments to the Loyal and Patriotic Society allowed the members to portray themselves as loyal citizens contributing to the provincial war effort. At the same time, however, the merchants never had to leave the comfort of their homes and shops.

The notes issued by the Kingston Association gained rapid acceptance and the society soon authorized the issuance of an additional one thousand pounds in three, two, one, and half-dollar denominations. Whitney was the first casualty of the merchant war and, by November 1813, he had been forced to stop extending credit and to ask that all unsettled accounts be closed immediately. Two months later the association announced that it would no longer accept private notes worth less than half a dollar. Until the next summer, Kingston Association bills enjoyed an unrivalled position as the paper money used by most area merchants. Finally, by July 1814, the supply of army bills of all denominations had increased to such a degree that the alliance began calling in its notes.[27]

Personal disputes revolving around paper money also divided the tiny community at York early in the war. Quetton St George, the richest merchant in the capital, at first offered discounts to those individuals who paid in specie. This discounting made army bills less attractive and St George was blamed for the high rate of inflation that put many essential goods out of the reach of "the great majority of the Population and army at and near York who could not command specie." After having nearly ruined the reputation of army bills, St George then proceeded to issue notes of his own "whereby he accumulated a large sum of money." In amassing this "handsome fortune," he may not have been operating solely out of a concern for money.[28] In addition to greed, the French immigrant may have wanted to repay York society for having previously snubbed him. St George conceded that his imperfect English may have marked him as an outsider, but he never forgave the outright rejection of his "presumptuous" marriage proposal to Anne Powell, daughter of Judge William Drummer Powell. If revenge for this slight was indeed his motivation, St George must have been pleased with his own success. At one point Powell remarked that his principal distress during the war years "arose from the incredible Expense of living."[29]

Wartime inflation brought rapid increases in the price of staple foods and these higher costs were a reflection of both shortages and increased profit-taking by middlemen. John Askin paid only $6 for every barrel of flour he bought in April 1812, but he quickly resold the flour for $7.50.[30] By the time that same flour reached York it could be sold to the government for $8.50. In December 1813 the price of a barrel of flour had reached the $12 mark and, two months later, it was selling in the Kingston market for $14 a barrel.[31] Prices for other items also more than doubled during the conflict. Hay, for instance, usually sold for between $12 and $15 a ton before the war.[32] By November 1813 those lucky enough to find suppliers were paying at least $30 for the same amount. John Clark, who was stationed at Kingston at that time, informed William Hamilton Merritt that his "poor horse was starving from a scarcity of forage." Clark bemoaned the fact that he had little to do at the garrison yet he was forced to accept an "extravagant rate" of inflation. "What they brought me here for God only knows," he complained to Merritt, "unless to get rid of what little pay I have."[33]

Many other residents, especially those restricted to fixed low incomes, also felt the pinch of high prices. Minor government officials at York, for example, experienced economic hardship since prices rose at uncontrolled rates while their incomes actually dropped. While inflation ate away at their yearly salary, the clerks found that the fees they relied on to supplement their pay had nearly disappeared because of the lack of immigrants seeking land patents. Gordon Drummond was eventually driven to appeal for increased salaries for his clerks because he feared they would quit the service. At the beginning of 1814, for instance, second-level clerks were paid just over £112 a year, and with the reduction in the amount of fees collected they were actually earning less than common labourers. Drummond considered increases in the region of one-third of their total salaries to be so "absolutely necessary" that he instituted the changes, retroactive to 1 January 1814, even before he received permission from his superiors.[34]

For the less fortunate, of course, the war years were even more difficult. Unprecedented numbers of Upper Canadians were unable to work because of illness or injuries during the war. These people felt the bite of inflation more than other colonists because labourers and farmers who continued to work received higher returns between 1812 and 1815. It has been estimated that, in peacetime, paupers needed £18–£22 a year to survive in Upper Canada, but that subsistence level was likely nearer £80 during the war. Especially hard-hit were the families of disabled flank veterans, and the widows and orphans of militiamen killed on duty. Even in peacetime the disability benefits of £9, and widows' pensions of £5, would have supplied only a fraction of what a family needed for survival.[35] Profit-taking by retailers during the war, however, put prices for staples completely out of the reach of some poorer colonists. In 1814 an inhabitant of Kingston noted that bakers in that town paid $14 for every barrel of flour they purchased. Taking into consideration overhead costs, he estimated that they made a daily net profit of more than $35 on the bread they sold. Annual profits of more than $12,000, or over £3000, were said to be derived chiefly from "the hard earnings of the poor." Unlike merchants, whose high prices could be excused because of the dangers involved in shipping, food retailers ran few risks and none justified gouging the public. This resident went so far as to suggest that Upper Canadians who were concerned only with the movements and actions of their American foes might be overlooking "some of our greatest enemies at home."[36]

There is little doubt that the widespread inflation of the war years was prompted, in large measure, by colonial merchants and retailers charging as much as the traffic would bear. By making life miserable for many in the colony, these "enemies at home" also hurt the war effort. At one point, the Loyal and Patriotic Society spent just over £38 in an attempt to subsidize the price of bread for the poorer inhabitants of York, but after what John Strachan described as "much trouble, vexation, and expense" the society gave up the venture.[37] Leaving aside the question of whether less than one-half of 1 per cent of an organization's budget can be considered "much expense," it is clear that the situation for the poorer inhabitants must have been desperate indeed if Strachan and his friends were willing to try to subsidize the price of their bread.[38] By the end of the war Strachan estimated that items were "four times their usual price" at York.[39]

For his part, Strachan did not feel the sting of high food prices as much as some of his poor parishioners did. Although he was prone to complain about his income, Strachan's annual salary amounted to at least £560.[40] Despite the hyper-inflation of the war years, £560 was still a significant amount of money. An ordinary private in the militia, for example, earned only six pence a day or, at best, just over £9 a year. At that rate, Upper Canadian militiamen would have had to fight well beyond the American Civil War of the 1860s if they intended to amass as much money as Strachan made in 365 days.[41] The chaplain's complaints seem even more absurd if we consider his family's total income. With Ann's pension included, the Strachan clan received at least £860 a year. In peacetime, an income of £150 to £200, along with the employment of a servant, conferred

Table 7
Merchant Sales to Garrison

Period	St George	Allan	Wood
1812–13	10.932	4,004	427
1814–15	15,799	9,000	5,528
Total £	26,731	13,004	5,955

Source: Fort York, Garrison Book Commissary Accounts

respectability on Upper Canadian families. Despite wartime inflation, therefore, Strachan never slipped below the requirements of his social position, and his means were more than adequate. Twenty years earlier, the whole civil administration of Upper Canada had operated on a budget of only £6700. Strachan's household income amounted to over one-eighth that amount.[42] Furthermore, as army chaplain at York, Strachan and his servant enjoyed the privilege of receiving garrison rations throughout the war. As noted previously, these meals bore little resemblance to their poor cousins in the field. Isaac Wilson found York garrison fare so filling that he later had to let out the seams on his civilian clothes.[43]

Wilson and Strachan were not the only York residents who lived well at the expense of the military. Three of the top merchants in the capital made good profits selling supplies to the garrison. Quetton St George, William Allan, and Alexander Wood sold at least £45,690 worth of merchandise to the military between December 1812 and January 1815.[44] Table 7 presents their sales, rounded to the nearest pound, during two twelve-month periods. These figures reveal that St George sold supplies worth more than both his nearest competitors combined. That information may help explain why he was disliked so much by other members of the York establishment. It also reveals why, after the war, St George was able to return to his homeland and purchase an estate near Montpellier where he spent the rest of his days as a "landed French gentleman."[45]

The figures produced in table 7, while impressive, do not tell us what the level of profit was. Wilson spoke of one merchant achieving a rate of return equal to more than 200 per cent, but that was probably unusual. A key to the riddle of how much the mercantile community expected the military to pay may be contained in the papers of Alexander Wood. In August 1813 he approached a friend, George Stuart, about the possibility of some British officers renting space in a storehouse. Stuart agreed, but he demanded a rent of £200 a year; he also remarked that he would settle for half that amount were the "occupants of a different description."[46] This

QUETTON ST. GEORGE AND CO.

Mr. St. GEORGE begs leave to return his thanks to his Friends and the Public for their very liberal fupport to him fince his firft eftablifh-ment in Bufinefs at this place ; and alfo to inform them that he has now taken Meffrs. JULIUS QUESNEL and JOHN S. BALDWIN into Copartnerfhip, and that the bufi-nefs of the Concern will in future be carried on under the name of *Quetton St. George & Co.*

The new Firm takes this opportunity of expreffing their hope that Mr. St. George's old Cuftomers will continue their favors towards them, and of affuring them that every attention fhall be paid to their wifhes and commands ; and alfo at the fame time to in-form them and the Public at large, that they have now an extenfive affortment of Goods of the firft quality immediately imported from England, from whence they will continue to import a conftant fupply—they flatter themfelves that their prices will not be higher than thofe of other Merchants.

York, December 10, 1814.

N. B. Mr. St. George requefts thofe indebted to him to make their payments with-out delay—and that all thofe to whom he is indebted will prefent their Accounts to him immediately, or at fartheft before the firft day of May next, as he purpofes to make a voyage to Europe in the courfe of the next Summer.

He has for fale a Mare and Colt ; a double Harnefs, plated ; a Pleafure Sleigh with Robes, Cufhions, &c.

Quetton St George announces plans for the expansion of his enterprises and for a triumphant homecoming, 10 December 1814.
Metropolitan Toronto Reference Library, Baldwin Room

discrimination can probably be attributed to Stuart's fears about the future condition of his building, but it also intimates that residents knew that the military had the resources to pay double the usual price and would do so if necessary. A researcher who has studied William Allan's transactions during this period has determined that his usual markup on goods sold to the commissariat was in the neighbourhood of 100 per cent.[47] Whether Wood and St George acquired similar profits remains unknown, but one suspects they would not have settled for less than what their competitor received. If all made that rate of return, Wood pocketed nearly £3000, Allan almost £7000, and St George an incredible £13,000 profit from the military. Whatever the markup, and despite inflation, it would be safe to say that these men managed to amass "small fortunes" through transactions with the army.[48]

Other businessmen in the capital also benefited from the presence of the garrison. The director of the York Association, Stephen Jarvis, sold items to the military throughout the conflict and in this he was joined by fellow members Thomas Deary and D'Arcy Boulton, Jr. Altogether, the commissariat paid out at least £351,238 to York suppliers between December 1812 and January 1815, or about £175,000 a year.[49] It has been estimated that between 1795 and 1806 the British government spent an average of about £65,500 in the province each year. During the conflict, therefore, the York garrison alone was responsible for distributing at least five times that amount of money.[50] For Strachan's flourishing neighbours, military spending between 1812 and 1815 represented the most important of the "many causes of joy" brought by the war.

Table 7 also reveals that all three of York's richest merchants conducted business with the military throughout the war. Of course, these shopkeepers likely had much more time to devote to mercantile activities after they were paroled in April 1813. Jarvis, who certified all the paroles granted after the battle, soon accommodated himself to the sacking of the capital. He later remarked that the defeat meant he was finally "able to pay strict attention" to his business.[51] Other merchants, like Major William Allan, also played a large role in the unsuccessful defence of York that spring. Immediately after the battle Allan helped negotiate the terms of surrender, which stipulated that private property was to be respected. Later, he was arrested and held until the articles of capitulation were ratified. At that time Allan was paroled, but his duty to his country was not over yet. On Thursday, 29 April, the Americans demanded that the public money be turned over to them as provided for in the articles of capitulation. Faced with the prospect of having to provide the difference from their own pockets, Allan, Strachan, and other town notables held a quick conference and immediately handed over more than £2000 from the provincial coffers.[52] It is worth noting that the actions of these men in regard to private property could be quite different. A few days after Strachan turned over the public purse, for example, he placed himself between two Americans and "some plundered property of a friend." In the altercation that followed, "one aimed his musket at his breast" and was prepared to fire, when another soldier rescued Strachan and ordered "the surrender of the booty."[53]

St George and Wood were mentioned in an official dispatch as two of the prominent York men who "gallantly volunteered" their services to defend the capital during the April invasion.[54] Yet it seems that neither of them was actually engaged in combat. St George may have arrived late on the scene because he had earlier "gallantly volunteered" to assist in gathering wagons "for the flight of the ladies."[55] For his part, Wood rushed home as soon as the fighting had ceased and that evening he wrote a few lines to an associate which dealt with both the recent excitement and the more pressing concerns of his business. Wood attributed the defeat to the superiority of American numbers, but he also felt that "a want of Judgement, indecision and shameful neglect of our own" had played a part in the loss. For the rest of the war Wood found little time for anything other than business activities. He battled with suppliers, wrestled with accounts, and spent the remainder of his days "receiving goods and attending to the examination of them" even after "every other person had gone to bed."[56]

It seems certain that Allan's own "indecision and shameful neglect" of his militia forces on that day contributed to the defeat at York in April 1813. Along with Wood and St George, moreover, his habit of gouging the military made the job of defending the province more difficult for the men in charge of the colony. At the same time, it must be admitted that none of these merchants was deliberately assisting the Americans. The same could not be said for all other Upper Canadians, since the fighting often resulted in a disregard for established laws and rules of conduct. During the capture of York in April 1813, for instance, dozens of citizens assisted the Americans in carting away government stores; it seemed to some leading figures in the capital that York's "mixed doubtful Population" believed the invasion had brought law and order to an end. So many inhabitants offered assistance and advice to the invaders that the magistrates could not decide "if the loyal or disaffected be most numerous."[57] Yet these citizens assisted the enemy, not only because some were sympathetic to the American cause, but more importantly because the invaders made it worth their while. For example, John Lyons, a distiller from Vaughan Township, acquired an "ox cart, a pair of large wheels for a gun carriage, a pair of small truck wheels, about one hundred weight of Iron, a large bathing machine, and other articles." Lyons enjoyed the use of these items for only ten days, however, because William Allan and other magistrates repossessed all government property given away by the Americans as soon as the enemy fleet left. Less than three months later the Americans landed again and Lyons took the articles back from the magistrates; he warned the "damned villians" not to bother him again. He told a neighbour, Michael Dye, that he had "made a fine hawl" of government property, which he estimated to be worth one thousand dollars. Lyons was also sure these items were more than enough compensation for the work he had done transporting flour. Feeling confident about having acquired items through such a profitable transaction, Lyons supposedly challenged anyone to "take them from me."[58]

Lyons's example was followed by others. In August 1813 the town jailer reported that all his prisoners had been liberated by the Americans. Before leaving the jail the prisoners took "several Green Rugs ... a pair of dog Irons and other articles." The jailer noted that the men had been given the goods when the Americans first landed at York in April and they considered the items theirs to do with as they pleased.[59] One of the prisoners had previously been incarcerated for refusing to serve in the militia when his name was balloted. On being released in the autumn of 1812, Gideon Orton found himself again liable for duty because of a general call of the militia. So "he had hidden himself in the woods to avoid serving" and he did not reappear until the following spring when the Americans captured the capital. At that time Orton boasted he had been given enough public property "to pay him four dollars a day for the time he kept out of the way." As his neighbours knew only too well, that was forty times the daily salary of a militia private.[60]

Others also saw the Americans as a potential source of booty and they immediately set out to acquire their share of public property. William Huff testified that Calvin Wood had given the enemy information about where guns and other stores were hidden at York; in return, he said, Wood had received seven barrels of flour.[61] For similar services, James Stevens was given "three barrels of Flour, half a Barrel of Pork, and nine pair or upwards of green Trowsers belonging to the militia."[62] Some residents, such as Jacob Clark, were said to have sold provisions to the Americans because the enemy offered specie in return.[63] In every instance where citizens of York assisted the invaders, they received or demanded some form of compensation. Nathaniel Finch, for example, managed to avoid militia service in the same manner that Gideon Orton had, by running to the bush. His father told Henry Mullholand that Nathaniel had made the right decision. John Finch said that his son had already received "iron and plough shares from the Americans and would get more." He advised everyone "to turn to the Americans and they will give you something worth the while, you see what I got already, but if you continue to serve with the British you will get nothing."[64] Like William Allan and Quetton St George, it appears that some York residents would try to profit from the war by whatever means available.

Outbreaks of hooliganism and a general disrespect for constituted authority were witnessed each time the enemy fleet appeared. In addition to acquiring public stores, Calvin Wood and Moses Martin were also accused of bullying their neighbours. Samuel Hatt said they kept residents in his locality in a state of "continual fear and alarm by reason of their threats and depredations and that they go about constantly armed." At one point American soldiers were forced to intervene when another citizen acted in the same manner.[65] William Knot testifed that a neighbour of his, Mr Howard, had seized him by the collar and demanded his boots. Before Howard managed to get them, however, a party of enemy troops arrived and "drove him out." Elijah Bentley, a Baptist preacher who had been warned about his inflammatory sermons in the past, supposedly heralded the arrival of the Americans by announcing that he would now "say and think what he pleased." Bentley also said that "he had been for some time in dread of his neighbours but now he should see them paid for it."[66]

In a society whose lower orders were expected to be deferential, such sentiments and activities proved worrisome to the authorities. In early May, after the Americans had withdrawn most of their troops, the inhabitants continued to steal from one another and members of the York elite were finally forced to appeal to the enemy commander. In consequence, General Dearborn issued a military order reminding both American soldiers and York residents that the invasion did not affect the normal administration of the law. William Drummer Powell remarked that this order "produced a good effect on the turbulent minds of some wretches of our own population whose thirst for plunder was more alarming to the inhabitants than the presence of the Enemy."[67] Still, a number of residents continued to defy the authorities and they became even bolder when the Americans invaded the capital for the second time in July 1813. R.N. Lacky reported that John Lyons had warned the magistrates not to attempt to repossess his new implements or he "would apply to General Dearborn for their return." Stephen Whitney testified that William Allan was singled out for having caused "a great deal of disturbance" by taking back public property after the first invasion in April.[68] Within a few days the news of Allan's activities had crossed Lake Ontario, where it reached the ears of American soldiers at Fort George. At least ten complaints were lodged with enemy officers about Allan's actions and they threatened to give "Major Allan such a parole the first time they caught him that he should never require another." During the July invasion of the capital, $500 rewards were posted for information on the whereabouts of Alexander Wood, Quetton St George, and William Allan. All three men had fled the town at the first sight of the enemy fleet. John Chilsom of Etobicoke was one of several inhabitants who announced that "he for one would not be backward in taking" any rewards offered.[69] It seems that resentment against prominent profiteers who had made life difficult for York residents extended beyond the polite company of William Powell and his family.

The redistribution of wealth achieved by the Americans through their handouts of public property was viewed with favour even by some persons who did not share in the bonanza. Isaac Wilson, for example, informed his brother that the British government had sent a large quantity of farming utensils to the province but the "authorities would not allow these to be given out except to favourites." Since the enemy distributed the items very "generally to all settlers," Wilson concluded that the first invasion "was very useful in that respect."[70] Not accustomed to seeing favourites going unrewarded, and alarmed that prosperous neighbours now had prices on their heads, John Strachan and other members of the colonial elite began to demand an effective response to the public disorder. Strachan's prized former pupil, Attorney-General John Beverley Robinson, suggested in August 1813 that Francis de Rottenburg appoint boards made up of "unprejudiced persons" to collect evidence against anyone suspected of wrongdoing. For the York area board, Robinson forwarded the names of William Allan, John Strachan, Duncan Cameron, Thomas Ridout, Alexander Wood, and Peter Robinson as candidates who would not hestitate to investigate any "character they deem suspicious."[71]

Although hardly "unprejudiced," it does appear that these "respectable gentlemen" did a thorough job of examining witnesses. The committee would later report that of the affidavits gathered on suspects, "some are mixed with prejudice & some with malice, others are clear and pointed." Altogether, testimony was received on the activities of thirty-two Home District residents. Ten of the men were accused of taking public stores illegally and the rest were said to have used "highly seditious expressions." Much of the evidence related to tavern conversations where imprudent inhabitants had given vent to repressed feelings by "drinking success to the enemy fleet" or toasting "Madison's health."[72]

In their first report to Major-General de Rottenburg the members of the committee informed their commander that warrants had been issued for the most prominent offenders, but the appointees feared that arrests might prove impossible. The board felt that the Americans would surely free the prisoners if they invaded again and, if not, their friends might. Even if the men remained in jail, however, the committee believed that convictions were unlikely since most of the potential jurors were "involved in the same guilt." Because of these problems, the committee finally declared that it was "at a loss how to proceed" since "there is little prospect of any person being convicted at the present crisis by the common operation of the law."[73] The obvious solution was to acquire extraordinary powers, but that would need legislative approval and would have to wait until the next session of the Assembly in the spring of 1814.

Other areas of the province also reported numerous incidents of wrongdoing. Like the events at the capital, however, most acts seem to have been related to concerns over money and do not appear to have been motivated by traitorous intentions. For example, in the Western District in the summer of 1812, Ebeneezer Allan joined other Upper Canadians in forming a cavalry unit. But Allan, who "changed his allegiance as often as other men change their shirts," simply spread word of the American offer to protect private property and never fought beside the invaders. Of course, these western "malcontents" were not given much of an opportunity and, as Donald McLeod has noted, "in consequence of Gen. Hull's disgraceful surrender, they were doomed."[74]

In the nearby London and Niagara regions, the lack of constituted authority also encouraged some inhabitants to take advantage of others. James Fleming of Middlesex County, for instance, had early on revealed that his loyalties ran mostly to his own pocketbook. One neighbour testified that in 1812 Fleming had taken one of Hull's proclamations on a "Grand parade" and had spent his time telling people "how happy they would be" if they stayed home since "they would not lose an apple." After Brock's advance, however, George Ward reported that "all was mute" from Fleming's corner until Procter evacuated his troops, "then the lad had sway again." While camping on Fleming's land several months later, a group of Kent militiamen set fire to piles of brush they found there. Underneath, the militiamen were startled to find eighteen wagon irons and cannons that the Americans had given him. After the Kent men left, Fleming hired a group of locals to ferry the items down the river to American-controlled territory. When the men completed the job, Fleming refused to pay, so the locals took "as much of the Iron as they thought would satisfy them." Angered by the requisitioning of his ill-gotten gains, Fleming approached the notorious Andrew Westbrook for assistance. Westbrook "got a party and took these young men prisoners," Ward testified, and offered them the choice of returning "poor Fleming the Iron" or going as prisoners to Detroit. The men wisely chose the former course and they delivered all the iron to the home of Fleming's daughter.[75] Local justices of the peace were aware of the real motives of Westbrook and his ilk. In May 1813, fearful that private property was in peril, eighteen magistrates from the London and Niagara districts appealed for a declaration of martial law. Among those who signed the petition were William and Thomas Dickson, Samuel Street, Jr, Thomas Cummings, Robert Nichol, and Thomas Clark. "As men of some standing and weight in this society and holding real property to a great extent," these magistrates felt that a "more rigid system" of regulations and punishment was needed if looting and disaffection were to be curbed.[76]

Even some of those magistrates, however, appeared to have engaged in questionable dealings. For instance, Samuel Street, Jr, a wealthy Niagara miller, justice of the peace, and nephew of the militia paymaster, was said to have sold flour to the enemy when they were in possession of Fort George in November 1813. William Lundy, a Quaker farmer and Street's neighbour, swore out two depositions relating to the incident, but nothing appears to have been done about it. Lundy testified that Street and an American named Lobden approached him to help transport flour to Fort George. The flour was owned by Street and his partner Thomas Clark, but Lundy at first refused to participate in the operation. At last, after his neighbour had used "threats and persuasion," the Quaker capitulated and reluctantly agreed to assist in the deed. Sometime later Street pulled Lundy aside and asked him for his opinion of recent events, "to which [Lundy] reply'd, that he thought and continued to think that the said Samuel Street had turned Yankee and that he would continue so as long as the Americans held the possession [of] the Province."[77] No doubt Street could have excused his actions by saying he was only being practical. One Upper Canadian would later admit that he had sold goods to the Americans "since he knew his property would have been taken forcibly if he refused."[78]

More worrisome to military authorities were the activities of other malcontents nearer to the capital. Sometime in 1812, about three hundred men took to the woods near the boundary of the Home and Newcastle districts. These men, it seems, only wished to avoid militia service and they had little desire to fight beside the enemy. E.A. Cruikshank believed these "Whitchurch rebels" merely hoped to retain their lands by proving to the victorious invaders that they had not taken part in the defence of the province.[79] By the next year the group seems to have dispersed, no doubt much surprised by British victories at Detroit and Queenston. Only when the capital fell in April 1813 did malcontents in the area east of York feel confident enough to again express their true feelings. P.A. Finan, who retreated eastward with Sheaffe, said the people between York and Kingston "evinced great disloyalty as we proceeded." As the British scrambled to leave the capital, they found the roads clogged with Upper Canadians rushing to the village to receive paroles. Finan said the residents "made no scruple to express themselves well-satisfied with our *success*, and their new masters."[80] In June 1813 W.D. Powell recommended that British dragoons make excursions into that same area to "keep down the turbulence of the disaffected who are very numerous." The next year, after a number of British victories, pro-American settlers in the Newcastle and Midland districts operated in a more discreet manner. Evidently some residents between York and the Bay of Quinte formed a "Loyalty Club" and the members maintained contact with "the boys who had hoisted the flag of liberty" in Whitchurch Township.[81] It was claimed by a number of other witnesses that American raiding parties in the Bay of Quinte region received information from those disaffected residents on possible targets. After the war, John Strachan admitted that, in addition to disturbances in the London District, there had also been many disaffected in the Home region and in "the NewCastle District the disposition to rebel was great but finding themselves too near Kingston and York they were afraid but they deserted in great numbers."[82]

Evidence of disloyal activity could be found even further east. The military depot at Kingston, for instance, was a prime target for thieves during the latter part of the war. Month after month the garrison ran advertisements offering rewards for information leading to the conviction of those involved in the "embezzlement of naval stores."[83] It is known that militiamen in the neighbouring district of Johnstown often refused to appear for service, and at least one incident appeared to involve an organized mutiny. Shirley Spragge has noted that on 10 August 1814 fourteen Augusta residents, most of them of Loyalist descent, refused to embark on a raid directed at targets in New York State. In addition to disobeying direct orders, it seems eastern Upper Canadians also fraternized with the enemy. An American from Ogdensburg said that by 1813 old neighbours were once again exchanging visits across the border as they had been accustomed to doing before the war.[84] The sympathies of many Eastern Upper Canadians seem to have been questionable, and it was rumoured that American foragers facing tenacious resistance from Upper Canadians in the Niagara region "expressed a sense of their error in not having landed in Augusta, where they knew they had numerous friends."[85] This was also the area where Charles Jones operated an "anti-Jacobin" movement to prevent impressment of private property by British forces and where Joel Stone said "seditious neighbours" were all around him. "It is a matter of general notoriety," Drummond remarked in 1815, "that of all the Districts of this

Province, the Johnstown District is, I am sorry to say, the most disaffected and disloyal."[86]

But to declare a whole region "disaffected" or "disloyal" simply
because of militia desertions, or because some residents traded with
the enemy, seems unreasonable. As has been shown, most inhabitants
of Upper Canada, wherever they lived, exhibited a reluctance to
serve in defence of the province. The people had few ties to government, the war was not their fault, and they were not soldiers. Commanding officers of the militia often understood this reluctance,
even if their counterparts in the regular army did not. At one point
the leaders of the Stormont, Dundas, and Glengarry regiments
begged that their men be allowed to go home because their minds
were "distressed with an anxiety for their families."[87] Moreover, ordinary colonists were not the only people trading with the enemy.
Throughout the war the province was dependent on supplies from
the United States; William Weekes estimated that 80 per cent of the
army's fresh beef came from Vermont and New Hampshire. Naturally, most of this trade took place along the eastern end of the
province. William Dunlop, for example, met a drover at Cornwall
who was "in the smuggling line" and had just brought over some
"fine critters, Colonel, as ever had hair on them." While this man
was ostensibly an enemy of Britain, Dunlop made no attempt to
arrest the visitor. Nor could the Upper Canadian claim ignorance of
the man's origins. After all, the drover had proven himself to be "a
kind of Yankee gentleman, for he wore his hat in the parlour, and
spit on the carpet."[88] Even commanders of the forces were not above
involving themselves directly in the thriving smuggling trade of
eastern Upper Canada. After the government printing press was
destroyed by invaders in April 1813, Gordon Drummond authorized
the purchase of another from Ogdensburg, in the United States,
"for the low price of Eighty four pounds."[89]

Much of the preceding evidence suggests that the questionable
activities of many Upper Canadians had more to do with greed than
with any affinity for republicanism. A number of so-called "rebels"
were motivated by neighbourhood disputes, others were driven by a
desire to avoid militia service, and more than a few were simply
drunk. In the strictest sense, the majority of people later accused of
being traitors were only guilty of sedition, speaking or acting against
public order, and not of treason, the betrayal of the government. It
might be argued that several prominent Upper Canadians who considered themselves loyal citizens were also guilty of the same offence.
Certainly those merchants who extracted obscene profits from a

military force that sometimes suffered as a result were acting against the best interests of public order and the war effort.

Other Upper Canadians, concerned with the lawful protection of property rights, were also accused of interfering with the war effort. Faced with a shortage of food for his forces in the autumn of 1813, Francis de Rottenburg instituted a version of martial law in the Midland, Johnstown, and Eastern districts. Usually depicted as the most loyal region of the province, many of the residents there were angered by de Rottenburg's decision and took measures to counteract it. In the spring of 1814 the area's representatives joined with other assemblymen in preparing a letter of protest over the imposition of martial law. Ultimately a vote of censure, moved by Levius Sherwood of Brockville, was passed by the legislature. The Assembly denounced de Rottenburg's measure as "arbitrary and unconstitutional" and said it was designed "to destroy the laws of the Province."[90] Donald McLeod, who served with the British army, observed that martial law was bitterly resented by all Upper Canadians: "Loyalists and malcontents, for once, were unanimous in damning the government; rebellion appeared inevitable, threats to this effect were publicly and boldly thrown out."[91]

To understand why such threats were uttered, one must remember that nearly all Upper Canadians considered private property to be sacrosanct. The acquisition of personal wealth, and its protection, was seen by most colonists as one of the important goals in life. De Rottenburg's actions, which appeared to overturn British traditions regarding private property, led people to refer to the administrator as the "Dutch tyrant." At one point W.D. Powell was forced to inform de Rottenburg that aspersions were being cast on his "origin" and he advised him "to show that the constitutional rights of His Majesty's people were at least as much respected by you as by natural born subjects."[92] For his part, Powell was well aware of the importance of private property to Upper Canadians. In 1812 he had drafted the British reply to Hull's offer to protect private property in return for promises of neutrality.[93] The widespread acceptance of the American terms forced Powell to remind residents that as "Canadian Freeholders" they owed allegiance to Britain. Nonetheless, few western Upper Canadians seemed to pay much attention to that warning. Only later, after it was discovered that enemy forces were prepared to engage in looting and destructive burnings, did the local population appear willing to take up arms. Eastern Upper Canadian experiences, of course, were somewhat different. American plundering parties were rarely seen in that area and, for a good portion of the war, many residents endured few hardships. It was a great shock to these colonists when they realized that private property rights could be ignored by British authorities. The anger of many otherwise loyal citizens is understandable since the burden of martial law was felt disproportionately by them. McLeod said Upper Canadians who sympathized with the enemy "suffered the least as they took the precautionary steps to secrete their property in the woods and swamps." Residents who made no effort to hide their possessions sometimes found them seized by military authorities.[94]

The first indication that British military commanders would have a real fight on their hands if they tampered with private property occurred early in 1813. At a meeting of the Lower Canadian legislature in February, George Prevost discovered that a number of assemblymen were opposed to any imposition of martial law that would affect the civilian populace. The leader of this early movement was James Stuart, an American who had been removed from the position of solicitor-general by the previous governor, Sir James Craig.[95] Stuart's campaign to limit martial law to the enforcement of discipline in the armed forces received support from a prominent Upper Canadian emigré, Samuel Sherwood. A former member of the Upper Canadian Assembly for the riding of Grenville in the Johnstown District, Sherwood had left the province for Lower Canada the moment war had been declared.[96] His brother, Levius P. Sherwood, represented the Leeds area in the Assembly for the upper colony and was to become a legislative councillor and a judge of the Court of King's Bench. Both men were sons of a well-to-do Loyalist, and Samuel Sherwood was one of the first lawyers in the province. He was also elected to the Lower Canadian legislature in 1814 and, while there, he spent most of his time objecting to the actions of the military authorities. These actions impinged on his own private business interests. Shirley Campbell Spragge has noted that Samuel's firm in Upper Canada, which relied on merchandise smuggled across the border, would have been adversely affected by proposed measures to control passage of goods on the St Lawrence.[97] Eventually, Sherwood managed to take over the leadership of Stuart's movement. Using the pen-name "Anti-Jacobin," Sherwood published a pamphlet which argued that it was illegal for a military commander to declare martial law without first getting the permission of the legislature. His influence was not restricted to Lower Canada, however, and Samuel was generally recognized as the "chief" of a "Junto" which aimed to limit the use of martial law in both provinces.[98]

Joel Stone believed that James Stuart and Samuel Sherwood had been in contact with Peter Howard, a former representative for Leeds in the Upper Canadian Assembly. Apparently Howard was active in attempts to undermine military authority in his district by having members of the commissariat arrested whenever they resorted to martial law to acquire provisions. Howard had refused to submit to unpopular measures in the past and, in 1808, he and two other assemblymen brought a legislative session to a halt by walking out of the House and depriving it of a quorum. This action was taken because all three were opposed to new rules that would have permitted bills to be rushed through the legislature without proper discussion. For his part in this protest Howard earned the enmity of Lieutenant-Governor Francis Gore, who immediately stripped the assemblyman of his position as magistrate. Howard was a man who refused to allow the rights of British subjects to be trampled on by members of the executive but, at the same time, he also refused to follow the dictates of Joseph Willcocks or anyone else. On 19 February 1812, for example, Howard supported Brock's new militia bill while Willcocks did not.[99]

Stone thought that Howard and some other prominent residents of eastern Upper Canada were part of a conspiracy led by Stuart and Sherwood, but he was unwilling "to say where the combination ends."[100] It is known that Sherwood sent letters of advice to old colleagues who found their property subjected to seizure by British troops. From his Montreal residence he sent a letter of inquiry to one of these associates asking him to forward any information he could gather on the activities of Lieutenant-Colonel Thomas Pearson, who was allegedly "violating the rights of individuals" near Prescott. Drawing on his legal knowledge, Sherwood informed others of their constitutional rights, even referring to specific statutes that quaranteed the sanctity of private property. "If you hear any ignorant military man ignorantly prattling in favour of old De Rottenburg's and Pearson's Martial Law," he told David Jones at the end of one of these legal lessons, "it will be in your power to stop his mouth very soon by citing authority."[101]

Another of Sherwood's admirers was a relative of his by marriage, Charles Jones, whose sister was the wife of Levius P. Sherwood. Jones was the son of a prominent Loyalist and had founded the village of Elizabethtown in the Johnstown District. A wealthy merchant and land speculator, Jones has been described by one historian as a real "wheeler-dealer" who would eventually cap his success with an appointment to the Legislative Council in 1828.[102] Ever the opportunist, Jones had changed the name of Elizabethtown to Brockville after the British victory at Michilimackinac but, because of the constant feuding which took place beteen the leading figures of the village, locals still referred to it as "Snarlington."[103] During the war years Jones was also continually involved in disputes with his commanding officer in the militia, Joel Stone, and he experienced one serious confrontation with regular soldiers. The incident may have led Jones to desert his post and leave the province before the war ended. On 4 April 1813 Jones said that he nearly lost his life trying to dissuade "half a dozen ruffians" belonging to a flank company of the King's regiment from impressing his prize horse. He lodged a formal complaint over the incident, in which he declared that if militia officers were to be treated in this "contemptuous way," "no militia situation ever so high can be desireable."[104]

Apparently Jones made good on his threat to leave the service and it was reported that he spent the rest of the war in Halifax. He left Guy Burnham, a member of his company of dragoons, in charge of his shop while he was gone. Burnham, it was said, resorted to smuggling goods from the United States to operate the store at even greater levels of profitability. Stone was of the opinion that most of the rumours about Jones were "highly colored from envy" until he again met up with the Brockville merchant. After the war Jones received a commission as justice of the peace and, at one of his court of quarter sessions, Stone was shocked to hear the new magistrate name Samuel Sherwood and James Stuart as "deserving the highest applause from all ranks of people for keeping down tyranny." The next day Jones and Stone got into an argument about which of them was more guilty of oppressing their neighbours. Jones declared that Stone was a "tyrant" who had fined militiamen for desertion and had assisted the government in acquiring forfeitures on the estates of suspected traitors. Stone maintained that the new magistrate was "the greatest tyrant" since he had acquired more lands from forfeitures on indebted customers than Stone had ever been "able to get to the Crown for treason."[105] It seems that both men were probably right in their opinions about each other. One of Stone's biographers has said his involvement in the war stemmed not from a wish to defend Upper Canada, but "from Joel's innate desire for self-glorification and compensation from a grateful government." Certainly his neighbours suspected Stone's motivation, and it was known that during the war he had "been making his fortune with his Mills."[106]

A resident of Lower Canada, John Richardson, wrote after the war that a deliberate and "nefarious plot" had been hatched by Sherwood and other disaffected citizens "to palsy our means of defence." Richardson believed that these men were guilty of treason – of aiding the enemy – because they resorted to legal measures to hamper the implementation of martial law. While men such as Howard claimed to be "patriots" defending British traditions, Richardson argued that their real motive "was to disconcert our military operations, by starving the troops." In addition to the work of these disaffected citizens, others engaged in similiar pursuits. Richardson believed that the "Junto" had achieved its greatest success "by operating upon the avarice of the well affected, by persuading them to withhold supplies in order to get higher prices."[107] Whether prompted by traitorous designs, simple greed, or by a concern for property rights, the end result of the prosecutions was the same. Richardson noted that soldiers were deprived of food as commissariat officers spent their time appearing in court and the defence of the province was made all the more difficult.

One of the "well affected" who followed Sherwood's advice was Allan McLean, a wealthy Kingston landowner and member of the Assembly for Frontenac. When he discovered that members of the commissary department had established a temporary headquarters on one of his estates, McLean took legal action. Thomas Osborne, deputy assistant commissary-general, was served with a declaration of ejection and McLean had three other members of that department charged with trespass. Always considered a "steadfastly loyal" subject, McLean had previously volunteered his services as an officer in a provincial corps, and his decision to sue the commissariat department surprised his associates. Christopher Hagerman, a fellow officer, was shocked by his friend's action and was at a loss to explain how such a "Zealous and Loyal subject" could set "an example of insubordination and resentment."[108] Yet for McLean the issue was undoubtedly more complicated and he was probably as concerned over the principles at stake as he was with any possible monetary loss. He had not given the commissariat permission to use his land, and the officials were violating his property rights. Loyal or not, Upper Canadians had always been quick to resort to the law when a contract was broken. McLean was no exception to that rule.

McLean's example was followed by other citizens in eastern Upper Canada who also had the means and contacts to undertake law suits against members of the commissary department. In May 1814 Gordon Drummond was worried that local juries would convict military men and he asked that the law officers of the crown defend any soldiers arrested while requisitioning supplies. Attorney-General John Beverley Robinson received an official request about the matter the next month, but at that time he was too involved in the prosecution of a handful of petty criminals charged with treason.[109] Most of those men had stolen goods from their neighbours or had disrupted the militia service by kidnapping senior officers to avoid serving themselves. Eventually, even without Robinson's assistance, the government managed to quash the lawsuits against the commissariat. On 17 October 1815 Lieutenant-Governor Gore reported that the prosecutions had finally "been checked by the prudence of the Judges," and any inhabitants who were still unsatisfied were directed to submit estimates to a board of claims appointed to hear such matters.[110] Although they had contributed to the difficulties of the British army in eastern Upper Canada, men such as Howard and McLean likely would not have felt guilty. They had been raised to believe that an individual had an inalienable right to the peaceful enjoyment of his private property and they were prepared to take the British government to court to defend that privilege.

Upper Canadians cared deeply about their own possessions, and those who dared to tamper with them had to be prepared to deal with the consequences. For instance, William Fitzpatrick, the barrackmaster at Fort Wellington in Prescott, was successfully sued by a militia deserter. In November 1813 Fitzpatrick was sent to Brockville to gather the militia together, but one merchant, Hiram Stafford, refused to leave his place of business. Eventually, Fitzpatrick forcibly entered the premises and grabbed hold of the reluctant militiaman. After the war, though, Stafford sued the former barrackmaster and charged him with having "broke open, broke down, broke to pieces, cut, damaged, prostrated, and destroyed the outer door" of his home. In his defence, Fitzpatrick argued that Stafford had illegally "absconded from duty and did not appear until after the conclusion of the war," but the jury awarded damages to the merchant.[111] In another incident, militiaman Daniel O'Reilly of Niagara found himself the victim of communal justice at the hands of his neighbours after the fall of Fort George in May 1813. At that time O'Reilly was ordered by General Vincent to requisition horses for the use of the artillery. Dutiful militiaman that he was, O'Reilly impressed the horse of a man named Huff who lived near Beaver Dams. That night, before O'Reilly could turn the animal over to the artillery officers, Huff "unimpressed" the horse. Daniel O'Reilly's troubles were not over yet, however, for a few days later Huff returned with some Indians and stole two of the militiaman's horses.[112]

While men like McLean and Stafford were quick to take British officials to court, some other colonists went so far as to sue individual members of the American army who had dared to violate private property rights. Christopher Arnold, a resident of Harwich Township in the Western District, managed to take an officer named Chittenden to trial in the United States. Arnold sued for the return of seven head of cattle worth £33, but he lost his suit when Chittenden was able to prove that he had taken the livestock "in his official capacity as an officer of the United States Army." John Misener of the Niagara District also resorted to the law in order to retrieve seven barrels of flour taken by the Americans. His attorney, George Keltz, apparently had even less luck than Arnold, since the case never reached trial. For some Upper Canadians the war remained a very private affair. Arnold and Misener refused to accept that property losses were an inevitable result of armed conflict between two nations. Chittenden and other identifiable individuals, not the United States of America, had taken their cattle and flour and the colonists wanted those items returned.[113]

The merchants at Kingston and York who overcharged commissary officials, and those citizens who assisted the Americans in return for government stores, also viewed the war in very personal terms, and most appeared unconcerned about loyalty and the war effort. Their primary goal was to improve their own economic situation and they seemed to care little if British officials or anyone else considered their actions immoral or even illegal. When the war offered an opportunity to acquire "a fine hawl," they seized the chance without hesitation. Respectable inhabitants such as John Askin and Samuel Street, Jr, were as prepared to trade with Americans as was John Lyons, except that he offered labour in return for booty while the businessmen received money for flour. Greed certainly motivated other residents, including those who sought to protect their possessions from forcible requisitioning, but there is little evidence to support John Richardson's belief that McLean and others were guilty of treason. They had not assisted the American invaders or betrayed the government, but they had placed their own concerns and rights above those of the state.

There were also "traitors" in the truest sense of the word and some of them were involved in government. Two members of the provincial legislature, Abraham Markle and Joseph Willcocks, and a former member, Benajah Mallory, deserted to the enemy in 1813 and were given positions in the American army. It is interesting to note the different backgrounds of each of these men since it suggests that traitors could originate from several segments of the population. Markle, for instance, was from a Loyalist family that had arrived in the colony before the American Revolution had ended. Four of his brothers had served in John Butler's Rangers, and Markle managed to establish a distillery and a mill near Ancaster and had acquired 1300 acres in the province by 1812. That summer he joined a dragoon company and carried dispatches for the British. But on 10 June 1813 Markle was called to headquarters at Burlington Heights and informed that numerous complaints had been lodged against him.

One week later, in captivity in Kingston, Markle complained to General Sheaffe that he had not yet been informed of the charges against him. He assured Sheaffe that any charges were "groundless" since it "has been hereditary from my forefathers to the Present age to be friends to the British government." Whatever his true feelings might have been, one week in the hold of a Royal Navy vessel on Lake Ontario apparently was enough to convince him that, for safety's sake, he was better off with the enemy. By 12 December 1813 Markle was serving in the company of Canadian Volunteers for the United States.[114]

When he joined that brigade, Markle found himself serving under Joseph Willcocks, a British subject from Ireland. One historian has suggested that Willcocks crossed over to the American side out of disgust over the activities of the Niagara and York elites. Elwood Jones believes that Willcock's loyalty was shaken in the summer of 1813 when prominent figures in those two places began demanding the imposition of harsh military measures to curb disaffection. "Firmly in the opposition whig tradition," Jones has written, "Willcocks opposed arbitrary and distant power" and was left with no choice but to repudiate his allegiance to the crown.[115] While it is true that Willcocks's decision to join the Americans in 1813 was prompted by the campaign to eradicate looting and disaffection, his actions were not based on lofty ideological concerns. Willcocks had been wooed by Brock to the British side in 1812 and he saw action at Queenston Heights. At that battle, however, Brock was killed and the Irishman lost another powerful ally. In early 1813 William Hamilton Merritt said that Willcocks "had changed about and become a zealous loyalist. He has behaved very well on all occasions and so have all his party, altho' they are trusted with no office whatever."[116] Proof of that came only weeks later when Willcocks tried to recruit a company for the Incorporated Militia. Like other hopefuls, he discovered there were few privates willing to serve and he was not one of the lucky men selected to lead the regiment.[117] His sincerity questioned on all sides, and his ambition to become an officer thwarted, Willcocks was soon to hear even more distressing news. Some residents of the district of Niagara claimed to have seen Willcocks acting as a guide for the American force which was defeated at Stoney Creek on 6 June 1813.[118] Along with Markle, therefore, the Irish immigrant stood accused of being a traitor and he faced the real possibility of being hanged because of these accusations. It was probably an earnest desire to avoid having his neck stretched, rather than offended sensibilities, which actually drove Willcocks to join the enemy. On 10 July 1813 he offered to form another "corps of volunteers," but this time the proposal was made to Henry Dearborn of the United States army.[119]

Unlike his Loyalist and Irish-born counterparts, Benajah Mallory had already fought for the Americans in the past. During the revolutionary war, Mallory had joined the rebel forces but, like thousands of other Americans, he came to Upper Canada some time later. By 1812 he had managed to acquire some 1220 acres of land in the province. In the fourth parliament from 1804 to 1808, Mallory represented the riding of Norfolk, Oxford, and Middlesex, and during the fifth parliament from 1808 to 1812 he sat for the counties of Oxford and Middlesex. All that time he consistently voted with Willcocks and in 1810, to cite one instance, he supported him on eighteen of the twenty-one divisions which took place. During the election of 1812, Mallory was defeated by Mahlon Burwell, a close associate of Thomas Talbot. Apparently, Talbot issued highly prized location tickets to anyone who would vote for Burwell. Mallory had also offended Robert Nichol, and the Scottish merchant sent reports to his friend Isaac Brock accusing Mallory of attending meetings "for bad Purposes." Like Willcocks and Markle, therefore, Mallory was rumoured to be a traitor and in the summer of 1813 such suspicions could lead to indefinite prison terms or worse. On 14 November 1813 Mallory enlisted in the company of Canadian Volunteers.[120]

At the opening of the spring session of the provincial legislature in February 1814, Gordon Drummond said that the news that Willcocks and other inhabitants had joined the Americans was "more a subject of regret than surprise." The assemblymen responded to Drummond's request for means "to punish such traitors" by passing several new pieces of legislation, including one that suspended Habeas Corpus. The third bill passed that session permitted arrests of individuals who were only suspected of treasonous acts, and two other bills allowed for the seizure and sale of lands held by inhabitants who had fled to the other side. Finally, the House modified the regulations dealing with treason to allow suspects to be tried outside the district in which they normally resided. The last measure was considered necessary since the British no longer controlled western Upper Canada and no trials could possibly be held there.[121]

On 24 March 1814 Gordon Drummond made use of one of the recent measures of the Assembly to empower boards to "secure and detain such persons as His Majesty shall suspect of treasonable adherence to the enemy." Drummond appointed fifty men to seven boards situated in every region except the Western and London districts, where the American raiding parties still operated. Among those selected were William Allan, Alexander Wood, and Thomas

Ridout for the Home District, Joel Stone for Johnstown, Thomas Markland from Kingston in the Midland District, and Samuel Street and Richard Beasley from Niagara.[122] The man most concerned with the proceedings of these boards, however, was the twenty-three-year-old acting attorney-general for the province, John Beverley Robinson. John Macdonell, the man who held that position at the start of the war, had been killed during the Battle of Queenston Heights. Soon after, William Drummer Powell and John Strachan put foward Robinson's name as a suitable temporary replacement, although he had not yet been admitted to practise law.[123] Robinson accepted the opportunity offered by Macdonell's misfortune and set out to make a name for himself in a manner that must have pleased his mentor Strachan.

The new attorney-general was to oversee the operation of a special commission, an inquiry reserved for those occasions that called for exemplary hangings to restore the public peace. In England, special commissions were usually granted at the request of wealthy gentlemen when riots threatened their authority. The assize judges would arrive from the capital, grave speeches would be made, evidence would be heard, and finally the sentence of death would be pronounced. It was thought that such "rituals of justice" helped to restore proper respect for authority and healed the "breach in the social and moral order."[124]

By 4 April 1814 Robinson had before him the names of sixty suspected traitors, but he had sufficient evidence to ensure the conviction of only thirty of these men. Unfortunately for the young attorney-general, the majority of those suspects were "out of the reach of punishment." What was worse, "the most notorious offenders," Willcocks, Mallory, Westbrook, and Markle, were among those safe behind enemy lines.[125] In fact, most of the men available for trial had been captured in the London District by vigilante forces led by Henry Bostwick and Henry Medcalf. In addition to this handful of looters, Robinson had in prison a number of York residents, including Calvin Wood, Elijah Bentley, and Gideon Orton, who were accused of having helped themselves to public stores in the garrison or of having counselled militiamen to acquire paroles. For these prisoners, however, the attorney-general thought he had sufficent proof to charge the men only with sedition. Although Robinson believed they had acted from "traitorous intentions," they had not actually rebelled against the crown. Finally, the jails also held a few men from the Niagara District who were charged with having assisted the enemy. None of these individuals was in the same league as Westbrook or Willcocks but, all the same, Robinson was determined to push forward with the trials. "It is wished, and very wisely," he informed Drummond's secretary, "to overawe the spirit of disaffection in the Province." The only way to do that, in Robinson's opinion, was through the "Execution of Traitors."[126]

Robinson originally objected to Drummond's suggestion that the trials be held near Burlington Heights, since he preferred that they take place in the areas where the offences were actually committed. That was particulary true for the looters from the London District who had endangered the lives and property of their neighbours to such a degree "that they voluntarily resorted to arms to subdue them." Robinson believed that men who "risqued their lives in the apprehension of traitors will be well satisfied to have them punished as they deserved." Eventually Robinson was forced to accept the Burlington location for all the trials, but he remained unhappy with it. On 20 April 1814 Robinson received the special commission which authorized the holding of trials. Only at that point was it realized that there was no township named "Burlington" and the trials would have to take place in Ancaster Township instead.[127]

The acting attorney-general was anxious to get convictions because he knew his reputation was riding on them. His meticulous attention to detail and his constant pestering of Drummond for permission to use troops from Burlington Heights for guard duty and to arrange for food for potential witnesses eventually brought a sharp rebuke from the commander of the forces. On 8 May 1814 Drummond's secretary, Robert Loring, reminded Robinson that the chief object of a special commission was to make immediate examples of wrong-doers by speedy convictions and public hangings. Whether by unavoidable delay or not, Drummond was convinced that an unacceptable amount of time had already elapsed. Moreover, if Robinson was really faced with difficulties in getting provisions and other items for the court, then Drummond suggested it might be better to postpone the trial until the next general assizes at York.[128] Fearing that his prized position might fall to another, Robinson quickly explained that he would be more than willing to use local constables for guard duty and went on to say that he had not actually promised provisions to anyone yet. Finally, Robinson apologized for bothering Drummond about such details but said that his only concern was preventing any possible disruption of the trials. Years later, Robinson would recall with pride how he had changed Drummond's mind about cancelling the commission by assuring him that "it was impossible the prosecutions could all fail."[129]

At last, on 23 May 1814, Chief Justice Thomas Scott opened the proceedings by reading the special commission. Over the next month, nineteen prisoners were paraded before Scott and the two other provincial judges, W.D. Powell and William Campbell. In the end, fifteen of the men were convicted of High Treason and four were acquitted. While only eight of the prisoners were hanged, several others died of diseases contracted while in custody.[130] None of the prisoners was well known, and ordinarily most would have been fined or sentenced to branding for common theft. These were not normal times, however, and the authorities were determined to produce examples to deter others.

Of the eight prisoners executed, five were from the London District. All of them had attempted to enrich themselves at the expense of neighbours by plundering them of property or had tried to disrupt the militia system by carrying off officers. John Dunham was described as one of the ringleaders of this band of rebels and it was at his home at Nanticoke Creek that Henry Bostwick captured most of the prisoners tried at Ancaster. Isaiah Brink was also captured in arms by Bostwick and it was said he was very active in all the plundering forays. Three of their associates, Dayton Lindsay, George Peacock, Jr, and Benjamin Simmonds, were also accused of making "prisoners of our militia officers and inhabitants" in the London region. All the other men held lands in the Niagara District. Adam Chrysler was from Thorold, but he was taken prisoner by Henry Medcalf at Chatham. Aaron Stevens had received land grants in both the Home and Niagara districts and was described as "a man formerly employed in the confidence of govt., of respectable family and property." Nonetheless, Stevens admitted to having spied on the garrison at Burlington Heights in return "for a large pecuniary reward." Finally, the last man convicted was Noah Payne Hopkins, a farmer from Queenston who was accused of acting "as a Commissariat for the Americans" since he had provided food to enemy soldiers.[131]

Part of the ritual of a special commission involved the granting of reprieves. Among those who escaped the noose during the Ancaster "Bloody Assize" were Samuel and Stephen Hartwell. These two American citizens had lived near Beaver Dams for ten years until the outbreak of war. At that point they left the province; they were later captured fighting for the American side at Queenston Heights and granted paroles. When the Americans gained possession of the Niagara District the Hartwells returned to their former residence, where they at one time endeavoured to prevent a neighbour from serving in the militia. Although Robinson felt both were technically guilty of treason, he reasoned that their status as American citizens made it prudent, for "political motives," not to "strain the law to its utmost rigour."[132] Also considered a suitable object for leniency was another Niagara District prisoner, Jacob Overholser, dismissed by Robinson as "an ignorant man" from Fort Erie. Overholser had been arrested because of a longstanding dispute with two members of the Anger family who have been described as "a thuggish lot." In December 1813 these men stole four horses from Overholser and then testified that he had been seen in company with the Americans. Overholser pleaded that he had been forced by the enemy to carry a rifle; John Beverley Robinson believed that if the charges were true, it was likely because Overholser had acted "from motives of personal enmity."[133]

The other four men granted reprieves were looters from the London District. Isaac Petit had been captured along with Chrysler and Brink by Henry Bostwick, but he had played only a minor role in the plundering of his neighbours. Garrett Neil and John Johnson were also involved in similar activities, but Robinson felt they were merely "two ignorant inconsiderable men." Johnson had apparently been deceived by his associates about their actual intentions, and the attorney-general noted that he "behaved with humanity to prisoners taken by the party."[134] Finally, the only prisoner to plead guilty, Cornelius Howey, was also granted a reprieve. Wounded during the Nanticoke Creek incident, Howey was described by Robinson as "languishing." Chief Justice Scott believed that he may have agreed with the charges simply to avoid the agony of having to stand to testify. Scott also ventured the opinion that a hanging might be superfluous since it was not thought Howey would "live to abide the sentence of the law."[135]

Before the hangings were carried out, petitions from family and friends of the condemned were considered by the authorities. Polly Hopkins, the wife of Noah Payne Hopkins, asked for clemency for her husband for the sake of her four children. Seven of Hopkins's neighbours joined in asking for mercy, since they knew "circumstances favourable to him." Samuel Street, Jr, a justice of the peace for the district, certified that the seven citizens were "loyal and respectable inhabitants." Street may have agreed to sign the petition because of his own personal knowledge of how easy it was to act as "a Commissariat for the Americans."[136]

Despite such appeals, Hopkins and the seven other condemned men were executed at Burlington Heights on 20 July 1814. It appears that a sizeable crowd assembled to see this unusual spectacle and the prisoners were placed in two wagons, four in each, and drawn under a hastily constructed gallows. An eyewitness said that when the wagons pulled away the condemned men "were left to strangle to death." John Ryckman, a sixteen-year-old youth at the time, described what happened next: "The contortions of the poor men so shook the loosely constructed gallows that a heavy brace became loosened and fell, striking one of the victims on the head and killing him instantly, thus relieving him of the tortures of the rope. After the men had been duly strangled their heads were chopped off and exhibited as the heads of traitors." Ryckman went on to observe that seven of the men seemed willing to die, but the eighth pleaded continually for his life. Noah Hopkins apparently announced that what he had done "was simply out of a feeling of hospitality and that he did not know who he was entertaining."[137]

From his vantage point atop the wagon, Hopkins may have been able to gaze out onto the lake, but it was unlikely that he would have seen the tiny village of York, which lay just over the horizon. Though we will never know for sure, it may be that poor Noah Hopkins spent his last moments cursing his decision to acquire a farm at Queenston rather than near York. The residents of the capital had recently become eligible for militia duty again and the sounds of crates being unpacked behind shops were now mixed with the noises of men marching to the garrison. On the walls of the fort were proclamations, freshly printed on Gordon Drummond's newly imported press, which gravely explained why martial law was necessary.[138] Yet the atmosphere in town was far from gloomy. Every two weeks the elite of the community gathered to drink teneriffe wines and partake of madeira cakes as "Lemon," the local violin player, provided background music. The first of these regular York Assemblies had been held on 19 December 1813 to celebrate the capture of Fort Niagara the night before. Every fortnight since that time, John Strachan, Alexander Wood, William Allan, Quetton St George, and other York notables met to rejoice over their good fortune and to discuss recent events. Strachan may also have taken the opportunity to chide his prosperous neighbours in a good-natured way about their contributions to the Loyal and Patriotic Society. Altogether, the three most powerful merchants in the capital had only promised to donate a total of £100 a year.[139]

Both the men who gathered at the York Assemblies and those who were placed in the wagons at Burlington Heights were of more or less ambiguous "loyalty." Leading colonists in the capital and in other garrison towns profited from military spending and they made a good living from their connections to the British government. Yet these men were quick to take advantage of military customers and they showed little hesitation about gouging the public. They were not selflessly devoted to ensuring the success of British arms, and more than one of these men proved capable of switching allegiance when

BY Lieutenant General GORDON DRUMMOND, Commanding His Majesty's Forces in the Province of Upper Canada, &c. &c. &c.

A Proclamation.

WHEREAS, it is found necessary for the Public Safety, that the most efficacious means should be used for supplying His Majesty's Troops, stationed in this Province, with Provisions, and Forage. which, though abounding in the Country, are withheld from the Commissariat, and their Agents, notwithstanding the most liberal prices have been offered for the same.——I do, therefore, hereby declare, that as far as relates to the procuring of Provisions, and Forage, for the said Troops, Martial Law shall be in force throughout the Province ; and the same is hereby declared to be in force therein ; and ordered to be acted upon accordingly.

Given under my Hand, and Seal at Arms, at Kingston, this Twelfth Day of April, One Thousand Eight Hundred and Fourteen.

GORDON DRUMMOND,
Lt. General,

Poster announcing martial law for food or forage, April 1814, produced on a press imported from the United States.
Public Record Office, Kew

that appeared to be the sensible thing to do. Most of the colonists who were accused of treason had also sought to profit by the war, but for many of them the only way they could do that was by stealing from their neighbours or by dealing with the enemy. In many respects, therefore, the difference in the actions of these "enemies at home" was often a matter of degree rather than of kind.

7 "Success to Commerce": Costs and Claims

In March 1815, more than two months after the negotiations for peace had come to an end, news of the Treaty of Ghent reached Upper Canada. William Hamilton Merritt observed that the announcement of the end of hostilities between Britain and the United States was warmly received in the province and that "joy and gladness beamed on every countenance." Some merchants may have beamed a little less brightly than their neighbours, since many colonial shopkeepers viewed the peace treaty as a mixed blessing. Alexander Wood quickly notified an out-of-province supplier that he would not be purchasing any items in the near future because the treaty had "opened the people's eyes" and had put an end to panic buying.[1] Wood was more fortunate than some other retailers, because he at least had not overextended himself. The sudden drop in demand for goods and provisions had left a number of colonial shopkeepers, including the director of the York Association, with excessively large inventories. Stephen Jarvis grumbled that when his shop finally started to make money "the Yankess got tired of the war and made a Peace by which I not only lost a profit but sank more than fifty per cent of the cost." Isaac Wilson informed his brother in August 1815 that colonial merchants "with goods on hand lost a great deal by the decline," and he knew of two men whose investment in provisions and other articles had dropped by more than one thousand dollars in value. Wilson was one of the luckier residents of York and he reassured his brother by writing, "I have fixed myself here now for some time to come if not for life."[2]

Other Upper Canadians also shared Wilson's good fortune and some continued to receive high returns in the immediate postwar period. In the same letter Wilson told his brother that the government had commissioned "a great many expensive undertakings at York," including new barracks, wharves, and a house for the returning lieutenant-governor, Francis Gore. As a result of the building boom, common labourers could command $1.50 a day with "victuals & grog" included. Many other colonists were hired to drive wagons for the military, "bringing back stores for the Government which were conveyed up at an immense expense during the war." Wilson also observed, however, that the demobilization activities meant there was "very little farming done."[3] Three years of relatively easy money may have left some Upper Canadians with no desire to return to the work of clearing bush and tending fields. Yet government construction and military demobilization would not last forever and, in the future, the colony would be forced to rely on its own resources to a much greater extent. When British spending began to decline, the real impact of the conflict on the provincial economy would become much more evident.

For thousands of colonists, wartime disruptions had entailed more than the abandonment of flourishing farms for lucrative employment in the towns. A British immigrant would later say that, in economic terms, the "people of the Niagara District, in particular, were torn to pieces by the war."[4] Thomas Verchères, who travelled through the region in June 1815, said "everywhere I saw devastation, homes in ashes, fields trampled and laid waste, forts demolished, forests burned and blackened, truly a most pitiful sight."[5] Naturally, the Niagara and Queenston Association merchants had not fared as well as their counterparts in York and Kingston. James Kerby and his partner Alexander Grant estimated their property losses at more than £240, but that did not include the potential earnings they might have realized had their warehouses and stores been able to continue operating.[6] Thomas Cummings, another Niagara merchant, had carried on his business until the 1813 invasions led to £3763 in damages, which "put a sudden and disastrous end to it."[7] George and Alexander Hamilton, who had inherited their father Robert's business after his death in 1809, saw the already troubled family firm completely destroyed by the war. Government contracts held by the brothers for supplying the army were suspended when the commissariat took control of provisioning, and their lucrative forwarding business was wiped out because of the indefensible position of the Queenston landing site. Destruction of valuable facilities by both enemy and friendly forces administered a *coup de grâce* to the

Hamilton enterprises, and the brothers estimated the family's losses to be in the neighbourhood of £3400.[8]

Further west, other merchants endured similar losses. Verchères, for instance, operated a shop at Amherstburg which made huge sums of money during the war. At one point during the summer of 1813 he risked a trip to York in order to stock his shelves. On his return he found "customers were all about the place, inside and outside, and each had to await his turn. You see by this time they were in need of everything." On the first day he brought in $2400, on the second $800, and on the third over $1600. Verchères noted that the citizens of Amherstburg had been collecting army bills for months and, because merchandise was preferable to paper money, the desire to obtain items "was overwhelming, regardless of the price." Only a few months later, however, he lost at least $8000 when his shop was looted by American invaders. What little money he had left was later lost in a business deal with Quetton St George in early 1815. "Peace with America was proclaimed," Verchères ruefully remarked, "and prices cascaded to one-fourth the existing scale."[9] It is useful to note that St George was not ruined by this misadventure. For some colonial shopkeepers the combination of wartime depredations and a lack of foresight proved to be overwhelming.

Other merchants who avoided wartime speculation still suffered tremendously because of the fighting. Robert Nichol's estate in Woodhouse Township, for example, was completely destroyed by the conflict, although he spent most of the war working for the commissariat. Before the fighting had ended he calculated that £5580 worth of his property had been lost, which he said was "nearly the whole fruit of twenty-two years' assiduous application to business." As he surveyed the destruction and prepared his claim for compensation in October 1814, Nichol might have had in mind Brock's assurance that "the British Government was never backward in rewarding faithful and meritorious services."[10] Thousands of other colonists also assumed they would be compensated for their losses, although they had never received the personal assurances of Isaac Brock. Upper Canadians certainly expected to be reimbursed for the damages caused by British soldiers and they also believed they had a strong case for compensation for other losses. It was common knowledge in the province that most of the earliest pioneers had been Loyalists who had been granted both land and money for their losses during the revolutionary war. Moreover, Upper Canadians always considered the more recent conflict to have been none of their doing in the first place. The war had been thrust upon them because of the British connection, and they considered compensation for the losses a debt owed to the province by the home authorities. John Strachan reminded an English friend in February 1815 that the "inhabitants of the Canadas had nothing to say about the Origin of the War," and the money needed to repay victims of the fighting "ought not therefore to be charged upon the Canadas."[11]

News of peace reached the colony when the sixth parliament was in its fourth session. Exactly half of the twenty-two members present for that session had lost property owing to the war, and by-elections would soon lead to thirteen Assembly seats being occupied by war sufferers. No sworn members of the Legislative Council had suffered any losses due to the fighting, but they still assisted in preparing a joint address to the Prince of Wales on the subject of war damages.[12] Early in March the politicians informed His Royal Highness that the colony had sustained "nearly the whole pressure of the Enemy's reiterated attacks" and, as a result, many of the colonists "had been reduced to great distress." The legislators asked that the "same generous determination" which had provided the inhabitants with money for their fight against the enemy now "be equally extended for their relief." Gordon Drummond, who admitted to being "a witness myself of their distress and suffering," forwarded the address to the secretary of state for war and the colonies, Earl Bathurst, with a favourable recommendation. Drummond suggested that Upper Canadians who had fallen prey to "the plunderers or the Flames" should be entitled to some of the aid being dispensed "in every quarter of the Continent of Europe."[13]

A few months later Bathurst's assistant, Henry Goulburn, informed Francis Gore that the joint address had not been rejected out of hand by the British Treasury. Since the principle of compensation for war losses had been admitted in the past, it was thought these Upper Canadians could not be denied "an opportunity of submitting their claims to the liberal consideration of parliament." Gore, who was about to leave for Upper Canada, was directed to appoint at least three "respectable" and disinterested colonists to prepare a report on the subject. Their findings were to be forwarded to Bathurst for his consideration, but no promises regarding payments were made.[14]

The pressing need for immediate compensation may have been undercut somewhat because of a letter written by Gore soon after his arrival in the province. After a quick tour through certain parts of the colony, and after conferring with members of his Executive Council, Gore informed Bathurst that the province was "labouring under no irreparable injury from the war." Gore admitted that much destruction had taken place in the Niagara District and areas to the west, but he stated that "any injury arising to the inhabitants has been much compensated by the means afforded to enrich themselves from the expenditure of the Army." The new lieutenant-governor even went so far as to affirm that, on the whole, "the general prosperity of the Province is greater than before the war." Unlike Drummond, who had first-hand knowledge of the war and its effects, Gore relied on others for most of his information and his opinions bore a striking resemblance to those expressed earlier by the province's newest executive councillor, John Strachan. There is little doubt that Strachan took a strong role in influencing Gore's outlook, and the lieutenant-governor ended his appraisal of the situation by observing that the Loyal and Patriotic Society had already "relieved great distress" through the "judicious application" of its funds. Thus, when the work of the claims commission was done, Gore believed "universal satisfaction" would prevail.[15]

Never hesitant when it came to personal advancement, Strachan had responded to rumours that he was to be selected for a senior government post by virtually accepting the position before it was offered. On 2 May 1814 he wrote to General de Rottenburgh that he would acquiesce to an appointment in the Executive Council "from the hope that I might be of some use during these troublous times." Strachan was sworn in as a member on 31 May 1815 and he was therefore in a perfect position to provide his old friend Francis Gore with a synopsis of his "many causes of joy" view of the war. Gore must have been pleased to find Strachan awaiting his arrival at York, for he had asked the ambitious Scotsman to leave Cornwall years before to be at his side. Along with "Bloody Assize" veterans William Drummer Powell and Chief Justice Thomas Scott, Strachan was selected as the third civilian member of the committee appointed to investigate war claims in 1815.[16]

The appointees met on 20 December 1815 and decided on the general principles that would guide the investigations. Only claims relating to losses caused by enemy forces, British troops and militiamen, and Indians serving with loyal forces were considered proper objects for compensation. Losses caused by negligence or from property placed at exceptional risk were considered unworthy of investigation; "trifling losses" and those sustained by "notoriously disaffected persons" were also to be dismissed without consideration. Finally, the members resolved that "as it is the object of Government to make the people content and happy the most liberal construction [will] be given to the different claims."[17]

The committee also reviewed submissions received during the summer of 1815 by five military boards assembled to hear claims for compensation. In August and September more than twelve hundred claimants submitted detailed accounts of their losses to officials at Amherstburgh, Fort George, York, Kingston, and Fort Wellington. For some of these claimants this was not their first appearance before a compensation board. In 1813 a group of militia officers had been appointed by Roger Sheaffe to examine outstanding claims against the commissariat. While preparing their final report, however, the officers were forced to flee the town of Niagara when the Americans invaded in 1813. The enemy burnt the home of James Crooks, a member of the board, and the only document from this first claims commission to escape the flames was the "scroll memoranda" of proceedings.[18]

With much of the preliminary work done for them by the military boards, the new claims commissioners were able to complete their investigation in a relatively short period of time. The job of sifting through hundreds of estimates based on various currencies was made easier when William Kemble was appointed secretary to the commission. A former assistant to George Prevost and later a paymaster for the Incorporated Militia, Kemble was described by Gore as a gentleman "conversant in accounts and business."[19] Kemble's talents sped up work considerably and by 1 May 1816 Gore sent a first draft of the war-claims commission report to Bathurst. It dealt with 2759 out of 2884 claims. The Upper Canadians had estimated their losses at over £390,152, but the commissioners certified only £256,815 as being worthy of compensation. In a letter to a friend in England, Strachan said that the amount owed to Upper Canadians was substantial, "but not so great as to frighten your Parliament from voting us remuneration."[20]

In comparison with the sums spent during the war, the amount of money required for compensation purposes was not large. The York garrison had disbursed more than £350,000 during the conflict, and additions to forts and the construction of naval vessels had consumed even greater sums. One of the warships built in the province, the *St Lawrence*, was said to require a crew of 1000. This flagship of the British fleet on Lake Ontario had cost £300,000 to build and the money spent on this vessel would have paid for all the claims certified by the committee. The *St Lawrence*, however, never saw action, and by 1816, when the report on war losses was sent to England, the ship had already begun to rot away in Kingston harbour.[21]

The efficient handling of the war claims and the expectation of speedy compensation set the minds of many colonists at ease. The declaration of peace had worried some merchants, but continued British spending and the likelihood that another quarter of a million pounds or more was on its way was cause for optimism. In 1816 a

A Brock token
Lossing, *Pictorial Field-Book of the War of 1812*

new copper token emerged which would become known as the "Brock half-penny." On one side of the coin were two cherubim holding a wreath over a monument inscribed with the date of the Battle of Queenston Heights and surrounded by the motto "Isaac Brock, the Hero of Upper Canada." On the obverse the inscription said, "Success to Commerce & Peace to the World."[22] Unfortunately, the merchant who commissioned the token would have had no way of knowing that both commercial success and internal peace would soon be in short supply.

There were several sources of potential discontent in the province and a number of them revolved around the militia. At its December 1812 meeting the Loyal and Patriotic Society promised "to reward Merit, excite Emulation, and commemorate glorious Exploits by bestowing medals or other honourary marks" on militiamen or soldiers "for extraordinary instances of personal courage or fidelity in defence of the province."[23] On 12 January 1813 the society set aside £100 sterling to purchase medals, but it was not until 2 December of the next year that the fifty "Upper Canada Preserved Medals" arrived in the province. A few weeks later a circular letter was addressed to officers commanding militia companies directing that they submit lists of individuals who were "considered fit recipients for such medals."[24]

Gordon Drummond submitted the names of seven individuals, including Robert Nichol, Colley Foster, Nathaniel Coffin, and Christopher Hagerman, all members of the general staff of the provincial militia. Four members of the Essex militia, three from Norfolk, and an equal number from the Fifth Lincoln Regiment, as well as six men from the Hastings and Dundas militia and ten from the Stormont and Glengarry regiments were also nominated by their officers. The Incorporated Militia nominees amounted to twenty-nine officers,

MEDAL OF GRATITUDE.

Upper Canada Preserved Medal
Lossing, *Pictorial Field-Book of the War of 1812*

nineteen sergeants, fourteen corporals, and fifty-two privates. Altogether, 147 militiamen were nominated for the fifty medals by May 1815 and that number was expected to rise, since reports from a number of officers, including those in charge of the other four Lincoln regiments from the Niagara District, had not yet been received.[25]

For some officers the task of selecting particularly deserving men was difficult. Lieutenant-Colonel Thomas Fraser of the Dundas militia eventually nominated five, but he felt that most of his subordinates were "equally deserving" of recognition. Many other nominees had also displayed extraordinary courage in the face of the enemy. Thomas Ross of the Glengarry militia, for instance, had been severely wounded during a raid on Ogdensburgh, but he simply "sat down upon a log & continued firing untill a Ball from the enemy made the lock of his musket useless." John Woolfe, another militiaman from the same regiment, also displayed bravery above and beyond the call of duty. During this attack on Ogdensburgh, Woolfe managed to overpower an enemy artillery position and single-handedly "continued firing his own and the captured gun alternately until the town of Ogdensburgh was taken." From the other end of the province came reports of the activities of two Essex militiamen, Thomas Martin and Michel Saumande, who risked their lives to spy on Hull's encampment at Sandwich "with a zeal rarely to be found."[26] One of the sergeants of the Incorporated Militia, Francis Lee, had kept fighting at Queenston Heights although wounded severely in the arm, and he "continued most active until disabled by a wound in his thigh."[27] The actions of these nominees were especially noteworthy considering that most other inhabitants managed to avoid militia service altogether. Major Samuel Wilmot of the York militia responded to the request for information by stating, "I do not know of one that comes under the above description."[28]

For members of the Loyal and Patriotic Society, the reports presented a number of problems. The first was that the number of nominees exceeded the quantity of medals on hand. That problem could be readily surmounted, and indeed later was, by the commissioning of an extra supply of medals. More troublesome was the vagueness of some of the reports. Lieutenant-Colonel Andrew Bradt of the Fifth Lincoln Regiment recommended Major Samuel Hatt, Lieutenant Robert Land, and Ensign Burnsey for their part in the battle of Lundy's Lane, but he said only that they "behaved with every mark of intrepidity."[29] The information provided on the activities of the Incorporated Militia nominees was even more limited. Some were simply listed as having been wounded in action, and for others no extra information was noted at all. This last problem could also have been surmounted by having the commanding officers forward further particulars, but there was another difficulty that proved to be the most intractable. No York residents were nominated for medals, which was hardly surprising, since most of the militiamen from the Home District had never seen action and they spent the better part of the war on parole. Some York citizens had been present at the fall of Detroit but, as no battle took place, the opportunity for noteworthy heroics never arose. Similarly, at the Battle of Queenston Heights, Brock suppposedly exclaimed, "Push on Brave York Volunteers," but few of the Home militiamen in attendance paid much heed. After one half-hearted charge, they fell back and awaited the arrival of reinforcements.[30] The next year, during the invasion of the capital, most of the Home District militia saw no action, and those close enough to feel the effects of the explosion of the magazine "melted away" soon after.

A two-man committee, consisting of John Beverley Robinson, a lieutenant in the Third York Regiment, and William Chewett, a lieutenant-colonel in the same unit, was appointed to deal with the question of who should receive the medals. In their report, Chewett and Robinson noted that most of the nominations appeared well-founded, but they said that Drummond's recommendations were too general and did not include specific instances of personal courage beyond stating that all the nominees had been "assiduous in their exertions." The same complaint was levelled against the recommendations for members of the Incorporated Militia, and the committee observed that the officer who submitted the names appeared "to consider a wound an unerring proof of courage or fidelity." They were concerned about that criterion, since it was believed that one of the privates nominated had lost his arm "accidentally, and not even while in action with the enemy." The list of Incorporated Milita nominees included almost every officer in the corps and eighty-six non-commissioned officers and privates. Chewett and Robinson remarked that there were "more persons recommended than there are medals to bestow."

Rather than seek additional information which might have allowed the society to whittle down the list of candidates, the committee decided to "revise the terms" on which medals were to be awarded. First, Robinson and Chewett dealt with the most glaring oversight – the lack of nominees from the Home District. They noted that Hull's invasion had "awed into inaction" the militamen from both the London and Western districts. "In this gloomy state of things, the Militia of the Home District were called forward," and the report said they "obeyed implicitly the summons" of General Brock. According to the committee this was a "prominent instance of the display of those principles which it is the wish of the Society to distinguish." After having expressed dissatisfaction with other reports that included too many names and too few particulars, the committee itself suggested adding a further 150 names, and these chiefly of men who had seen little or no action. Since Hull surrendered at Detroit without making a stand, most Home militiamen had spent their time marching about in cast-off redcoats trying to intimidate the enemy force by appearing to resemble battle-hardened regulars. Perhaps aware that this blatant attempt to award themselves with medals might provoke discontent, particularly among veterans of the Incorporated Militia who had survived real fighting at Lundy's Lane and Chippawa, Robinson and Chewett suggested that all members of that corps should receive "some mark" of the society to commemorate their services. It was not likely that those men would receive medals, however, since the committee also added the names of nine other nominees. Needless to say, General Brock was the first mentioned, but also included on the list was Henry Botswick for his actions in affecting "the suppression of a dangerous Rebellion in the district of London." Finally, Chewett and Robinson suggested that a medal might be given to the family of Tecumseh, "of which, the meaning might be explained to them."

Instead of easing the task of deciding who should receive medals, the members of the committee had complicated matters immensely. By their actions, all the members of the Incorporated Militia, some four hundred men, were now in line for awards. In addition to the nine other deserving candidates, however, the committee had nominated all the Home militiamen who went to Detroit, about 150 men, including Robinson and Chewett. The report was adopted by the unanimous vote of the society and £750 sterling was voted to purchase an additional 562 medals. The original 50 silver medals were to be given to non-commissioned officers, and 500 more of a similar but smaller design were ordered for privates. A further fifty gold medals for general and field officers was also commissioned, and twelve large gold pieces, presumably for Brock and other prominent heroes, were ordered as well. On 26 August 1815 John Beverley Robinson was given the £750 sterling because he was soon to leave the province for England, where he intended to pursue his law studies at the Inns of Court.[31]

As the medals were being struck in England, other issues arising out of the war continued to occupy Gore's attention. During the summer of 1815 the Colonial Office authorized the granting of land to Incoporated Militia veterans who had been promised the awards for enlisting. The maximum grant allowable, however, was only fifty acres, and Gore warned the home authorities that this amount was considered an insult. No applications were made for the lands since, prior to the war, ordinary settlers had received two hundred acres, and Gore reported that the latest offer placed the services of the militiamen in a light "which cannot be flattering." He suggested minimum grants of one hundred acres to privates and two hundred acres to officers.[32]

Rumours of dissatisfaction over backpay owed militiamen also reached Gore, who directed that a report be prepared so he could "form a correct judgement of the complaints so universally prevailing on that head." In addition, officers from the Incorporated Militia were also demanding to be placed on half-pay in the same manner as senior members of the Lower Canadian Voltigeurs had been. The Incorporated Militia officers argued that they were not permitted to leave the service and that they were selected because they were prominent men who could influence others to join the regiment through the promise of "a small Bounty and [by] large Personal Expenditure."[33] Gore forwarded the memorial with a favourable recommendation, since he thought it unfair that individuals who were "connected with all that is Loyal and Influential in this Colony" should receive less than their counterparts to the east.[34]

Gore's quick actions on the war claims and his favourable handling of militia grievances earned him the respect of assemblymen such as Robert Nichol. During the fourth session of the sixth parliament in early 1815, Nichol emerged as a leader in the House and it was he who proposed that the province grant £1000 for the erection of a monument in memory of Isaac Brock. At the same session, Nichol also helped draft the joint address dealing with the claims of the war sufferers. The next year, during the fifth and final session of the sixth parliament, Nichol again emerged as a force to be reckoned with. While the war-claims commission was completing its investigation, the Assembly met on 6 February 1816. Gore found the proceedings cordial enough, but there was also a hint of some of the discontent that would rock Upper Canadian politics for more than two decades to come. Dissatisfied with what they rightly perceived to be a general indifference to colonial affairs, the assemblymen granted the sum of £500 to pay for the appointment of a provincial agent. This civil servant was to reside in England and was expected to lobby for greater attention to provincial affairs. Gore agreed to the measure since he believed that he "could direct its course to be harmless." His solution was to appoint William Halton, his private secretary, to the post. Gore described him as a "discreet and honourable man," well-qualified to "conciliate and protect the Colonial Intercourse from all Embarassment." Halton, who was in failing health, had already requested to be sent home.[35]

In private meetings, Nichol pressed his case for receiving one of the gold medals recently issued by the British army. Only officers who had taken part in three events – the capture of Detroit and the battles of Chateauguay and Crysler's farm – were eligible for these awards. Nichol, who had served as quartermaster-general of the militia throughout the war and who had supervised the supply situation at Detroit, felt entitled to the award.[36] His anger at being passed over would have been undoubtedly sharpened had he known that John Beverley Robinson would acquire a "Fort Detroit" clasp for his war service. Robinson would later reminisce that his "short experience of soldiering was uncommonly lucky," since he received both a medal and a share of the Detroit prize money amounting to over £90. Gore sympathized with Nichol's position and he recommended that this "painful" oversight be rectified as soon as possible through a series of awards to all meritorious militiamen.[37]

Gore's willingness to address the concerns of Nichol and other veterans earned him much goodwill among that segment of the population. His readiness to reinforce the myth that Upper Canadians had been primarily responsible for the defence of the colony also contributed to his popularity. In every speech he would praise those inhabitants who had been "employed with so much credit and effect during the war."[38] Optimistic that the war claimants would soon be paid, and that outstanding issues such as land grants and backpay would be resolved quickly, the Assembly ended its 1816 session by voting Gore £3000 for the purchase of silver plate.[39] This act, which would later be derided as the "Spoon Bill," refected the confidence of the assemblymen in Upper Canada's future and was meant to recognize Gore's part in fostering the atmosphere of optimism. On 26 March 1816 the speaker of the Assembly, Allan McLean, joined with his counterpart from the upper house, William Powell, in presenting the money "as a demonstration of our gratitude."[40]

Yet over the next few months there were increasing signs that the hopes of the assemblymen would remain unfulfilled. Prior to 1812 the Upper Canadian economy had relied on four sources for its major infusions of capital: profits on exports, import duties, British government spending, and funds brought in by immigrants. The two least important of these sources were the money raised through exports of flour and other staple products and the money collected in Lower Canada on imports destined for the upper province.[41] The war years, however, brought disruption to the regular rhythms of agricultural life and, between 1812 and 1815, any surplus production was immediately consumed by the military forces stationed in the colony. The cessation of hostilities brought an end to militia service but, as Isaac Wilson noted, some men chose to pursue other occupations rather than return to their neglected farms. For quite a few settlers, of course, that decision may have been forced on them since many homesteads no longer existed. For these and other reasons, Upper Canada would not begin large-scale exports of produce until the 1820s. At the same time, the province had not received its proper share of duties on goods arriving in Lower Canada from 1812 to 1815.[42] The combination of a loss of export capabilities and a reduction of import revenues meant that the colony was increasingly dependent on British spending. For that reason, the steady decline in military expenditures from 1815 onward would prove almost catastrophic for the colony.

The gradual completion of public works during 1816, together with massive troop withdrawals, brought about a rapid dimunition in government spending. In January 1815 the York garrison disbursed more than £53,747 to merchants, suppliers, and workmen in the area. Over the next five months the military's expenditures declined substantially but, on average, the garrison was still spending more than £20,000 a month in the capital. Two years later, however, monthly expenditures averaged under £5000, or less than one-tenth of what was spent in January 1815.[43] The large military establishment at Kingston was also reduced after the war. During the conflict the military population at Kingston had risen from 100 men to some 5000 soldiers and sailors, and the civilian population had doubled to more than 2000.[44] The shipyard employed as many as 1200 labourers, and it was reported that the naval establishment alone spent £47,327 in 1814.[45] One authority has estimated that, at the mid-point of the war, disbursements from the military chest in Kingston amounted to £1000 a day. With the termination of hostilities, however, the garrison was reduced and, by 1817, there were fewer than one thousand troops in the town. Naturally, the level of spending declined accordingly and the garrison disbursed only about £6000 a year from then on, outside of military pay and money devoted to fortifications.[46] Demobilization meant that the size of the town's wartime population would not be equalled again until the 1840s, and the end of the fighting inevitably led to tougher economic times.[47] In comparison with some of their counterparts in western Upper Canada, however, many residents of Kingston also had much for which to be thankful. Money pried from the military during the war was later reinvested in stone mansions for the Cartwright, Macaulay, and Markland families, and a postwar building boom continued in Kingston until at least 1817.[48]

Reduced military spending was favoured by British authorities who found themselves saddled with an unprecedented national debt. In 1815 Britain owed more than £900 million sterling to creditors, and the interest and charges on this debt constituted about one-third of the total annual government revenue. Even after embarking on a program of retrenchment, the national debt continued to consume a huge proportion of government expenditures. By 1818, two-thirds of all revenues were directed towards servicing these obligations.[49] Not surprisingly, the near-bankrupt position of the imperial treasury had a direct impact on colonial affairs. Without the resources to meet its own needs, the British parliament directed scant attention towards Upper Canadian demands. Moreover, once the fighting was over, British officials naturally considered the conflict done with, and the concerns of the colonists appeared to merit little attention. That was especially so since some members of the home government were under the impression that all claims for damages and for services rendered to the British military had been discharged before the troops returned to England.[50] Thus, representatives of the crown in Upper Canada faced incessant demands for reimbursement, but their appeals on behalf of those claimants were repeatedly ignored. In April 1817, for instance, Gore was forced to remind British officials once again that the provincial militia was still clamouring for back pay which amounted to at least £28,784. Yet Gore felt that even that sum would not placate all the veterans, since Lower Canadian militiamen had been offered exactly the same pay as regular soldiers. He therefore suggested that Upper Canadians receive an equivalent amount of money in order to avoid "a Sense of Injustice" that would only be aggravated "by a Jealousy of distinction between them and their fellow subjects in the Lower Province."[51]

Of much greater importance than unpaid militia salaries were the direct effects of nearly three years of fighting and wartime losses on the deepening economic malaise. For example, an examination of submissions made to the 1823–26 committee of revision reveals that a staggering number of farm animals were consumed or taken during the conflict without compensation. Of the 2055 claims examined, information on what was lost was provided in 1650 cases. The number of horses, cattle, sheep, and hogs, and an estimate of their value are presented in table 8. If we assume that the 405 claims for which information was not recorded included a proportionate share of livestock, the figures rise appreciably. The projected losses amount to 1626 horses, 1297 cattle, 2524 sheep, and 4184 hogs worth, in total, at least £41,000.[52] All these animals were stolen, or impressed without payment, and most were taken from farmers in the Niagara District and areas to the west. Having been hard hit by other property damage, many of those settlers were forced to borrow money to replenish their stock after the war. At first, few would have worried about those loans, since they expected to be repaid any day for the losses they had suffered. As time went on, however, some colonists found they could not escape from the cycle of debt caused by wartime depredations. For a man such as Robert Nichol, who was hounded by creditors until the day he died, the war was blamed for "the ruin of his family and the annihilation of his hopes and prospects."[53]

Already seriously affected by the retrenchment campaign and by a decline of revenue-producing trade, the colonial economy was further undermined when Upper Canadians sought to replace their losses from sources outside the province. In 1815 Isaac Wilson noted that instead of exporting pork and flour, the colony was receiving shipments from Ireland and Lower Canada. Prices for livestock in the province remained high – cows were selling for more than £12 a head and oxen for as much as £45 – while on the American side of the border provisions of all kinds were said to be "plentiful and cheap." One of Wilson's associates "had been over and brought in a quantity of flour and 100 fat sheep and was gone again," but those not fortunate enough to have prospered by the war had to rely on credit from merchants to begin again.[54] The next year the Upper

Table 8
Value of Livestock Lost

Livestock Type	Number Claimed	Average Cost (£)	Total Value (£)
Horses	1,306	15	19,590
Cattle	1,042	5	5,210
Sheep	2,027	1	2,027
Hogs	3,361	2	6,722
Total	7,736		£33,549

Source: NA, RG 19, E5 (a), Board of Claims

Canadian wheat crop was very poor and the province was again forced to spend money to import flour. One York resident noted in July 1817 that "altho the Farmers expect a very abundant harvest this Season" it would "hardly make up for the deficiency in the article of cash."[55] In January 1818 William Crooks of Grimsby noted that the number of farm animals in the country had only barely reached prewar levels. Crooks said that the conflict had "drained the country of horses, horned cattle, and sheep," and prices for livestock had "continued high" because of the scarcity.[56] Later that year the *Niagara Gleaner* reported that little livestock had come to market over the summer, and it glumly noted that the local farmers "had not got into a sufficient stock of cattle and hogs since the destruction that was made during the late war."[57] It appears that by this point the colony had already been drained of its hard-earned specie and any money accumulated during the conflict had been sent into the pockets of external suppliers. Despite the apparent prosperity of the war years, therefore, the province actually progressed very little after 1812.

The disruptions to the colony's nascent export trade and the decline in military spending could have been compensated for by the fourth, and most important, source of capital in the prewar period. During the conflict immigration had come to a complete halt and, for the first time since the 1780s, the population of the province had actually declined. With the end of the fighting in 1815, many inhabitants assumed that the lucrative business of land and implement sales to settlers from the United States would be renewed immediately. In this expectation, as in many others, the colonists were to be sorely disappointed. Plans to prevent further immigration from south of the border had been made while the war was still raging. In 1814 Gordon Drummond had supported Bathurst's proposal to introduce Scottish settlers into the colony, since he thought they would serve as "counterpoise to that ill-disposed and disaffected part of the population" which had "crept from time to time" into the province.[58] In this view Drummond was supported by John Strachan, and the priest advised that no Americans should be allowed in at all. Even though as late as 1812 Strachan had considered going to the United States, he now suggested that other British subjects who had first settled in the republic should only be admitted with "great caution." Strachan was adamant that no Quakers or Tunkers be allowed in because they had hurt the war effort by refusing to fight and by "holding back their produce or selling it at exhorbitant prices – refusing to transport stores – crying down the Government paper issue." Those already in the country should be allowed to stay, but Strachan warned that the population was "too small to allow a large proportion to be non-combatants."[59] He spoke from experience, of course, since he and most of the rest of the "parcel of Quakers" in the colony had failed to shoulder a gun during the contest.

On the advice of Drummond and Strachan, and after months of reading reports of rampant disaffection, the British authorities moved to reduce American immigration only days after the Treaty of Ghent was signed. On 10 January 1815 Bathurst ordered Drummond to withhold land grants to all American immigrants.[60] Even arrivals rich enough to buy land soon found themselves excluded from the province. After Gore arrived in the colony the justices of the peace were directed to report on "the Character of Aliens coming from the u.s. or elsewhere" and not to administer the oath of allegiance without special permission.[61] While this move was perhaps pleasing to Strachan, Gore reported that it proved "particularly offensive to certain Land Speculators who had become possessed of vast tracts of land." The new lieutenant-governor went on to report that one of the landowners who resented the change in rules was William Dickson, a cousin to the Hamilton brothers and Robert Nichol.[62] Dickson was a justice of the peace and a legislative councillor who had lost an estimated £3668 in property during the war. After the peace treaty, Dickson counted on land sales to revive his fortunes, since he had recently purchased 94,000 acres of Indian lands on the Grand River. He had spent £4000 on opening roads and building mills and had settled forty families on the tract by the time Gore arrived in the colony. With his back to the wall, Dickson felt he had no choice but to ignore the new regulations, and he was dismissed from the magistracy as a result.[63] The appointment of new justices of the peace who were willing to follow orders did not eliminate the controversy over American immigration. Large landowners such as Robert Nichol, Thomas Clark, and William Dickson considered the decision to exclude all settlers from the United States to be impractical and, as a result, questions about new policies relating to the oath of allegiance and immigration would bedevil the province for more than a decade.

By 1817, therefore, the province was on the verge of an economic crisis, while in the neighbouring United States a postwar boom that was destined to last another two years was still underway. For Upper Canadians this prosperity must have appeared particularly galling since they could see with their own eyes that certain measures contributed to economic growth. The American boom was fuelled by massive immigration and speculation in land, by government-spending on national roads and canals, and by an abundance of bank notes, easy credit, and even by restitution for war damages.[64] North of the border the administration had curbed immigration, and this had caused the value of land to plummet. The government had also scaled-down or cancelled most public works, and the army bills were no longer in widespread circulation. The currency had last been issued in December 1815 and the interest-earning power of the notes ceased that same month. The next year commissary officials announced they would no longer redeem the notes in Upper Canada, and the province was gradually drained of its major supply of currency.[65] At the same time, Upper Canadians enviously observed their former enemies in New York receiving compensation payments from Washington for damages caused by British forces.[66] Even residents of eastern districts who had been spared the worst effects of the war soon discovered that the impact of this "made in Upper Canada" recession could not be avoided. By 1817 the increasing numbers of paupers had prompted the creation of the "Kingston Compassionate Society" and the York "Friends of Strangers Society." From all reports, both were soon doing a brisk business providing poverty-stricken pioneers and new unemployed arrivals with outdoor relief.[67]

Despite the potential for strife, expressions of discontent were, at first, somewhat muted. When the newly elected seventh parliament first met for its introductory session on 4 February 1817, for example, little was said about the declining state of affairs in the colony. It may have been that members expected the economy to improve as spring approached, and at least some assemblymen were distracted by personal disputes. The session began on an acrimonious note after James Durand had taken his seat as the representative for the riding of Wentworth. During his election campaign, Durand had reminded the electors how "the Military domineered over the community" around Burlington Heights at the end of the war. While the suspension of Habeas Corpus had served to "close the lips" of most assemblymen, Durand had dared to speak out against the abuses that were taking place at that time. He asked the electors to remember John Vincent's threat to burn the homes of reluctant militiamen, and he pointed to the conduct of Colonel James of the Thirty-Seventh Regiment "who placed military guards on all the various roads, with orders to stop all sleighs having provisions on board and in consequence the farmers' grists and the travellers' bags of oats were equally precipitated into the military depots, though perhaps a large hungry family were waiting the good man's return from the mill to be fed." Durand had been involved in the movement to censure de Rottenburgh for his declaration of martial law in 1813, but the next year his attempts to do the same with Drummond's measure met with less success. Tempted by "good contracts" for supplying the military or afraid they might be imprisoned for sedition, no other representatives would join Durand. Warned by a fellow representive, John Willson, "that times were too dangerous for a man to open his mouth," Durand continued his attacks against the "versatile chameleons of corruption" after peace had been declared.[68]

Durand's election speech was printed in the *Niagara Spectator* and came to the attention of the new Assembly, where several re-elected "chameleons" had taken their seats. Robert Nichol branded the speech a "scandalous and seditious libel," likely because Durand had said that commissariat officers had made use of martial law "to tread down the people."[69] On 4 March 1817 Nichol led a successful campaign to have Durand jailed, but the latter fled York before the arrest warrant was issued. Meanwhile, the House promptly voted to have him expelled from his seat. Durand's constituents took up a crusade on his behalf and sixty of them sent a petition to the colonial newspapers attesting to his "Loyalty and uniform tenor" of conduct.[70]

Once the members had ceased squabbling among themselves they turned their attention towards legislative business. Chief among the concerns facing the representatives was the postwar recession. The Assembly finally took the unusual step of forming itself "into a committee of the whole to take into consideration the present state of the province." On 3 April 1817 the members sat down to discuss four issues: the exclusion of American settlers, the continuance of the crown and clergy reserve system, the granting of land to members of the flank companies and the Incoporated Militia, and the state of the post office. On Saturday, 5 April 1817, eleven resolutions were adopted, the first eight of which concerned the policy of restricting American immigration. The members asked that the measure be rescinded because "many respectable and valuable settlers have been prevented from emigrating to this province."[71] The passage of that resolution calls into question the assertion sometimes made by

historians that widespread anti-Americanism was created and reinforced by the War of 1812. It is true some colonists despised Americans, but the level of anti-American sentiment in postwar Upper
Canada has been exaggerated. A number of researchers have relied
solely on the writings of John Strachan or John Beverley Robinson
for information on postwar colonial attitudes, but their views were
not typical.[72] Others have even mistakenly assumed that all Upper
Canadians, inflamed with a renewed sense of anti-Americanism,
favoured a ban on further immigration.[73] The movement to halt
arrivals from the United States, however, was imposed on the province by outside authorities and, when given an opportunity, the
majority of elected representatives signified their decided opposition
to the measure.

To understand why colonists would remain in favour of American
immigration, one should consider the nature of the war that had just
been fought. Unlike Strachan and Gore, most of the men who voted
in favour of the Assembly resolutions had actually served for
extended periods during the conflict and some had suffered extensive material losses. In 1816 the *Niagara Spectator* claimed that nineteen out of twenty-five assemblymen in the sixth parliament had
been members of the militia, and the proportion appears to have
risen to twenty-two of twenty-five in the next parliament. Several
members of both legislatures had "their houses and property burnt"
during the war and, while the editor failed to mention who was
responsible for those damages, one can determine that from the
claims submitted in 1823–6.[74] It has already been shown that about
50 per cent of all plundering incidents involved British forces, and
an investigation of the twelve submissions made by members of the
seventh parliament reveals a similar pattern. Of the ten claims that
mentioned responsibility for damage, nine blamed at least part of
the destruction on British troops or native warriors and only one,
Robert Nichol's submission, accused enemy forces alone.[75] Veterans
in the Assembly, like many Upper Canadians, may have evinced little
anti-Americanism because it had actually been their allies who had
robbed them of much of their hard-earned property.

Support for American immigration was also a product of the
Upper Canadian sense of practicality, and Nichol provides a perfect
example of that pragmatism. While he could have harboured real
anger over the devastation wrought by the invaders, and might have
been expected to "hate the Yankees, as the Devil," this does not
appear to have been the case.[76] Like most other Upper Canadians,
Nichol knew that thousands of knowledgeable farmers, who had
taken no part in the fighting, were located just south of the border.

As one prewar observer noted, American pioneers were "endowed with a spirit for adventure, activity, industry, and perseverance, rarely to be equalled." Since the United States remained the only source of newcomers with those attributes, as well as "money and stock," even men wounded or taken prisoner by enemy forces still favoured the resolutions.[77] During the conflict, Mahlon Burwell had been seized by a party of American marauders and, after "being stripped almost naked was placed upon a horse with his face towards the tail and carried away prisoner." Yet he and William McCormick, who was wounded and taken prisoner by the enemy at Frenchtown, also voted to increase American immigration.[78]

Whatever their true feelings about their former enemies, these assemblymen certainly felt the best interests of the province were being neglected, and the last three resolutions called for the sale of crown and clergy reserves. The respresentatives announced that the present policy of leasing had proved unworkable and they admitted that the lands were considered "insurmountable obstacles to the forming of well-connected settlements." The land set aside for the maintenance of the Protestant clergy came in for special abuse and was described as "an appropriation beyond all precedent lavish," which should be reduced before sales commenced. Although the members were discussing several of the key provisions of the Constitutional Act of 1791, they did not disagree with the basic premise of that legislation. In fact, they were merely asking for the better administration of the resources that had been granted.[79]

Alarmed by the tone of the proceedings, Gore immediately prorogued the legislature the next morning before "such dangerous Resolutions ... should be promulgated to the Public through the medium of the Press." In a letter to his superiors, Gore blamed Dickson for having urged Nichol to begin the proceedings. Gore thought Dickson's actions could easily be explained because of his status as a speculator, but he was less sure about Nichol's motives since "until this session he has led the loyal and rational part of the Assembly." Gore believed that the Scottish merchant was probably "indignant at some disappointment of a medal" and may have been angered by the lieutenant-governor's refusal to provide any "special interference in his favour on the subject of his claim" for war losses.[80] Gore failed to appreciate the real distress that Nichol was in, and it may have been because he was distracted by the support the resolutions had received. Among those who voted in favour of what was the equivalent of a vote of non-confidence in the administration were such prominent Loyalists as Mahlon Burwell, John Cameron, Jonas Jones, and Peter Robinson.[81]

The drafting of the resolutions was a clear indication that the two-year honeymoon in postwar colonial politics had come to an end. For the first time, a majority of elected representatives had declared that the executive was mishandling the affairs of the colony, and the members had gone so far as to offer advice on how the province might be better administered. A shocked John Strachan wrote to Nichol expressing a hope that tales of unprecedented developments in the Assembly were only the "fabrications of your enemies." Strachan pointed to the "absurdity" of the resolutions dealing with the reserves and he warned against censuring Gore for proroguing the House, because the lieutenant-governor had every right to do so.[82] The rupture between these two old friends shows that the work of the 1817 Assembly committee had actually created additional grievances in the province. Some representatives were very angry that their inquiry had been cut short, and it seems that Gore was equally upset over their actions. Apparently Sir John Sherbrooke, the commander of the forces at Quebec City, had requested that Gore forward a list of those claimants still waiting for payment for goods requisitioned by the British army during the war. The 1815–16 commission had revealed that 277 Upper Canadians were owed more than £9590 for such claims, and Sherbrooke proposed to settle the account from the colonial military chest. Angered by the activities of the Assembly, and advised to withhold payment by one of his executive councillors, Gore prevented any payments from being made. According to William Kemble, the commission accountant, "Strachan worked Mr. G. up to a rage by presuading him that his dignity was insulted, & the Sufferers [were] deprived of their relief." Kemble admitted that this knowledge was not something he would wish Gore's enemies to know, but he could only regret that the lieutenant-governor "should have allowed his violent temper to hearken to such unchristianlike advice."[83]

Perhaps Gore and Strachan would have been more sympathetic had they faced war-related hardships common to so many other Upper Canadians. The lieutenant-governor, for example, had managed to be in England for all the fighting, although his personal property was looted by American invaders during the April 1813 occupation of York. Immediately after his return to the province, however, Gore received a warrant for £1600 to replace the lost goods and in 1816 he sought another £379 to pay the shipping charges on new items brought from Britain.[84] At the same time, while the fortunes of many of his fellow subjects continued to decline, John Strachan's career soared to new heights. Worried that the recent Assembly resolutions would lead to further attacks on clergy reserves,

Strachan solicited a position on the Legislative Council where he could influence government policy. In a letter to Gore on 22 May 1817, he claimed that it was his "duty to offer [his] services" although he also allowed that his "motives [were] not altogether disinterested."[85] Strachan was eager to receive Gore's recommendation since the latter had announced he would soon be sailing for England to defend himself against a libel suit brought by Robert Thorpe. On his departure, Strachan and other prominent York citizens, including William Powell and D'Arcy Boulton, presented an address thanking Gore for being a "friend and protector of this province."[86] Before the silver plate tucked away in his luggage had time to tarnish, however, Gore had reason to question the sincerity of at least one of those men. Two years later, having lost his case with Thorpe, Gore informed Powell that the "Archdeacon of York does not write to me now – I am in disgrace – or rather I am no longer Lt. Governor of Upper Canada."[87]

Within a few days of Gore's departure, Robert Nichol also set sail for England to deal directly with his claim for compensation. Although the Treasury had received the report of the 1815–16 commission on 22 July 1816, no promise of full payment had yet been made.[88] Since that time the prince regent had told officials at the Colonial Office that the proceeds from sales of estates confiscated from traitors could be applied for compensation purposes, but no one who was well-acquainted with the province seriously believed that this measure would raise a significant amount of money. William Halton had visited the office of the secretary of state but was directed to see Lord Bathurst at the Colonial Office who, in turn, suggested he discuss matters with Treasury officials. Already nearly lame from repeated attacks of gout, Halton was worn out by the process. Finally, on 9 July 1817, he was told by employees at the Treasury that they were only going to recommend that the forfeited estates be used to pay the claimants.[89]

That news so angered Nichol that he requested a personal meeting with Bathurst in order to explain why even the prospect of "partial indemnification from that source" was completely "illusory." Nichol also believed that his claims merited more particular attention and he told Bathurst that the "sufferers generally … My Lord, have a strong claim on the generosity of the Nation, *Mine* is on its *justice*." Nichol's entreaties were given a sympathetic reception but he made little headway with his claim. Six months later he informed Bathurst that he had not abandoned his lucrative civilian career for a position in the militia because of any desire for profit or reward: "No my Lord, I was activated by far Nobler motives, for as to emolument that was to be obtained, as it was by hundreds of my fellow subjects in the Province with more ease and less work by attending to my private affairs at home."[90] Unfortunately, noble sentiments were about all Nichol had left, and he was forced to sail for home without the money he had hoped to get.

Another native of Scotland, Robert Gourlay, had already embarked for Upper Canada by the time Nichol had met with Bathurst. Although Gourlay was destined to spend only a short time in the province, he would manage to influence the character of Upper Canadian politics in an unprecedented and indelible manner. At forty years of age he left his home in Fifeshire to view a tract of land in Upper Canada that belonged to his wife, née Jean Henderson. She was Robert Hamilton's niece and, through his marriage, Gourlay was connected to some of the most prominent men in the province, including William Dickson and Thomas Clark. A cantankerous individual, Gourlay was constantly casting about for projects to administer and for perceived grievances to redress. Even before he arrived in the province he had decided to write a book about his journey by collecting answers to a series of questions about the colony. He entered Upper Canada in June 1817 and arrived at Thomas Clark's home at Queenston in mid July. While there Gourlay was treated to lengthy lectures about the grievances of his relatives; he would later say that "Councillor Dickson was loudest in these complaints."[91]

What most annoyed Gourlay's relatives was that few newcomers were arriving in the province and there were no customers for the large tracts of land owned by speculators. Between 1794 and 1811 the provincial population had more than doubled, but during the war the province appears to have lost about one-sixth of its inhabitants through deaths and emigration. Only a large influx of newcomers could have immediately replaced those losses. At first, the resumption of peace brought a renewed flow of Americans, and the population increased more than 20 per cent between March 1814 and June 1817. As the restrictions against American immigration were applied more stringently, the growth rate slowed and eventually stalled and the population total for 1818 was actually lower than in 1817.[92] Many of the immigrants who did arrive were in no position to buy land. In 1817, for example, a number of arrivals from the United Kingdom required charitable donations to make it through the winter.[93] Figure 6 shows population growth for the period 1809–21 and it indicates why many thoughtful observers felt that the province was being administered poorly. It also offers a projection of what the population could have been if the prewar growth rate

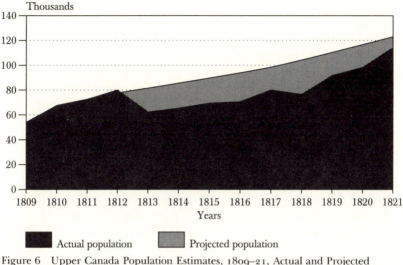

Figure 6   Upper Canada Population Estimates, 1809–21, Actual and Projected
Population
Source: NA, RG9, Militia Returns 1809–21; NA, RG5, B26, Upper Canada Returns of Population
and Assessment

from 1794 to 1811 had been maintained. At that pace, the population in 1818 would have been about 104,500 instead of 76,688.

Gourlay made good use of the fears over the province's slow rate
of growth when he published an address, "To the Resident Landowners of Upper Canada" in the York *Gazette* of 30 October 1817.
He asked that township meetings be held in order that suitable
answers could be given to a series of questions appended to the
address. Gourlay intended to gather the results into a statistical
account that, instead of appealing to paupers, would "tempt able
adventurers from home." An increased flow of settlers from Europe
would revive the failing colonial economy and might even make the
exclusion of American farmers a matter "of small importance."[94] The
questions themselves appeared harmless enough: Gourlay simply
requested that the respondents provide the number of churches,
stores, taverns, and medical practitioners in each township, as well as
offer information about soils and agricultural practices. The thirty-
first query, which would soon land Gourlay and his supporters in a
great deal of trouble, asked: "What, in your opinion, retards the
improvement of your township in particular, or the province in general; and what would most contribute to the same?"[95] When Gourlay
first proposed issuing the address he approached the members of

the government at York for their approval. Only Strachan was opposed to the questionnaire; it was said that he saw within it a "wicked tendency," but he was overruled by the other councillors.[96] No doubt, after the legislative resolutions of April, Strachan was well aware that the elimination of the clergy reserves would rank high as an answer to query thirty-one.

Gourlay at first ignored Strachan and his protests, but he underestimated the intelligence and influence of his enemy. At one point he contemptuously dismissed Strachan as "a lying little fool of a renegade Presbyterian," a characterization that hit the mark except the priest was no fool.[97] Indeed, Gourlay found that his time was increasingly spent defending the very concept of township meetings. In a letter to the *Niagara Spectator* of 8 January 1818, he argued that his plans were designed only to benefit Upper Canada, and he singled out Strachan as one of those men "who will run in the face of common sense and discretion to gratify their envy and their spleen." Yet as the township reports began to trickle in, Strachan's influence made itself apparent. From the Niagara, Gore, London, and Western districts, Gourlay received fifty-five reports from sixty-three townships; but no meeting was held at York and only eleven townships east of Gore dared to submit answers to the questionnaires.[98]

Gourlay blamed the poor response from the east on Strachan's "unrighteous" campaign against him, but a closer examination of those involved in the township meetings suggests that more was at work than clerical influence.[99] In the Western District, twenty of twenty-five individuals who signed their names to the township reports, or 80 per cent of the respondents, were listed as war sufferers by the 1823–6 committee appointed to investigate damages. The proportions fell somewhat as one went east, but over 13 per cent of respondents from the London District, more than 49 per cent of the Gore signatories, and over 36 per cent of the Niagara respondents also had submitted claims to the final commission. In total, more than 33 per cent of the 261 signatories from the four western districts appear to have been war sufferers. To the east, where damages were slight and where postwar grievances were less evident, only two of the ninety respondents, just over 2 per cent of the total, had submitted claims. Altogether, the ninety claimants who were listed on the township reports had estimated their losses to be £55,723, or an average claim of more than £619. That amount was about three times the size of the average submission examined by the 1823–6 war-claims commission.[100]

Although only a minority of his supporters were war sufferers, Gourlay considered them a very important part of his constituency.

They often took the lead in forming local organizations and they included magistrates and militia officers who could not be stigmatized as disloyal radicals. In February 1818, while Gourlay was preparing his second address to the people of Upper Canada, news reached the colony that the prince regent was offering only the proceeds from the sale of confiscated estates to indemnify the thousands of claimants. Gourlay excused the regent's actions by saying they were the product of ignorance fostered by an inept system of colonial management. "Were he apprized of the truth," Gourlay claimed, "the public property of the province might not only defray every claim, but yield to England a handsome revenue."[101] Here for the first time was the suggestion that the sale of public lands, such as crown and clergy reserves, might serve to pay war sufferers. If any doubts lingered in Strachan's mind about the dangers of Gourlay's activities, they must have been immediately swept aside by this article.

In 1819, writing under his brother's name, Strachan would deride Gourlay's actions and claim he had only tried to address two grievances: war losses and militia land grants. Strachan said that both issues were being dealt with by the ministry at that time and he went on to declare that "the people of Upper Canada lost nothing by the war compared to their fellow subjects in Great Britain." Strachan also deliberately lied about the township reports, saying that all of them ended with a demand for the payment of war losses, even those "from places in the interior, where the war never reached."[102] But only the representatives from Wellington Square in the Gore District actually rated losses by the conflict as a serious impediment to the prosperity of their township. About three-quarters of the signatories from all the townships were not war claimants, and unpaid damages stood fourteenth on the list of twenty-three factors that were said to be retarding economic prosperity. Yet Gourlay paid an inordinate amount of attention to the war claims because they offered a key to solving a great number of the province's problems. The lands held by non-residents were mentioned in twenty-four township reports as a significant grievance. Crown and clergy reserves were cited in another nineteen, and a lack of immigrants was rated as an important factor in retarding economic growth in fourteen township reports. Yet, if the lands lying idle were sold to pay war damages, all of these grievances could be eliminated. The sufferers would be compensated, obstacles between settlements would be removed, and a large influx of newcomers would gain access to fertile lands.[103]

While Gourlay was tabulating the figures from his township reports, the seventh provincial Assembly met for its second session at York. These proceedings proved no less tumultuous than the last. Jonas Jones, the member for Grenville, submitted a claim for payment for the time he had served as a member of a commission dealing with the division of import duties gathered by Lower Canadian authorities. The administrator in Gore's absence, Samuel Smith, complied with the Assembly's request for payment, but members of the upper council objected saying that the Assembly could only authorize payments for ordinary expenses of the House. What had started out as a simple request for reimbursement eventually turned into a vexing constitutional question over who controlled the colony's finances. With public business again at a standstill, Smith prorogued the session on 1 April 1818. He later defended that action by pointing out "how uncertain the peace of the colony must be" if such "pretences of privilege" could lead to protracted disputes.[104]

Gourlay seized the opportunity offered by the second dismissal of the Assembly in as many years. In his third address to the inhabitants of Upper Canada he declared that the fault did not rest with the elected representatives but with "the *system* which blasts every hope of good," and the situation would continue that way "till the system is overturned." Gourlay called for a second round of township meetings to select representatives who would meet at a convention. At this gathering, Gourlay proposed that a petition be drafted which would be presented directly to the prince regent. Gourlay cautioned that every "eye should be resolutely bent on the one thing needful – a radical change in the system of Government of Upper Canada." If this plan was followed, he promised that "every just claim may be paid by next Christmas," and the colony would become the "most flourishing and secure spot" on the globe.[105]

For some, of course, things were fine as they were, and Samuel Smith was approached by Strachan and others who were alarmed at the possibility of a convention. All were convinced that the American Revolution had grown out of similar meetings and they were determined to prevent any assembly that might lead to "radical change." Persuaded by these men that to ignore the proceedings would only "add fuel to the flames," Smith ordered Attorney-General John Beverley Robinson to follow Gourlay's actions closely and to "seize the first proper occasion to check by criminal prosecution the very threatening career now entered upon." Strachan would later take full credit for this decision, informing Bathurst that "had I passively followed up the system of permitting the Convention to proceed, there is no saying where it would have it would have ended." As it turned out, however, it was Gourlay's relatives who actually put an end to his career in Upper Canada. The idea that Strachan had rid the colony of Gourlay was much like the fable that he had saved York from the torches of the American invaders. Strachan was often the hero of his own tales, and most grew taller in the telling as the years passed.[106]

Township meetings were organized immediately in the Niagara region under the guidance of men such as Robert Hamilton. Following these meetings, a preliminary convention of Niagara delegates was held on 4 May 1818 in St Catharines. Fifteen prominent citizens, several of whom were local magistrates, assisted Gourlay in the preparation of a petition. Among those present were three justices of the peace – William Hamilton Merritt, John Clark, and George Keefer – as well as a number of senior militia officers including Robert Hamilton, Major William Robertson, and John Baxter, all of whom were also war sufferers.[107] The petition drafted by these representatives explained that "raw battalions" of Upper Canadians had thrown back the invading foe when the British army in the province was too weak to deal with the Americans. The representatives pointed out that the militiamen had acted out of loyalty since the "invader would have spared them their property" had they remained at home. After three years of peace, however, the inhabitants were still in distress because government construction had ceased, troops had been withdrawn, and fortifications were being allowed to "go to ruin." Although an investigation of war damages had taken place, the Prince Regent was reminded that "nothing has followed, but delay and insult." Militiamen had been promised lands, but so far the grants had been "unjustly withheld." Instead of a practical policy of land management which might eliminate such grievances, the inhabitants had been forced to accept a "system of patronage and favouritism." These evils, and those "which have their root in the original Constitution of the Province," had to be removed, and the petitioners requested that a commission be sent to investigate these and other matters.[108] Unlike previous critics, such as Thorpe and Willcocks, Gourlay and the Niagara delegates went further in their suggestion of what was wrong with the colony. In their view it was the whole system of government with its appointed councillors, rather than the appointees themselves, which stood in need of change.

After the meeting in St Catharines, Gourlay ventured east to drum up support for the proposed general convention at York. On 11 June Gourlay reached Kingston and, while dining with friends, he was approached by Thomas Markland, one of the magistrates of the district, with an arrest warrant. Robinson had issued the warrant on a charge of libel relating to the petition drawn up at St Catharines. Gourlay believed that two of his earliest supporters, William Dickson and Thomas Clark, were involved in the campaign to have him arrested because they did not wish to jeopardize their positions as legislative councillors. A few days later, Gourlay was involved in a fight with Duncan Fraser, a magistrate from Johnstown, and was arrested and jailed in Brockville. After paying a fine, Gourlay was released and eventually made his way to York, where the meeting of the "Upper Canadian Convention of the Friends of Enquiry" was scheduled to begin on 6 July 1818.[109]

At York, fifteen delegates from seven districts – the Home, Eastern, and Ottawa regions were not represented – spent five days discussing measures that might improve the colonial administration. Richard Beasley, a justice of the peace for the Gore District, was elected chairman, and another magistrate, William J. Kerr, was appointed secretary. Also in attendance were Robert Hamilton, John Clark, and Major William Robertson, all three of whom had submitted war claims and were owed, collectively, more than £2000.[110] The petition drafted at the St Catharines meeting was adopted by the York convention, but since a new lieutenant-governor, Sir Peregrine Maitland, was expected to arrive shortly, the plan to appeal directly to the Prince Regent was abandoned. The delegates decided to approach Maitland first and ask for an inquiry into provincial affairs by the local parliament in the belief that a "new and better era would commence."[111]

On his arrival, however, Maitland appeared completely unsympathetic to the plight of the war sufferers. In a reference to two British radicals, Maitland described Gourlay as "half Cobbett and half Hunt," and he refused to accept the petition. In a private letter to his superior, Maitland told Bathurst that he hoped Gourlay would lose the libel suit and be forced to pay a heavy fine which would "cripple him." Yet at the trial, which was held on 15 August 1818, Gourlay conducted his own defence and he managed to gain an acquittal in spite of prosecutor Henry John Boulton's eloquence and abilities.[112] Undeterred by this setback, Maitland took other measures to put an end to Gourlay's career in Upper Canada. At the opening of the third session of the seventh parliament on 12 October 1818, Maitland asked the members to ban further conventions with what was to become known as the "Gagging Bill." Having seen the York meeting as a threat to their positions, and angered by some of Gourlay's statements about their abilities, the assemblymen agreed with Maitland's request and they denounced the York Convention as "highly derogatory and repugnant to the spirit of the constitution of this Province."[113]

A little over a month later Gourlay was again arrested, this time on a charge of sedition. William Dickson, who now believed Gourlay threatened his position in the colony, had his relative arrested under the terms of the Sedition Act of 1804. This little-used statute provided for the detention of anyone who had resided in the province for less than six months and who had not taken the oath of allegiance. Isaac Swayze swore out a deposition which described Gourlay as an "evil-minded and seditious person," and Dickson and another legislative councillor, William Clark, ordered Gourlay to leave the province within ten days. Considering the whole affair absurd, Gourlay refused; he was arrested and promptly put in jail on 4 January 1819.[114] At his trial more than seven months later, Gourlay defended himself by arguing that he was a loyal British subject and that he was not required to take an oath of allegiance. Robinson, who considered the defendent to be a "wicked and unprincipled incendiary," proved to be a more able prosecutor than Boulton. Robinson ignored Gourlay's protests about the oath of allegiance and maintained that the only issue before the court was that the prisoner had been ordered to leave the colony and had failed to do so. Judge William Drummer Powell agreed with his "Bloody Assize" associate and, on 20 August 1819, he ordered Gourlay to leave the province on pain of death for disobedience. The next day, having had his fill of colonial prisons and politics, the dejected Scottish immigrant crossed over to the United States.[115]

Those who had supported Gourlay were also punished. In his address to the Assembly on the opening of the provincial parliament on 26 June 1819, Maitland announced that he was authorized to bestow lands on certain members of the militia and provincial navy but, at the same time, said that no individuals who had been involved in the "late Convention of Delegates" would be granted "this mark of approbation." A British immigrant to the colony noted that all the militia officers and magistrates who had supported Gourlay "were to a man deprived of their commissions."[116] One of these was Thomas Merritt, the magistrate who had supervised the hangings at Burlington Heights and in whose jail Gourlay spent most of 1819. Maitland justified the dismissal of this "old Servant of the Crown" on the grounds that Merritt had delivered Gourlay's letters to the newspapers for publication and at one point had proofread them before he left the jail for the editor's office. For such "notoriously improper" conduct, Merritt was removed from his post as a justice of the peace, a position he had held since 1803.[117]

Richard Beasley also paid a price for his role in the Gourlay agitation. Beasley had served as chairman for the York Convention and, along with Merritt, he was dropped from the magistracy as a result. When he was also removed from the command of the Second Regiment of the Gore militia, Beasley demanded an inquiry but he soon found himself facing a general court martial. At the trial he was accused of having disobeyed two minor requests made by Francis Gore. There were more serious charges as well. During the capitulation of York in April 1813, Beasley was alleged to have "voluntarily placed himself in the hands of the enemy," and at the 25 July 1814 Battle of Lundy's Lane he was said to have "withdrawn himself and remained at the rear during action." Beasley was found not guilty of all charges except for having disobeyed Francis Gore's request to call out his men for inspection on 4 June 1816. Nonetheless, he was dismissed from his militia post and Abraham Nelles was promoted to take his place.[118]

The official crackdown on Gourlay and his supporters did not put an end to controversy. The war claims had proven to be a veritable "Pandora's Box," and questions that had been raised about the crown and clergy reserves would continue to be asked even after Gourlay was silenced. On 30 March 1819 the congregation of the Presbyterian church in Niagara informed Maitland that, since the war, the faithful had been forced to worship in a temporary shelter. Unable to pay for a full-time rector, the congregation asked Maitland if he would direct the annual sum of one hundred pounds "out of the funds arising from the clergy Reserves." Recognizing the implicit threat to the Church of England's monopoly over these lands, Strachan wrote directly to the home authorities. He warned Bathurst that to allow Presbyterians access to the funds would only prompt "all sorts of Sectaries" to seek equivalent status. The original act had merely stated that the proceeds were to be used for the support of the "Prostestant" clergy, and Strachan clung to the most narrow definition of that term. "If the Act had meant to include Dissenters generally, or even the Church of Scotland," he told Bathurst, "to me it appears that it would have said so."[119]

Strachan's motives in defending the reserves from the demands of other religious groups had much to do with his personal plans. In 1819 William Powell remarked that the "venerable politician has attained all of the objects of his ambition, short of the mitre." Strachan believed that he might eventually be appointed bishop of Upper Canada and, with one-seventh of all the lands in the province at his disposal, he would be a powerful individual indeed. He had certainly already done much better for himself than other men of the cloth in the colony. In 1819 one Roman Catholic priest, Alexander Macdonell, prefaced his appeal for payment of his war losses by observing that during the conflict he had "constantly attended the militia in the field & even in action." He had done this without having received "a sixpence of pay or allowance, while other clergymen who never quitted the bosom of their families the whole time received both."[120]

It is unlikely that Strachan was overly concerned by such petty insults since he had far more important matters to deal with. In addition to the time he was devoting to the defence of clergy reserves, he was also occupied in directing the affairs of the "Friends of Strangers" association. The new organization had grown out of the Loyal and Patriotic Society which had ceased formal operations in October 1817. Since the end of the war, the society had spent almost all the money it had received and, after issuing its final report only £212 remained in the hands of the directors. That money was supposed to be kept in reserve "for the purpose of purchasing Medals should those already ordered be found to be insufficient in number."[121] Near the end of its existence, support was being extended to citizens who had been "mutilated and afflicted" by the war and also to the increasing number of pauper immigrants arriving from Britain. Some members felt it was improper to expend funds on newcomers when the money had been raised for war sufferers, but John Strachan did not share in that belief. Nonetheless, he was overruled and it was decided that a distinct organization should be created for the support of Upper Canada's new class of indigents. On 17 October 1817 the Patriotic Society closed its books and the money left over was transferred to the new organization.[122] Although questions continued to be asked about the 612 medals that had been ordered, the former directors refused to discuss the matter. Strachan had helped to foster the myth that all Upper Canadians had played a heroic role in the war and to distribute medals to some would have inevitably excited jealousy in others. Even before the medals had arrived, Colley Foster, one of Drummond's nominees, had warned that he would "feel particularly hurt" if he was passed over for an award.[123] Other deserving recipients might have been more than disappointed had they known that Chewett and Robinson had awarded medals to themselves and then had recommended that only ribbons or "other honourary marks" be given to Incorporated Militia veterans.

A way out of the medal dilemma appeared in 1819 when an additional £4000 arrived from England. This money had been collected on behalf of the Loyal and Patriotic Society and, with it, the former directors could have purchased enough medals to award one to nearly every man who had shouldered a musket. Instead, the society used the money to construct an institution that was to become known as the Toronto General Hospital. The directors apparently gave some thought to erecting a number of hospitals at York, Kingston, and Niagara, but they eventually decided to restrict the project to the capital. On 24 November 1819 an invitation for tenders was published in the *Upper Canada Gazette* and construction began the

following spring.[124] On 22 February 1820 Chief Justice William
Campbell proposed that the society melt the medals on hand and
use the proceeds from the sale of the bullion for the Hospital Fund.
For some reason, this resolution was passed but not carried into
effect, and the medals remained in the possession of William Robinson, John Beverley's brother.[125] In January 1822 former society
member William Warren Baldwin asked for both the medals and the
list of nominees, and the attorney-general was more than happy to
oblige, although he reminded Baldwin of the "difficulties" the society
had already experienced over the question of distribution. Apparently Baldwin though better of the idea, perhaps after realizing that
Robinson and Chewett's report had made the task impossible. Later
that year the medals were placed in the vault of the Bank of Upper
Canada, where they would remain for almost two decades.[126]

In York, on 21 April 1821, the Bank of Upper Canada had opened
its doors. Some four years earlier a group of eastern merchants,
including former members of the Kingston Association, had sought
approval for the first chartered bank in the colony. In their 1817
application they pointed out that "the want of such an establishment
was severely felt before the late war" and that the imminent withdrawal of all army bills made it necessary to keep "up a circulating
paper to meet every demand."[127] Although the Assembly agreed to
charter the bank, the deepening depression prevented the Kingston
merchants from raising the £20,000 subscription required by the
Assembly and, in consequence, a competing group began the first
colonial bank in the capital.[128] The president of the York organization
was William Allan, and another of the "heroes of the capitulation,"
John Strachan, was made a director.[129] Thomas Gibbs Ridout, on
half-pay from the British army and with his onion-attacking days
now long behind him, was elected general manager at a salary of
£200 a year. His father Thomas was also appointed to the board,
and this may have made up for his disappointment over the peace
treaty. Several years ealier he had expressed a willingness to "see the
war prolonged if it had meant continued advancement for his
family."[130] Other prominent men such as Henry John Boulton, James
Crook, and James Baby also served as directors at various times. Nine
of the bank's first directors were members of the Executive or Legislative councils, or occupied important positions in the provincial
government, and most of the other six were appointed to similar
posts later. Over the years the bank would become a target for
reformers who suspected that favouritism, rather than strict business
practices, dictated many of the policies of the institution.[131]

The emergence of a permanent opposition in the Assembly that
would criticize the actions of Strachan and his associates owed much

to Robert Gourlay and the heavy-handed measures used to persecute him and his followers. John Howison, a vocal opponent of Gourlay, felt that the Scotsman deserved some credit for finally stirring up interest in politics among ordinary Upper Canadians. Howison believed that Gourlay had arrived in the province at the right time, however, since he received much of his support from individuals who were driven by personal grievances that might not have existed earlier. "A man is seldom interested in the political affairs of his country," Howison wrote in 1818, "until they begin to affect him individually."[132] E.A. Talbot, who also considered Gourlay a dangerous radical, found that almost every colonist he spoke to rejected that view. "He was in truth," Talbot admitted, "the idol of the people."[133] Andrew Heron, publisher of the *Gleaner*, also felt that Gourlay was an unprincipled agitator but he still opposed some measures, such as the "Gagging Bill," which were used against the turbulent Scot. In an editorial on 24 June 1819 Heron observed that it was not only Gourlay's supporters who were offended by the act, "but the whole community that are disgusted by the law." Heron went on to warn that since "nine-tenths of the freeholders of the province view it in that light, it will therefore have a decided influence at the ensuing elecion."[134]

The results of Gourlay's activities were dramatically displayed in the 1820 provincial elections. The Assembly, which had previously been restricted to twenty-five members, expanded to forty seats. Among the men elected who would become staunch government supporters were John Beverley Robinson and Charles Jones. The attorney-general represented York in the house while the Brockville "tyrant" sat for Leeds. A new group of men were also elected and they would often find themselves opposed to the government faction. In the Niagara District, four of Gourlay's supporters topped the polls. The first three Lincoln ridings elected John Clark, William J. Kerr, and Robert Hamilton. In the fourth riding Issac Swayze, who had assisted in having Gourlay arrested, lost his seat to Robert Randal.[135] These men were joined in the Assembly by five other "Gourlayites," William Chisholm for Halton, George Hamilton for Wentworth, Samuel Casey for Lennox and Addington, Thomas Horner for Oxford, and Paul Peterson for Prince Edward.[136] At least eight of these men had been delegates to the York Convention and all had taken an active part in the township meetings.[137] While Casey, Horner, and Peterson were not war sufferers, each of the Niagara representatives had submitted a claim for losses and so had many of their constituents. Yet concern for war claimants did not guarantee election. In the eastern riding of Frontenac, Anthony McGuin failed to win his seat, although he had addressed the electors as friends and

Veterans of 1812 begin to enjoy public notice nearly half a century after the war.
Photograph by William Armstrong taken at Rosedale, 23 October 1861.
Archives of Ontario

"fellow sufferers" whose relief he stood pledged to obtain if elected. At the polls, however, Allan McLean, justice of the peace and former foe of the commissariat department, was able to exert sufficient influence to retain the seat he had held for sixteen years.[138]

When the Assembly met in 1821, the old political veteran Robert Nichol was able to rely on the support of Gourlayites when he called for quick action on war claims, pensions, land grants, and other issues that had arisen out of the conflict. Uppermost in the minds of all colonists, however, was the deepening economic depression which affected every aspect of business in the province. Hard economic times began in Britain and the United States early in 1819, but Upper Canada had already been in the grip of a recession for nearly two years by that time. A good harvest in Britain in 1820 only worsened matters because the 1815 corn law was applied against imports of colonial wheat to prevent a glut.[139] With no market for their most valuable commodity, farmers in Upper Canada were unable to purchase manufactured goods and, by 1821, colonial merchants were forced to hold weekly auctions to reduce their unsold inventories. That summer Isaac Wilson informed his brother that "all is barter and traffic" since real money was rarely seen.[140] John

Howison observed that most merchants were owed huge sums by colonists and he thought that if they tried to collect it would mean the "ruin of two-thirds of the farmers in the Province."[141] Private financial embarrassments were matched by those facing government. Up to 80 per cent of the province's revenue was derived from duties levied on imports entering Lower Canada, but a constitutional crisis in that colony had held up payments for two years.[142] In July 1821 a senior government official reported that the "crisis is pressing, the Province of Upper Canada is in a State of Bankruptcy."[143] In the face of such difficulties the optimism of 1816 had evaporated long before, leaving behind only a few worn and devalued half-penny tokens.

8 "The Most Puzzling Question": War Losses Politics

At the opening of the eighth provincial parliament at York on 31 January 1821, Robert Nichol took his seat in the new brick legislature located on Front Street. Over the past few months the representative for Norfolk had spent his time haggling with creditors, courting constituents, and writing letters to old acquaintances such as Roger Sheaffe.[1] On occasion he met with a group of Niagara contractors who had agreed to build a monument in memory of Isaac Brock. The structure under consideration, a 130-foot-high Tuscan column, had been designed by engineer Francis Hall and was expected to be financed by both public and private contributions. One thousand pounds had been voted for that purpose by the Assembly in 1815, but it was believed that individual donors would soon pledge a far greater amount. After six years, however, fund raising had brought in less than £1000, with private donations slowing to a trickle as the postwar slump in the provincial economy worsened after 1817.[2] Although disappointed by the response, Nichol knew he could not turn to his fellow assemblymen for assistance. The Upper Canadian treasury was unable to meet the ordinary expenses of the government, and the commemoration of the greatest hero of the war would have to be postponed until the province had overcome its economic dislocation.

Even the granting of land to deserving militiamen, which should have been cause for much celebration, somehow managed to contribute to the financial difficulties of the colony. Constant complaints about Britain's failure to fulfil this wartime promise had led home authorities to announce reluctantly in 1819 that grants would be forthcoming. But only members of the general staff of militia, the first flank companies, the Incorporated battalion, and those who served in provincial artillery, driver, or marine corps were eligible for the lands. Ordinary members of sedentary regiments who had failed to volunteer for service in the flank companies in 1812 were over-looked and a large number of active militiamen were thereby excluded from the awards. A single notice in the colonial press in February 1820 was the only indication that the process was underway. Government officials presented a complicated list of due dates for the various militia regiments, and applicants were warned bluntly that deadlines would not be extended.[3] In order to cover the survey costs on these grants, Maitland had intended to use the proceeds from the sales of crown reserves. However, despite the narrow terms of the offer, the militia grants had led to "not less than 500,000 acres" being "unavoidably alienated," and Maitland found there was little demand for tracts on the crown reserves.[4] As more grants were surveyed the province was driven deeper into debt, and the glut "so diminished the expected demand for land from the Crown" that the administration had no money to pay for even minor obligations such as the annual presents to Indian groups.[5] When the new Assembly met in January 1821 it was again forced to deal with these issues and other problems that were directly related to the War of 1812.

The constitutional crisis which had prevented Lower Canadian authorities from forwarding a share of the import duties in 1819 and 1820 had left Upper Canada with no means to pay militia pensions. Grand plans for a veterans' hospital, which first surfaced in 1820, were immediately shelved and the men who might have been residents of the "Royal Invalid Asylum" were forced instead to solicit proof that they deserved the meagre pensions provided by government.[6] To reduce the number of recipients, the Assembly decreed in April 1821 that all pensioners would have to appear before a board of medical inspectors to prove that they were incapable of earning a "living by hard labour."[7] Aware that a more rigid enforcement of eligibility criteria would not eliminate every claimant, the Assembly was also forced to authorize Maitland to borrow money to pay the remaining pensioners. While the sums involved were minor, amounting to less than £2000, this move initiated a pattern of borrowing which eventually drove the province into bankruptcy.[8]

Two other war-related issues – claims for damages and half-pay for militia officers – also continued to occupy an important place on the legislative agenda. On 13 April 1821 a second joint address on war losses was presented to Maitland. The Assembly wished to remind

British authorities that the United States had attacked Upper Canada because of "certain principles of National Policy affecting the whole Empire." Legislators pointed out that the first joint address on this topic had been sent in March 1815, but little had been done for the sufferers and it was clear that the proceeds from the sales of confiscated estates would likely amount to less than £15,000.[9] The two branches of parliament also asked that half-pay be granted to officers who had served with the Incorporated Militia battalion. The petition noted that members of the Voltigeurs in Lower Canada had received that allowance, and the politicians observed that Upper Canadians were entitled to "at least equal consideration."[10]

On 19 April 1821, only six days after the submission of the second joint address on war damages, Maitland surprised the Assembly by announcing that one class of claims, those for services and property provided to the British army, would be paid immediately. For more than a year military officials had been contemplating the propriety of settling these direct claims, which amounted to over £9000. Finally, on 27 December 1820 the decision was made that such charges had been erroneously "mingled with the General Claims for losses."[11] While applauding this decision, the legislators made it clear that they still wished to see the other claimants repaid as soon as possible. Maitland said he would forward their view on the topic "with great pleasure."[12]

The news that part of the claims would soon be discharged must have pleased Robert Nichol. Along with Thomas Clark and Robert Grant, Nichol had been approached a few months earlier by what he described as a numerous body of war claimants. The sufferers wanted the three men to act as agents on their behalf, and Nichol and the others were offered 5 per cent of whatever award was made as a commission for their work. On 1 December 1820 the agents met at Niagara Falls for the purpose of addressing letters to several well-known British figures. The first was sent to Earl Bathurst and it contained a full restatement of the various categories of losses. Its authors pointed out that in many cases private property had been used for public purposes in a "war that was altogether a national one." Yet after more than five years, "individuals whose properties were thus sacrificed" were still anxiously awaiting reimbursement fearful that they might be forever "consigned to universal poverty and distress." To reinforce their appeal, Nichol and the others included an extract from *Hansard*, dated 20 June 1783, which dealt with the topic of Loyalist claims. There was no mistaking the obvious intent of the enclosure, and it was clear that the colonists felt those earlier payments had set a precedent that should be followed.[13]

Aware that similar requests had been denied by the Colonial Office in the past, the agents hit on the idea of subcontracting the task out to three other prominent British citizens. Each was asked to act as a lobbyist on behalf of the sufferers in return for a two-third share of the 5 per cent commission. Of those approached, Edward Ellice and Alexander Gillespie refused the offer, but John Galt accepted at once. Although he was a relatively successful novelist, Galt's writings had not made him a wealthy man and the chance to earn extra money as a paid lobbyist was tempting.[14] Galt has been described as a "tall pensive man" with a "nose which seemed too large for even his massive frame," but his imposing physique and robust health made him an ideal candidate for the job.[15] William Halton, the province's official agent in England, had suffered another attack of gout and was completely incapacitated by this time.[16]

Early in the new year, Galt was shuttling back and forth between the Colonial Office and the Treasury. He first drafted an application for funds which emphasized that the British government was ultimately responsible for the claims, but officials at the Treasury responded by saying they could not justify the "grant of any Public Money." Galt characterized the reply as a "very dignified evasion" and he continued to press his case.[17] Making use of his writing talents, Galt prepared another application that was sure to gain the attention of British officials. On 25 July 1821 he told Bathurst that the government "might as well expect to silence the falls of Niagara with a Treasury minute as to stifle the Canadian claims." He also warned that if the sufferers were not soon paid there was a possibility of the "colonists becoming rebels."[18] This letter seems to have jolted the bureaucrats into action and Galt was granted an immediate interview with Bathurst. A few days later a preliminary agreement was reached by which Galt was to raise a loan in Britain in order to pay off the claimants. The Treasury balked at guaranteeing repayment, however, and the uncertain state of the financial markets made Upper Canada a poor risk for an unsecured loan.[19]

Several other meetings with the president of the Board of Trade, Frederick Robinson, led to a new plan. Robinson at first proposed that the colony should agree to pay half of its own civil expenses. If this were done, Galt was assured that the "United Kingdom should undertake to discharge the claims."[20] Unfortunately by this time the colony was hard-pressed to meet even the most basic demands on its treasury and there was simply no way it could assume a further share of the burden of government. When this was realized, a third round of talks was held. This time the participants agreed that a loan of £200,000 sterling should be raised, with both the British and the colonial governments being responsible for half of the annual interest of 5 per cent. At the end of twenty years both parties would be expected to pay half the principal. In many respects this was an ideal solution to the problem. The claimants would be reimbursed immediately and the province would have two decades to accumulate sufficient capital to discharge its half of the debt.[21]

But while Galt was finally achieving a measure of success with the compensation question, some "enemies at home" were undermining his work. At least one member of the York elite had informed Maitland that some claims submitted to the 1815–16 commission were fraudulent or much exaggerated. Although it is not known for certain, the source for that information was likely John Strachan, who had served on the commission, or his student John Beverley Robinson, who Maitland increasingly relied on for advice. One can only speculate as to why either would suddenly begin a campaign to discredit the 1815–16 commission. Neither of them were owed money personally, and this could have led to indifference about the plight of war sufferers or even jealousy, since some claimants were expecting large payments. Such sentiments would not satisfactorily explain why Strachan would campaign against the sufferers, however, for after certifying all the claims and issuing a report on the 1815–16 commission he expressed a wish for speedy payments, and his sentiments appeared genuine.[22] Robinson's motivation was not likely jealousy either, since years later he would try to ensure that payments were made. More likely, considering when these objections first surfaced, the movement to undermine the claims of certain sufferers was probably related to Gourlay's agitation and the development of a permanent opposition group in the postwar Assembly. Some prominent Niagara area claimants, like the Hamilton brothers, were part of both movements, and the activities of other men like Nichol were viewed with disdain by Maitland's supporters in the capital. Robinson, the chief spokesman for the administration in the legislature, had quickly tired of the activities of the loose faction of oppositionists gathered around Nichol. During the first session of the eighth parliament in February 1821, Robinson suggested to John Macaulay that, if the troublesome conduct of "the little Colonel" could only be controlled, the Assembly would function quite smoothly. "Without that little animal," Robinson predicted, "all would certainly be harmony."[23]

A few months later, Peregrine Maitland informed Bathurst that if the British government was to pay the awards granted by the 1815–16 commission it "would give success to some of the greatest impositions ever attempted." Maitland suggested that a team of officials should be sent out from England to establish a new commission that would only "examine evidence upon Oath." If this path were followed, Maitland believed that the "amount of the losses would not be very heavy."[24] This advice was, at first, ignored and on 20 April 1822 Maitland was forced to repeat the same charges. He warned again that some of the claims were clearly fraudulent and this time he offered a specific example. After being approached by Robert Nichol with yet another appeal for compensation, Maitland agreed to forward the application, "but without recommendation." Actually, Maitland went much further and actively campaigned against Nichol's claim for £6025 in damages. He said that one of the original board members, most likely John Strachan, had declared that Nichol's losses were not worth £1500.[25] But, having a high regard for Nichol's wartime activities, and not authorized to take depositions on oath, the member of the board now claimed they had accepted Nichol's estimates because "they had no expectation that their decision would be final." According to Maitland, the only solution was to create "a new inquiry into these claims with full power to ascertain their just and fair amount previous to proceeding with payment."[26] The next month Galt was told by Treasury officials that the home government was willing to guarantee half the interest on a loan of £100,000 sterling to discharge "claims of sufferers by the invasion as may be established before a new Commission to be immediately appointed by Sir P. Maitland."[27]

The case against the 1815–16 commission was strengthened further in November 1822 when John Beverley Robinson told officials at the Colonial Office that he believed "the claims were in some instances much exaggerated." Robinson was then in England as a representative of the Upper Canadian government, which was seeking a solution to the import duty problem with Lower Canada. Although Robinson admitted that he should say "nothing on the subject" of war losses because he was only empowered to deal with the duty issue, he nonetheless proceeded to give his private opinions on the topic. He said he had no "interest unfavourable to the claimants – quite the contrary – many of my friends are among them." If the British government saw fit to pay all the costs without another inquiry, Robinson said he would "have no reason to resent it."[28] Such statements obviously did little to bolster British confidence in the 1816 report. Not only were they told that some claims were wildly exaggerated, but Robinson had also implied that the British government was more than welcome to pay these fraudulent claims as long as it did not expect the colonial administration to do likewise.

Galt was infuriated by Robinson's meddling and, in reference to the Gourlayites and Robert Nichol, he attributed the campaign against the 1815–16 commission to the "dissensions" and "virulence of party spirit in Canada."[29] He also pointed out that of the original 2884 claims, 561 had been rejected and so it could not be said that all submisssions had been accepted without due consideration of their worth. He went on to observe that the board members had assumed "monstrous and impeachable powers" in deciding that "notoriously disaffected" persons could not submit claims. Galt also noted that the eighth principle decided upon by board members had provided for the exclusion of claims with "grossly exaggerated" prices and that the tenth permitted the commissioners to reduce awards by deducting the value of any "benefits" that claimants may have obtained by the war. These principles, Galt said, were "repugnant to justice" since they amounted to a trial without a jury. But, more importantly, he also thought it was unlikely that many fraudulent submissions would have survived such rigid scrutiny.[30]

Despite Galt's sensible objections, it was decided that a new commission would be appointed. At the opening of the next session of the provincial legislature on 15 January 1823, Peregrine Maitland announced that a "gracious scheme" for the elimination of the war claims had been received from England."[31] Only two days before Maitland made this announcement, however, the "gracious scheme" had undergone yet another change. On Galt's assurances that immediate payments were desperately required, the Colonial Office had directed Maitland to pay all claimants one-quarter of the amount awarded them by the 1815–16 commission. It was thought that a payment of five shillings on the pound would reduce much unnecessary distress since it was believed that no claim would be reduced by more than 75 per cent. The obvious problems with this decision, such as the possibility of some claimants being utterly rejected by the committee of revision after having pocketed a 25 per cent award from the former commission, quickly brought about another new policy announcement. On 15 February 1823 Maitland was informed that one-quarter of the original award, a total of £57,412 10s sterling, was still going to be paid, but that the money would be given only to those claimants who submitted new lists of damages to the committee of revision.[32]

The constant changing of plans in 1823 left Upper Canadian claimants and legislators confused and angry. Debates over the various "gracious schemes" also revealed that some old grievances simply refused to fade away. William Baldwin, the member for York and Simcoe, was originally opposed to voting any money until it was determined who was eligible. He cautioned the members to move slowly; they had already signified a disposition to grant £250,000 for canal construction, and he shuddered at the thought of voting thousands more for the claimants. This brought a sharp rebuke from his friend Robert Nichol, who noted that Baldwin had been a director of the Loyal and Patriotic Society which had misappropriated funds destined for war sufferers to build a "hospital in Little York." Nichol went on to declare that "Little York swallowed up everything. If a man had a claim not of generosity but of justice and applied to the board at York, they would tell him your claim is not good, you don't belong to little York, go to the Western or Niagara District, or go to the Devil." The impassioned nature of this speech is indicative of how deeply Upper Canadians were divided by wartime experiences. Resentment against those citizens who had profited by the war was a natural emotion for settlers residing in regions that were devastated by the fighting. Nichol admitted that inhabitants from the Niagara District and areas to the west "not only suffered in their property but in their minds."[33]

On 12 March 1823, after hours of heated debate, the Assembly passed an act to defray half the interest on a loan of £100,000.[34] In the end, only two members voted against raising the money and both represented constituencies in the east where war damages were slight. One of them, Philip VanKoughnet, sat for the riding of Stormont and Russell and had first been elected to the legislature in 1816. The son of a Loyalist, VanKoughnet had attended Strachan's grammar school at Cornwall and, during his years in politics, he was recognized as a staunch defender of the colonial administration.[35] The other negative vote was cast by one of the newer faces in the House, the "tyrant" Charles Jones, who represented Leeds. Jones had fled the province during the war, but a smuggling operation that made him wealthy continued in his absence. Both men had little reason to fear the wrath of their constituents since few war claimants were in their districts. Within five years Jones's friendship with John Beverley Robinson and John Strachan would earn him an appointment to the Legislative Council.[36]

Despite the overwhelming nature of the vote in the Assembly, Peregrine Maitland refused to grant the act royal assent. In his opinion the legislators had failed to fulfil their part of the bargain since no new duties had been instituted to cover the annual interest payments. The act only stipulated that the money was to come from "rates and duties raised, levied and collected, or hereafter to be raised, levied, and collected." Maitland noted that the province was already spending more money than it collected through such measures, and he suspected that the assemblymen would be forced to cover the interest payments with money granted for other purposes by the British parliament.[37] Robert Nichol complained in a letter to

John Galt that Maitland's actions were typical of a provincial administration which had always "shewn the greatest apathy and indifference toward the claims." Nichol noted that several of the "principal
Ministerial Members," such as VanKoughnet and Jones, had opposed
the bill from the start, and he stated that the decision to withhold
royal assent was unwarranted because the Assembly had always followed the same procedure. No one had been told that a specific fund
was required, and Nichol claimed that the administration officials
"meant from the very first to do everything they could to counteract
us." Ministerialist members, who usually introduced new legislation
on behalf of the government, apparently "took no concern" in the
matter, and Nichol claimed he had been forced to handle the job
himself. Only when it came to the associated Commission Bill did
the administration take an interest and, at that point, the assemblymen could have done without the interference. Nichol had originally
wished to add the names of the new commissioners to the bill, but
he was told to replace this clause with another which empowered
Maitland to add the names. "I was obliged to consent to this to
ensure its passing," Nichol angrily informed Galt, "as I was expressly
told it would not pass the Legislative Council, or receive the Royal
Assent in any other shape." Maitland, of course, wished to appoint
men whom he could trust, and among the commissioners nominated
were William Allan, Thomas Ridout, Alexander Wood, and John
Beverley Robinson.[38]

Although Robinson declined to serve on the committee, he was
very active in the attempt to acquire control of the more than £57,412
sterling which the British government had granted to the sufferers.
In January 1823 Robinson lobbied for the Bank of Upper Canada
at York to be chosen as the agent to disburse the fund. He pointed
out that postwar financial difficulties had led to the formation of the
bank at York. To ensure the respectability of the institution, direc-
torships were offered to members of the colonial administration;
Robinson said that through this process the "*Government* are *themselves
made stockholders*." Robinson argued that the acquisition of the compensation grant would reinforce the solid image of the bank and
make it "useful to the country." He claimed that the actual transaction
would afford the directors only a "trifling" profit, but he thought it
"might yet be an object to them in the infancy of their institution."[39]
One researcher who has studied the history of the bank has declared
that the "transaction was far from trifling" since the payment would
be made in sterling and the exchange rate would have provided for a
healthy profit.[40] Another firm vying for the loan expected to
clear more than £5000 on the deal, since the premium on sterling,

compared with provincial currency, was 12½ per cent in 1823.[41] Galt objected to Robinson's plan because he believed "the Bank would keep the specie it received for the Bills & pay the claimants with its own notes."[42] Eventually he defeated this "attempt to seduce Government into an arrangement ... by which the Banking Speculators at York could alone have benefitted," and the transaction was carried out directly by the provincial receiver-general, John Henry Dunn, and his Montreal agents, Forsyth and Richardson.[43]

The work of the committee of revision, which began in 1823, lasted much longer than that of any of its predecessors. By 23 December 1824 the committee had completed 1874 claims, and it issued a preliminary report on its activities a few weeks later.[44] The process had been slowed considerably by the necessity of acquiring sworn affidavits and because the committee sometimes called witnesses to offer testimony about various submissions. In the preliminary report, which was issued on 6 January 1825, the commissioners admitted that certain classes of claims had been rejected without consideration. Among those dismissed were claims for goods and vessels in transit. It was decided that "mercantile adventurers" had placed their property at exceptional risk in order to reap huge profits, and any losses sustained were their responsibility. The second class rejected involved claims for property lost beyond the borders of the colony. The committee members said such claims could not be considered because the government had directed the commission to investigate only "losses sustained within the province." Also rejected were claims involving burglary or other "felonious takings" because such acts were "not necessarily confined to a state of warfare." The fourth class deemed inadmissable were claims for lost army bills or specie, since exact amounts would have been impossible to verify. Any claims for horses or oxen lost in the service, or for teaming done under military orders, were deemed inadmissable since the onus was on the owner to ensure that his animals were properly cared for and that vouchers for work completed were submitted to military departments in a timely fashion. Other claims, such as those for crops lost because the owner was serving in the militia, were also considered unworthy of consideration. The committee believed that this type of loss was unavoidable during wartime and that paying the claims might set a dangerous precedent.

In the general abstract which accompanied this preliminary report, the commissioners noted that 1874 claimants had valued their losses at over £404,828. Of that amount, the committee had determined that only £194,038 was worthy of repayment. Still to be examined were ninety new claims that had not been submitted to the 1815–16

board; 509 submissions that had been preferred to the former commission remained to be investigated because no new application had
yet been made.[45] The board's final report would not be issued for
some time since it did not complete its investigations until 15 March
1826. At that point, 2055 claims had been examined, 236 had been
rejected, and 1819 accepted. The total amount awarded was
£182,180 17s 6½d sterling and the average individual payment was
to be more than £100 sterling.[46]

The question of where the province would find its share of the
money for the award was not settled for several years. At first Nichol
and other members of the colonial legislature hoped to raise funds
through the levying of export duties on products leaving the lower
province or through an increase in the rate of import duties collected
at Quebec and Montreal. This was a popular idea among some Upper
Canadians, since it was felt that legislators in the neighbouring colony
had spent most of the war as only "indifferent or idle spectators."[47]
During the conflict, moreover, unprecedented sums of money had
been collected on imports arriving at Quebec and Montreal, but the
Upper Canadian legislature had not received its proper share of the
duties. "Why should not Lower Canada be called upon to pay her
proportion?" Nichol asked. "She reaped all the benefits of our suf-
ferings and exertions."[48] The next year the Assembly and the Legislative Council presented a joint address requesting that duties be
increased on wines and sugar entering Lower Canada. But the representatives in the neighbouring colony refused to agree to the
proposal.[49]

In December 1823 Galt was visited by Alexander Macdonell, now
bishop of Rhesina, who was seeking compensation for his wartime
services and who had recently applied for a portion of the lands
being granted to militia veterans. Macdonell pointed out to Galt that
thousands of acres of land were contained in the crown and clergy
reserves.[50] The Roman Catholic bishop, perhaps aiming to deflate
Strachan's power, suggested that profits from the sales of the reserves
could be used to discharge the claims of the war sufferers.[51] A few
days later Galt approached Bathurst with an outline of this plan and
was encouraged to proceed with the work. On 14 May 1824 a pro-
visional committee of interested investors met in London and, by the
next month, Galt had a list of wealthy men who were willing to
purchase the land. At stake was more than two million acres of
reserves, valued at £348,680 sterling, which were to be paid for by
annual instalments of £20,000.[52] On 6 August 1824, after having
laid the groundwork for what was to become known as the Canada
Company, Galt was informed that the British government did not

consider the money involved "to be applicable to the relief of the sufferers by the late war with the United States." The funds were to be used instead to pay the provincial civil list and for pensions.[53] For the rest of his life Galt harboured a grudge against the British officials who had perverted the intention of his plan and who had also robbed him of the opportunity of acquiring a large commission.

John Strachan was in England when he first heard of the proposed sale of the reserve lands. He still hoped that he might be appointed bishop and had just completed construction of a new stone house reputed to be the finest in York.[54] In the sumptuous study of this colonial palace, he had spent countless hours preparing a defence against other denominations that were demanding a share in the reserves. On 22 April 1823 he had put the finishing touches to his "Ecclesiastical Chart," which attempted to prove that the Church of England was the most important religious institution in the colony. The task required some creative book-keeping. Strachan added the totals of those who attended no church to the number who professed to be Anglicans, to suggest that the established church had more adherents in the province than all other religions combined. Strachan declared that the Methodists had only ten or twelve itinerant preachers in the province, and clergymen of other faiths were described "as seemingly very ignorant."[55] This fabrication brought about a howl of protest, but for Strachan the continued control of the reserves justified such lies.

When rumours began to circulate near the end of 1823 that a separate Church of England bishopric might be established for Upper Canada, Strachan gathered his papers and made arrangements to sail for England. When he left early in 1824 he carried with him a letter of introduction from Maitland, who had spent the war in Europe, which claimed that Strachan's "exemplary loyalty" during the fighting had done much to "alleviate the miseries" of those who suffered by the conflict.[56] On his arrival, Strachan quickly arranged for a meeting with representatives from the Colonial Office so he would be the first to apply for the £3000-a-year post. He told Bathurst that his pupils and their friends had accompanied Brock to Detroit, "by which he was enabled to capture General Hull." Perhaps sensing that this might be an insufficient recommendation for receiving the mitre, Strachan went on to list other wartime activities, including an address for the Assembly and his work with the Loyal and Patriotic Society. To cap this litany of great deeds, Strachan also mentioned that it was his "determination, aided by my friends and pupils, that gave the first check to Mr. Gourlay's seditious plans." Although he claimed to "feel ashamed" about recounting these services, he also assured Bathurst "that they are far from being exaggerated."[57] Bathurst was sympathetic to Strachan's appeal, but he was unable to comply with the request since no funds had been voted for the establishment of a new bishopric.[58]

Strachan's disappointment at that news turned to dismay when he was informed that the clergy reserves might be sold to pay war losses. He quickly met with officials at the Colonial Office and listed a number of objections to Galt's plans. Galt had proposed that all the crown reserves and one-half of the clergy reserves should be sold to investors, but the provincial Church of England was to receive only a small share of the £20,000 annual payments. Strachan noted that this would amount to an increase of only 50 per cent over what the institution already received, and he suggested an alternate plan whereby the investors would pay for half the clergy reserves immediately. He thought a lump-sum payment of more than £250,000 might be a fair price.[59] In the end, however, neither plan was adopted. Strachan's objections to the low prices offered by investors prompted the authorities to withdraw the clergy reserves from the transaction, and a further one million acres of recently acquired Indian lands were substituted instead.[60]

While Strachan was in England, Maitland was busy preparing a series of documents designed to show why Incorporated Militia officers should not be granted half-pay. That topic had been a perennial favourite of the Assembly and, between 1816 and 1823, at least three formal requests for such an award had been made. In February 1824 Maitland sent a confidential dispatch to Bathurst which warned of the "pretensions that would be awakened should the allowances prayed for be granted in the present instance." A memorandum included with the dispatch offered a point-by-point comparison between the Incoporated battalion and the Voltiguers which revealed that the Lower Canadians had served for three years, but that their counterparts to the west had served "less than two years and scarcely a year after they were embodied." Saying that it was "entirely a matter of grace" whether the British gave half-pay to officers of either corps, Maitland nonetheless stressed "that the Voltiguers have superior claims." He feared that granting half-pay to some veterans would encourage others, such as flank company officers, to submit similar requests, which he believed were completely unwarranted.[61] By such means, veterans of Lundy's Lane and other hard-fought contests were again denied the recognition they deserved. The "Upper Canada Preserved" medals remained in the vault of the York bank and the presentation of ceremonial colours to the Regiment of Incorprated Militia, which took place on 23 April 1822, had seen the award placed in the hands of militiamen from the East and West regiments of York militia. Most of those men had spent a large part of the conflict on parole, but they acquired the honours because the original Incorporated battalion had been disbanded immediately after the war.[62]

Robert Nichol was one of the few militia veterans who was rewarded for wartime services. After years of pestering British authorities, he was granted an annual allowance of £200 in lieu of half-pay.[63] He did not enjoy this bounty for long. On 3 May 1824 Nichol was returning from an inspection of the Brock monument site when his horse and wagon took a fatal plunge over the cliffs at Queenston Heights. A coroner's inquest later determined that Nichol's death was an accident, but the foreman of the jury thought it might also have been the work of "some secret enemy." Nichol was very familiar with the territory and the incident had occurred well away from the regular path. More troubling was the fact that Nichol's scarf was wrapped around his head and part of it was found in his mouth, giving him the appearance of having been gagged and strangled.[64] For the conspiracy-minded, the scarf may have symbolized the administration's desire to see Nichol "sit silent" and cease his "indecorous" activities.[65]

Nichol died before receiving his share of the British grant, but the 1823–6 committee of revision eventually determined that he should be compensated for more than £4205 in losses. Apparently Strachan had been wrong, since Nichol's submission for £6684 in damages had only been reduced by one-third, the standard rate of revision for most claims.[66] His widow received a share of the money pledged by the British government, but all of it was directed towards creditors who had numerous claims against the estate. She immediately applied to Maitland for relief as the widow of a militia veteran and he forwarded her application with a favourable recommendation. Maitland said the family had been "left in extremely distressed circumstances." Several years later Theresa Nichol was placed in charge of Brock's monument in the hope that she could earn at least a modest income from leading tours around the site. The position had originally been offered to another woman, Laura Secord, but Theresa's case was considered more pressing.[67]

Robert Nichol's passing marked the end of an era in Upper Canadian affairs. He had entered the Assembly in 1812 as a staunch supporter of the government, but the war and its legacy of economic hard times led him to become the chief critic of the administration for almost a decade. By the time of his death, however, the economy of Upper Canada was showing definite signs of revival.

The depression which had gripped much of the Atlantic world since 1819 was coming to an end, and both business and agricultural activities in the colony would eventually benefit. A relaxation of the British corn laws would soon permit large-scale exports of flour from North America, and thousands of immigrants would be on board the ships when they returned from England. Unemployment, low wages, and a scarcity of arable land would prompt the British government to encourage emigration to the colonies.[68] What started as a trickle – the colonial population would increase by only 6444 between 1824 and 1825 – would later become a flood, and in 1832 more than 66,000 immigrants would arrive in the province.[69] This explosive growth contributed to a renewed sense of optimism, but it also meant that unresolved issues arising out of the war were sometimes pushed farther into the background. In 1828 the provincial population stood at 186,034, or more than double the estimated figure for 1812; by that time newcomers outnumbered those who had lived in the colony during the conflict.[70] By 1837, when the compensation issue was finally settled, there were more girls under the age of sixteen in the province than there had been settlers in 1812.[71]

William Lyon Mackenzie was one of the many immigrants who entered Upper Canada after the war and he was destined eventually to fill the role that Nichol had left vacant. A native of Scotland, Mackenzie was only twenty-five when he arrived in the colony in 1820, and like many of his fellow countrymen in the province, he eventually embarked on a mercantile career. In partnership with John Lesslie, he opened a general store in Dundas but, by 1824, he had moved to Queenston where he established a newspaper, the *Colonial Advocate*. In the first edition on 18 May 1824 Mackenzie provided a detailed account of the inquiry into Nichol's death. He had gathered the information while serving as foreman on the coroner's jury and he was only one of many Upper Canadians who suspected that foul play might have been involved.[72]

The inaugural issue also had an editorial which criticized the executive government for having delayed distribution of the compensation award and attributed the tardiness to the "*degree of accountability* which must exist between a government and a governor separated [by] three thousand miles." Similar statements had been made by Robert Gourlay during his short stay in the colony, and Mackenzie left no doubt where his sympathies lay; he said that a copy of the first number of the *Colonial Advocate* had been sent to the "Banished Briton." Subsequent editions also took up old Gourlayite complaints, such as the exclusion of American settlers, with

Mackenzie questioning why "fat rich Dutch farmers" from Pennsylvania were turned back in favour of penniless Irish immigrants.[73]

Mackenzie was also responsible for having a copy of the inaugural edition of the *Colonial Advocate* placed in the base of Brock's monument. During a conversation with Robert Nichol, Mackenzie had learned that the cornerstone of the structure was to be installed on 1 June 1824. The two men had agreed that a time capsule should be included; after Nichol's death, Mackenzie visited Thomas Dickson, one of the commissioners in charge of the project, who also thought highly of the idea. No public announcement about the cornerstone laying was made and only a handful of contractors were on the site that day. Most of the leading figures of the colony, including Peregrine Maitland, were in Kingston attending the ground-breaking ceremony for the new town jail. Mackenzie also declined to appear for the laying of the monument's cornerstone, and a young assistant was sent to deliver the time capsule to Queenston Heights. Inside the bottle were a few coins, some press-clippings, and a rolled-up copy of the first issue of the *Colonial Advocate*. More than a month later, after Maitland learned of what had gone on in his absence, he ordered the time capsule removed. Needless to say, the *Colonial Advocate* devoted a great deal of ink to this "silly conduct," and readers were treated to vivid reports of the alarmed reactions of Queenston residents who thought all the fuss "was a sure sign of a new war with the Yankees."[74] Mackenzie suspected that John Beverley Robinson and other members of the York elite had been offended by the editorial slant of the newspaper and had counselled Maitland to destroy the monument. It is true that Robinson disliked the sharp-tongued Scot and had earlier dismissed him as another "reptile of the Gourlay breed."[75] It should be noted that the attorney-general had good reason for his low opinion of the editor of the *Colonial Advocate*. One edition described Robinson as a "subservient tool of [his] ... schoolmaster."[76]

In the months after the demolition of the monument, Mackenzie's newspaper continued to raise the ire of colonial authorities. The journal often published letters dealing with both old and new grievances, including some which stemmed from the war. In the 30 September 1824 edition, for example, a correspondent asked fellow readers to consider the career of a certain "Cardinal Alberoni," William Powell, who had sat in "judgement upon some unfortunate wretches" at the Ancaster assize. According to the writer, Alberoni had his sights set on the position of chief justice and he therefore ignored any pleas for mercy, saying that it was "necessary to make examples in order to strike fear into the hearts of others."[77] Another correspondent from Sandwich complained that a number of claims rejected by the committee of revision were from "some poor people not aware" that a second application was required. This writer also complained that the more recent committee had reduced every claim accepted by the former board, although the new members had no real knowledge of the area since they were *"all strangers to the District."*[78]

When the committee issued its preliminary report in January 1825, Mackenzie criticized the principles on which certain claims had been rejected. Those who had been refused compensation for crops lost while on militia service earned the editor's deepest sympathy, and he prayed that the ruthless souls who had made that decision might "never sit in judgement on the affairs of me or mine."[79] In another article Mackenzie derided the pretensions of the "gentlemen" of Upper Canada who often were placed in such positions. He claimed they lacked both education and refinement, but they demanded respect "on account of newly acquired wealth, a seat on a bench at quarter sessions, or a commission in the militia or the like." Mackenzie claimed that these "gentlemen" were "disliked by the farmers & are by them rarely trusted."[80]

The *Colonial Advocate* set a new standard for criticism of powerful individuals. Maitland occasionally forwarded clippings to British officials to give them some idea of what was being printed in the colonial press. In one article entitled "A Favourite of the Governor," Mackenzie described a fictional visit to York by a traveller from Oswego in neighbouring New York. On his arrival the American enters the customs house and encounters the collector, William Allan. He then proceeds to mail a letter and discovers that the postmaster is none other than William Allan. Bewildered, he next enters the Bank of Upper Canada and once more runs into William Allan, the president of that institution. Later he accompanies a friend who wants a tavern licence and he meets Allan again in his role as inspector of licences. On the way home they pass a militia muster headed by the same individual. Several more improbable meetings occur, one with the treasurer of the Society for Strangers in Distress, another with a hospital trustee, and still another with the treasurer of the Home District. Finally he met "a friend from Niagara in a doleful mood– enquired the cause, and was informed that the COMMISSIONERS *for War Losses* had cut off half his claim – who are the Commissioners, asked he of Oswego: the reply was A. B. C. D. and – Mr. William Allan!!!" At once "amazed, astonished, and confounded" by his experiences, the visitor expresses pity for the overworked Allan and wonders why a colony would allow "one man to hold such a number of trusts." An Upper Canadian quickly tells him to hold his tongue because Allan is a friend of Maitland and an "Aberdeensman ... – a townsman of the Hon. & Rev. owner of the palace there."[81]

Mackenzie's brash style was soon emulated by other editors and choice bits of criticism were often reprinted in the *Colonial Advocate*. Andrew Heron's *Niagara Gleaner*, for example, questioned why certain "*gentlemen* who long evinced a hostility to the *claims* of the sufferers" always seemed to be placed on boards to investigate the damages. Heron referred specifically to the "Honorable Reverends & Co." and he observed that the same men had collected and distributed the funds of the Loyal and Patriotic Society. "How *partially* that was done is well known to the sufferers on this frontier," Heron wrote, and "it was, with little exception, *dealt* out to their FRIENDS, who were least in need." After the war, "the *Honorables* and Reverends" refused to distribute the money on hand and instead built a hospital which only provided "a rendezvous for the birds and brutes."[82] A similar complaint was levelled by the *Canadian Freeman*, which said that the directors had taken "it upon themselves to misapply the good charity of the people of England" by deciding to build a hospital. "This compact" had also failed to reserve money for staff salaries or medicine, and the hospital remained the preserve of "bats and owls" except when occupied "as a DANCING SCHOOL HOUSE by Madam Harris for the use of the children of the *Venerable* Archdeacon Strachan, Judge Sherwood, Mr. Attorney Robinson, the Solicitor, etc.!!"[83]

The creation of the *Colonial Advocate* in 1824 marked the dawning of a new age for the provincial press. From that point on, Upper Canadian publications devoted an increasing amount of space to discussions of colonial affairs. Earlier newspapers were comprised mostly of advertisements and news of Old World affairs, but Mackenzie and his imitators introduced lengthy editorials, sarcasm, and scathing critiques of government policies. These attacks on the colonial administration did not go unanswered. Other journals, such as the *Canadian Emigrant*, entered the fray on the side of government. The development of a reform-conservative dichotomy in the Assembly was reflected in, and spurred on by, the evolution of a thriving, indigenous, provincial press, and the change in journalistic style was accompanied by an explosive growth in the number of journals printed. On the eve of war Upper Canada had three newspapers, and only the *Kingston Gazette* managed to publish continuously throughout the conflict. It was not until 1816 that the number of newspapers in the colony reached prewar levels. But by 1836 there were at least thirty-eight newspapers published in twenty-one different locations, and Upper Canadians in all regions were provided with information about both local and provincial concerns.[84]

The development of a flourishing fourth estate contributed to the growth of a "national" consciousness in the colony, and the mid-1820s witnessed important changes to the Upper Canadian political landscape. While political parties in the modern sense still did not exist, and members continued to vote independently on all issues, candidates across the colony were increasingly identified as either "conservative" or "reform." That development, as well as the transformation in interest from purely local concerns to a "province-wide political awareness," was fostered by the maturation of colonial journalism.[85] Various newspapers might disagree sharply over different issues, but most advocated Upper Canadian solutions to Upper Canadian problems. One researcher has suggested that "a deep, horizontal comradeship" is an inevitable result of such an occurrence. Members of a community, separated by distance and personal experiences, are joined together through a discussion of common situations.[86] The sharing of ideas and opinions through the medium of the press widened the horizons of the average settler. While still surrounded by "thick woods," Upper Canadians increasingly knew more about their neighbours and were aware that they were part of a larger community that extended beyond the boundaries of their own farms.

Of course, the colonial population had always agreed on the need for economic advancement: one reader of the *Colonial Advocate* said that Upper Canada remained "a country of speculators and GAIN, the grand main chance of their beings, end and aim."[87] Reformers and conservatives, who seemed to be at odds on almost every issue facing the colony, often exhibited a surprising degree of consensus on the need for new canals and roads. At one point Mackenzie declared that self-interest was behind this drive for internal improvements. "Patriots in the west," who were eager to complete the Burlington canal, offered support to "patriots from Kingston and Belleville" who sought new roads for their region. "Self is at the bottom" of such demands, declared the editor of the *Colonial Advocate*, and throughout the land the cry was heard: "It will double the value of our property."[88] That drive for economic advancement saw the province lavish huge sums of money on internal improvements, but it also meant that the legitimate claims of war sufferers were to be consistently ignored during the 1820s.

Owing to the rate of exchange, the award from the British parliament had amounted to over £63,791 in 1824, and each claimant received a share of that sum equivalent to approximately 35 per cent of what was lawfully due them.[89] The British government had pledged to make another payment of £57,412 sterling, but not until the Upper Canadian legislature voted an equivalent amount. If this was done, officials at the Treasury had promised to contribute "a moiety of whatever further sum may be required" to satisfy all the claims. The professed inability of colonial legislators to fulfil the terms of the agreement angered Wilmot Horton, undersecretary of state for war and the colonies. He complained in 1824 that the "delay in satisfying these claims has already produced great positive mischief & inconveniences, & has given an opportunity to the disaffected to hold very injurious language toward the Mother Country."[90]

Despite Horton's complaints, little was done to solve the compensation problem over the next few years. The oppositionists who had entered politics in the early 1820s had sought to have the British government and colonial administration deal with real issues, such as claims for losses, pensions, and land grants, in a timely fashion. It appeared to them that postwar administrators were ignoring important problems, and they and their supporters were determined to see that change. In this endeavour the representatives were quite successful, and many war-related issues, as well as other problems, were speedily dealt with by the eighth parliament between 1821 and 1824. Pleased by the handling of these affairs, some Gourlayites, like John Clark and William Chisholm, would eventually became conservative supporters of the administration.[91] A number of other Gourlayites, including W.J. Kerr, Samuel Casey, and Robert Hamilton, did not return to the ninth parliament (1824–8). Those who remained to join the expanding reform group in the legislature after 1824, however, soon realized that in politics there are sometimes no easy answers. The decision by the British government in 1823 to fund only part of the war claims, and to make further payments contingent on Upper Canadian contributions, complicated that issue immensely. No longer was it a simple matter of prying money from coffers located overseas, and the question of whether the province really should pay a share of the compensation eventually divided later groups of colonial reformers. Some disagreed with the 1823 imperial decision because they disliked the idea of raising taxes to liquidate the claims. That was not a popular idea among many Upper Canadian voters and the *Niagara Gleaner* observed that, when it came to war losses, the "body of the Electors are averse to have anything paid out of the public funds of the province."[92] That may have been more true in eastern regions of the colony where war sufferers were fewer in number. For former Gourlayite Paul Peterson, who represented Prince Edward County until 1830, this meant joining other radical reformers in opposing any payments by the colony. Two other old Gourlayite reformers, George Hamilton and Robert Randall, were war sufferers themselves and they consistently cast votes in favour of Upper Canada paying a share of the claims.[93]

Another problem arising out of the war was to preoccupy the minds of many assemblymen in the mid 1820s. The issue that dominated the ninth parliament – the alien question – had actually been simmering since the war. Its origin dated from January 1815 when land grants were no longer offered to newcomers from America. On his arrival in the colony a few months later, Francis Gore exceeded his powers and ordered magistrates to refuse the oath of allegiance to all Americans, even those who had merely purchased land.[94] This, as we have seen, prompted opposition from many sectors of the population; when the law officers of the crown were solicited for their opinions on the issue in 1817, they announced that the "governor has not any discretion to refuse to administer such oaths." But the law officers also observed that simply taking an oath of allegiance did not entitle a migrant from the United States to possess land in a British colony. According to these officials, any American arriving in the colony after 1783 was also required to make several other declarations, including an "oath of intention to reside and settle," and then live "within the colony 7 years before he can be entitled to hold lands as a natural-born subject."[95] The information contained in that memorandum shocked colonial administrators since it insinuated that the vast majority of settlers in Upper Canada were holding land illegally. Most arrivals had acquired grants immediately after arriving, and few had taken all the oaths and made every declaration required by law. The majority of Upper Canadians mistakenly assumed that being born in the Thirteen Colonies while they were still British territory had made them British subjects legally entitled to hold land anywhere in the empire. Afraid of the potential for upheaval should the truth become known, the administration disavowed knowledge of the memorandum and claimed that colonial officials were not competent to judge questions about "the indelible quality of birth to impart allegiance."[96]

The issue remained dormant for several years until Barnabas Bidwell took his seat in the eighth parliament as a representative for Lennox and Addington. In November 1821 his right to the seat was called into question by a defeated opponent, who noted that Bidwell had been accused of criminal acts in the United States and had never completed all of the steps needed to become a "natural-born subject" in Upper Canada. His son, Marshall Spring Bidwell, then ran for the same seat in 1822, but the returning officer refused his nomination because he had been born in the United States. The furore aroused over the case of the Bidwells subsided somewhat after the issue was submitted to the law officers of the crown for their verdict. The decision, that Loyalists were entitled to hold land but all other American immigrants in the colony would have to make a declaration to acquire citizenship, arrived in the summer of 1825.[97] Although the administration immediately created a bill for the "relief" of the people affected, the decision of the law officers created an invidious distinction between Loyalists and those who followed after them, and it effectively called into question the right of an estimated 80 per cent of the adult male population to hold land or vote.[98] For the next three years the alien issue reopened old wounds and created new divisions in the colony. At different times it pitted Loyalists against newcomers, reformers against tories, easterners against westerners, and even veterans against shirkers.

Debate over a naturalization bill began in late 1825 during the second session of the ninth parliament. In response to assertions that Americans had been invited to settle by Simcoe in the 1790s, John Beverley Robinson declared that he had never seen such a proclamation, "nor did he believe that it existed." He argued instead that "thousands and thousands of stragglers" had come, not because of affection for Britain, but to "elude the pursuit of their creditors." He dismissed many other Americans in the province as men "who left their wives behind them, runaway husbands."[99] These insults brought a response from Niagara veteran Edward McBride, who denounced any restriction on American immigration and who saw the naturalization bill as an affront to residents who "had fought nobly by his side in the day of battle."[100] Conservative William Morris, who had spent the war years in the Johnstown District well away from most fighting, still felt entitled to dismiss McBride's stories about the bravery of Americans in the late war. Morris noted "it was not true and he did not like to see such things reported to the country in fine eloquent speeches."[101] Robinson agreed and said Americans inside the province had offered aid to invading forces; he declared "that for one old country man who deserted our colours during the last war, a hundred Yankees had gone over to the enemy." Furthermore, he noted that many Americans were still entering the country, and he was not sure that was a good idea. Among the new arrivals might be former soldiers, and Robinson plaintively argued "they MURDERED our wives, they destroyed our families ... they made our homes a desert." Reformer John Rolph, a member of the Norfolk militia from 1812 to 1814, dismissed the attorney-general's histrionics; he warned that wealthy immigrants would be discouraged from coming to the colony and that such "inflammatory language as this was the way to keep it a desert."[102] Robinson's comments also brought a cutting retort from reformer John J. Lefferty, an American who had served throughout the war in the Lincoln militia. Dr Lefferty declared that former enemy soldiers would surely fight for their adopted country and would likely defend Upper Canada "in a future war better than those poltroons who in the late war staid at home."[103]

Eventually, a number of reformers were successful in having new instructions sent from Britain, and in 1828 a revised bill was submitted to the legislature. This new document avoided any mention of the word "alien" and merely decreed that all people who held land grants or served in public office, or who had taken the oath of allegiance and had been settled in the province before 1820, were to be considered "natural-born subjects."[104] Since the legislation had the approval of the home authorities, John Beverley Robinson and other supporters of the administration acquiesced to its passage and did not further impugn the reputation of all American residents. The protracted debates over the alien issue, however, had involved open discussion of topics that some Upper Canadians would have rather avoided. There certainly was a measure of truth to some of Robinson's claims, since hundreds of Americans had fled at the first sign of trouble while others offered comfort to the invaders. But for militia veterans like Lefferty and Rolph, who resided in areas where real fighting had occurred and where some residents of American origin had fought bravely on the British side for most of the war, the blanket denunciations offered by supporters of the administration provoked bitter resentment. There is little doubt that debate over the alien question soured the views of many other colonists, and the next election saw the defeat of no less than twenty-one representatives, including Charles Jones and Philip VanKoughnet, who had been willing to see some constituents declared non-citizens.[105]

The intense interest in the alien issue precluded much discussion about the claims for war losses during the ninth parliament. Over time, of course, issues arising out of the war would gradually occupy less space on the legislative agenda of the Assembly. That decline was partly a reflection of the increasing numbers of young representatives who began entering the House after the eighth parliament. Some of these newer assemblymen had been only boys when the conflict erupted, and their limited interest in the war is understandable. For example, Marshall Spring Bidwell, who took his seat as the representative for Lennox and Addington on 11 January 1825, had been thirteen years old when the war began.[106] Even for more mature administration critics, however, the conflict was of less interest than it had been for predecessors like the Gourlayites. These newer oppositionists were more concerned to tackle issues like internal improvements or the control of finances and, unlike the critics of the adminstration who preceded them, newer reformers had not pledged to do their utmost to relieve the war sufferers.[107] In the first two sessions of the ninth parliament, therefore, the loosely linked group of reformers in the House drafted only one address on war claims, composed another on half-pay for militia officers, and passed a memorial condemning the administration for having withheld land grants to militiamen who had been involved in Gourlay's movement.[108] An editor from Niagara excused the relative inactivity of the House in regard to the losses because even committed reformers had failed to solve the problem in the past. In late 1825 Andrew Heron blamed the lack of a solution on the "hostility of the leading characters at York, to claims of sufferers on this frontier." He predicted that so "long as they retain their influence, nothing from that quarter can be expected."[109]

Another reason why the problem remained unsolved was that no agreement could be reached on the best method of discharging the claims. Some colonists continued to agree with Nichol's original position, that the British should be "obliged to pay the money from the National Treasury."[110] Early in 1826 the *Canadian Freeman* expressed the opinion that Britain had entered the conflict "without consulting the people of this Colony" and that the home authorities were liable for all damages sustained because of the war.[111] Others felt that Upper Canadians should also shoulder the burden because the losses had been sustained in defence of the colony. But even assemblymen who held to that position appeared reluctant to impose new taxes to pay sufferers. The province was already in debt and, if more money was to be spent, most would prefer that it be used to provide the colony with concrete improvements for the future like canals or highways. Thus, although the ninth Assembly cried poverty when the subject of war losses was raised, it was willing to authorize a loan of £25,000 to fund the construction of William Hamilton Merritt's Welland Canal project.[112]

On 23 January 1826 the Assembly and the Legislative Council submitted another joint address on the subject of war losses. The politicians thanked the British government for its contribution to the sufferers, but went on to declare that the colonial treasury had been drained of more than £40,000 to pay for militia pensions and the province was too poor to fulfil the terms of the agreement. The politicians noted they had been unsuccessful in acquiring the assistance of the Lower Canadian parliament, and "extreme hardship" was the result for some residents of the province. That was particularly true for the inhabitants of western Upper Canada, who "inevitably suffered in consequence of the destruction of the buildings, the devastation of their farms, and the spoilation of every description of their personal property." The address ended with an appeal to the "well-known generosity of the British Nation," and the legislators petulantly noted that money was often sent to "the people of foreign lands."[113] Apparently, after more than a decade, Upper Canadians were still willing to pin their hopes on a possible British bailout. Over the next two years officials overseas would continue to ignore pleas for assistance, and it became increasingly obvious that the British authorities did not intend to shoulder the burden alone.

During the last session of the ninth parliament in 1828, John Beverley Robinson was placed in charge of a committee established to investigate the status of the claims for losses. During this exercise the attorney-general came to the conclusion that the sufferers should be paid as soon as possible. In the early 1820s the actions of Nichol and the Gourlayites had prompted Robinson to work against the interests of some sufferers, but much had changed since then. Nichol was dead, several Gourlayite war claimants were now supporters of the administration, and the 1823–6 committee of revision had closely scrutinized submissions to eliminate fraudulent requests. Also of importance was Robinson's belief that the economic potential of Upper Canada was nearly limitless. Like many other members of the colonial elite, the attorney-general favoured borrowing large sums of money because the wealth of the province would esure repayment of all debts.[114] In Robinson's opinion, the colony could well afford to borrow money for both internal improvements and war sufferers, and he felt the claimants had "good ground" to expect the province to share in the compensation payments. He reminded the Assembly on 19 March 1828 that members of the eighth parliament had resolved to pay a portion of the debt in 1823 and, on principle, future representatives could not repudiate that promise. According to the attorney-general, proceeds from the sales of confiscated estates and the grant from England had permitted payments totaling £63,763 6s 1½d sterling. Since the committee of revision had declared that £182,180 17s 6½d sterling was due the sufferers, a further £118,417 11s 5d sterling was required for the full indemnification of the claimants. Robinson said that a duty on salt imported from the United States might permit the government to meet at least a part of that obligation, and he announced "that it is the present disposition of the Assembly to apply such duties to that object."[115]

By the time legislation designed to deal with the compensation issue was introduced, that spirit of cooperation had evaporated. In the wake of the alien debate an election had been held and, for the first time, there was a clear majority of reformers in the Assembly. In the new tenth parliament, which met for its inaugural session in January 1829, reformers outnumbered conservative members thirty-five to thirteen.[116] Among the new faces in the Assembly was William Lyon Mackenzie. During his election campaign the *Colonial Advocate* published extracts from a "Black Book" that detailed such past abuses of executive power as the "Gagging Bill," the "Spoon Bill," and the threats made against James Durand for his opposition to martial law. Mackenzie also listed the names of "Positively Ministerial or Court Canadidates" so his readers might recognize their enemies and defeat them at the polls.[117] Although he would never become the leader of the reform group in the House – the moderate William Baldwin held that post – Mackenzie did serve as a spokesman for the more radical members of the Assembly. Unfortunately for the war sufferers, he also held to Nichol's old position – that the British should pay for all damages or allow proceeds from the sale of reserves to be used instead. Like most assemblymen, Mackenzie wished to see the sufferers compensated, but he disagreed with Robinson about the need for colonial involvement in the process. At one point Mackenzie argued that the imperial parliament was responsible for all costs because the British army had forcibly taken food and other property during the war and had kept "them sixteen years out of payment."[118] Statements like that suggest Mackenzie was not fully versed on the subject, and he apparently believed that British troops had caused all the damage. This may be attributed to the fact that the editor of the *Colonial Advocate*, like increasing numbers of other residents in the province, had arrived in Upper Canada years after the war had ended. A real fear about increasing the public debt, and perhaps an imperfect understanding of the major issues involved, combined to lead William Lyon and some other assemblymen to oppose measures aimed at relieving hundreds of war sufferers. Although they often portrayed themselves as "friends of the people," the actions of the radical reformers on this issue angered many ordinary Upper Canadians who happened to have suffered because of the fighting. This may be why Mackenzie considered the war-losses problem to be "the most puzzling question" in Upper Canadian politics.[119]

During his first session of parliament in 1829, Mackenzie indicated he would hamper any move by the province to pay a portion of the compensation required. His announcement angered war sufferers, of course, because the imperial government had indicated it would withhold further payments until the colonial Assembly contributed a share. Threat of a deadlock also made Robinson livid, since he had already prepared legislation for liquidation of the claims. According to Mackenzie, a spiteful Robinson endeavoured to "sow seeds of discord" between the editor of the *Colonial Advocate* and many important colonists. Before the legislature gathered for its second session in January 1830, Mackenzie admitted to his readers that the widespread criticism of the radical reformers over the claims issue had "wounded our feelings last winter." Still, he argued that if the British assumed all the costs, they could forgo further expenditures on fortifications. Compensation payments, the *Colonial Advocate* said, would provide a better defence: "a fortress built up in the hearts." Mackenzie, perhaps aware of Robinson's role in discrediting the 1815–16 commission, even hinted that the "day may come when the sufferers will learn to know and apppreciate their true friends."[120]

A war losses compensation bill was finally introduced to the Assembly in January 1830. Mackenzie remained true to his word and immediately sought to amend the measure so that no loan could be raised until after the British government had agreed to provide another award of £57,412 sterling. This amendment was seconded by Robert Baldwin, son of William Warren, who had won the seat for York vacated when John Beverley Robinson was appointed chief justice on 31 July 1829. Baldwin and Mackenzie were unable to muster sufficient support for their position, however, and the vote to amend the bill was lost by a majority of nine.[121] The unamended act, which was soon voted on by the House, directed that proceeds from duties on salt and whiskey imported from the United States were to be appropriated for the relief of war sufferers.

Opinion on Mackenzie's "most puzzling question" transcended nascent party boundaries. An examination of the voting on the final reading of the 1830 compensation bill shows that the Assembly was not simply split between reformers and conservatives. Altogether, of the thirty-nine members present for the vote, twenty-four favoured passage while fifteen did not. It is true that all of the conservatives wanted Upper Canadians to pay a portion of the claims, and every one of the ten ministerialist members present voted in favour of the bill. The fifteen opponents of the measure, in contrast, were all supporters of the reform movement. But fourteen other oppositionists joined with their traditional enemies to support the measure, and this reform-conservative coalition ensured passage of the act. Why did nearly half the reformers support a motion forcing Upper Canadians pay a portion of the costs? Undoubtedly, some members followed their conscience and voted on the bill according to firmly held principles. Varying degrees of enthusiasm for the measure, however, may also have been related to private concerns. For instance, the fifteen reformers who believed the British should pay all the costs were apparently willing to see payments delayed in order to defend that principle. But this position was obviously easier to maintain if personal finances were not involved. Seven of the fourteen reformers who voted in favour of the province paying a portion of the costs were claimants themselves. At the same time, none of the fifteen reformers who voted against the bill were war sufferers.[122]

The debate over the merits of the 1830 war-losses bill, like those over the alien issue years before, clearly revealed that other divisions were also at work in the Assembly. For example, Peter Perry, who was known as the "Parliamentary Bull Dog" of the reform group, said that he was against increasing the duty on salt because it would only hurt the "labouring part of the community."[123] One of the members for Prince Edward, James Wilson, also argued that "men who work for a living" should not be forced to pay the claimants. He favoured sales of clergy reserves instead, and Wilson felt that Strachan and his colleagues should sacrifice their resources for the war sufferers. "Do the clergy defend the country? Do the clergy of any denomination fight the battles of the country? No Sir, no Sir, by no means," he reminded the Assembly. "Let us have the revenue and we can pay and we will pay for all the war losses," Wilson further declared, "and we will make our roads, build bridges and make canals."[124] Another member from eastern Upper Canada, William Morris, declared that the provincial debt was already too large to permit any new expenditures. Such statements prompted a sharp rebuke from John J. Lefferty, who sat for one of the Niagara area constituencies. "Members will sit and look at each other and laugh when the distresses of those who suffered in the war are brought forward," Dr Lefferty said, but that was because they had not witnessed the suffering first-hand: "Had you been at Niagara, had you been at Chippawa you would have known how they suffered ... Yes sir, people in Niagara not only sacrificed their property but their lives for their country. They not only gave their property but their blood for the seats you hold." To this impassioned speech fellow reformer Hugh C. Thomson, a founding member of the Kingston Association and the representative for Frontenac in eastern Upper Canada, said that he "thought the hon. member's remarks were uncalled for."[125]

Lefferty's outburst was a reminder that the conflict had touched various regions in strikingly different ways. All the reformers who voted against the compensation bill, except for John Rolph of Middlesex, represented ridings from York eastward.[126] Most of these opponents of immediate reimbursement, therefore, came from areas where war damages were slight, and the one exception to that rule, Rolph, was not a war sufferer either. Naturally their perception of the conflict was vastly different from colonists who were not so lucky and, according to Lefferty, the mere mention of war-related hardships was enough to prompt smiles and laughter among some. For hundreds of western Upper Canadians, however, the conflict had involved more than record profits, and any discussion of losses was sure to bring old antagonisms to the surface. At one point during the same session, George Hamilton from Wentworth declared that eastern Upper Canadians appeared to be heartless "pitiable creatures" who had never "witnessed the distress of war." Fellow reformer Paul Peterson, who sat for the riding of Prince Edward, immediately rose to defend the reputation of his constituents. Peterson denied that the only "good soldiers" were those who had participated in battles, and he said he had seen men marching on patrol at the "bay of Quinte, with as much bravery and cheerfulness as any man who marched to Niagara."[127] Hamilton was apparently too much of a gentleman to suggest that the cheery attitude reflected a certain knowledge that no enemy troops would ever bother to set foot in Prince Edward County.

Despite the passage of the 1830 compensation bill by both houses of the legislature, the claimants remained unpaid because the duties collected under the act proved insufficient for the purposes intended. When the Assembly again dealt with the issue two years later, a conservative majority held power in the House but the attitudes of some representatives had changed very little. Peter Perry, the member for Lennox and Addington, still refused to support any attempts to raise a loan, "as it would launch the province into debt." Marshall Bidwell, another reformer from eastern Upper Canada, was also opposed to raising a loan, and he reminded his fellow members that the public debt was already too large. The Assembly had before it another proposal to borrow fifty thousand pounds for the construction of canals on the St Lawrence, and Bidwell felt that "so young a country" as Upper Canada could not continue to spend beyond its means. Other members, including Charles Duncombe from Oxford, expressed more moderate views. Duncombe believed that the British ought to pay for all damages since "the war was a war about maritime rights." But if the authorities in England were determined not to bear the burden alone, Duncombe thought that Upper Canada should provide the money required. The tory view, as elucidated by

Henry John Boulton from Niagara, was that the province could afford both canals and war-claim payments. Tolls at each lock would generate revenue, and the new attorney-general had calculated that the St Lawrence system would pay for itself and the war losses in only twenty-five years. Boulton also remarked that the Assembly's failure to solve the war-losses problem in the past "was a fact which he could not contemplate without feelings of shame," and he pointed to the plight of David Secord to illustrate the need for immediate action. He noted that this "respected and venerable old man" had "lost his all during the war." As a former member of the Assembly, Secord was still "looking to that House to do him justice."[128]

Passage of the 1832 war-claims compensation bill was guaranteed because conservatives outnumbered reformers forty to nineteen in the 1830–4 parliament. On 28 January 1832 the Assembly appropriated the money collected from salt and whiskey duties for the payment of war losses.[129] If those funds proved insufficient to service the loan, the province stood pledged to "make good any deficiency" from other revenues.[130] An unrelated disagreement with the Legislative Council, however, prevented the war-claims bill and several other pieces of legislation from receiving royal assent that session.[131] The pressing need for such legislation was soon made evident when Mackenzie called for township meetings to be held in western Upper Canada. Claims from that region dated from Brock's march and, after nearly two decades of broken promises, the sufferers were demanding to be heard. Thomas Talbot, who was a war claimant himself, was the first to respond to the "imagined grievances" presented during the township gatherings, and he called for a general meeting of his settlers to be held at St Thomas on 23 April 1832. Talbot claimed that he wished to hear the "real sentiments of the inhabitants" so he might "put down the fire." A similar gathering was called for Sandwich, where rumours that the executive government was witholding payments were countered by damaging evidence showing "Mr. Mackenzie and his party" had actually been obstructing passage.[132]

For his part, Mackenzie continued to blame the executive for the lack of proper war-losses legislation. While on his tour of the countryside in the spring of 1832, Mackenzie had interviewed hundreds of Upper Canadians and had acquired thousands of signatures on petitions. One result of Mackenzie's vernal perambulation was a lengthy document dealing with the war-claims problem. In January 1833 he presented a package to Lord Viscount Goderich, secretary of state for war and the colonies, that contained eleven petitions. The ninth dealt with the war-losses issue and, according to Mackenzie, the blame for delays in payment did not rest with his faction. "The present House endeavoured to provide for the payment of the War Losses," Mackenzie argued, "but were checked by the Legislative Council, which is to say the Government." A few years later, in his famous 1835 report on grievances, Mackenzie included the opinions of reformers who felt the administration had mishandled the war claims. Gilbert McMicking, an assemblyman from Niagara, agreed with Mackenzie that the crown and clergy reserves should have been used to provide compensation. Fellow reformer James Wilson maintained his old postion and said that instead of borrowing money or increasing duties, the crown and clergy reserves should have been sold to liquidate the claims. Upper Canadians, Wilson noted, "did not provoke the war with the United States" and should not be expected to pay "the war losses out of their hard labour."[133]

By the 1830s, however, the war claims were not an issue of importance to vast numbers of Upper Canadians and, for most inhabitants, problems arising from the conflict must have appeared remote indeed. Because of the fighting, a total of 2884 claims for damages had been submitted to the 1815–16 commission. That number represented about one-quarter of the adult male wartime population, and probably one in every four or five pioneer families, as much as 25 per cent of the population, orginally had a real interest in the payment of those claims.[134] But natural increases in population, as well as great numbers of immigrants, had reduced that ratio substantially. So too had the work of the 1823–6 committee of revision which declared that only 1819 claims were valid. By 1837, when the losses were liquidated, the war sufferers awaiting payment represented about 1.8 per cent of the adult male population; only one in every fifty families, or about 2 per cent of Upper Canadians, would likely have been directly interested in the results.[135]

Like the people they represented, the interests of assemblymen in the issue also declined over time. More than 54 per cent of the assemblymen in the first postwar parliament had been war sufferers, but the proportion dropped to 48 per cent for the seventh parliament (1816–20), declined even further to 40 per cent in the eighth parliament (1820–4), and fell below 23 per cent in the next Assembly. In 1837 only six assemblymen received payments for losses, and they accounted for less than 10 per cent of the representatives in the thirteenth parliament.[136] Moreover, most of the war claimants present in the Assembly during the 1830s were owed comparatively small sums of money. The average award for members of the thirteenth parliament (1836–41) amounted to less than £377. In the immediate postwar period, however, members of the sixth parliament (1812–16) were granted awards averaging more than £1160.[137]

Both political manoeuvring and sincere disagreements about the best mode of liquidating the claims combined to prevent the payment of war losses for several years. Older issues, of course, had to compete with newer questions, and many of the more current controversies stemmed from the unprecedented number of immigrants entering the province. Questions about internal improvements, control of revenue, settlement policies, relief systems, schools, public health, and penetentiaries occupied the time of most legislators. In an ironic twist, the influx of newcomers who arrived in the 1830s may also have contributed to the solution of the war-losses problem. Among the thousands of postwar arrivals were many staunchly conservative immigrants, including Irish Protestants renowned for their sense of loyalty to the crown. Tory members gained support as a result and, because conservatives expressed a greater willingness to borrow funds to liquidate the claims, these immigrants also assisted the cause of the war sufferers.[138] Thus it was the tory-dominated eleventh parliament that finally authorized a loan of £55,000 sterling to help indemnify the sufferers on 13 February 1833.[139]

Despite the best efforts of local politicians, payments to war claimants were once again delayed because of stalling overseas. In addition to the loan of £55,000 sterling, the Assembly had at its disposal other money collected by taxes and from the sale of confiscated estates. By 1835 the province was prepared to make its payment of £57,412 sterling and had nearly another £4000 sterling that could be applied to the losses.[140] The British Treasury department had promised previously to advance half the outstanding balance, which would have amounted to £28,955 sterling out of a total of £57,910 sterling, but on 26 January 1835 Lieutenant-Governor John Colborne notified the legislature that authorities at the Colonial Office had determined on a new plan. The British government indicated it would provide £17,910 sterling if the Assembly appropriated a further £40,000 sterling. After several months of negotiations the province agreed to the deal, half the amount being paid out of the casual and territorial revenue of the colony and £20,000 sterling pledged by the legislature, and the appropriate measures were passed on 28 November 1836.[141] Payments were delayed, however, because the Upper Canadian legislation had stipulated that funds were to be withheld until all the money required was "in the hands of the Receiver General." On 19 December 1836 the Assembly was informed that no money had yet been received from England and the £40,000 appropriated by the province was therefore sitting idle.[142] Finally, on 4 March 1837, new legislation was enacted to allow for the immediate payment of all outstanding claims.[143] The "most puzzling question" in colonial politics had at last been solved.

For many war sufferers, of course, the award had come too late. One hundred and thirty of the claimants had died by the time the committee of revision began its work, and a number of other sufferers, including Robert Nichol, would die before the 1825 preliminary report was issued. In 1832 Henry John Boulton lamented that "numbers of grey headed sufferers had gone down with sorrow to the grave," without having received full compensation.[144] Five years later so many claimants were either dead or had assigned the rights to their awards to creditors that the representatives who drafted the war-losses bill were forced to include a specific clause dealing with powers of attorney.[145]

In one sense, the decision to liquidate the remaining claims also came too late for the government. Near the end of 1836 the Upper Canadian economy began to feel the effects of a worldwide depression and, as one historian has observed, the province "was in a very poor position to weather the resulting storm."[146] The colony's finances had never completely recovered from the postwar recession, and even the resumption of duty payments from Lower Canada did not have an appreciable impact on the provincial debt. By 1828 the province owed creditors more than £112,166, and that figure rose steadily over the next few years.[147] Part of the problem stemmed from inadequate sources of revenue. In 1830 a provincial finance committee reported that the colony had spent £49,695 in 1829 but had received only £29,149 as its share of duties levied in Lower Canada.[148] That shortfall in ordinary income was compounded by the pattern of borrowing initiated in 1821 when the legislature found itself unable to pay militia pensions. From then on the Assembly borrowed heavily for canal projects and road construction, and the province gradually saddled itself with an enormous debt. After approving an initial grant of £25,000 for the Welland Canal, for example, the province continued to pour money into the project: £50,000 in 1827; £25,000 in 1830; £50,000 in 1831; £7500 in 1833; and £50,000 in 1834. Once the process had begun, the province seemed incapable of putting a stop to it and, in 1837, the Assembly promised a further £245,000 to the company.[149] The sums voted for war losses were paltry in comparison, but the decision to borrow thousands of pounds to meet the outstanding claims of the sufferers only made the later financial crisis more pressing.

The economic downturn in 1837 prompted demands from some quarters for more frugal government. For other colonists, including William Lyon Mackenzie, the only solution to the myriad problems of the colony seemed to lie in armed rebellion. Mackenzie's supporters were few in number and he drew many of his followers from Whitchurch township north of York. During the war large numbers of American settlers in that region had refused to serve in the militia, and two of Mackenzie's lieutenants, Silas Fletcher and Jesse Lloyd, were among them. Fletcher had arrived in the province in 1806 but, after the outbreak of war, he was listed as a deserter from the Markham militia. Lloyd was of Quaker stock and, during the conflict, he had refused to serve and was later fined for having ignored a press warrant for his sleigh.[150] On 5 December 1837 a small party of rebels proceeded south towards the capital, where they were met by a handful of government supporters. Both sides exhibited the same sort of steely reserve shown by most militiamen during the war and, after firing once, each group took to its heels and Mackenzie's revolt quickly collapsed.[151]

Rumours that the rebellion had succeeded, however, prompted more than four hundred settlers near Brantford to take up arms. The leader of this revolt was Charles Duncombe, who had represented Oxford in the Assembly since 1830. At first Duncombe had sided with the tory faction in the legislature, but by 1835 he was recognized as a "moderate reformer." The shift in his political views may have occurred when Duncombe was refused a patent for land he had bought. In 1835 the Executive Council decreed that the property, which had originally belonged to Benejah Mallory, could not be transferred to Duncombe since it should have been confiscated along with the estates of other traitors.[152] A few other western rebels may have harboured similar grievances against the administration, and members of the Malcolm family, who took a prominent part in the revolt, had suffered extensive property damage during the war. Finlay Malcolm and his sons, Finlay and John, had submitted claims for more than £2800 worth of losses to the committee of revision, and the long delay in receiving payment may have soured their views towards the colonial government.[153] Most of the other rebels had no connection to the war-claims issue, and the majority of the men would have been only about five years old when the conflict began.[154] Like the rising to the east, Duncombe's revolt soon fizzled. The "Boy Hero" of the war of 1812, Allan MacNab, was given the responsibility of rounding up those insurgents who had failed to flee to the United States.[155]

The original Brock monument after the 1840 explosion
Morden, *Historical Monuments*

Over the next few years the province was menaced by rebel raiding parties operating out of American bases. The provincial militia was called out on a semi-permanent basis and, as in the War of 1812, the men deserted in droves. In an attempt to stem the tide, a suggestion was made that rewards be offered for the capture of militia fugitives. British authorities refused to sanction the action, however, because they were "fearful of the enormous expense this would entail."[156]

Benjamin Lett was one of the raiders who menaced the province, and his work earned him a measure of fame. At four o'clock in the morning on Good Friday, 17 April 1840, the citizens of Queenston were awakened by the sound of a terrific explosion. Lett had somehow "contrived to introduce a large quantity of Gunpowder" into the column of Brock's monument, and the subsequent detonation of that charge destroyed most of the structure.[157] A little over three months later more than 5000 Upper Canadians assembled on Queenston Heights to plan for the reconstruction of the monument. This time the lieutenant-governor was in attendance, and Sir George Arthur was joined by men of all parties in a meeting that revealed the first stirrings of nationalistic emotions. Arthur was surprised at the enthusiasm of the crowd and he later admitted that he had "never expected to have seen such a scene in the Province."[158] Usual distinctions were forgotten, reformers joined with conservatives, easterners mingled with westerners, and one newspaper reported that the "great meeting went off with the highest degree of unanimity and enthusiasm."[159]

Those who attended the gathering at Queenston Heights were told of the illustrious past of the colony. In speech after speech, Upper Canadians were asked to recall the glorious exploits of the "brave little band" who had stood shoulder to shoulder with Brock at Detroit. Well-known veterans, such as William Hamilton Merritt, John Beverley Robinson, and Alan MacNab, preferred their accounts of great events for those too young to possess their own memories of the conflict. No mention was made of disaffection, desertion, profiteering, or treason, and the hardship, jealousy, and discord engendered by the fighting were also ignored. This was a time for rejoicing, an opportunity for celebration and not recrimination, and under the forlorn wreck of the old column the citizens vowed that they would erect an even larger monument. To Sir George Arthur this was proof that, whatever divisions might still exist in the colony, "there is unanimity in U[pper] Canada when the National Honor is concerned."[160]

9 "A Greater Degree of Patriotism": Developing Nationalism

On 21 July 1840, a little over a week before the great meeting on Queenston Heights, William Allan, Alexander Wood, and a young blacksmith by the name of Paul Bishop met at the head office of the Bank of Upper Canada.[1] Thomas Gibbs Ridout, the cashier at the institution, greeted the men and presented Allan and Wood with a handful of papers he had prepared. Once the forms were signed, Bishop and his assistants carted away two dusty boxes that had been in the vault for more than fifteen years. A few hours later, Bishop and his two helpers were busily engaged in the work of defacing hundreds of Upper Canada Preserved medals. The work was done in the garden behind Alexander Wood's stately home, where a temporary blacksmith shop had been established. Bishop would later say he had set up an anvil in the backyard and the "medals were brought in successive trayfuls, and were, one by one, smashed on the anvil with a large hammer."[2] The scraps were then gathered together and sold to two watchmakers in the town. On 11 November, a date that later generations of Canadians would reserve for the remembrance of war veterans, Allan and Wood deposited the proceeds from this work, £393 12s ½d, in the bank account of the Toronto General Hospital.[3]

The Upper Canada Preserved medals had been a source of controversy in the province for decades. An inquiry into the subject had been launched by the Assembly in 1831 and William Allan was one of a number of witnesses asked to testify. Allan explained that most of the medals had been deposited in the bank in 1823 or 1824 and that those in his possession were sent there some time later. When asked why the decorations had never been distributed, Allan said he believed that much "jealousy and discontent" would have arisen because "no previous means had been taken to ascertain who were the persons most entitled to receive them."[4] Either Allan was lying or he had a faulty memory, since he and other directors of the Loyal and Patriotic Society had appointed John Beverley Robinson and William Chewett to report on "the persons most entitled to receive them."

No action was taken by the Assembly in 1831, probably because the Legislative Council would have blocked any move to force a distribution of the awards, and there the matter rested until February 1840. By that time Strachan's influence over the upper council had been greatly reduced. In 1838 the new lieutenant-governor, Sir George Arthur, had taken an instant dislike to Strachan, and his poor opinion of the archdeacon was reinforced when he examined the accounts of the local college. Arthur discovered that Strachan had used his position as trustee to borrow public funds for his personal use.[5] Convinced that such impropriety was inexcusable, Arthur recommended that Strachan not be appointed bishop of Upper Canada. Arthur thought William Armstrong was a more suitable candidate, but British authorities disagreed and Strachan's patent was issued in July 1839. As bishop, he devoted an increasing amount of time to concerns of the church and he resigned from the Legislative Council in 1841; his influence in colonial politics waned rapidly. This development pleased Arthur, but he deeply regretted that his friend Armstrong had been overlooked: "not only on my account, but for the sake of this community."[6]

The power of the upper council was further reduced when Charles Poulett Thomson arrived to take over Arthur's post temporarily in November 1839. Thomson convinced the Assembly to accept a legislative union with Lower Canada by promising that the huge public debt of the province, which amounted to more than £1 million, would be relieved through access to the Lower Canadian treasury. He also appointed moderate reformers to influential positions, made Robert Baldwin solicitor-general, and even managed to solve the clergy reserve issue. One-half the income from land sold was to be appropriated for the Church of England and the Church of Scotland, according to their numbers, and the rest was divided among other denominations on the same principle.[7] Having eliminated this old bone of contention, the Assembly then turned its energies towards resolving the grievances associated with the Upper Canada Preserved medals.

On 8 February 1840 Alexander Wood and John Strachan were called to appear before a select commmittee established to investigate the medal issue. Wood proved to be a hostile witness, however, and he told the committee that the operations of the Loyal and Patriotic Society were "wholly of a private nature" and were not the concern of the Assembly. The committee disagreed, noting that money had been donated to relieve suffering and for the creation of awards; the objects of the society, therefore, were "entirely of public nature." The bishop of Toronto proved to be no less hostile when he appeared before the board. Strachan lied to the members, claimed that he did not possess a copy of Chewett and Robinson's report, and said that the medals were never distributed because of the "extraordinary lists sent in by the Commanding Officers."[8] Strachan knew full well that originally only 147 men had been nominated for the awards and that the "extraordinary lists" had actually been compiled by Patriotic Society members. After receiving the report of the select committee on 8 February 1840, the Assembly resolved: "That this House is of the opinion, that it is most desireable that the Medals referred to should be distributed according to the original intention, among the Militia entitled to them and who are living, and the children of such as are dead, that they may be retained, as a distinquished memorial." The House speaker, Allan MacNab, was directed to transmit a copy of the Assembly's resolutions so "that they may be complied with."[9]

Determined to see that the medals did not "fall into unworthy hands," an emergency meeting of the surviving directors was held on 7 July 1840. Among those in attendance were John Strachan, John Beverley Robinson, William Allan, and Alexander Wood. Former members who might have agreed with the Assembly's resolution, such as William Baldwin, were not informed that a meeting had been called. At this gathering the directors ordered the medals defaced as soon as possible. The men who were present would later claim they had no idea of the select committee's recommendations, although they had appeared as witnesses before the board. They said too that knowledge of the Assembly's wishes would not "have led to passing of a different resolution."[10]

Through their actions, the directors of the Patriotic Society had ensured that deserving candidates would never receive the awards for which they had been nominated. In the years that followed, as the true heroes of the War of 1812 passed away, the controversy over the medals would be forgotten. In its place flourished the militia myth – all colonists had risen as one to defend the country and all were deserving of recognition. A few individual Upper Canadians, however, were remembered for their heroic deeds. One of them was John Strachan, "the fighting bishop," who "saved" York from "wholesale burning."[11] Another of the "heroes of the capitulation," William Allan, was even luckier, since he acquired both recognition and – unique among all militiamen – a number of Upper Canada Preserved medals.[12] C.W. Robinson, John Beverley's son, would later reminisce that he had seen two of the medals, one gold and one silver, at the Allan household long after the defacement party had taken place.[13] Hamilton Craig, who examined the controversy over the awards, has asked: "If William Allan did really retain two medals as mementos, who could find it in his heart to point the finger of accusation?"[14] One is tempted to speculate that the militiamen who served under Allan during the April invasion, and the 147 candidates who were deprived of awards, might have an answer for Craig.

The men who were cheated out of their awards had little to show for their wartime services. Members of select militia units, like the first flank companies and Incorporated battalion, had received land grants in the 1820s, but pensions for all militiamen were not instituted until 1875. In that year the parliament of Canada voted $50,000 for "militia survivors," and the search for eligible veterans revealed that most were "in indigent circumstances, many having no one to depend upon for support, and living entirely on public charity."[15] While the memories of some had "let many a fact slip away," at least one sedentary militia veteran vividly recalled his postwar experiences. Robert McAllister, a member of the Burford militia, said that he had fought at the vicious Battle of Lundy's Lane, but after hostilities had ceased he "got no marks of distinction, no grant."[16]

The decision to grant pensions in 1875 was a product of a renewed interest in the War of 1812. For more than a generation, students in the schools of the province had been taught of the valiant efforts of the colonial defence forces. Spurred into action by the rebellions of 1837, Upper Canadian legislators passed the first proposal for tax-supported schools in 1838. The financial embarrassment of the colonial treasury, however, prevented immediate implementation of the plan and tax-supported schools did not become a reality until 1841. All parties in the Assembly believed that state-run schools would inculcate proper values in youngsters. Conservatives believed that children would learn to respect authority, while reformers saw the schools as a means of preventing the return of oppressive administrations. A proper education, available to all, would preserve the province from the "twin evils of aristocratical domination and popular tyranny."[17]

The inauguration of a public school system was one indication that Upper Canada, or Canada West as it was known after 1841, was no longer a primitive, frontier society. Before the war, travellers often found the colony's few roads to be impassable, and in many places fallen trees, commonly referred to as "racoon bridges," were the only means of crossing streams.[18] Even pioneers who avoided overland travel found that trips between villages could be extremely time-consuming. In the 1790s, for instance, a journey from Niagara to Kingston by sailboat sometimes required two or three days.[19] Fifty years later the provincial road network, while still a source of numerous complaints, was much improved, and a trip from Kingston to Niagara could be accomplished in a matter of hours on board one of the fifty or more steamboats operating on Lake Ontario.[20]

Changes in the provincial education and transportation systems mirrored developments within colonial society and the empire as a whole. Duelling and the days of the "old code of honour" were gone forever by the time the war sufferers were paid in 1837. The last recorded duel in the province had taken place four years earlier at the military settlement at Perth.[21] If arrested for any criminal act, including duelling, Upper Canadians no longer faced being branded or placed in a pillory.[22] In 1835 a penetentiary had opened at Kingston, and the public humiliation of criminals was replaced with a more modern routine of confined prisoners quietly moving in lockstep. In addition to a prison, Kingston boasted a new legislature since it had also been chosen capital of the United Province of Canada. The seat of government had finally been pried from "muddy York," which was now known officially as the City of Toronto.[23] One of the first acts passed by the new Legislative Assembly in 1841 was a pardon for Robert Gourlay. True to his nature, he found fault with the colony's offer of a pension and refused to return to Canada.[24] One can hardly blame Gourlay, since so much had changed since the "Banished Briton" had last set foot in the colony. The province now boasted a population of nearly half a million inhabitants and, in June 1837, those colonists had celebrated Queen Victoria's accession to the throne. Three other sovereigns had ruled since the War of 1812 and the colony had entered the war under George III, the man who had reigned during the American Revolution.

Students who attended schools in Victorian Canada West learned that their ancestors had played a crucial part in preventing the complete dissolution of the empire. Major John Richardson, a veteran of the War of 1812, had been approached by a group of politicians who wanted suitable textbooks for the new school system. Richardson agreed to write three volumes, and in 1842 the first volume of the "Historical Narrative Series for the Use of Schools in Canada" was published in Brockville. In his preface to this work, Richardson noted that young people should be made aware of the real facts of the war instead of being left to acquire knowledge through the "corrupt channel of American party publications." This first volume dealt with the "Operations of the Right Division of the Canadian Army," and the "gallant deeds" of the inhabitants, as well as the actions of British regulars, were the focus of the book. Students were informed that the "French and English races" were "knit together in one common bond" and that all colonists had done their duty nobly.[25]

Richardson's work, and others by writers such as Gilbert Auchin-leck which followed in later years, perpetuated many of the myths originated by John Strachan. Readers in mid-nineteenth-century British North America were told that all Upper Canadians had taken to arms at the first signs of danger and that the citizens had fought bravely until the province was free of invaders. By 1857 even members of parliament were repeating such fabrications. A committee appointed to investigate the propriety of granting half-pay to flank officers reported that the "entire population of Canada, both Militia and Indians, came forward and tendered their services." The report went on to recommend that pensions be granted since "few instances are recorded where the inhabitants of any country evinced a greater degree of patriotism."[26]

A closer examination of events, however, has clearly revealed that later histories often bore little relation to actual events. The prospect of war frightened most Upper Canadians and the vast majority seemed to want no part in the conflict. Divided by race, origins, and religion, separated by huge tracts of forests, Upper Canadians had no sense of unity, no concept of a shared nationality. During the war these divisions were intensified, westerners and residents of the Niagara region were angered that they bore the brunt of enemy attacks, and those rare individuals who volunteered their services were disgusted when thousands of others raced to acquire exemptions. Those who profited by the war were marked as targets by others who did less well and, whenever British control over a territory was lost, favourites of the government found that jealousy could endanger their lives. Some colonists derided the military skills of the regulars, many soldiers in the British army scorned the value of militiamen, and most whites appeared to agree that native warriors were more trouble than they were worth. Each segment of the population tried to take advantage of the other. A small group of merchants made enormous profits from military contracts, and combatants robbed citizens of every item imaginable, including those that were nailed down. Hundreds of colonists died from wounds or disease and thousands more, especially in the west and in the Niagara region, suffered terrible financial hardship when their crops and farms were destroyed.

After the war the province remained divided and new disputes arose once the long-term economic effects of the conflict began to be felt. Within a few years, a variety of contentious issues arising out of the war helped foster the creation of an opposition group in the Assembly. Concerned for the colony's future, a number of elected representatives in the postwar period first voted to appoint a provincial agent and then formed a committee which recommended that significant changes be made to the colonial administration. When the actions of the legislators were cut short, some inhabitants turned to Robert Gourlay and his novel methods of agitation. While official efforts to repress the activities of the "Banished Briton" were successful, they did not eliminate any of the real sources of discontent in the province. Some disputes, such as those over war losses, militia backpay, pensions, land grants for veterans, and American immigration, were directly related to the fighting. Others, including the lengthy controversy over the control of reserved lands, stemmed from the original constitution of the colony, yet the conflict seems to have served as a catalyst in promoting debate. For a number of reasons the compensation question also remained a divisive issue in the province until the 1830s, when it was finally resolved. The decision to borrow money to pay the war sufferers, however, was made only after the colony had already borrowed beyond its means to finance other expensive projects. Ironically, that immense financial burden made union with the flush treasury of the lower province far more attractive to many Upper Canadian legislators. It was imperial policy and bankruptcy that "knit together" the two provinces, not common wartime experiences.

The sense of a shared national identity, which began to emerge in the 1830s, did not flower until the memories of wartime grievances had begun to fade away. Only when the truth was obscured or forgotten could Upper Canadians join together as one. Desertion, profiteering, and treason provide infertile ground for the growth of such sentiments, and these traits were conveniently omitted from the standard nineteenth-century works on the war. Prior to 1812 the term "Canadian" was reserved for those settlers whose origins could be traced to Quebec. Most inhabitants would have identified themselves as Irish, Scotch, English, Indian, American, Loyalist, or German, but few would have declared themselves Canadians. By the time the second Brock monument was completed in 1857, however, all that had changed. One resident of the province who attended the celebrations held at Queenston Heights on 13 October 1857 later wrote to a friend in England: "You may be assured we had a great day on the Heights to do honour to him, of your country, who

The second Brock monument, built in the mid-1850s.
Lossing, *Pictorial Field-Book of the War of 1812*

sacrificed his valiant life in defending our home, Canada ... I was
among those present on the heights and I enjoyed the day as a native
Canadian ought to."[27] Naturally, sacrifices were required to achieve
this development. One hundred and forty-seven men were deprived
of the recognition that was due them so that all could share in the
glory of victory. Those who lost everything they had strived to create
before the war were also forgotten. In the place of potentially divisive
truths, Upper Canadians and their descendants supped a soothing
mixture of distortions and myths.

APPENDIX A
Colonial Accounts

Colonial accounts were tabulated using four different valuations. The most common was the provincial or Halifax currency and all values quoted in this work are in provincial currency unless stated otherwise. Also in use were New York currency and sterling. All three of these systems were based on the pound, with one pound equal to twenty shillings and one shilling equal to twelve pence. Finally, prices were sometimes expressed in American dollars. The exchange rate for each of these currencies fluctuated over time. The rate of exchange in effect during the war was as follows:

Upper Canadian Currency Values

Provincial Currency	Exchange Factor	Result
£1	0.9	18s sterling
£1	1.6	£1 12s New York cy
£1	4.0	$4

One pound provincial currency was equal to 0.9 of a pound sterling or eighteen shillings sterling. The New York pound was worth much less; one pound provincial currency was equal to £1 12 shillings New York currency, while four dollars were needed to purchase one provincial pound.

Gourlay's Township Meetings

A comparison of the list of war claimants who submitted claims to the committee of revision in the 1820s suggests that ninety of them were involved in Gourlay's township meetings. The names of those who attended the meetings in each district can be found in the first volume of the *Statistical Account*. The names of these claimants and their claim numbers are presented below.

WESTERN DISTRICT

Claim	Name	Claim	Name
423	John McGregor	127	Angus McIntosh
119	F. Baby	841	G. Jacobs
460	J.B. Baby	673	William Caldwell
1765	A. Maisonville	534	William McCrae
675	Thomas Crow	747	James Forsyth
1105	Hezek Wilcox	871	John Williams
656	Jacob Dolsen	703	Daniel Dolsen
1022	William Stirling	981	John Peek
1348	John Laird	698	Joshua Cornwall
1853	John Dolson	965	Samuel Osborne

LONDON DISTRICT

Claim	Name	Claim	Name
1470	Daniel Springer	143	Peter Teeple
84	John Robins	1915	John Bray
115	Morris Sovereene	1160	William Culver

Claim	Name	Claim	Name
196	Daniel Freeman	585	Samuel Brown
1437	Abraham Smith	1546	Simeon Davis
1599	James Nevills	507	Daniel Rapelje
1317	M. Burwell	1579	Alex Ross
1594	Leslie Patterson		

GORE DISTRICT

Claim	Name	Claim	Name
1061	Benjamin Smith	249	John Brant
1366	Augustus Bates	783	Thomas Ghent
917	Ralph Morden	664	Asahel Davis
916	James Morden	1245	Nicholas Kern
1637	George Chisholm	1607	John McCartey
7	James Crooks	274	William Hare
959	William Nevills	1307	John Keagy
290	Andrew VanEvery	517	H. Lyons
509	Robert Nichol	951	Jacob Erb
72	James Durand	530	John Wilson
503	Richard Hatt	1893	Wm. Rymal
537	Chris Almost	338	Jacob Rymal
800	Peter Hogeboom	166	Joseph House
490	Danl. Showers	209	Lot Tisdale
461	Richard Beasley	592	Alexander Brown
616	George Chisholm, Jr		

NIAGARA DISTRICT

Claim	Name	Claim	Name
1143	Christian Zavitz	1139	J. Warren
904	Andrew Miller	326	Henry Warren
977	William Powell	451	John Applegarth
1419	Ben Hardison	807	Mathias Haun
632	Thomas Cummings	788	John Garner
167	William Chisholm	1036	Paul Shipman
1188	John Clark	633	William Crooks
987	Elijah Phelps	1888	Thad Davis
362	Jacob Upper	421	John Decou
635	Calvin Cook	1117	Richard Yokum
366	Shubal Park	164	William Robertson

EASTERN DISTRICT

Claim	Name	Claim	Name
1922	John Cameron	1967	Donald McPherson

APPENDIX C
A Note on Methods and Sources

Altogether, there were four commissions appointed to investigate war claims. The first, in 1813, involved militia officers examining claims against the commissariat, but most records from this committee were destroyed by American invaders during the war.[1] The second began work in 1815 when military boards were again established to investigate claims against the army commissariat. This commission collected evidence at Niagara, Fort Wellington, Kingston, York, and in the London and Western districts. The investigators soon discovered that hundreds of Upper Canadians also expected payment for damages done during the war, and not just for goods or services provided to the military. Since that was beyond their mandate, the officers rejected any claim for damages by enemy forces.[2] Not surprisingly, some claimants demanded a broader investigation, and later in 1815 the third commission was established. This was a civilian committee appointed to examine all war losses, not just commissariat claims. The 1815–16 commission began its work in December 1815 and eventually 2884 claims were examined.[3] Seven years later, after complaints about fraudulent submissions, a committee of revision was appointed. This fourth commission began its work in 1823, and by 1826 it had reviewed 2055 claims for losses.[4]

I have made use of the final reports of the third commission from 1815–16 and the complete records of the fourth commission from 1823–6. The earlier commission was useful because its final reports offered precise accounts of how much damage (in monetary terms) was done by British troops, enemy soldiers, and warrior allies. The 1823–6 committee of revision did not always note who was responsible, and its final report did not divide the damages according to perpetrators. Still, information for the SPSS* computer survey used for chapters 6, 7, and 8 was derived from that commission. There were several reasons why the 1823–6 committee of revision was selected: most of the documents for that investigation had survived intact and were relatively undisturbed; the committee was thorough in examining submissions; and, most importantly, final payments were based on its report. Claims 365 to 1121 are found in volume 4357, while claims 1116 to 1874 are in volume 4358. Information on claims 1 to 364 can be found in volumes 3735 and 3736. Full records do not appear to exist for claims 1875 to 2055, but minutes regarding the submissions, which detail names, location, and amounts owed, can be found in volume 3729. The records of the various war-claims commissions are located in NA, RG 19, E5 (a), but the documents are arranged in a haphazard fashion and in many cases are quite jumbled. Unfortunately, the finding aid for the reports is of little use since it often confuses one commission for another.

In 1828 John Beverley Robinson announced that more than £182,180 sterling was owed the sufferers according to work done by the 1823–6 committee of revision. But the total from the computer-generated survey was just over £195,908, or a little more than £176,172 sterling.[5] That discrepancy of £6008 sterling is likely the product of several factors. First, simple coding errors and mistakes in keypunching may have played a part. Second, fluctuating exchange rates may also have affected the total. The raw data used for the survey was usually presented in provincial currency, and submissions were made between 1823 and 1826. Minor changes in the rate of exchange between 1823 and 1828, therefore, may account for some of the difference between the survey results and Robinson's official total. Finally, there were also mistakes in the original data and at times, for example, it was not made clear whether the submission was in sterling or provincial currency. In 1825 an accountant reported the existence of at least six tabulating errors in the first 1726 claims, and there were probably others in the final 329.[6] Unfortunately, only the rough minutes exist for claims 1875 to 2055, and the majority of errors may stem from those last submissions. Without more complete records, however, there is no way to cross-check the information to ensure greater accuracy.

Notes

1 See, for example, Finlay and Sprague, *The Structure of Canadian History*, 99. Similar statements are to be found in Coles, *The War of 1812*, 265; and Brode, *Sir John Beverley Robinson*, 25–6. In 1914 Laurence Burpee went so far as to suggest that even the Canadian Pacific Railway owed its origin to the fighting; "Influence of the War of 1812 upon the Settlement of the Canadian West." Only recently have researchers begun to examine the impact of campaigning on Upper Canada. See, for instance, Dennis Carter-Edwards, "The Battle of Lake Erie and Its Consequences: Denouement of the British Right Division and Abandonment of the Western District to American Troops, 1813–1815," in *War on the Great Lakes*, 41–55.

2 These ideas existed before 1880. As early as 1862, Gilbert Auchinleck, one of the editors of the *Anglo-American Magazine*, noted that with the help of "a mere handful of British troops the Canadian militia achieved the expulsion of the invading foe." Auchinleck felt that all Canadians should be thankful that earlier colonists, with "true hearts and strong arms," had managed to preserve the British connection; *A History of the War between Great Britain and the United States*, 5. Those sentiments were echoed two years later by William Coffin, a Canadian soldier and civil servant who feared that the Civil War in the United States might lead again to invasions of British North America. Like Auchinleck, he stressed that earlier inhabitants had gladly shouldered the burden of military service: "They thronged to

the banner of Brock. The Province rose as a man. Numbers for whom arms could not be provided, returned disappointed to their homes. The rest did their duty nobly." Those men had shown that the successful defence of the region was possible, and Coffin believed Victorian Canadians should remember the war "as an example and a warning"; *1812; The War and Its Moral*, 18–19, 41. See Bell, "The Loyalist Tradition in Canada," for some other examples of these ideas.

3 Ryerson, *The Loyalists of America and Their Times*, 2: 379, 471.

4 Edgar, *Ten Years of Upper Canada*, 6–7.

5 Evidence for this can be found in R. A. Bowler's dissertation "Propaganda in Upper Canada," 130, and his article "Propaganada in Upper Canada in the War of 1812," in *War along the Niagara*, 77–92.

6 Berger, *The Sense of Power*, 90. The growth and role of historical societies in the 1800s is dealt with in Killan, "Preserving Ontario's Heritage," 108–11.

7 McConnell, "The Effect of the War of 1812 on Canada," 183.

8 Stacey, "The War of 1812 in Canadian History," in *The Defended Border*, 332–3.

9 Stanley, "The Contribution of the Canadian Militia during the War," in *After Tippecanoe*, 44–5.

10 McConnell, "The Effect of the War of 1812 on Canada," 182.

11 Shortt, "The Economic Effect of the War of 1812 on Upper Canada," in *The Defended Border*, 296–302.

12 Wood, *The War with the United States*, 171; Mahant and Mount, *An Introduction to Canadian American Relations*, 92.

13 See, for example, Glazebrook, *Life in Ontario*, 92.

14 Hammond, "Banking in Canada before Confederation, 1792–1867," in *Approaches to Canadian Economic History*, 141.

15 For the view that economic troubles really began in 1819 see Jones, *History of Agriculture in Ontario 1613–1880*, 38–9; Baskerville, introduction, *The Bank of Upper Canada*, xxxi; Fraser, "Like Eden in Her Summer Dress," 105.

16 See Shortt, *Adam Shortt's History of Canadian Currency and Banking*, 66, and A.R.M. Lower, "The Character of Kingston," in *To Preserve and Defend*, 19.

17 Shortt, for instance, seems to have relied on the papers of Richard Cartwright for most of his information on the financial aspects of the war; "The Economic Effect of the War of 1812," in *The Defended Border*, 297–300. See also Sheppard, "Deeds Speak," 207–8, 224–6, for an example of how Strachan's views on the war have been incorporated by later writers.

18 Fear of further American invasions led to lavish expenditures on projects like the Rideau Canal system which were destined to remain

military "white elephants." The Rideau system drained the British treasury of more than one million pounds by 1834. That figure was four times the amount needed to pay for the war claims; Craig, *Upper Canada*, 153.

19 It should be noted that prewar Upper Canadians were not uniformly opposed to paper money; its widespread use was reported upon by many visitors to the province. See, for example, Gray, *Letters from Canada*, 229; and Douglas, *Lord Selkirk's Diary 1803–1804*, 138–9.

20 Two recent works on early Canadian economic history have ignored the dramatic impact of the fighting on Upper Canada's population. Although the population total in 1814 was actually less than in 1811, both McCalla's "The 'Loyalist' Economy of Upper Canada," 285, and Norrie and Owram's *A History of the Canadian Economy*, 164, 173, insist that the population increased by nearly 25 per cent over the course of the war.

21 Ryerson, *The Loyalists of America and Their Times* 2: 472.

22 Stanley, *The War of 1812*, 414–15.

23 Dunham, *Political Unrest in Upper Canada*, 60. Bethune, *Memoir of the Right Reverend John Strachan*, 64–7.

24 For examples of lengthy discussions of the alien question see Mills, *The Idea of Loyalty*, 35–44; Romney, *Mr Attorney*, 82–104; and Brode, *Sir John Beverley Robinson*, 125–41. Dunham, *Political Unrest in Upper Canada*, devotes one whole chapter to the alien question but mentions the claims for damages only twice.

25 E.A. Cruikshank, "Postwar Discontent at Niagara"; Riddell, "Robert Fleming Gourlay."

26 Johnson, *Becoming Prominent*, 129.

27 A number of historians have ignored the close connection between Gourlay and the war-claims grievances. See, for example, Craig, *Upper Canada*, 93–100, Romney, *Mr. Attorney*, 85–7; Brode, *Sir John Beverley Robinson*, 52–7.

28 Craig suggested Gourlay was merely "stirring up the public to express opinions" rather than harnessing popular discontent, *Upper Canada*, 94. Dunham, in contrast, did note that there were grounds for popular discontent, but she dismissed Gourlay as a "demagogue." She also suggested that Upper Canada had simply "imbibed ... political hysteria" from him; *Political Unrest in Upper Canada*, 59–60. Not all historians have dismissed Gourlay, and some have mentioned the war claims and stressed his role in advancing the state of colonial politics. See Milani, *Robert Gourlay, Gadfly*, 91, 109; and Bowsfield, "Upper Canada in the 1820s," 6.

29 In light of the fluid nature of colonial politics this is not a surprising development. S.F. Wise has shown how conservative members of the

Assembly often disagreed with both colleagues in the legislature and Tories on the councils; "Upper Canada and the Conservative Tradition," in *Profiles of a Province*, 26–9.

30 Richardson, *War of 1812*, 1. Ryerson, *The Loyalists of America and Their Times*, 2:471.

31 Finlay and Sprague, *The Structure of Canadian History*, 99; Wise and Brown, *Canada Views the United States*, 8–9, 128; Francis, Jones, and Smith, *Origins: Canadian History to Confederation*, 212; Johnson, *Becoming Prominent*, 68.

32 Stanley, *The War of 1812*, 411.

33 *Kingston Gazette*, 11 May 1816, 3.

34 Jane Errington, for example, has written that the elite members of the Kingston community identified with supporters of the American Federalist party, and that those ties were actually strengthened by a shared opposition to the war; "Friends and Foes," 58–9.

35 *Colonial Advocate*, 12 January 1826, 3; Dunham, *Political Unrest in Upper Canada*, 82; Read, *The Rising in Western Upper Canada*, 21–3

36 Robert Fraser has shown that members of the Upper Canadian elite assumed that prosperity would ensure loyalty, and this was why they championed extensive public works in the postwar period; "Like Eden in Her Summer Dress," 160–5. Ironically, their efforts might have been better served had they permitted more liberal immigration from the United States in the immediate postwar period. The money brought by the hundreds who could have taken up residence would have lessened the severity of the recession that began in 1817.

37 For a discussion of this style of writing see Keegan, *The Face of Battle*, 27–78; and Tim Travers, "The Development of British Military Historical Writing and Thought from the Eighteenth Century to the Present," in *Military History and the Military Profession*, 23–32.

38 For example, J. Mackay Hitsman's 1965 work, *The Incredible War of 1812: A Military History*, sought to rehabilitate Sir George Prevost's "greatly maligned" reputation. G.F.G. Stanley's *The War of 1812*, published in 1983, delved into logistics, but it, too, emphasized tactics and operations. Pierre Berton has described his most recent works on the war, *The Invasion of Canada* (1980) and *Flames across the Border*, (1981), as "social history." While the books provide accounts of wartime events, they do not focus on civilians or the economic and political impact of the fighting. A handful of more recent articles on specialized aspects of the War of 1812 have moved beyond these conventions. See the works collected in *War on the Great Lakes* and *War along the Niagara*.

39 See Allan R. Millet, "American Military History: Clio and Mars as Pards," in *Military History and the Military Profession*, 12–15.

40 See Don Higginbotham, "The New Military History: Its Practioners
and Their Practices," 131–44, and Donald Graves, "'Naked Truths
for the Asking': Twentieth-Century Military Historians and the
Battlefield Narrative," 45–55, in *Military History and the Military Profession*. An early example of this fusion was Royster's A *Revolutionary
People at War* (1979), which investigated the tensions that developed
between the civilian population and George Washington's Continental
Army over provisioning and enlistment. Stephen Porter's publications,
"The Fire-raid in the English Civil War," 27–40, and "Property
Destruction in the English Civil War," 36–41, have dealt with punitive
fire-raids and property destruction and they revealed how army requisitioning and plundering led to the dislocation of trade and industry
even after hostilities had ceased. Both Christopher McKee and John
Keegan have continued to study battles, but they have avoided opera-
tional concerns in favour of investigating how soldiers dealt with the
reality of combat. McKee's work, "The Pathology of a Profession," 1–
25, for example, discussed the casualty rates for American naval officers during the early years of the force, while Keegan's pioneering
effort, *The Face of Battle*, 27–9, examined camaraderie, wounding, and
the changing demands of warfare due to technological advancement.

41 An explanation of the methodology and sources employed for this
part of the work can be found in appendix C.

42 Howison, *Sketches of Upper Canada*, 77–8.

CHAPTER 2 "A Motley Population"

1 For Brock's appointment, see National Archives of Canada (NA), Colonial Office (CO) 42/351, Gore to Liverpool, 8 October 1811, 117.
Information on Brock's life is in NA, CO42/353, John Brock to Bathurst, 28 November 1812, 216; concern over his career is in NA, CO42/
353, Brock to brothers, September 1812, 226.

2 Information on the comet is in Metropolitan Toronto Library (MTL),
Breakenridge, "Some Account of the Settlement of Upper Canada of
Robert Baldwin," 1859, 21; and Goldie, *Diary of a Journey through
Upper Canada*, 13.

3 There has been a great deal of debate over the size of the antebellum
population, and some individuals even contradict themselves. In 1815,
for instance, Joseph Bouchette said the colony had a population of
95,000; *A Topographical Description of the Province*, 596. In 1832, however, he said that calculations based on "more correct sources" (assessment returns) yielded a figure of 77,000; *The British Dominions in
North America*, 1:103. For a discussion of the numerous estimates
made over the years see Akenson, *The Irish in Ontario*, 110–12. In

1983 Douglas McCalla estimated that the population was closer to
60,000, and he based this figure on the number of households in the
colony in 1811; "The 'Loyalist' Economy of Upper Canada," 285.
Militia musters may offer a more precise method of estimating colonial populations. In the 1820s, when district returns become available,
the militia muster amounted to about 17.5 per cent of the total population (or a factor of 5.7 or so). In 1821, for example, the population
was 113,066 and the militia amounted to 19,737; in 1828 the population was 185,391 and the militia amounted to 32,438. NA, RG 9,
Upper Canada Militia, IB2, volume 1, General Annual Returns,
1808–38 (hereafter NA, RG 9 UCM); NA, RG 5, B26, Upper Canada,
Returns of Population and Assessment, 1821 population, 111 (hereafter NA, RG 5, B26, UCRPA); Upper Canada, *Journals*, 10th Parliament, 2d session, 1828 census, appendix, 4. If that ratio held true a
decade earlier, the colonial population in June 1811 would have
amounted to about 73,000 (12,801 adult males × 5.7). NA, RG 5, A1,
Upper Canada Sundries, vol. 13, 4 June 1811 Militia Return, 5437
(hereafter NA, RG 5, A1, UCS). Owing to natural increase, and because
native people, soldiers, and what Michael Smith called "sojourners"
were not counted, the figure for late 1811 would probably be closer
to 80,000; Smith, *A Geographical View*, 59–60.

4 John Howe Senior, quoted in *Eleven Exiles*, 43.

5 Thomas Jefferson quoted in Hickey, *War of 1812*, 73.

6 NA, CO42/352, Brock to Prevost, 3 December 1811, 55–8. For a less
favourable view of Brock's strategy see Hyatt, "The Defence of Upper
Canada in 1812," 39–45.

7 NA, CO42/136, Gore to Craig, 5 January 1808, 167.

8 *The Correspondence of ... Simcoe*, 1:77.

9 *The Constitutional History of Canada, 1791–1818*, 267. We can offer an
estimate of the population in the early 1790s by using the 1793
militia return, which lists 4213 men aged 16 to 50; Chambers, *The
Canadian Militia*, 35. An 1816 return was used to determine the
number of male colonists aged 50 to 60. In three companies from
across the province in 1816 (Lincoln, York, and Leeds), colonists aged
16 to 50 amounted to 1254 of 1355 or 92.6 per cent of the total. If
the ratio of the male population aged 16 to 60 in 1793 was the same,
there would have been 4552 militiamen altogether. That figure, multiplied by a factor of 5.7, produces a total population in 1793 of about
26,000; NA, RG 9 UCM, IB2, vol. 2, Annual Returns 1795–1816, partial
return 1816. Cruikshank mistakenly assumed that 4213 was the
militia total for 1788; *The Origin and Official History of the Thirteenth
Battalion*, 6.

10 *The Correspondence of ... Simcoe*, 1:27

11 Bothwell, *A Short History of Ontario*, 23.
12 *Documents Relating to the Constitutional History of Canada 1759–1791*, 1031–51. Simcoe quoted in *Constitutional History of Canada, 1791–1818*, 207.
13 *Documents Relating to the Constitutional History of Canada 1759–1791*, 1031–51.
14 Cartwright, *Life and Letters*, 95–7.
15 *Lord Selkirk's Diary 1803–1804*, 141.
16 Hayes, *The Historical Evolution of Modern Nationalism*, 6.
17 Spragge, *The John Strachan Letterbook: 1812–1834*, 24.
18 Mills, *The Idea of Loyalty in Upper Canada*, 4.
19 For information on the number of clergymen see NA, CO42/355, Drummond to Bathurst, 30 April 1814, 69. *Kingston Gazette*, 25 September 1810, 3.
20 Smith, *A Geographical View*, 79. As Akenson notes, however, Smith's estimates varied from edition to edition. At one point he claimed the British element made up 20 per cent, yet later he said it was 40 per cent; *The Irish in Ontario*, 110–12.
21 These occurrences are discussed in Craig, *Upper Canada*, 8; MacFarlane, "The Loyalist Migrations: A Social and Economic Movement," in *Manitoba Essays*, 107–20; Gates, *Land Policies of Upper Canada*, 15.
22 Gates, *Land Policies of Upper Canada*, 28; Craig, *Upper Canada*, 24.
23 *The Correspondence of ... Simcoe*, 1:108. Hansen, *The Mingling of the Canadian and American Peoples*, 1:81–2.
24 Gates, *Land Policies of Upper Canada*, 29. The population estimate of 25,803 in 1793 in note 9 above amounts to about one-third the 1811 estimate in note 3.
25 Weld, *Travels through the United States* 1:407–9.
26 Cartwright, *Life and Letters*, 95–7.
27 *Canadian Letters: Description of a Tour*, 53; Heriot, *Travels Through the Canadas*, 151.
28 Fleming, "Negro Slaves with the United Empire Loyalists," 28; Winks, *The Blacks in Canada*, 33–4, 96–7.
29 Estimates can be found in Surtees, "Indian Land Cessions," 18; and Tanner, *Atlas of Great Lakes Indian History*, 66.
30 Smith, "The Mississauga, Peter Jones, and the White Man," 35–6; Patterson, *The Canadian Indian*, 81–6; Craig, *Upper Canada*, 4–5.
31 *The Valley of the Six Nations*, xl.
32 This policy is discussed in Johnson, "The Mississauga – Lake Ontario Land Surrender of 1805," 233–53, and Firth, "The Administration of Peter Russell," 167–8.
33 For internal disputes see *The Valley of the Six Nations*, xli; information on the threat of attack and land sales is in Smith, "The Mississauga,

Peter Jones, and the White Man," 72; Patterson, *The Canadian Indian,* 8.

34 For the Delaware see O.K. Watson, "Moraviantown," 125. C.M. Johnston discusses Six Nations relations with western groups in "An Outline of Early Settlement in the Grand River Valley," in *Historical Essays on Upper Canada,* 5.

35 Tindall, *America: A Narrative History,* 1:344.

36 Archives of Ontario (AO), Richardson Family Papers, James Richardson "Incidents," MU 7534. The origins of those attitudes are discussed in Demos, *A Little Commonwealth,* 14–16; Sheehan, *Seeds of Extinction* and *Savagism and Civility*; and Salisbury, *Manitou and Providence.*

37 See Smith, "Disposession of the Mississauga Indians," 80–1, for a discussion of suspicions about the native element of the population. Carl Benn's "Iroquois Warfare 1812–1814," explains that the Iroquois viewed death as a horrible calamity, so they valued skill in battle, not reckless bravery; *War along the Niagara,* 61–7.

38 "Thomas Douglas," *Dictionary of Canadian Biography,* 5:265.

39 For Cartwright's offer see Stewart, *True Blue,* 247; for Strachan's arrival see Smith, "John Strachan and Early Upper Canada 1799–1814," 159; for the possible U.S. move see Henderson, *John Strachan: Documents and Opinions,* 23.

40 For these events see Spragge, *John Strachan Letterbook,* iv-vi; Henderson, *John Strachan: Documents and Opinions,* 23.

41 Quoted in Spragge, *John Strachan Letterbook,* vi.

42 AO, Strachan Papers, volume 1, 1794–1822, Strachan to James Brown, 27 October 1803.

43 Campbell, *Travels in the Interior* 157. AO, Strachan Papers, vol. 1, Strachan to Brown, 27 October 1803.

44 AO, Strachan Papers, Strachan to Brown, 27 October 1803; for Mortimer see Gray, "From Bethlehem to Fairfield: 1798 – Part Two," 107. The self-absorbed nature of pioneer life is also discussed in Muir, *Petticoats in the Pulpit,* 199.

45 T.G. Anderson, in *Loyalist Narratives,* 13–15. Case quoted in Moir, "Early Methodism," 55.

46 Craig discusses many of these groups in *Upper Canada,* 42–8; information on the Tunkers is in Leibbrandt, *Little Paradise,* 2–3, and Sider, "The Early Years of the Tunkers in Upper Canada," 121–9. The Society of Friends are dealt with by Dorland, *The Quakers in Canada,* 52.

47 *Public Archives of Canada Annual Report* (1892), Gore to Windman, 1 October 1806, 37. Melish, *Travels through the United States,* 494.

48 Henderson, *John Strachan: Documents and Opinions,* 21–2; NA, CO42/351, Brock to Liverpool, 3 December 1811, 146.

49 Melish, *Travels through the United States*, 494. See also Stanley, *The War of 1812*, 51.

50 *Public Archives of Canada Annual Report* (1893), 38.

51 *The John Askin Papers*, 1:436–8.

52 Landon, "The Evolution of Local Government in Ontario," 2.

53 *Canadian Letters*, 42–3; NA, CO42/352, Brock to Liverpool, 31 August 1812, 138.

54 Melish, *Travels through the United States*, 502.

55 For land granting see Gates, *Land Policies of Upper Canada*, 66–7. Talbot is discussed by Hamil, "Colonel Talbot's Principality," 183–92, and "Thomas Talbot," *Dictionary of Canadian Biography*, 8:860.

56 *Canadian Letters*, 83.

57 Henderson, *John Strachan: Documents and Opinions*, 21–2; "Henry Allcock," *Dictionary of Canadian Biography*, 5:17.

58 Romney, "The Spanish Freeholder Imbroglio of 1824," 43.

59 Burns, "True Patriotism," 14.

60 *Public Archives of Canada Annual Report* (1892), Thorpe to Gordon, 14 July 1806, 49.

61 Gates, *Land Policies of Upper Canada*, 68–9.

62 "Peter Hunter," *Dictionary of Canadian Biography*, 5:439–43.

63 *Public Archives of Canada Annual Report* (1892), Thorpe to Shee, 2 December 1806, 57; Thorpe to Cooke, 24 January 1806, 39.

64 The slogan is mentioned in *Public Archives of Canada Annual Report* (1892), William Willcocks, 8 January 1807, 68. S.R. Mealing has discussed changes to UE lists in "Francis Gore," *Dictionary of Canadian Biography*, 8:337.

65 *Public Archives of Canada Annual Report* (1892), Thorpe to Shee, 2 December 1806, 57.

66 Craig, *Upper Canada*, 63. NA, CO42/354, petition, 24 October 1811, 57.

67 "Joseph Willcocks," *Dictionary of Canadian Biography*, 5:854–5.

68 Guest, "Upper Canada's First Political Party," 289.

69 "Joseph Willcocks," *Dictionary of Canadian Biography*, 5:856–7.

70 Graves, "Joseph Willcocks and the Canadian Volunteers," 35.

71 See Bowsfield, "Upper Canada in the 1820s," 306, for further discussion.

72 Mills, *The Idea of Loyalty*, 6, 19–20.

73 Patterson, "Whiggery, Nationality," 25–31.

74 For information on legal tender in the colony see *Canadian Letters*, 75; Shortt, *Adam Shortt's History of Canadian Currency and Banking*, 53.

75 Gray, *Letters from Canada*, 229. Wilson, "The Struggle for Wealth and Power at Fort Niagara, 1775–1783," discusses the enormous problems facing early traders, 137–52.

76 Wilson, *The Enterprises of Robert Hamilton*, 60.

77 *Canadian Letters*, 56–7.

78 "Robert Nichol," *Dictionary of Canadian Biography*, 6:539–41; and Cruikshank, "A Sketch of the Public Life and Services of Robert Nichol," 6–9.

79 NA, CO42/352, Nichol to Halton, 25 April 1811, 31.

80 Ibid., Brock to Liverpool, 23 March 1812, 10.

81 *Canadian Letters*, 56; Gates, *Land Policies of Upper Canada*, 60.

82 "Richard Cartwright," *Dictionary of Canadian Biography*, 5:169.

83 Talbot, *Five Years' Residence in the Canadas*, 2:20–1; 1:413–15. Talbot's observations reflect the rudimentary nature of the prewar colonial social structure. Historian Peter Russell says, for the period 1815 to 1840, colonists recognized that there were at least three different classes in Upper Canada. The elite were the "respectable" people and these were merchants, senior government officials, and well-to-do farmers with two or more servants. Below them were the independent class of small-scale farmers and journeymen, and the dependent class of squatters, servants, and paupers; *Attitudes to Social Structure and Mobility*, 9.

84 Spragge, "John Strachan's Contribution to Education, 1800–1823," in *Historical Essays on Upper Canada*, 75–6.

85 The role of schools is described in Errington, *The Lion, the Eagle, and Upper Canada*, 52, while the patriotism of the elite is dealt with in Beasley, *The Canadian Don Quioxte*, 14; Modris Ecksteins has noted that many soldiers vounteered for service in the Great War because they considered it their duty to their nation. By the twentieth century, notions of duty and public good had been inculcated through the medium of compulsory primary education, which stressed civics and national history; *Rites of Spring*, 176–86.

86 Upper Canada, Journals of the Legislative Assembly, 11 February 1812, in Ontario Bureau of the Archives, *Report* (1912), 16 (hereafter OBA *Report*).

87 *Loyalist Narratives*, 266; Brode, *Sir John Beverley Robinson*, 10.

88 Machar, *The Story of Old Kingston*, 153, records Clark having died in 1795, but Armstrong says he died in 1793; *Handbook of Upper Canadian Chronology* 58; Wyatt-Brown, *Southern Honor*, 26.

89 Errington, *The Lion, the Eagle, and Upper Canada*, 203.

90 Conant, *Life in Canada*, 84–5.

91 AO, Strachan Papers, Strachan to Brown, 31 March 1801; Demos, *Entertaining Satan*, 377–9.

92 Spragge, *John Strachan Letterbook*, 24.

93 Wallace, "Pioneers of the Scotch Settlement," 173–4. Havran, "Windsor – Its First Hundred Years," 179.

94 NA, RG 19, E5 (a), Board of Claims for War Losses, volume 4358,
    claim 1301, evidence of Bartheaume (hereafter NA, RG 19, E5 (a)
    Board of Claims); Wallace, *The Periodical Literature of Upper Canada*,
    5, 9.
95 Mortimer quoted in Gray, "From Bethleham to Fairfield," 61. Douglas,
    Medical Topography of Upper Canada, 4.
96 NA, CO42/354, Militia Memo, 1808, 189.
97 Garland and Talman, "Pioneer Drinking Habits," 342–4.
98 Swainson, "Chronicling Kingston: An Interpretation," 305.
99 For York see Edgar, *Ten Years of Upper Canada*, 27; Dunlop, *Recollec-
    tions of the War of 1812*, 89–90; *York Gazette*, 28 July 1812, 4.
100 For Newark see Weld, *Travels Through the United States*, 1:63; Bouch-
    ette, *A Topographical Description of the Province*, 612; *Canadian Letters*,
    54; Douglas, *Medical Topography of Upper Canada*, 6.
101 *The Correspondence of … Simcoe*, 1:21.
102 *Kingston Gazette*, 25 September 1810, 1.
103 Ibid., 31 October 1812, 4.
104 MacGillivray, *The Mind of Ontario*, 25. Information on the Street
    family is in Darling, "John Darling of St. Johns U.C.," 53–4.
105 Jones, *History of Agriculture in Ontario*, 26–7.
106 Douglas, *Medical Topography of Upper Canada*, 4.
107 Berton, *The Invasion of Canada*, 19. Another writer has recently con-
    cluded that the majority of Upper Canadians were "apathetic to the
    war"; Graves, "The Best Means of Suppressing the Growing Evil," 1.
108 *Kingston Gazette*, 8 February 1812, 2.
109 Ibid., 11 February 1812, 2.
110 Ibid., 12 May 1812, 2.
111 NA, CO42/352, Brock Address, 5 February 1812, 14; Assembly
    response, 5 February 1812, 2.
112 *Kingston Gazette*, 26 May 1812, 3.
113 NA, CO42/352, Hull's Proclamation, 12 July 1812, 122.
114 *The John Askin Papers*, Askin to James McGill, 17 July 1812, 2:79.

CHAPTER 3 "Cool Calculators"

1 Selby quoted in Ermatinger, *The Talbot Regime*, 47.
2 *St David's Spectator* quoted in *Kingston Gazette*, 11 May 1816, 2.
3 AO, Eli Playter Diary, 27 June 1812, 397.
4 NA, RG 8, C Series, British Military Documents (hereafter NA, RG 8, C
   Series), volume 675, Brock to Prevost, 22 April 1812, 3; CO42/146,
   Barclay to Prevost, 5 May 1812, 209.
5 NA, CO42/352, Brock to Prevost, 3 December 1811, 55.

6 Hitsman, *Safeguarding Canada*, 57. There were unofficial militia musters prior to the passage of the 1793 act.

7 HPL, Jones, "The Militia," 3–4.

8 *Documentary History*, "Militia Law of 1808," 3:3–18.

9 HPL, Jones, "The Militia," 5.

10 NA, CO42/352, Brock to Prevost, 3 December 1811, 58–9.

11 Ibid., Brock to Liverpool, 23 March 1812, 8; Smith, *A Geographical View*, 80–1.

12 *Documentary History*, Brock to Prevost, 25 February 1812, 3:43.

13 Ibid., "An Act to Amend the Militia Act," 6 March 1812, 4:5–11; NA, UCS, vol. 14, 1811, Clenche to Shaw, 8 June 1811, 5456.

14 *Documentary History*, "An Act to Amend the Militia Act," 6 March 1812, 4:5–11.

15 NA, UCS, vol. 13, 4 June 1811 Militia Return, 5437. Altogether the militia numbered 12,801 in 1811. That was an increase of 924 from 1810 and, therefore, it is safe to assume that by 1812 the total was at least 13,000.

16 *Documentary History*, "An Act to Amend the Militia Act," 6 March 1812, 4:5–11.

17 *Kingston Gazette*, 24 March 1812, 3.

18 Ibid., 19 May 1812, 2.

19 NA, CO42/146, Brock to Prevost, 16 May 1812, 215.

20 At least three militia officers submitted claims for the loss of swords and belts; NA, RG 19, E5 (a), Board of Claims, Thomas Humberstone, claim 443; Nathaniel Bell, claim 467; Eli Playter, claim 1328. One historian has noted that officers sometimes purchased other items including special uniforms; Johnson, *Becoming Prominent*, 71–9.

21 Stanley, *Canada's Soldiers*, 146; NA, UCS, Edward Baynes's Notice, 22 February 1812, 5990.

22 NA, CO42/146, Prevost to Liverpool, 26 May 1812, 205.

23 For Armstrong see *Kingston Gazette*, 26 May 1812, 205; information on recruits and desertions is in Cruikshank, "Records of ... The Glengarry Light Infantry," 13.

24 McLeod, *A Brief Review of the Settlement of Upper Canada*, 41.

25 Brock to Prevost, 22 April 1812, quoted in HPL, Jones, "The Militia," 7–8. Prevost discussed the 15 May call in NA, CO42/146, Prevost to Liverpool, 9 June 1812, 237.

26 NA, CO42/352, Brock to Executive Council, 19 May 1812, 101; Eneas Shaw circular, 23 May 1812, 103.

27 *Documentary History*, Brock to Prevost, 11 December 1811, 3:25–6; NA, UCS, vol. 13, 4 June 1811 Militia Return, 5437. The return lists only 1926 weapons brought by the 12,801 men.

28 *Kingston Gazette*, 19 May 1812, 2.

29 AO, Abraham Nelles Papers, June memorandum.

30 NA, CO42/352, Brock to Liverpool, 23 March 1812, 9.

31 NA, CO42/146, Prevost to Liverpool, 18 May 1812, 197.

32 *Documentary History*, Nichol to Glegg, March 1812, 3:15.

33 The description of Nichol is from Scott, *John Graves Simcoe*, 206, while his philosophy on government work is from NA, CO42/352, Nichol to Halton, 25 April 1811, 31. Brock's assurance is in Cruikshank, "Sketch," 22.

34 *Documentary History*, Brock to Prevost, 28 July 1812, 4:148–9.

35 Richardson, *Richardson's War of 1812*, 11.

36 Smith, *A Geographical View*, 81.

37 The pay offer is in NA, RG 9 UCM, IB3, vol. 1, General Orders, 1812–16, 2 July 1812, 58. *Documentary History*, Brock to Prevost, 3 July 1812, 3:97, discusses the attitudes of the men.

38 *Documentary History*, Militia General Order, 1 July 1812, 3:97–8.

39 NA, RG 9 UCM, General Orders, vol. 2, 1811–21, 4 July 1812, 8; 10 July 1812, 12.

40 *Documentary History*, Brock to Prevost, 12 July 1812, 3:65.

41 Stanley, "The Significance of Six Nations Participation," 218; *Documentary History*, Brock to Prevost, 3 July 1812, 97.

42 Stanley, "The Indians in the War of 1812," 155–6.

43 NA, CO42/352, "Hull's Proclamation," 12 July 1812, 122; Smith, *A Geographical View*, 82–3.

44 Stanley, "The Contribution of the Canadian Militia," in *After Tippecanoe*, 33; *Documentary History*, spy to Van Rensselaer, 16 September 1812, 3:268.

45 NA, CO42/352, "Brock's Proclamation," 22 July 1812, 124.

46 Stanley, *The War of 1812*, 6–7; Stanley, "The Indians in the War of 1812," 150–2.

47 NA, RG 9 UCM, IB3, vol. 2, General Orders, 1811–21, 22 July 1812, 17; *Documentary History*, Militia General Order, 22 July 1812, 3:138.

48 NA, C.676, Elliot to Claus, 15 July 1812, in Stanley, "The Contribution of the Canadian Militia," 33.

49 NA, CO42/147, Prevost to Liverpool, 30 July 1812, 31–2, St George to Brock, 15 July 1812; CO42/352, Brock to Liverpool, 29 August 1812, 105.

50 T.B. St George to Brock, 15 July 1812, in *Documents Relating to the Invasion of Canada*, 61.

51 *The John Askin Papers*, Charles Askin's Journal, 24 July to 12 September 1812, 713.

52 AO, Percy Band Collection, no. 238, G. Hamilton to A. Hamilton, August 1812; no. 237, Charles Askin to A. Hamilton, 21 July 1812.

53 NA, CO42/352, Brock to Liverpool, 29 August 1812, 105.

54 "Ebeneezer Allan," *Dictionary of Canadian Biography*, 5:13–15.

55 Ermatinger, *The Talbot Regime*, 44–6, discusses the failed partnership; *Documentary History*, Brock to Prevost, 26 July 1812, 3:145–6.

56 "Andrew Westbrook," *Dictionary of Canadian Biography*, 6:808–9, notes the business deals between Talbot and others. In his fictional work *Westbrook the Outlaw; Or the Avenging Wolf*, 1, John Richardson said that Westbrook harboured a grievance over being refused a militia commission.

57 Springer to Brock, 23 July 1812, in *Documents Relating to the Invasion of Canada*, 85–6.

58 *Documentary History*, Brock to Prevost, 26 July 182, 3:45–6.

59 Ibid., Brock to Prevost, 28 July 1812, 3:148–9; Brock to Prevost, 26 July 1812, 3:145–6.

60 NA, CO42/352, Assembly Reply, 27 July 1812, 115.

61 Ibid., Executive Council Minutes, 3 August 1812, 109.

62 Ibid., Assembly Reply, 27 July 1812, 115; Brock to Liverpool, 29 August 1812, 105.

63 The address is in York *Gazette*, 5 September 1812, 2; and the new regulations in *Kingston Gazette*, 19 December 1812, 4; 26 December 1812, 4.

64 *Documentary History*, Brock to Baynes, 29 July 1812, 3:152–3; Brock to Prevost, 28 July 1812, 3:148–9.

65 NA, MG 23, H14, vol. 3, W.D. Powell Papers, "First Days in Canada," 1058. The composition of the force is discussed in NA, CO42/352, Brock to Liverpool, 29 August 1812, 105; and Stanley, *The War of 1812*, 106–7.

66 Stacey, "The Defence of Upper Canada," in *The Defended Border*, 18; Verchères in *War on the Detroit*, 107.

67 Verchères, *War on the Detroit*, 107.

68 NA, CO42/353, Brock to Brothers, 3 September 1812, 226.

69 NA, UCS, vol. 13, 4 June 1811 Militia Return, 5437. The militia of those four districts amounted to 5850 men in 1811. These calculations are an overestimate of the proportion of active men, since the total number of militiamen would have increased over the previous twelve months.

70 NA, RG 9 UCM, IB3, vol. 2, General Orders, 14 August 1812, 22.

71 *Documentary History*, Militia General Order, 18 August 1812, 3:188–9; Militia General Order, 23 January 1813, 5:46–7.

72 Ibid., Myers to Prevost, 17 August 1812, 3:185–6.

73 AO, Eli Playter Diary, August Muster Roll, 401–2.

74 *Documentary History*, Buffalo Gazette, 11 August 1812, 3:170; New York *Gazette*, 24 July 1812, 3:127.

75 McLeod, *A Brief Review of the Settlement of Upper Canada*, 44; Cruikshank, "A Study of Disaffection in Upper Canada," in *The Defended Border*, 223.

76 NA, CO42/352, Brock to Liverpool, 29 August 1812, 105; CO42/353, Brock to Brothers, 3 September 1812, 226.

77 Cruikshank, "The Battle of Queenston Heights," in *The Defended Border*, 22.

78 *Documentary History*, Militia General Order, 26 August 1812, 3:212–13; Smith, *A Geographical View*, 92.

79 McLeod, *A Brief Review of the Settlement of Upper Canada*, 44.

80 Smith, *A Geographical View*, 82.

81 *Documentary History*, Brock to Prevost, 7 September 1812, 3:243.

82 Ibid., Militia General Order, 21 September 1812, 3:285. NA, CO42/353, Brock to Brothers, 18 September 1812, 227.

83 *Kingston Gazette*, 31 October 1812, 3; *Documentary History*, Return of Casualties, 13 October 1812, 4:73; Brett, *The Wars of Napoleon*, 115–16.

84 Stacey, "The Defence of Upper Canada," in *The Defended Border*, 19.

85 Smith, *A Geographical View*, 90.

86 McLeod, *A Brief Review of the Settlement of Upper Canada*, 42.

87 This group is discussed in Smith, *A Geographical View*, 90, and *Documentary History*, *Baltimore Whig*, 5 June 1813, 5:269.

88 AO, Playter Diary, October 1812, 405.

89 York *Gazette*, 10 October 1812, 2.

90 For examples of substitution and costs see AO, Abraham Nelles Papers, John Frennett's Deposition, 11 September 1812; NA, Upper Canada RG 5, A1, UCS, Traitors and Treason, vol. 6, 6646; CO42/355, Baynes to Prevost, 18 June 1814, 404.

91 The Philips case is in AO, Military Records, Miscellaneous no. 5, Cameron's Company, 3d York, 1812.

92 *Kingston Gazette*, 9 January 1813, 3.

93 Peacetime figures for gross income are from Russell, *Attitudes to Social Structure*, 21, 75. Assumptions about wartime incomes are based on prices of goods sold to the commissariat; see chapter 6.

94 NA, RG 19, E5 (a), Board of Claims for War Losses, vol. 3735, file 3, claim 116, Job Lodor testimony. *The Constitutional History of Canada, 1791–1818*, Drummond to Bathurst, 27 February 1816.

95 AO, Captain James Mustard Papers, 26 March 1813.

96 *Kingston Gazette*, 1 December 1812, 2.

97 Cruikshank, "A Study of Disaffection in Upper Canada," in *The Defended Border*, 210; McLeod, *A Brief Review of the Settlement of Upper Canada*, 50.

98 Smith, *A Geographical View*, 90.

99 *Kingston Gazette*, 1 December 1812, 2.

100 Cruikshank, "A Study of Disaffection in Upper Canada," in *The Defended Border*, 212.

101 HPL, Special Collections, "Estimate of Sums Wanted," 25 September to 24 October 1812.

102 *Documentary History*, Sheaffe to Prevost, 3 November 1812, 4:176; Militia General Order, 13 November 1812, 4:207–8; Militia General Order, 14 November 1812, 4:211–12.

103 Ibid., Militia General Order, 28 October 1812, 4:169.

104 Ibid., District General Order, 29 October 1812, 4:170.

105 NA, CO42/354, Sheaffe to Prevost, 23 November 1812, 5.

106 Mann, *Medical Sketches*, 1. Battle casualties were determined from pension lists published in the *Niagara Spectator*, 11 December 1817. Since pensions were granted to widows or orphans, the pension lists did not include the names of single men who died on duty. For example, at least two other militiamen died in battle in late 1812 according to lists in CO 42/354, Sheaffe to Prevost, Return of Casualties, 30 November 1812, 16.

107 NA, RG 9 UCM, IB3, vol. 2, General Orders, 1811–21, District General Order, 27 September 1812, 30; *Documentary History*, District General Order, 1 October 1812, 4:27; *Niagara Spectator*, 11 December 1817.

108 AO, Abraham Nelles Papers, Field Reports 1812–14. The experiences of Crook, Macklem, and Applegarth were shared by other commanders. Captain Hatt's flank company had 35 men fit for duty on 30 November 1812 but only 26 by 11 December. Abraham Nelles's company had 53 present on 24 November but only 38 six days later.

109 *Documentary History*, Merritt to Pendergrast, 8 December 1812, 4:4.

110 Ibid., Shaw to Talbot, 11 December 1812, 296; Militia General Order, 16 December 1812, 324; NA, CO42/352, Sheaffe to Bathurst, 31 December 1812, 176.

111 *Documentary History*, New York *Evening Post*, 11 November 1812, 4:179–80.

112 Ibid., Bill Sherman's statement; David Harvey's statement, 3 December 1812, 4:247–9.

113 Ibid., Nichol to Talbot, 18 December 1812, 327; Robinson, *The Life of John Beverley Robinson*, 61.

114 AO, Strachan Papers, draft constitution, 15 December 1812.

115 Ibid., society history, 1813?; Spragge, *The John Strachan Letterbook*, Strachan to Stewart, winter 1814, 58.

116 Walden, "Isaac Brock: Man and Myth," iii. The deification of Brock began as early as 1813 when John Rolph informed a friend that the former administrator was a man "who ardently loved the country and whom every lisping child would follow into the field." NA, MG 24, J48, J.W. Whittaker Papers, 1813.

117 AO, Strachan Papers, society history, 1813?

chapter 4 "A Parcel of Quakers?"

1 Harkness, *Stormont, Dundas, and Glengarry*, 104.
2 *The Report of the Loyal and Patriotic Society*, 26–7.
3 Stanley, *Canada's Soldiers*, 149. Stanley felt that in spite of insufficient training and improper weapons, the flank members were able to "prove their worth" when war was declared.
4 *Documentary History*, Evans to Powell, 6 January 1813, 5:29–30; Prevost to Sheaffe, 27 March 1813, 5:135.
5 Pearson to Shaw, 19 January 1813, in Cruikshank, "The Militia of the Eastern District," 86.
6 NA, CO42/354, Sheaffe Address, 13 March 1813, 33.
7 Ibid., 17 March 1813, 52.
8 NA, CO42/372, Maitland to Bathurst, 1 March 1824, 23.
9 According to Brock, between 1809 and 1811 the annual provincial revenue amounted to less than £7300 or about $29,200 a year. NA, CO42/352, Brock to Liverpool, 31 August 1812, 10.
10 NA, CO42/354, Sheaffe to Prevost, 13 March 1813, 74, Sheaffe to Prevost, 18 March 1813, 76.
11 Ibid., Sheaffe to Bathurst, 20 March 1813, 72–3.
12 *Kingston Gazette*, 6 April 1813, 3.
13 Spragge, *The John Strachan Letterbook*, Strachan to Brown, 9 October 1808, vi. *Public Archives of Canada Annual Report* (1896), "Annual Militia Return," 5 January 1808, 38. Only 177 companies existed and there should have been only an equivalent number of lieutenants. There were 606 commissioned officers between the ranks of ensign to colonel, and a further 49 from coronets to assistant surgeons. In addition, there were 525 sergeants.
14 HPL, Special Collections, "Estimate of Sums Wanted," 25 September to 24 October 1812. The sixty-three officers who led four militia companies on the Niagara frontier were paid, on average, about £7.14 a month or just over 5s 2d a day.
15 Ermatinger, *The Talbot Regime*, 47.
16 *Documentary History*, "An Act to Amend the Militia Act," 6 March 1812, 4:5–11. Article xi increased the limit of a company from fifty to one hundred men. For the authorization of the regiment and for the number of men in Talbot's companies see Ermatinger, *The Talbot Regime*, 68, appendix, 336.
17 *Documentary History*, Nichol to Glegg, March 1812, 4:15.
18 Pearson to Shaw, 19 January 1813, in Cruikshank, "The Militia of the Eastern District," 86.
19 *Documentary History*, Harvey to Baynes, 16 November 1813, 8:205–6.
20 NA,CO42/355, Baynes to Prevost, 18 June 1814, 408.

21 Strachan to Coffin, 19 March 1813,in Spragge, *The John Strachan Letterbook*, 17.

22 The promise of rations is mentioned in "Joseph Seely," *Dictionary of Canadian Biography*, 5:747–9. Sheaffe quoted in Cruikshank, "The Militia of the Eastern District," 87–8.

23 Pearson's proposal called for the formation of two battalions of 500 men each for the Eastern District alone; Cruikshank, "The Militia of the Eastern District," 86. Such an optimistic proposal might have influenced Sheaffe to believe that one or two battalions could be formed in each district and, according to William Hamiltion Merritt, three regiments were sanctioned in the spring of 1813; AO, Merritt Family Papers, additional, MU4375, 9.

24 Permission to grant fifty acres per volunteer was received that summer; *Documentary History*, Bathurst to Sheaffe, 10 July 1813, 6:214; *St David's Spectator* quoted in *Kingston Gazette*, 11 May 1816, 2.

25 For information on the number of recruits in 1813 see NA, CO42/355, Drummond to Bathurst,20 March 1814, 19.

26 Information on the origins of the Incorporated Militia is in NA, CO42/372, Maitland to Bathurst, March 1824, 23.

27 NA, RG 23, H14, vol. 3, William Drummer Powell Papers, "First Days in Upper Canada," 1058.

28 The case of the four rejected militiamen is mentioned in *Report of the Loyal and Patriotic Society*, 233–4.

29 NA, CO42/372, Maitland to Bathurst, March 1824, 23.

30 Smith, *A Geographical View*, 99.

31 Richardson, *Eight Years in Canada*, 87.

32 "Allan Napier MacNab," *Dictionary of Canadian Biography*, 9:519; Beer, *Sir Allan Napier MacNab*, ix.

33 Williams, *Merritt*, 2. Merritt was born on 3 July 1793 in New York. The family had moved to New Brunswick after the revolution, but returned to the United States when they found that winters were too cold in British North America. In 1796 the family relocated in Upper Canada and Thomas Merritt managed to qualify as a United Empire Loyalist. Presumably Merritt believed the free land and other "UE" benefits compensated for the more frigid climate of Canada. For information on the origins of the dragoons see AO, Merritt Family Papers, additional, MU4375.

34 Aitkin discusses Merritt's dominant goal in "The Family Compact and the Welland Canal Company," in *Historical Essays on Upper Canada*, 157. Merritt's own account of his militia service is in AO, Merritt Family Papers, additional, MU4375.

35 Humphries, "The Capture of York," in *The Defended Border*, 251–70.

36 NA, CO42/354, Sheaffe to Prevost, 5 May 1813, 119, 132.

37 AO, Isaac Wilson Diary, Isaac to Jonathan, 5 December 1813; Humphries, "The Capture of York," in *The Defended Border*, 255; Benn, *The Battle of York*, 57.

38 *Documentary History*, William Allan, 8 May 1813, 5:194–5.

39 These events are described in NA, CO 42/354, Sheaffe to Prevost, 5 May 1813, 119; *Documentary History*, Lieutenant Fraser, May 1813, 5:182.

40 AO, Strachan Papers, Strachan to Brown, 14 June 1813.

41 Williams, *Sketches of the War*, 197.

42 AO, Strachan Papers, Strachan to Brown, 14 June 1813.

43 NA, CO42/354, "Terms of Capitulation," 27 April 1813, 21, Sheaffe to Prevost, 5 May 1813, 132.

44 The agreement on exchanging parole lists and pledging parolees not to fight is in NA, UCS, vol. 14, 1812, Prisoner Treaty, 12 November 1812, 6488. Ratios for returning prisoners are in United States National Archives, War of 1812 Papers, U.S. Marshals' Returns of Enemy Aliens and Prisoners of War of 1812–15, Part Two, 483.

45 AO, Isaac Wilson Diary, Isaac to Jonathan, 5 December 1813.

46 Beaumont's account is in *Town of York 1793–1815*, 306–7, and Miller, *William Beaumont's Formative Years*, 47. His diary was not used for propaganda purposes and it was not published until 1912 by J.S. Myer, in the *Life and Letters of Dr. William Beaumont* (St Louis 1912).

47 In September 1813 John Strachan reported that the whole Home District considered itself paroled; Strachan to de Rottenburgh, 6 September 1813; Spragge, *The John Strachan Letterbook*, 45–6. The population of York is in Edgar, *Ten Years of Upper Canada*, 27.

48 Stephen Jarvis in *Loyalist Narratives*, 253–4.

49 NA, UCS, vol. 13, 4 June 1811 Militia Return, 5437. The total number of men eligible for service in 1811 in the Home District was 1587. That number would have increased by 1812, but dropped again when people fled to the United States. It seems likely that residents from the nearby districts of Newcastle and Niagara made special trips to acquire paroles, and this could account for a total of 1700 paroles in only three days.

50 *Documentary History*, Abraham Nelles's Parole, 22 December 1813, 9:39.

51 AO, Eli Playter Diary, 27–30 April 1813.

52 Stanley, *The War of 1812*, 179.

53 AO, Robert Nelles Papers, Series B-2, Orders, Militia District Order, 1 May 1813.

54 *Documentary History*, Burwell to Talbot, 21 May 1813, 5:239.

55 AO, Robert Nelles Papers, Series B-6, Returns and Statements, "Morning States." The word "present" includes men listed as "present,"

"on duty," and "on fatigue," since all these designations concerned active duty. *Documentary History*, Vincent to Prevost, 19 May 1813, 5:237.

56 *Documentary History*,, Prevost to Bathurst, 26 May 1813, 5:137.

57 AO, Merritt Family Papers, additional 1860s, MU4375, 28 May 1813.

58 For the number of militia prisoners taken at Fort George see Lossing, *The Pictorial Field-Book of the War of 1812*, 600. For the number of paroles granted see USNA, RG 94, volume 426, 167, "List of Prisoners Paroled after Taking of Fort George," 27 May 1813, quoted in Graves, "Joseph Willcocks and the Canadian Volunteers," 38. The actual number of residents and militiamen paroled was 1193.

59 *Documentary History*, Dearborn to secretary of war, 8 June 1815, 6:55; *Kingston Gazette*, 8 June 1813, 3.

60 AO, Merritt Family Papers, additional 1860s, MU4375, 20 June 1813.

61 "Address to Canadians," in *Kingston Gazette*, 7 July 1813, 2; Cruikshank, "A Study of Disaffection in Upper Canada," in *The Defended Border*, 213. The *Buffalo Gazette* said the residents between those villages appeared well suited to the recent changes; 8 June 1813, *Documentary History*, 6:29.

62 Cruikshank, *The Fight in the Beechwoods*, 7; Cruikshank, *Documentary History*, New York *Statesman*, 21 June 1813, 5:268.

63 NA, RG 19, E5 (a), Board of Claims, claim 1298.

64 *Kingston Gazette*, 15 June 1813, 2–3.

65 For a description of the battle see *Kingston Gazette*, 15 June 1813.

66 Stanley, *The War of 1812*, 192.

67 Graves, "Joseph Willcocks and the Canadian Volunteers," 107.

68 Stanley, *The War of 1812*, 192.

69 Only about 13 per cent of the volunteers held land according to assesments made by British authorities; see Graves, "Joseph Willcocks and the Canadian Volunteers," appendix 6, 137–8. For information on Dearborn's attitudes see Stanley, *The War of 1812*, 192. Donald Graves has assembled a list that names 163 of 164 recruits.

70 In addition to the sixty-five militiamen, Vincent had other companies that were made up of Upper Canadians. Also assembled at the head of the lake were sixty-six Glengarries, twenty-nine Dragoons, and thirty members of the Coloured Corps, a group of black colonists. See *Documentary History*, "State of Troops Burlington Bay," 3 June 1813, 6:331. Altogether, probably 190, or just under 12 per cent of the troops were Upper Canadians.

71 About 1700 residents were paroled at York in April, as well as another 1200 at Fort George and 500 more at Fort Erie. Paroles were also distributed throughout western Upper Canada after the Battle of Moraviantown in October 1813. See Stanley, *The War of 1812*, 276;

Macewen, *Excerpts from the Letters*, Macewen to wife, 13 August 1813, 9–10.

72 *Kingston Gazette*, 10 August 1813, 1.

73 NA, UCS, vol. 16, Traitors and Treason, War of 1812–14, James Lymburner Testimony, 23 August 1813, 6640.

74 Ibid., Examination of Elijah Bentley, 24 August 1813, 6644.

75 Spragge, *The John Strachan Letterbook*, Strachan to de Rottenburgh, 6 September 1813, 45–6.

76 NA, UCS, vol. 16, Traitors and Treason, Examination of Elijah Bentley, 24 August 1813, 6644.

77 *Kingston Gazette*, 7 September 1813, 1–2.

78 Stephen Mecredy has shown that news of a potential American attack on Kingston in 1813 prompted the authorities to call out about four hundred militiamen, and that at least that many appeared. Mecredy also shows that others often stayed on their farms to avoid service; "Some Military Aspects of Kingston's Development," 117–18. More important than exceptional calls are the patterns of long-term service. Captain William Morgan's Flank Company of the 1st Stormont, for instance, had only seventy of ninety-four rank-and-file members in attendance in March 1813. More than 25 per cent of his men were missing (13 sick, 9 AWOL, and 2 discharged); NA, MG 19, A39, Duncan Clark Papers, journal, 21–2.

79 Akenson's study, *The Irish in Ontario*, 123–4, revealed a desertion rate of almost 29 per cent among members of one of the Leeds flank companies; Spragge, "Organizing the Wilderness," 193. Stone quoted in Akenson, *The Irish in Ontario*, 124.

80 Spragge, "Organizing the Wilderness," 193; NA, Upper Canada RG 5, A1, UCS, vol. 13, Militia Return, 4 June 1811, 5434; vol. 16, Traitors and Treason, Stone to Drummond, 27 January 1814, 6710–11.

81 Militia General Orders in NA, RG 9 UCM, IB3, vol. 2, 1811–21, 58–139, contain information on the removal of Lincoln officers and the Essex Court of Inquiry. They also include the results of six court martials held between 1813 and 1815. Twenty-two militiamen stood trial and all but four were tried for desertion. The results of Simpson's trial were announced on 14 February 1815. An additional court martial of a Lincoln deserter, John MacMillan, is noted in *Documentary History*, Militia General Order, 28 October 1814, 2:279.

82 Vincent's threat is recorded in Cruikshank, "A Sketch of The Public Life," 54; *Documentary History*, Vincent to Rottenburg, 11 October 1813, 8:50.

83 Procter's activities are outlined in Stanley, *The War of 1812*, 202–3.

84 Procter's decision to dispense with the militia is in Stanley, "The Contribution of the Canadian Militia," in *After Tippecanoe*, 39. While the

disarming of the force is noted in NA, RG 9 UCM, IB2, vol. 2, Militia Returns, 1795–1816, 1st Essex Return, 4 June 1816.

85 Stanley, *The War of 1812*, 281.

86 *Documentary History*, Brock to Glegg, 11 November 1813, 7:156–7.

87 Ibid., Examination of Mabee Brothers, 2 November 1813, 7: 183–5.

88 Ibid., Bostwick to Glegg, 14 November 1813, 8:181–2. The Militia General Order quoted is in Stanley, "The Contribution of the Canadian Militia," 40. Medcalf's exploits are in J.J. Poole, "The Fight at Battle Hill," in *The Defended Border*, 131.

89 *Documentary History*, Spencer to Tompkins, 16 October 1813, 8:65.

90 Ibid., MacFarland to wife, July 1814, 1:73. See Stanley, "The Contribution of the Canadian Militia," for an example of this letter being used as proof of the zeal of the Upper Canadian militia.

91 *Documentary History*, Drummond to Prevost, 8 February 1814, 9:189–90.

92 NA, CO42/355, Drummond Address, 14 February 1814, 22.

93 AO, RG 4, Attorney-General's Correspondence, Robinson to Foster, 20 April 1814 (hereafter RG 4, AGC).

94 *Documentary History*, Drummond to Bathurst, 20 March 1814, 9:250; AO, RG 4, AGC, Robinson to Foster, 20 April 1814.

95 *Documentary History*, Militia General Order, 24 April, 9:307–8.

96 NA, CO42/355, Drummond to Prevost, 27 April 1814, 97; *Documentary History*, Return of Right Division, 22 June 1814, 1:28–30. In the summer of 1814 the number of Upper Canadians serving from Fort Erie to York amounted to 527. The units were the Provincial Light Dragoons (39), the Incorporated Artillery (12), the Coloured Corps (23), Kent Volunteers (47), and the Incorporated Militia (406). In addition, there were 3939 British troops, or a ratio of about seven regulars for every Upper Canadian serviceman.

97 These calculations, which are based on pension lists, do not include single men who died while serving in the militia and they are therefore not an accurate total of Upper Canadian casualties. The pension lists probably record more than half the militia deaths. A casualty list compiled for the Lincoln Regiments contains the names of 108 who died, while the pension lists note only sixty-three from those companies; AO, Military Records Collection, 1812, no. 10, Lincoln Militia. If that ratio held true for all regiments, the total number of deaths would have been in the region of 269. The list presented below, which is derived from pension records, is not comprehensive, but it does provide insight into trends and it offers a large sampling of the provincial casualties; *Niagara Spectator*, 11 December 1817.

Deaths	Non-Action	Battle	Total
July to Dec. 1812	46	3	49
Jan. to June 1813	49	9	58
July to Dec. 1813	16	1	17
Jan. to June 1814	9	0	9
July to Dec. 1814	11	13	24
Total	131	26	157

98 Stanley, *The War of 1812*, 313.

99 For the 25 July totals see Cruikshank, *The Battle of Lundy's Lane*, 42, and *Documentary History*, District General Order, 26 July 1814, 1:93–5.

100 Cruikshank, *The Origin and Official History of the Thirteenth Battalion*, 19.

101 *St David's Spectator* in *Kingston Gazette*, 11 May 1816, 2.

102 NA, Upper Canada RG 5, A1, UCS, vol. 13, Milita Return, 4 June 1811, 5437. There were 2577 militiamen in the Niagara District in 1811, but Drummond only managed to draw out 150 in September 1814; see NA, CO42/355, Drummond to Prevost, 21 September 1814, 159.

103 NA, RG 9, IB3, vol. 2, Militia General Orders, 31 October 1814.

104 Stanley, "The Significance of Six Nations Participation," 228–30.

105 Stanley, "The Contribution of the Canadian Militia," 44. Upper Canadians who had their horses and carts impressed were paid ten shillings a day if they drove themselves, and seven shillings if left to the military; *York Gazette*, 10 October 1812, 2.

106 Spragge, *The John Strachan Letterbook*, Stachan to Stewart, winter 1814, 30; Canada, *Statement Showing the Name*, iv.

107 NA, CO42/355, Drummond's Address, 14 February 1814, 22; Assembly Response, 17 February 1814, 30.

108 Assembly Petition, 14 March 1814, 41–2.

109 Spragge, *The John Strachan Letterbook*, Strachan to Stewart, winter 1814, 59. The similarities between this letter and the Assembly's petition are striking, and Strachan used the same phrases in both compositions.

110 Ibid., Strachan to Clifford, 27 April 1816, 107; Strachan to Stewart, winter 1814, 59.

CHAPTER 5 "A Grand Attack on the Unions"

1 *Documentary History*, T.G. Ridout to T. Ridout, 4, 16, 21 September 1813, 7:99–100, 137, 153–7.

2 Christie, *Military and Naval Operations*, appendix D, General Smyth's proclamation, 17 November 1812, 233. Private plundering was forbidden by the conventional rules of war, but the taking of lawful booty was not. Horses, materiel, and money belonging to the losing

army were considered prizes and the usual practice was to sell the items and divide the proceeds among the victors. *Documentary History*, District General Order, 27 July 1813, 6:287, warned British soldiers not to loot since they would be punished and forced to repay owners.

3 The total number of claims is mentioned in NA, CO42/369, Galt to unknown, 12 December 1822, 127–30. The provincial militia in 1814 amounted to 11,489, and the 2884 claimants would equal about 25 per cent of the total adult male population; NA, RG 9 UCM, IB2, vol. 1, General Annual Returns, 24 March 1814.

4 NA, RG 19, E5 (a), Board of Claims, volume 3730, file two, 1816 commission report.

5 In 1812 Brock reported the annual provincial revenue had averaged £7261 sterling; CO42/352, Brock to Liverpool, 31 August 1812, 138.

6 *Documentary History*, unknown to Powell, 4 December 1812, 5:17–18.

7 *Select British Documents*, Strachan to Baynes, 2 August 1813, 2:193.

8 NA, CO42/355, Thomas Clark to Gore, 20 July 1814, 394; AO, John Strachan Papers, Strachan to Brown, 26 April 1813, reel 1.

9 *Select British Documents*, Murray to Vincent, 12 December 1813, 2:481–2.

10 *Documentary History*, Armstrong to McClure, 4 October 1813, 7:193.

11 Descriptions of the destruction are in Edgar, *Ten Years of Upper Canada*, 258–9, and Stanley, *The War of 1812*, 218–19. Total damages are estimated in *The Report of the Loyal and Patriotic Society*, 379–82.

12 Macewen, "Excerpts from the Letters," Macewen to wife, 31 March 1814, 12–13.

13 *Kingston Gazette*, 1 February 1814, 2.

14 Hein, "The Niagara Frontier and the War of 1812," 201.

15 NA, CO42/355, Response to Opening, 17 February 1814, 29.

16 AO, Merritt Family Papers, additional, 1860, 5 July 1814.

17 *Documentary History*, MacFarland to wife, July 1814, 1:73.

18 Damage estimates are in the *The Report of the Loyal and Patriotic Society*, 383.

19 *Select British Documents*, Riall to Drummond, 19 July 1814, 3:138.

20 Watson, "Moraviantown," 130.

21 AO, Isaac Wilson Diary, Isaac to Jonathan, 5 December 1813.

22 "Andrew Westbrook," *Dictionary of Canadian Biography*, 6:809.

23 *The Report of the Loyal and Patriotic Society*, 385.

24 *Select British Documents*, Talbot to Riall, 16 May 1814, 3:89.

25 Amelia Harris in *Loyalist Narratives*, 147.

26 Quoted in Stanley, *The War of 1812*, 279–80.

27 *Documentary History*, Drummond to Prevost, 31 May 1814, 1:16–17.

28 *The Report of the Loyal and Patriotic Society*, 384.

29 *Documentary History*, Drummond to Prevost, 31 May 1814, 1:16–17.

30 Amelia Harris in *Loyalist Narratives*, 148.

31 NA, CO42/355, Drummond to Bathurst, 20 November 1814, 129.

32 Ibid., Clark to Gore, 20 July 1814, 394.

33 Macewen, "Excerpts from the Letters," Macewen to wife, 6 June 1813, 3; 26 July 1813, 8–9; 3 July 1813, 6–7.

34 This is what a soldier would have eaten from September 1813 onward. A district general order dated 13 August 1813 specified these amounts of food; NA, RG 8, C Series, vol. 1170, District General Order, 13 August 1813, 365–6. A second order on 6 September 1813 specified that half a gill of rum would be given only "whilst actually encamped"; Irving, *Officers of the British Forces*, 242.

35 Fort York, "Domestic Training Manual," 169.

36 Kilborn quoted in Leavitt, *History of Leeds and Grenville*, 69.

37 At one point only one "lad" out of eight officers was well enough to work; NA, RG 8, C Series, vol. 117, Couche to Robinson, 27 September 1813, 145.

38 Mann, *Medical Sketches*, 37. Evidence of widespread use of liquor during the war is in [An Ohio Volunteer] *War on the Detroit*, 187–8, 284–5.

39 NA, RG 9 UCM, IB3, vol. 2, Militia General Orders, 1811–21, 3 April 1813, 77–9.

40 One pound of whole wheat bread, soft crumb type, equals 1095 calories. One pound of lean cooked beef, at 56 calories to the ounce, would equal 896; Robinson, *Normal and Therapeutic Nutrition*, 631, 621. A half gill, or 2.5 British imperial fluid ounces, of rum would equal 71 milliliters. At 111 calories to 50 millilitres, the liquor ration contained 158 kilocalories; *Nutrient Value of Some Common Foods*, 30. A number of assumptions have been made in order to complete these calculations. First, lean stewing beef was chosen, rather than lean and fat rib roast or other cuts, to reflect the realities of the time. Beef served to enlisted men was never of the choicest variety and, in the case of Upper Canada, the cattle may have first been driven hundreds of miles overland from Vermont. As to the bread, whole wheat was selected, although other varieties would not have affected the total in a significant manner. Finally, this is likely an overestimate of the real nutrient value of the ration. For example, because of the high cellulose content of grain, only about 90 per cent of kilocalories can be absorbed by the body; Altman and Dittmer, *Metabolism*, 281–2.

41 For Canadian and American allowances see Robinson, *Normal and Theraputic Nutrition*, 684, 98. See also Briggs and Calloway, *Nutrition and Physical Fitness*, 41–2.

42 Engels, *Alexander the Great*, 123.

43 Meat rations in the U.S. army were more generous than in the British, and Americans received 20 ounces of beef or 12 ounces of pork; Hickey,

The War of 1812, 78. Archeological evidence from bodies uncovered at Fort Erie revealed evidence of disease and stress "caused probably by heavy work and long marches;" Turner, *The War of 1812*, 99. For more information on daily routine see Joseph Whitehorne, "Fort Erie and u.s. Operations on the Niagara Frontier, 1814," in *Snake Hill*, 30–1.

44 For an athlete's requirement see Robinson, *Normal and Theraputic Nutrition*, 322; Briggs and Calloway, *Nutrition and Physical Fitness*, 32; and also Guitard, *The Milita of the Battle of Chateauguay*, 40. However, Guitard's calculations regarding army nutrition are hopelessly flawed since they also include substitutions that were added only when the primary article could not be procured. By adding the values for salt pork, Guitard (41) estimated the daily intake to be 4793 kilocalories.

45 Objections to these estimates may arise because of the widespread assumption that "spectacular" growth in average stature has occurred recently; Jana Parizkova, "Interrelationships between Body Size, Body Compostiton and Function," in *Nutrition and Malnutrition*. The typical British field soldier of 1812, however, was likely a mature man of about thirty years of age who stood nearly as tall as men do today; Stagg, "Enlisted Men in the United States Army," 634. It seems adult male heights have not changed significantly for people of European extraction since the early nineteenth century. For example, I have determined the statistically weighted, average height of 5732 Scottish militiamen in 1817 from figures presented in Stigler, *The History of Statistics*, 208. At 172.5 centimetres, these men were shorter than u.s. soldiers in the Second World War, who were of an average height of 176.5 centimetres. But the u.s. result was slightly biased because the American forces were created through selective service, not unavoidable military obligation, and candidates considered too short were rejected. Long-term studies of Italian men, who faced *universal* military service, have shown a steady rise in the average height of twenty-year-old conscripts born between 1854 and 1929 (162.4 cm to 167.4 cm), but this is not proof that final heights were greater. It may only be an indication of an earlier onset of puberty; see Clark and Haswell, *The Economics of Subsistence Agriculture*, 9. In 1974 the Food and Nutrition Board of the u.s. National Research Council used 172 centimetres as a standard height for modern adult males to determine nutrition requirements – that is, just under the average height of the Scottish militiamen in 1817; Burton, *Human Nutrition*, 154.

46 NA, RG 8, C Series, vol. 117, Smyth to Sherbrooke, 7 May 1813, 64; vol. 1170, District General Order, 13 August 1813, 365–6.

47 Bigelow, "The War of the Gulls" 23.

48 Verchères, *War on the Detroit*, 93.

49 *Select British Documents*, Procter to Prevost, 4 July 1813, 2:43–4.

50 Stanley, *The War of 1812*, 202–4.

51 NA, RG 8, C Series, vol. 117, Couche to Robinson, 27 September 1813, 145.

52 *Documentary History*, Return of right division, 22 June 1814, 1:28–30.

53 These calculations are based on information from Van Creveld, *Supplying War*, 34, and the results are expressed in short tons of 2000 lbs.

54 Weekes, "The War of 1812," 157. Each barrel would have held 196 lbs of flour; see AO, Abraham Nelles Papers, Miscellaneous, commission prices, 5 September 1814. Twenty-five barrels times 196 times 30 days = 147,000 lbs of flour, or about 73.5 tons.

55 Weekes, "The War of 1812," 157. The Indians were supplied with 25 barrels (25 x 196) or 4900 lbs of flour. That flour would have produced about 6533 lbs of bread or about 4356 rations. Therefore, approximately 4400 Indians required sixteen cattle per day, and the 4466 soldiers and militiamen would have required at least the same amount. The cattle near Burlington are mentioned in NA, RG 8, C Series, vol. 117, Couche to Robinson, 27 September 1813, 145.

56 Procter's army of 1127 men required 99 horses (one horse for every 11.38 men); Christie, *Military and Naval Operations*, 59. At that ratio, 4466 men would need about 392 draught animals.

57 NA, RG 8, C Series, vol. 116, Robinson to Freer, 12 June 1812, 244. The draught animals would have required some 335,160 lbs, or 167.6 tons of forage a month (392 × 28.5 lbs. × 30 days).

58 AO, Isaac Wilson Diary, Isaac to Jonathan, 5 December 1813.

59 Steppler, "A Duty Troublesome beyond Measure," 187.

60 AO, Abraham Nelles Papers, unknown to Nelles, 20 August 1814 discusses extortion, while NA, RG 8, C Series, vol. 119, 6–7, Turquand to Couche, 9 January 1815, explains that magistrates were involved.

61 AO, Abraham Nelles Papers, Miscellaneous, commission prices, 5 September 1814.

62 *Documentary History*, "Proclamation," 26 September 1814, 2:292; "Proclamation," 5 November 1814, 2:292.

63 NA, RG 8, C Series, vol. 119, Turquand to Roche, 9 January 1815, 5–10.

64 *Select British Documents*, Drummond to Prevost, 6 October 1814, 3:207–8.

65 NA, RG 8, C Series, vol. 119, Turquand to Couche, 8 January 1815, 12–14; Turquand to Roche, 9 January 1815, 9–10.

66 *Documentary History*, Drummond to Prevost, 5 march 1814, 9:209; Steppler, "A Duty Troublesome beyond Measure," 171, 104–5.

67 *Kingston Gazette*, 1 April 1815. See also *St. David's Spectator* in *Kingston Gazette*, 11 May 1816, 2.

68 NA, RG 5, A1, UCS, 1814, volume 19, Prevost to Drummond, 19 March 1814, 8139.

69 *Documentary History*, Izard to secretary, 31 July 1814, 2:114–15.

70 Errington, *Greater Kingston*, 17.
71 According to J.W. Spurr, 167 officers, 3549 rank and file, and two companies of artillery (approximately 100 all ranks) were in Kingston in 1815; "Garrison and Community 1815–1870," in *To Preserve and Defend*, 104.
72 Mecredy, "Some Military Aspects," 117.
73 These calculations are based on the garrison ration of 1 lb flour and 9.5 ounces pork issued daily; Fort York: Domestic Training Manual, 58. For flour in 1812 the garrison would have needed (100 men × 1 lb × 30 days) 3000 lbs, or (3000 ÷ 196 lbs) 15.3 barrels a month. The 1812 pork requirements were (100 men × 9.5 ounces × 30 days) 28,500 ounces or 1781.3 lbs, or (1781.3 ÷ 200 lbs) 9 barrels. 1813 totals can be derived by multiplying by 50, the ratio by which the garrison population increased (765 barrels of flour a month and 445 barrels of pork). The barrel sizes are from AO, Abraham Nelles Papers, Miscellaneous, Commission Prices, 5 September 1814.
74 The garrison ration included 1 lb. flour; 1 lb fresh beef or 9½ ozs pork; a ³⁄₇th of a pint of peas, one and ¹⁄₇th oz of rice, and ⁶⁄₇th of an oz of butter. If peas were unavailable, a substitution of 1 lb flour or 6 shillings would be given every week. Irving, *Officers of the British Forces*, 242. *Kingston Gazette*, 16 March 1813, 5 January 1814.
75 Weekes, "The War of 1812," 157.
76 NA, CO42/355, Drummond to Bathurst, 5 April 1814, 49.
77 Ibid., Drummond to Bathurst, 5 April 1814, 49–50, says 5000 rations were needed – about 25 barrels. See also NA, CO42/355, Drummond to Prevost, 28 April 1814, 99.
78 *Documentary History*, Drummond to Prevost, 25 April 1814, 1:11.
79 Bret-James, *Life In Wellington's Army*, 107.
80 Macewen, "Excerpts from the Letters," Macewen to wife, 26 July 1813, 8–9.
81 NA, RG 19, E5 (a), Board of Claims, volume 4375, file 3, case of John Farmer, claim 31.
82 Macewen, "Excerpts from the Letters," Macewen to wife, 13 August 1813, 9–10.
83 Conant, *Upper Canada Sketches*, 47.
84 Leavitt, *History of Leeds and Grenville*, 39.
85 Stuart, "Refutations of Aspersions," 39.
86 Hein, "Niagara Frontier," 139–40.
87 NA, RG 19, E5 (a), Board of Claims, volume 4357, claim 427; volume 3735, file 3, claim 48.
88 Ibid., volume 3735, claim 244; Dunlop, *Recollections of the War of 1812*, 63.
89 E.A. Cruikshank, *The Battle of Lundy's Lane*, 7–8.
90 NA, RG 19, E5 (a), Board of Claims, volume 4358, claim 1319.

91 Ibid., volume 4357, claim 889.

92 Ibid., claim 503.

93 Ibid., Peter Swartz claim 424; volume 4358, Robert Biggar claim 102.

94 *Hamilton Spectator*, 4 October 1880, 2.

95 NA, RG 19, E5 (a), Board of Claims, volume 4357, claim 499.

96 Ibid., volume 4358, claim 141.

97 AO, Isaac Wilson Diary, Isaac to Jonathan, 5 December 1812.

98 Stacey, "Upper Canada at War," 41.

99 Cruikshank, *The Battle of Lundy's Lane*, 7–8.

100 NA, RG 19, E5 (a), Board of Claims, volume 4357, claim 457.

101 These figures are based on a computer-generated survey and they differ from the official totals. See appendix C for an explanation.

102 NA, RG 19, E5 (a), Board of Claims, volume 4357, claim 752.

103 The Gore District is an anachronism since it was not created until after the war. However, the third commission was appointed in 1823 and made use of existing districts. Western, London, Niagara, and Gore = £342,405 or 92.5 per cent of £370,051.

104 £182,169 ÷ 382,427 = 47.63 per cent versus 0.69 per cent for Newcastle.

105 The militia total for the Gore District was created by combining the numbers for the 2nd York and 5th Lincoln. The Gore District militia was formed in the summer of 1816 and combined those two regiments; Rogers, *History of the Lincoln & Welland Regiment*, 17. The militia totals and population estimates (militia multiplied by 5.7) for each district are: Western – 971 (5535); London – 1068 (6088); Niagara – 1747 (9958); Gore – 907 (5170); Home – 887 (5056); Newcastle – 590 (3363); Midland – 1956 (11,149); Johnstown – 1,243 (7085); Eastern – 1676 (9553).

106 NA, RG 19, E5 (a), Board of Claims, volume 3730, file two, 1816 commission report.

107 AO, Strachan Papers, package o, reel 8, Fitzgibbon to Strachan, [nd].

108 AO, Isaac Wilson Diary, Isaac to Jonathan, 5 December 1813.

109 Excluding acts outside the province, the incidents of single-perpetrator cases per district are:

	Enemy	Indian	British Troops
Western	124	52	6
London	92	11	6
Niagara	156	27	50
Gore	19	118	20
Home	21	15	16
Newcastle	5	0	1
Midland	2	0	3
Johnstown	7	0	9
Eastern	29	1	6

110 *Documentary History*, Drummond to Prevost, 5 March 1814, 9:209.

111 Bret-James, *Life in Wellington's Army*, 40.

112 Hibbert, *Recollections of Rifleman Harris*, 74.

113 Robinson, *The Life of John Beverley Robinson*, 61.

114 These figures were compiled from lists in the *The Report of the Loyal and Patriotic Society*.

115 Verchères, *War on the Detroit*, 171–2.

116 Powell, for one, said the militia was only used well when it was "under the eyes of Brock"; NA, MG 23, H14, vol. 3, W.D. Powell Papers, "First Days in Upper Canada," 106. Strachan also had a low opinion of most officers other than Brock. In December 1813 he lamented the "ignorance and stupidity" of soldiers who felt "terrour" was the only way to encite compliance; "Memorial for Col. Bishoppe," December 1813, in Spragge, *John Strachan Letterbook*, 7–8.

117 *St David's Spectator* in *Kingston Gazette*, 11 May 1816, 2.

118 See, for example, Ryerson, *The Loyalists of America*, 2:471, and Richardson, *War of 1812*, 1.

119 Osborne and Swainson, *Kingston Building on the Past*, 52.

120 Spragge, "Organizing the Wilderness," 162–9.

121 Mecredy, "Some Military Aspects," ii; Errington, *Greater Kingston*, 17.

122 *Kingston Gazette*, 22 June 1814, 2.

123 AO, Isaac Wilson Diary, Isaac to Jonathan, 5 December 1813.

CHAPTER 6 "Enemies at Home"

1 *Kingston Gazette*, 11 May 1814, 3; Strachan, "A Sermon Preached at York," 33–5.

2 AO, Isaac Wilson Diary, Isaac to Jonathan, 5 December 1813.

3 NA, RG 19, E5 (a), Board of Claims, volume 3729, claim 466; Russell, "Wage Labour Rates in Upper Canada 1818–1840," 65.

4 NA, RG 19, E5 (a), Board of Claims, volume 3735, file 3, claim 12; volume 4357, claim 457.

5 *The John Askin Papers*, John Askin to Charles Askin, 28 April 1812, 2:707–8; *Kingston Gazette*, 15 February 1814, 2–3.

6 Verchères, *War on the Detroit*, 176; Spragge, *The John Strachan Letterbook*, Strachan to Bishop, 15 September 1816, 90.

7 *The John Askin Papers*, John Askin to Charles Askin, 28 April 1812, 2:707–8; John Askin to James McGill, 17 July 1812, 2:709–10.

8 MTL, Alexander Wood Business Book, 1810–12, Wood to Irvine & Leslie, 8 August 1812.

9 Smith, *A Geographical View*, 94; Hein, "Niagara Frontier," 254.

10 Lossing, *Pictorial Field-Book*, 283.

11 La Rochefoucault-Liancourt, *Travels in Canada 1795*, 18; Redish, "Why Was Specie Scarce in Colonial Economies?" 716.

12 *Documentary History*, Brock to Noah Freer, 23 April 1812, 3:58–9.

13 *Kingston Gazette*, 14 September 1813, 1.

14 Steppler, "A Duty Troublesome beyond Measure," 101–2.

15 NA, CO42/352, Brock to Liverpool, 29 August 1812, 105.

16 Neufeld, *Money and Banking in Canada*, 41–2.

17 Christie, *Military and Naval Operations*, 59; Steppler, "A Duty Troublesome beyond Measure," 101–2.

18 Stevenson, "The Circulation of Army Bills," 63.

19 *Kingston Gazette,*, 31 October 1812, 1; 12 December 1812, 3.

20 Weekes, "The War of 1812," 157.

21 *Kingston Gazette*, 15 January 1814, 1.

22 Ibid., 31 August 1813, 3; 14 September 1813, 1.

23 Ibid., 31 August 1813, 3.

24 Ibid., 13 November 1813, 4.

25 Ibid., 14 September 1813, 1–2.

26 Ibid., 31 August 1813, 3; 14 September 1813, 1.

27 Ibid., 7 September 1813, 3; 13 November 1813, 3; 25 January 1814, 4; 22 July 1814.

28 NA, RG 19, E5 (a), Board of Claims, volume 3734, file 4.

29 "Laurent Quetton St. George," *Dictionary of Canadian Biography*, 6:623; "Anne Powell," ibid., 6:604; "William Drummer Powell," ibid., 6:609.

30 *Documentary History*, Brock to Freer, 23 April 1812, 3:59.

31 Ibid., T.G. Ridout to T. Ridout, 4 September 1813, 7:99–100; *Kingston Gazette*, 15 February 1814, 3.

32 NA, RG 19, E5 (a), Board of Claims, volume 3735, file 3, claim 12.

33 *Documentary History*, John Clark to Merritt, 16 November 1813, 8:203–4.

34 NA, CO42/355, Drummond to Bathurst, 2 May 1814, 73–4.

35 Russell, *Attitudes to Social Structure and Mobility*, 9.

36 *Kingston Gazette*, 15 February 1814, 2–3.

37 Ibid., 4 November 1817, 2.

38 Craig, "The Loyal and Patriotic Society of Upper Canada," 32. Craig has determined that by October 1817 the society had collected £13,841; therefore, £39 represents 0.28 per cent of that sum.

39 Spragge, *The John Strachan Letterbook*, Strachan to Bishop, 15 September 1816, 90.

40 For an example of his complaining see ibid., Strachan to Bishop, 15 September 1816, 90. His salary was derived from the chaplaincy (£150), clerical position (£310) (AO, Strachan Papers, Strachan to Brown, 24 May 1812), and, beginning in the fall of 1812, a position as district school teacher (£100 grant) and any fees collected; *York Gazette*, 10 October 1812, 3; Russell, *Attitudes to Social Structure*, 34.

41 HPL, Special Collections, "Estimate of Sums Wanted," 25 September to 24 October 1812. At 0.025 of a pound a day, an ordinary militiaman

who served 365 days would earn £9 2s 6p. To amass £560, he would have to serve continuously for more than sixty-one years.

42 Peacetime incomes are from Russell, *Attitudes to Social Structure and Mobility*, 79–80. The 1793 budget is referred to in "Our First Legislative Assembly," 2.

43 Fort York, Account Book of the Garrison of York, "Abstract of Stoppages," 1812–15; AO, Isaac Wilson Diary, Isaac to Jonathan, 5 December 1813.

44 Fort York, Account Book of the Garrison of York. These figures do not include the months of May 1813 and September 1814, which were not recorded.

45 "Quetton St. George," 624.

46 MTL, Alexander Wood Papers, S113, 1813–16, Stuart to Wood, 24 August 1813.

47 "William Allan," *Dictionary of Canadian Biography*, 8:6.

48 For information on how the war affected the lives of two of these men see Magill, "William Allan and the War of 812," 132–41; and Firth, "Alexander Wood, Merchant of York," 5–28.

49 Fort York, Account Book of the Garrison of York.

50 McCalla, "Loyalist Economy," 291. McCalla has estimated that annual expenditures were between £54,000 and £77,000.

51 *Loyalist Narratives*, 253–4.

52 Humphries, "The Capture of York," in *The Defended Border*, 262; NA, CO42/354, Sheaffe to Bathurst, 13 May 1813, 107. Sheaffe informed Bathurst that the money was turned over when the Americans threatened to burn the village, but since Sheaffe was not there at the time he must have been informed of this by residents who were – and who perhaps had reason to want to excuse their actions.

53 Bethune, *Memoir of the Right Reverend John Strachan*, 49.

54 *Kingston Gazette*, 15 June 1813, 3.

55 MTL, Breakenridge, "Some Account of the Settlement of Upper Canada of Robert Baldwin," 18.

56 If he had been fighting, Wood should have been held as a prisoner until the next day; MTL, Wood Business Book, 1810–22, S114, Wood to Stevens, 5 May 1813, Wood to Stuart, 21 February 1815.

57 NA, Powell Papers, Notes, 1813, 12223.

58 NA, RG 5, A1, UCS, Traitors and Treason, vol. 16, George Culver Testimony, 10 August 1813, 6538; Michael Dye Information, 16 August 1813, 6542.

59 Ibid., William Knot Information, 17 August 1813, 6563.

60 Ibid., Edward Sauders Information, 16 August 1813, 6557. Four dollars equals one pound a day, while six pence = 0.025 of a pound.

61 Ibid., William Huff Information, 17 September 1813, 6658.

62 Ibid., William Wills, Sr, Information, 20 August 1813, 6602.

63 Ibid., Jacob Anderson Information, 20 August 1813, 6591.

64 Ibid., Henry Mullholand, 24 August 1813, 6646.

65 Ibid., Samuel Hatt Information, 1 September 1813, 6656.

66 Ibid., William Knot Testimony, 21 August 1813, 619–20; Betsy Osborne Information, 21 August 1813, 6622.

67 NA, Powell Papers, Powell to son, May 1813, 1234.

68 NA, RG 5, A1, UCS, Traitors and Treason, vol. 16, R.N. Lacky Testimony, 21 August 1813; Stephen Whitney Testimony, 20 August 1813, 6611.

69 Ibid., Stiles Stevens, Testimony, 23 August 1813, 6626.

70 AO, Isaac Wilson Diary, Isaac to Jonathan, 5 December 1813.

71 NA, RG 5, A1, UCS, Traitors and Treason, vol. 16, Robinson to de Rottenburg, 20 August 1813, 6534.

72 Ibid., Committee to de Rottenburg, 20 September 1813, 6664–5; 16 August 1813, 6670.

73 Ibid., 16 August 1813, 6670; 20 September 1813, 6664–5.

74 Miller, "The Notorious Ebeneezer Allan," 77; McLeod, *A Brief Review of the Settlement of Upper Canada*, 42.

75 NA, RG 19, E5 (a), Board of Claims, volume 3730, file 3, George Ward to Maitland, 1 April 1823.

76 Riddell, "Joseph Willcocks," 498; Cruikshank, "John Beverley Robinson and the Trials for Treason in 1814," 195.

77 AO, Samuel Street Papers, Declaration of William Lundy, 14 October 1824.

78 NA, RG 19, E5 (a), Board of Claims, volume 4357, claim 423.

79 McLeod, *A Brief Review of the Settlement of Upper Canada*, 42; Riddell, "An Echo of the War of 1812," 445; Cruikshank, "John Beverley Robinson and the Trials for Treason," 193.

80 *Recollections of the War of 1812*, 98, 93.

81 *Documentary History*, Powell to Prevost, 28 June 1813, 6:160–1; Information of Tapley, 24 April 1814, 9:296–7.

82 NA, RG 19, E5 (a), Board of Claims, vol. 3735, file 3, John Farmer and Thomas McCormic information; Spragge, *John Strachan Letterbook*, Strachan to Harvey, 22 June 1818, 166.

83 *Kingston Gazette*, 26 April 1814.

84 Spragge, "Organizing the Wilderness," 193, 165.

85 Richardson, "The Letters of Veritas," 84.

86 Spragge discusses the anti-Jacobin movement in "Organizing the Wilderness," 226–7; Stone's description is in QA, Joel Stone Papers, Stone to Drummond, 1814. NA, CO42/356, Drummond to Bathurst, 2 January 1815, in Steppler, "A Duty Troublesome beyond Measure," 229.

87 Quoted in Spragge, "Organizing the Wilderness," 203.

88 Weekes, "The War of 1812," in *Defended Border*, 198; Dunlop, *Recollections of the War*, 33.

89 NA, CO42/355, Drummond to Bathurst, 12 April 1814, 57.

90 NA, CO42/354, Drummond to Bathurst, 5 April 1814, 49; *Kingston Gazette*, 22 March 1814, 3.

91 McLeod, *A Brief Review of the Settlement of Upper Canada*, 47.

92 Ibid., 47; *Documentary History*, Powell to de Rottenburg, 8:229.

93 "William Drummer Powell," *Dictionary of Canadian Biography*, 6:609.

94 McLeod, *A Brief Review of the Settlement of Upper Canada*, 47.

95 Stanley, *The War of 1812*, 226.

96 Armstrong, *Handbook of Upper Canadian Chronology*, 76–82; *The Constitutional History of Canada, 1791–1818*, Drummond to Bathurst, 22 February 1816; Fryer, *King's Men*, 342–3.

97 Spragge, "Organizing the Wilderness," 225–7.

98 Richardson, "The Letters of Veritas," 80.

99 QA, Stone Papers, Stone to Coffin, nd; "David MacGregor Rogers," *Dictionary of Canadian Biography*, 6:666; Upper Canada, Journals of the Legislative Assembly, 19 February 1812 militia bill, in OBA *Report*, (1912), 37.

100 QA, Stone Papers, Stone to Coffin, nd.

101 NA, RG 5, A1, UCS, vol. 19, Sherwood to Jones, 10 July 1814, 8165–6.

102 Richards, "The Jones of Brockville and the Family Compact," 171; "Ephraim Jones," *Dictionary of Canadian Biography*, 5:456.

103 Cole, "The Local History of the Town of Brockville," 33–41; Matthews, "By and for the Large Propertied Interests," 18.

104 AO, RG 22, series 26, box 1, envelope 2, Charles Jones, 5 April 1812.

105 QA, Stone Papers, Stone to Coffin, [nd].

106 Morgan, "Joel Stone: Conneticut Loyalist," 173; QA, Stone Papers, Stone to Coffin, April 1815.

107 Richardson, "The Letters of Veritas," 79–83.

108 Armstrong, *Handbook of Upper Canadian Chronology*, 77–9; AO, RG 4, AGC, 1814, box 1, Hagerman to Robinson, 28 June 1814.

109 NA, CO42/355, Drummond to Bathurst, 28 May 1814, 82; AO, AGC, 1814, box 1, Loring to Robinson, 16 June 1824.

110 NA, CO42/356, Gore to Bathurst, 17 October 1815, 122.

111 NA, RG 1, E3, Submissions to the Executive Council on State Matters; RG 1, E3, vol. 30A, Fitzpatrick to Colborne, November 1832, 227–30.

112 NA, RG 19, E5 (a), Board of Claims, volume 3728, claim 232.

113 Ibid., volume 4358, claim 1335; claim 1628.

114 Upper Canada, Journals of the House of Assembly, 10th parliament, 2d session, 8 January–6 March 1830, appendix 1, "Return of Forfeited Estates," 146; OBA *Report* (1912), 37; NA, RG 5, A1, UCS, Traitors and Treason, Vol. 16, Abraham Markle appeal, 18 June 1813; "Abraham Markle," *Dictionary of Canadian Biography*, 6:488–9.

115 "Joseph Willcocks," *Dictionary of Canadian Biography*, 5:857.

116 Colquhoun, "The Career of Joseph Willcocks," 292.

117 Murray, "A Recovered Letter," 54.

118 Cruikshank, "John Beverley Robinson and the Trials for Treason," 196.

119 Graves, "Joseph Willcocks and the Canadian Volunteers," 4.

120 Upper Canada, Journals of the House of Assembly, 10th parliament, 2d session, appendix 1, "Return of Forfeited Estates," 146; Armstrong, *Handbook of Upper Canadian Chronology*, 76–82; "Benajah Mallory," *Dictionary of Canadian Biography*, 8:607–9.

121 NA, CO42/355, Drummond to Assembly, 14 February 1814, 22; "Acts of 6th Parliament," 14 March 1814, 35.

122 Ibid., "Acts of 6th Parliament," 14 March 1814, 35; *Kingston Gazette*, 11 May 1814, 2.

123 "D'Arcy Boulton," *Dictionary of Canadian Biography*, 6:79; Cruikshank, "John Beverley Robinson and the Trials for Treason," 191.

124 Douglas Hay, "Property, Authority, and the Criminal Law," in *Albion's Fatal Tree*, 25–30.

125 NA, RG 5, A1, UCS, Traitors and Treason, vol. 16, Robinson to Loring, 4 April 1814, 6761–71.

126 AO, RG 4, AGC, A-I-1, box 1, Robinson to Scott, 30 March 1814; NA, RG 5, A1, UCS, Traitors and Treason, volume 16, Robinson to Loring, 4 April 1814, 6761–71.

127 NA, RG 5, A1, UCS, Traitors and Treason, vol. 16, Robinson to Loring, 4 April 1814, 6761–71; Robinson to Loring, 20 April 1814, 6776.

128 AO, RG 4, AGC, A-I-1, box 1, 1814, Loring to Robinson, 8 May 1814.

129 NA, RG 5, A1, UCS, Traitors and Treason, vol. 16, Judges to Robinson, 13 May 1814, 6793; Robinson, *The Life of John Beverley Robinson*, 6.

130 Riddell, "The Ancaster 'Bloody Assize' of 1814," in *The Defended Border*, 249; Garret Neil, Jacob Overholser, and Isaac Petit died of "jail-fever" or typhus.

131 AO, RG 4, AGC, Robinson Report, A-I-1, box 1, July 1814; AO, Black, "Register of Persons Connected with High Treason during the War of 1812–14 with U.S.A.," 1926.

132 AO, RG 4, AGC, Robinson Report, A-I-1, box 1, July 1814; NA, CO 42/355, Robinson to Loring, 18 June 1814, 106.

133 AO, RG 4, AGC Robinson Report, A-I-1, box 1, July 1814; "Jacob Overholser," *Dictionary of Canadian Biography*, 5:642.

134 NA, CO42/355, Robinson to Loring, 18 June 1814, 106.

135 AO, RG 4, AGC, Robinson Report, A-I-1, box 1, July 1814; NA, CO42/355, Scott to Drummond, 28 June 1814, 108.

136 Riddell, "Bloody Assize," 113; NA, RG 5, A1, UCS, Traitors and Treason, vol. 16, petition, July 1814, 7021–22.

137 *Hamilton Spectator*, 4 October 1880, 2.

138 NA, CO42/355, Proclamation, 1 April 1814, 84.

139 Robinson, *The Life of John Beverley Robinson*, appendix 2, "York Assembly subscribers," 411; *The Report of the Royal and Patriotic Society*, 332–3.

CHAPTER 7 "Success to Commerce"

1 AO, Merritt Papers, package 1, MS 74, volume 1; MTL, Wood Business Book, Wood to Maitland Garven, 15 March 1815.

2 Jarvis in *Loyalist Narratives*, 257. AO, Isaac Wilson Diary, Isaac to Jonathan, 20 August 1815.

3 AO, Isaac Wilson Diary, Isaac to Jonathan, 20 August 1815.

4 Gourlay, *Statistical Account of Upper Canada*, 2:414.

5 Verchères, *War on the Detroit*, 168–9.

6 Cruikshank, *A Memoir of the Honourable James Kerby*, 38; NA, RG 19, E5 (a), Board of Claims, Alexander Grant, claim 1738; Grant and Kerby, claim 1183.

7 NA, RG 19, E5 (a), Board of Claims, Cummings, claim 632; Cruikshank, "A Country Merchant in Upper Canada," 188.

8 "George Hamilton," *Dictionary of Canadian Biography*, 7:379–83; Wilson, *The Enterprises of Robert Hamilton*, 165–70; NA, RG 19, E5 (a), Board of Claims, Hamilton family claims 1315, 1210, 163, 827.

9 Verchères, *War on the Detroit*, 133–4, 174.

10 NA, CO42/355, Nichol to Bathurst, 3 January 1815, 264; Brock quoted in Cruikshank, "A Sketch of the Public Life and Services of Robert Nichol," 42, 22.

11 Spragge, *The John Strachan Letterbook*, Strachan to Harvey, February 1815, 84.

12 Because of defections to the enemy the house was reduced in size. Members present in 1815 and their claim numbers are Chrysler 1385, Pattison 262, Macdonell 334, Young 1498, McGregor 527, Fairfield 1517, Clench 324, Dickson 1274, Swayze 1033, Nichol 509, Burwell 1317. Nelles 1241 and Durand 72 would be present in February 1816. Thomas Talbot, who submitted a war claim, was never a sworn or commissioned member of the Legislative Council and he never attended meetings. NA, RG 19, E5 (a), Board of Claims and Armstrong, *Handbook of Upper Canadian Chronology*, 79–80, 56.

13 NA, CO42/356, Joint Address, 13 March 1815; Drummond to Bathurst, 24 March 1815.

14 Ibid., Treasury to Goulbourn, 18 July 1815, 272.

15 Ibid., Gore to Bathurst, 17 October 1815, 121.

16 Spragge, "Dr. Strachan's Motives for Becoming a Legislative Councillor," 337.

17 NA, RG 19, E5 (a), Board of Claims, volume 3732, file 1, General Principles, 20 December 1815.

18 *Kingston Gazette*, 1 August 1815; NA, RG 19, E5 (a), Board of Claims, volume 3726, files 1–6; CO42/365, Clarke to Maitland, 6 March 1820, 45.

19 "William Kemble," *Dictionary of Canadian Biography*, 7:462; CO42/357, Gore to Bathurst, 23 February 1816, 33–4; Gore to Bathurst, 1 May 1816, 210.

20 NA, RG 19, E5 (a), Board of Claims, volume 3730, file 2, 1816 Commission Report, 46; Spragge, *The John Strachan Letterbook*, Strachan to Clifford, 25 April 1816, 105.

21 R.A. Preston, "The Fate of Kingston's Warships," in *The Defended Border*, 285; Hounson, *Toronto in 1810*, 16.

22 Sandham, *Coins, Tokens and Medals of the Dominion of Canada*; Charlton, *1971 Standard Cataloque of Canadian Coins, Tokens and Paper Money*, 32–3.

23 *Kingston Gazette*, 23 February 1813, 2; AO, Strachan Papers, draft constitution, 15 December 1812.

24 *The Report of the Loyal and Patriotic Society*, 196,148–9.

25 AO, Strachan Papers, Wilmot to Foster, 19 January 1815.

26 Ibid., Fraser to Foster, 18 January 1815; Wilmot to Foster, 19 January 1815.

27 Ibid., Report of the Medal Committee, 1 May 1815.

28 Ibid., Wilmot to Foster, 19 January 1815.

29 Ibid., Bradt to Foster, 25 January 1815.

30 *Kingston Gazette*, 12 October 1812, 2. Stanley denies that the words ever left Brock's lips and, if so, the reports published in the colonial press must have been fabrications; *The War of 1812*, 127–8.

31 AO, Strachan Papers, Report of the Medal Committe, 1 May 1815; *The Report of the Loyal and Patriotic Society*, 166–7, 217–18.

32 NA, CO42/356, Gore to Bathurst, 17 October 1815, 122–3.

33 NA, CO42/357, Kerby Petition, 22 February 1816, 50–2.

34 Ibid., Gore to Bathurst, 28 February 1816, 48–9.

35 Ibid., 13 April 1816, 131–2.

36 Stanley, *The War of 1812*, 422.

37 Robinson, *The Life of John Beverley*, 31; NA, CO42/357, Gore to Bathurst, 15 April 1816, 137–8.

38 Upper Canada, Journals of the Legislative Assembly, Gore Proclamation, 6 February 1816, OBA *Report*, (1912), 169; NA, CO42/356, Gore to Bathurst, 17 October 1815, 122–3.

39 "Francis Gore," *Dictionary of Canadian Biography*, 7:339.

40 Gourlay, *Statistical Account*, 2:443.

41 For discussions of these aspects of the economy see Talman, "Life in the Pioneer Districts of Upper Canada 1815–40," 2–3; and Heriot, *Travels through the Canadas*, 151.

42 Upper Canada, Journals of the Legislative Assembly, Assembly peti-tion, 14 March 1814, OBA *Report*, (1912), 155.

43 Fort York, Account Book of the Garrison of York, Turquand – in Account." The monthly totals in 1815 were January £53,747; Feb-ruary £24,018, March £29,651; April £7298; May £16,437; July £24,889. For 1817 see Garrison Book, "Robinson – disbursements," July £5180, August £4857, September £4,546 (shillings and pence excluded).

44 Population estimates are from Osborne and Swainson, *Kingston: Building on the Past*, 53–4, and Mecredy, "Some Military Aspects of Kingston's Development," ii.

45 Osborne and Swainson, *Kingston: Building on the Past*, 53–4.

46 J.W. Spurr, "Garrison and Community 1815–1870," in *To Preserve and Defend*, 104, 115.

47 The wartime high of 6000 to 7000 people was not matched until 1842 when the population reached 6292; A.R.M. Lower, "The Char-acter of Kingston," in *To Preserve and Defend*, 23.

48 J.C. Morgan, "The Emigrant's Notebook," in *Kingston! Oh Kingston!*, 246; Osborne and Swainson, *Kingston: Building on the Past*, 50.

49 Webb, *Modern England from the Eighteenth Century to the Present*, 161.

50 Upper Canada, Journals of the Legislative Assembly, Goulbourn to Halton, 15 January 1819, OBA, *Report* (1913), 150.

51 NA, CO42/359, Gore to Bathurst, 8 April 1817, 115.

52 Individual estimates of the value of specific animals varied widely. Horses, for example, ranged from £10 to £50, but £15 or £20 was the usual value cited. The category "cattle" includes cows, oxen, steers, and calves, while the "hog" category total includes all pigs from shoats (which might be valued at only 10 shillings or so) to full-grown adults (at £6 or more). The 1650 cases which provide information amount to 80.3 per cent of the total number of claims. To arrive at the projected numbers of livestock claimed, each actual total was multiplied by 1.245. So 1306 horses × 1.245 = 1626 horses (£24,390); 1042 cattle × 1.245 = 1297 cattle (£6485); 2027 sheep × 1.245 = 2524 sheep (£2524); and 3361 × 1.245 = 4184 hogs (£8368).

53 NA, CO42/361, Nichol to Bathurst, 4 June 1818, 377.

54 AO, Isaac Wilson Diary, Isaac to Jonathan, 20 August 1815.

55 MTL, Baldwin Papers, Deltor to St George, 11 July 1817.

56 Gourlay, *Statistical Account*, 1:441.

57 Cruikshank, "The News of Niagara a Century Ago," 55.

58 NA, CO42/355, Drummond to Bathurst, 12 July 1814, 118.

59 Spragge, *The John Strachan Letterbook*, Strachan to Murray, [nd], 92.

60 NA, CO42/359, Gore to Bathurst, 7 April 1817, 103–4.

61 NA, RG 9 UCM, IB2, vol. 2, Militia Annual Returns, 1795–1816, 1st Lennox Return 1816.

62 NA, CO42/359, Gore to Bathurst, 7 April 1817, 103–4.

63 RG 19, E5 (a), Board of Claims, Dickson claim 5; Wilson, *The Clergy Reserves of Upper Canada*, 57.

64 Divine et al., *America Past and Present*, 262–73.

65 *Kingston Gazette*, 9 December 1815, 352; NA, CO42/357, Gore to Bathurst, 12 April 1816, 129–30.

66 OBA, *Report* (1913), Halton to Goulbourn, 25 August 1818, 148–9.

67 Rainer Baehre, "Paupers and Poor Relief in Upper Canada," in *Historical Essays on Upper Canada*, 307–9; Patricia Malcolmson, "The Poor in Kingston 1815–50," in *To Preserve and Defend*, 291.

68 Upper Canada, Journals of the Legislative Assembly, 1 March 1817, in OBA, *Report* (1913), 336–43.

69 "James Durand," *Dictionary of Canadian Biography*, 6:230; Upper Canada, Journals of the Legislative Assembly, 1 March 1817, in OBA, *Report* (1913) 337.

70 *Upper Canada Gazette*, 17 April 1817.

71 Gourlay, *Statistical Account*, 2:286–8.

72 See, for example, Johnson, *Becoming Prominent*, 68–9; Wise and Brown, *Canada Views the United States*, 42.

73 Finlay and Sprague, *The Structure of Canadian History*, 99.

74 NA, CO42/358, extract of *Spectator*, 26 April 1816, 149. According to information contained in Johnson's *Becoming Prominent*, 169–238, only Cornwall, Howard, and Casey did not serve in the War of 1812; Armstrong, *Handbook of Upper Canadian Chronology*, 80–1.

75 Three assemblymen, Durand no. 72, Macdonell no. 1283, and Chrysler no. 38, mentioned only friendly forces as being responsible; Cameron no. 1922 and Burwell no. 1317 blamed no specific agent; and six others, Hatt no. 503, Cornwall no. 698, Nelles no. 1241, Clench no. 324, Secord no. 1516 and no. 501, and Swayze no. 1033, blamed both enemy and friendly forces; NA, Board of Claims, RG 19, E5 (a); Armstrong, *Handbook of Upper Canadian Chronology*, 80–1.

76 Goldie, *Diary of a Journey through Upper Canada*, 33.

77 Heriot, *Travels through the Canadas*, 151–2.

78 *St David's Spectator* in *Kingston Gazette*, 18 May 1816, 2. McCormick is dealt with in Johnson, *Becoming Prominent*, 206.

79 Gourlay, *Statistical Account*, 2:286–8.

80 NA, CO42/359, Gore to Bathurst, 7 April 1817, 104–5.

81 Gourlay, *Statistical Account*, 2:288.

82 Bethune, *Memoir of the Right Reverend John Strachan*, 74–5.

83 The total owed is from NA, RG 19, E5 (a), Board of Claims, 1816 Report, volume 3730, file 2, 46; MTL, Jarvis Papers, Kemble to Jarvis, 20 January 1820.

84 NA, CO42/356, Treasury to Goulbourn, 18 July 1815, 272; CO42/357, Gore to Bathurst, 28 April 1816, 183.

85 "John Strachan," *Dictionary of Canadian Biography*, 4:755.

86 Gourlay, *Statistical Account*, 2:441.

87 Powell Papers, Gore to Powell, 10 May 1819, quoted in Quealey, "The Administration of Sir Peregrine Maitland," 114.

88 NA, CO42/357, Gore to Bathurst (notation), 1 May 1816, 210.

89 CO42/359, Gore to Bathurst, 4 January 1817, 4; Upper Canada, Journals of the Legislative Assembly, Halton Correspondence, 15 July 1817, OBA *Report* (1913), 446.

90 NA, CO42/360, Nichol to Bathurst, 10 December 1817, 221; NA, CO42/361, Nichol to Bathurst, 4 June 1818, 376.

91 Riddell, "Robert Fleming Gourlay," 15–16; Gourlay, *Statistical Account*, 2:334.

92 The population figures for the period 1809 to 1821 are based on militia muster totals multiplied by 5.7. The annual totals are: 1809 9561; 1810 11,886; 1811 12,801; 1812?; 1813 10,819; 1814 11,489; 1815 ?; 1816 12,640; 1817 13,884; 1818 13,454; 1819 16,021; 1820 17,250; 1821 19,737; NA, RG 9 UCM, IB2, vol. 1, General Annual Returns, 1809–21. The mathematical procedures employed to produce the projected population estimates are in Petersen, *Dictionary of Demography*, 296. In the seventeen years between 1794 and 1811 the militia increased from 5350 to 12,801; Cartwright, *Life and Letters*, 105, and NA, RG 5, A1, UCS, vol. 13, 1811 Annual Militia Return, 5437. Projected figures are produced by deriving the exponential growth rate (r) for the seventeen (n) years from 1794 (P_o) to 1811 (P_n). The formula used includes the symbol e, which is approximately equal to 2.71828 and is the base of natural logarithms. The formula was $P_n = P_o e^{rn}$. The results are: 1812 13,470; 1813 14,180; 1814 14,926; 1815 15,711; 1816 16,538; 1817 17,388; 1818 18,325; 1819 19,290; 1820 20,305; 1821 21,374. The population in 1821 was 113,066; NA, RG 5, B26, UCRPA, 111.

93 *Upper Canada Gazette*, 9 October 1817, 3.

94 Gourlay, *Statistical Account*, clxxvi–cxcvi.

95 Gourlay, ibid., 2:270–4.

96 NA, CO42/362, Maitland to Bathurst, 25 June 1819, 226.

97 Dent, *The Story of the Canadian Rebellion*, 17.

98 *Niagara Spectator*, 8 January 1818, in Riddell, "Robert Fleming Gourlay," 17. The township reports are in Gourlay, *Statistical Account*, 1:274–579.

99 Riddell, "Robert Fleming Gourlay," 17.

100 Of the ninety claimants identified as Gourlayites, there may be some inaccuracies due to identical names. Eight of the correspondents from the Western District, for example, signed the petition for a township next to the one listed as their principal residence by the 1823–6 committee of revision. That commission investigated the claims more than

five years later and it is quite possible that these were the same war claimants, but they may have moved in the interim period. Also, it was not unusual for a settler to own several tracts of land in various townships. See appendix B for a list of the ninety claimants.

101 Gourlay, *Statistical Account*, 2:554.

102 Strachan, *A Visit to the Province of Upper Canada in 1819*, 187–8, 192.

103 Gourlay, *Statistical Account*, 1:369, 623–5; 90 of 381 signatories equals 23.62 per cent.

104 NA, CO42/361, Smith to Bathurst, 6 April 1818, 40.

105 Gourlay, *Statistical Account*, 2:581–7.

106 NA, CO42/361, Smith to Bathurst, 18 April 1818, 68–9; CO 42/362, Strachan to Bathurst, 2 June 1819, 209.

107 Gourlay, *Statistical Account*, 2:609–10; NA, Board of Claims, Merritt claim 1208; Clark claim 1188; Keefer claim 1518; Hamilton claim 827; Robertson claim 164; Baxter claim 581.

108 Gourlay, *Statistical Account*, 1:571–7.

109 Riddell, "Robert Fleming Gourlay," 29–30.

110 Ibid., 30.

111 Gourlay, *Statistical Account*, 2:610.

112 NA, CO42/361, Maitland to Bathurst, 19 August 1818, 115–16; Riddell, "Robert Fleming Gourlay," 34.

113 NA, CO42/361, Assembly resolutions, 22 October 1818, 120.

114 NA, CO42/369, Gourlay petition, 10 August 1822, 137; Dent, *The Story of the Canadian Rebellion*, 26–8.

115 Ibid., Maitland to Bathurst, 25 June 1819, 228; Craig, *Upper Canada*, 98; Riddell, "Robert Fleming Gourlay," 54.

116 NA, CO42/362, Maitland to Bathurst, 26 June 1819, 213.

117 Talbot, *Five Years' Residence in the Canadas*, 418–19.

118 *Upper Canada Gazette*, 9 March 1820, 3; "Richard Beasley," *Dictionary of Canadian Biography*, 7:58.

119 NA, CO42/362, petition to Maitland, 30 March 1819, 196; Strachan to Bathurst, 2 June 1819, 208.

120 Powell Papers, Powell to Gore, 1819, in Quealey, "The Administration of Sir Peregrine Maitland," 114; NA, CO42/363, Macdonell to Bathurst, 17 August 1819, 139.

121 *Kingston Gazette*, 4 November 1817.

122 *Upper Canada Gazette*, 9 October 1817, 3; Craig, "The Loyal and Patriotic Society," 33.

123 AO, Strachan Papers, Foster to Strachan, 13 December 1815.

124 Clarke, *A History of Toronto General Hospital*, 17–23;

125 AO, Strachan Papers, Robinson to Baldwin, 29 January 1822.

126 Upper Canada, Journal of the House of Assembly, 13th parliament, 5th session, "Report … in Relation to Certain Medals," 10 February 1840, 33.

127 NA, CO42/3357, Gore to Bathurst, 12 April 1816, 129–30.
128 Shortt, "The First Bank in Upper Canada," in his *History of Canadian Currency and Banking 1600–1880*, 86, 84; Peter Baskerville, introduction to *The Bank of Upper Canada*, xxix.
129 This description is from *Dictionary of Canadian Biography*, 8:5.
130 "Thomas Gibbs Ridout," *Dictionary of Canadian Biography*, 9:661; "Thomas Ridout," *Dictionary of Canadian Biography*, 6:648. The disappointment of the elder Ridout is discussed in Burns, "God's Chosen People," 222.
131 Vaughn, "The Bank of Upper Canada in Politics," 188–9. A complete list of directors can be found in *The Bank of Upper Canada*, appendix B, 321.
132 *Kingston Gazette*, 7 April 1818, 2.
133 Talbot, *Five Years Residence in the Canadas*, 416–17.
134 Cruikshank, "The News of Niagara a Century Ago," 63.
135 Armstrong, *Handbook of Upper Canadian Chronology*, 81–2; Cruikshank, "Postwar Discontent at Niagara," 46.
136 The list of 1820 Gourlayites has been compiled from Milani, *Robert Gourlay, Gadfly*, 227, and *Colonial Advocate*, 22 May 1828, 3.
137 *Colonial Advocate*, 26 January 1826, 2. Unfortunately, no mention was made of which man had not attended the convention.
138 *Kingston Gazette*, 7 July 1820, 3.
139 Brode, *Sir John Beverley Robinson*, 61–2.
140 AO, Isaac Wilson Diary, Isaac to Jonathan, 7 September 1819, 24 June 1812.
141 Howison, *Sketches of Upper Canada*, 81.
142 *The Bank of Upper Canada*, xxviii.
143 NA, CO42/366, Commission on Duties, July 1821, 251. 474

CHAPTER 8 "The Most Puzzling Question"

1 The building is discussed in Brode, *Sir John Beverley Robinson*, 61, while Nichol's activities are dealt with in NA, CO42/367, Sheaffe to Bathurst, 10 February 1821, 255.
2 Upper Canada, Journals of the House of Assembly, 9th parliament, 1st session, "Brock Monument Committee," 15 March 1825, 71; *Colonial Advocate*, 10 June 1824, 1.
3 *Kingston Chronicle*, 18 February 1820, 3; Jarvis, "Military Land Granting in Upper Canada," 131–3.
4 NA, CO42/368, Maitland to Bathurst, 18 March 1822, 55–6.
5 NA, CO42/365, Maitland to Bathurst, 18 November 1820, 183.
6 The pension problem is discussed in NA, CO42/366, Report on Duties, July 1821, 251, while the asylum is noted in CO42/365, Maitland to Bathurst, 8 March 1820, 73.

7 *Upper Canada Gazette*, 30 April 1821, 1.

8 Upper Canada, Journals of the House of Assembly, 9th parliament, 2d session, App., 1825 pension list; Craig, *Upper Canada*, 100; NA, CO42/371, Robinson memorandum, 28 January 1823, 229.

9 NA, CO42/366, Joint Address, 13 April 1821, 169.

10 Ibid., Maitland Address, 19 April 1821, 170.

11 MTL, Jarvis Papers, Kemble to Jarvis, 20 January 1820; NA, CO42/365, Treasury to Bathurst, 27 December 1820.

12 NA, CO42/366, Maitland to Assembly, 31 May 1821, 167.

13 NA, CO42/365, Nichol to Bathurst, 1 December 1820, 225–9.

14 Timothy, *The Galts*, 50.

15 C.G. Karr, "The Two Sides of John Galt," in *Historical Essays on Upper Canada*, 279.

16 NA, CO42/367, Gore to Goulbourn, 28 September 1821, 194.

17 Ibid., Treasury minute, 17 July 1821, 90; Galt, *The Autobiography of John Galt*, 1:279–80.

18 *Public Archives of Canada Annual Report* (1897), xxii; Galt, *The Autobiography of John Galt*, 1:278–9.

19 NA, CO42/367, Treasury minute, 17 July 1821, 90; Galt, *The Autobiography of John Galt* , 1:279–80.

20 Galt, *The Autobiography of John Galt*, 1:282.

21 NA, CO42/369, Galt to Vansittart, 15 March 1822, 107.

22 Spragge, *The John Strachan Letterbook*, Strachan to Clifford, 25 April 1816, 109.

23 Robinson to Macaulay, February 1821, in Brode, *Sir John Beverley Robinson*, 62–3.

24 NA, CO42/369, Maitland to Bathurst, 10 May 1881, 199.

25 NA, CO42/368, Maitland to Bathurst, 20 April 1822, 98. Since Thomas Scott had retired six years before, and Powell and Maitland had quarrelled earlier in the year, it seems Strachan was the source for that information as he was the only board member still in the lieutenant-governor's inner circle. "Thomas Scott," *Dictionary of Canadian Biography*, 6:698; and Brode, *Sir John Beverley Robinson*, 75.

26 NA, CO42/368, Maitland to Bathurst, 20 April 1822, 98.

27 NA, CO42/369, Treasury to Galt, May 1822, 75.

28 Ibid., Robinson to unknown, 19 November 1822, 121.

29 Galt, *The Autobiography of John Galt*, 1:291–2.

30 NA, CO42/369, Galt to unknown, 12 December 1822, 127–30.

31 Upper Canada, Journals of the Legislative Assembly, 15 January 1823, in OBA *Report* (1914), 204.

32 NA, CO42/371, chronology of events, 1823, 180.

33 Patrick Brode has noted that Nichol headed the opposition, but Baldwin served as his adjunct; *Sir John Beverley Robinson*, 62. Clearly, the two did not agree on all issues; *Niagara Gleaner*, 15 March 1823, 2.

34 Upper Canada, Journals of the Legislative Assembly, 12 March 1813, in OBA *Report* (1914), 405.

35 Armstrong, *Handbook of Upper Canadian Chronology*, 80–1; "Philip VanKoughnet," *Dictionary of Canadian Biography*, 10:693.

36 Armstrong, *Handbook of Upper Canadian Chronology*, 80–1; "Charles Jones," *Dictionary of Canadian Biography*, 7:455.

37 Upper Canada, Journals of the Legislative Assembly, 19 March 1823, in OBA *Report* (1914), 430–1; NA, CO42/370, 1823 Act, March 1823, 130; NA, CO42/370, Maitland to Bathurst, 24 March 1823, 128.

38 NA, CO42/371, Nichol to Galt, 26 May 1823, 171–2. Neither Robinson nor Wood actually served on the committee – the former because of time constraints and the latter because of a scandal "of a very disgusting nature"; W. Drummer Powell, "A Letter from W.D. Powell, Chief Justice, to Sir Peregrine Maitland, lieutenant-governor," [1831], 1, 5.

39 NA, CO42/371, Robinson to Wilmot, 20 January 1823, 225.

40 Peter Baskerville, introduction to *The Bank of Upper Canada*, lxiii.

41 NA, CO42/371, Gillespie, Moffat, & Finlay, 10 January 1823.

42 Ibid., Galt to Treasury, 27 January 1823, 157.

43 Ibid., Galt to Bathurst, 14 July 1823, 178; *The Bank of Upper Canada*, lxiii.

44 NA, RG 19, E5 (a), Board of Claims, vol. 3729, file 6, 58.

45 Upper Canada, Journals of the House of Assembly, 9th parliament, 1st session, app. A-2, Report of the Commissioners.

46 NA, RG 19, E5 (a), Board of Claims, vol. 3729, file 7, 2–6. The total owed, £182,180 17s 6½p sterling, divided by 1819, equals £100 3s 1p sterling.

47 *St David's Spectator* in *Kingston Gazette*, 11 May 1816.

48 NA, CO42/371, Nichol to Galt, 26 May 1823, 174.

49 NA, CO42/372, Joint Address, Janurary 1824, 112.

50 NA, CO42/368, Maitland to Bathurst, 18 March 1822, 55; CO42/374, claim correspondence, 7 May 1824, 249.

51 Information on the competitive nature of the relationship between these two men is in Rea, *Bishop Alexander Macdonell and the Politics of Upper Canada*, 51–3.

52 Galt, *The Autobiography of John Galt*, 294–8; Coleman, *The Canada Company*, 12; NA, CO42/374, Galt to Bathurst, 31 July 1824, 257.

53 Galt, *The Autobiography of John Galt*, 296–8.

54 Talbot, *Five Years' Residence in the Canadas*, 101.

55 NA, CO42/370, Strachan Chart, 22 April 1823, 141.

56 NA, CO42/372, Maitland to Bathurst, 11 February 1824, 32.

57 CO42/374, Strachan to Bathurst, 8 June 1824, 428.

58 "John Strachan," *Dictionary of Canadian Biography* 4:757.

59 NA, CO42/375, Strachan to Bathurst, 7 January 1824, 42.

60 Craig, *Upper Canada*, 136.

61 NA, CO42/372, Maitland to Bathurst, 5 February 1824, 42; Maitland to Bathurst, 1 March 1824, 25.

62 Fitzgibbon, *A Veteran of 1812*, 147; *Kingston Chronicle*, 10 May 1822, 3.

63 NA, CO42/372, Maitland to Bathurst, 24 June 1824, 221; Cruikshank, "A Sketch of the Public Life and Services of Robert Nichol," 78.

64 *Colonial Advocate*, 18 May 1824, 1.

65 *Kingston Chronicle*, 3 March 1820, 3.

66 NA, RG 19, E5 (a), Board of Claims, claim 509. Andrew Heron complained that the near-universal deduction of one-third left honest men, like Nichol, "wofully in the lurch!" *Niagara Gleaner* in *Colonial Advocate*, 7 January 1830, 2.

67 NA, CO42/372, Maitland to Bathurst, 24 June 1824, 221; McKenzie, *Laura Secord*, 75.

68 Bowsfield, "Upper Canada in the 1820s," 227.

69 *Colonial Advocate*, 22 December 1825, 2; McNaught, *The Pelican History of Canada*, 77.

70 Upper Canada, Journals of the House of Assembly, 10th parliament, 1st session, app., 1828 population returns, 4.

71 Canada, *Census*, 1870–1, 4:120.

72 Biographical information is from Dent, *The Story of the Canadian Rebellion*, 115; *Colonial Advocate*, 18 May 1824, 1.

73 *Colonial Advocate*, 18 May 1824, 13, 1; *Colonial Advocate*, 3 June 1824, 3.

74 Morden, *Historical Monuments and Observatories*, 71; *Colonial Advocate*, 8 July 1824, 3.

75 Killbourn, *The Firebrand*, 30.

76 *Colonial Advocate*, 3 June 1824, 3.

77 *Colonial Advocate*, 30 September 1824, 3; Romney, "The Spanish Freeholder Imbroglio of 1824," 33.

78 *Colonial Advocate*, 8 July 1825, 2.

79 Ibid., 27 March 1825, 2.

80 Ibid., 8 July 1824, 2.

81 NA, CO42/374; *Colonial Advocate*, 25 October 1824, 125.

82 *Colonial Advocate*, 8 July 1830, 2.

83 Ibid., November 1828, 2.

84 Wallace, *The Periodical Literature of Upper Canada*, 5, 9.

85 Romney, *Mr Attorney*, 106; see also Johnson, *Becoming Prominent*, 137.

86 Anderson, *Imagined Communities*, 14, 19, 44.

87 *Colonial Advocate*, 10 March 1825, 2.

88 Ibid., 1 May 1828, 10.

89 NA, CO42/375, Treasury to Horton, 12 August 1824, 109.

90 NA, CO42/374, Horton to unkown, January 1824, 210.

91 Johnson, *Becoming Prominent*, 182.

92 *Niagara Gleaner* in *Colonial Advocate*, 7 January 1830, 2.

93 Information on assemblymen can be found in Johnson, *Becoming Prominent*, while voting divisions are in Upper Canada, Journals of the House of Assembly, 10th parliament, 2d session 1830, 70.

94 NA, CO42/359, Gore to Bathurst, 7 April 1817, 103–4.

95 NA, CO42/360, Law Officers to Bathurst, 15 November 1817, 22–3.

96 NA, CO42/361, Smith to Bathurst, 23 February 1818, 30.

97 Dunham, *Political Unrest in Upper Canada*, 75–9.

98 Errington, *The Lion, the Eagle, and Upper Canada*, 172–3.

99 *Colonial Advocate*, 15 December 1825, 2.

100 Ibid., 15 December 1825, 2.

101 Errington, *The Lion, the Eagle, and Upper Canada*, 179.

102 *Colonial Advocate*, 2 February 1826, 2.

103 Ibid., 12 February 1826, 3.

104 Dunham, *Political Unrest in Upper Canada*, 80–1.

105 *Colonial Advocate*, 21 August 1828, 3.

106 "Marshall Spring Bidwell," *Dictionary of Canadian Biography* 10:60–4; Armstrong, *Handbook of Upper Canadian Chronology*, 82–4.

107 See *Kingston Chronicle* 7 March 1823, 2, for example of a pledge to constituents to see speedy payments made.

108 Upper Canada, Journals of the House of Assembly, 9th parliament, 1st session, half-pay report, 31 March 1825, 80; Gourlay memorial, 14 January 1826, 76.

109 *Niagara Gleaner*, in *Colonial Advocate*, 15 December 1825, 2.

110 NA, CO42/371, Nichol to Galt, 26 May 1823, 173.

101 *Canadian Freeman* in *Colonial Advocate*, 2 March 1826, 1.

112 Williams, *Merritt*, 41–2.

113 Upper Canada, Journals of the House of Assembly, 9th parliament, 2d session, Joint Address, 23 January 1826, 1; Upper Canada, Journals of the House of Assembly, 9th parliament, 4th session, Maitland Address, 23 January 1826, 101.

114 Fraser, "Like Eden in Her Summer Dress," 165.

115 Upper Canada, Journals of the House of Assembly, 9th parliament, 4th session, Robinson report, 19 March 1828, 11.

116 Johnson, *Becoming Prominent*, 137–8.

117 *Colonial Advocate*, 22 May 1828, 3; 3 April 1828, 3.

118 Ibid., 4 February 1830, 2; 11 February 1830.

119 Ibid., 4 February 1830, 2.

120 Ibid., 24 December 1829, 3.

121 Upper Canada, Journals of the House of Assembly, 10th parliament, 2d session, amendment division, 26 February 1830, 70; Armstrong, *Handbook of Upper Canadian Chronology*, 85.

122 The voting on the war-losses bill is in Upper Canada, Journals of the House of Assembly, 10th parliament, 2d session, 26 February 1830, 70. Political affiliations are from Johnson, *Becoming Prominent*, 169–238. Below is a list of the "yea" voters with their political affiliation ("r" for reformer and "c" for conservative) along with claim number if applicable: Yeas – Baby (r) no. 1196; Dr Baldwin (r) no. 520; Berczy (c); Bethune (c); Blacklock (r); Dalton (r); Dickson (c); Fraser (c); Hamilton (r) no. 1210; Henderson (c); Hopkins (r) no. 1237; Hornor (r); Lefferty (r); McCall (r); McLean (c); McMartin (c); Malcolm (r) no. 442; Randall (r) no. 1145; G. Rolph (r); Shaver (r) no. 416; Terry (c); Wilkinson (c), John Willson (c) no. 530; Woodruff (r). All the "nays" were cast by reformers and none were war claimants: R. Baldwin, Buell, Cawthra, Ketchum, Lockwood, Longley, Lyons, McDonald, MacKenzie, Morris, Perry, Peterson, Radenshurst, J. Rolph, Thompson.

123 Craig, *Upper Canada*, 197; *Colonial Advocate*, 4 February 1830, 1.

124 *Colonial Advocate*, 11 February 1830, 1.

125 Ibid., 4 February 1830, 1.

126 Armstrong, *Handbook of Upper Canadian Chronology* 84–5; Upper Canada, Journals of the House of Assembly, 10th parliament, 2d session, 70.

127 *Colonial Advocate*, 11 February 1830, 1.

128 *Western Mercury*, 2 February 1832, 1–3.

129 Estimates of political strength are from Johnson, *Becoming Prominent*, 138, while the bill is described in the *Western Mercury*, 2 February 1832, 3.

130 *Canadian Emigrant*, 14 April 1832, 2.

131 *Western Mercury*, 2 February 1832, 3.

132 *Canadian Emigrant*, 17 April 1832, 2, 1.

133 Upper Canada, *7th Report from Select Committee*, Mackenzie to Goderich, 9 January 1833; appendix 71, 12.

134 The militia numbered 11,489 in 1814, and 2884 claims represents 25.1 per cent; NA, RG 9 UCM, IB2, vol. 1, General Annual Returns, 1814 militia muster; CO 42/369, Galt to unknown, 12 December 1822, 121.

135 There were 103,797 males over sixteen in Upper Canada in 1837 and the total population was 397,489. The 1819 recipients represented about 1.8 per cent of the adult male population; Canada, *Census*, 1870–1, vol. 4, 121.

136 These figures were derived from a comparison of the submissions made to the 1823–6 committee of revision and Armstrong's *Handbook of Upper Canadian Chronology*, 79–92. Of the sixty-two members in the thirteenth parliament from 1836–41, for example, the six recipients

were Shaver £500, Cook £54, Chisholm £210, McCrae £25, Woodruff £642, and Burwell £830.

137 Of the twenty-four members who sat in the sixth parliament after the war, thirteen submitted claims, but those by John Chrysler and Benjamin Fairfield were rejected. The sums paid the rest were Pattison £1625, Macdonell £25, Young £671, McGregor £226, Nelles £350, Clench £239, Dickson £1292, Swayze £3223, Nichol £4202, Burwell £830, and Durand £86.

138 Craig, "The American Impact on the Upper Canadian Reform Movement before 1837," 348; Houston and Smyth, *The Sash Canada Wore*, 146–7.

139 Upper Canada, *Statutes of Upper Canada*, chap. xxv, 611.

140 In 1830 a special receiver had some £4000 sterling that was to be applied to the losses; *Colonial Advocate*, 11 March 1830, 3. Over the years that sum increased and the province was able to attach £2412 sterling to its 1833 loan of £55,000 to fund its £57,412 sterling share of the debt. Robinson had reported in 1828 that £118,417 sterling was outstanding; Upper Canada, Journals of the House of Assembly, 9th parliament, 4th session, 111. After the provincial payment of £57,412 sterling was applied, £61,005 sterling would have remained unpaid. Since the 1836 instructions to Colborne dealt with a total debt of £57,910, another £3095 sterling must have been applied from interest on taxes and sales of confiscated estates; Upper Canada, *Statutes of Upper Canada*, chap. xxxvii, 756.

141 Upper Canada, *Statutes of Upper Canada*, chap. xxxvii, 756.

142 Upper Canada, Journals of the House of Assembly, 13th parliament, 3rd session, 19 December 1836, 756.

143 Upper Canada, *Statutes of Upper Canada*, chap. lxxix, 846.

144 *Western Mercury*, 2 February 1832, 1.

145 NA, RG 19, E5 (a), Board of Claims, 130 of the 2055 claims listed the claimant as deceased; Upper Canada, *Statutes of Upper Canada*, chap. lxxxix, 846.

146 Craig, *Upper Canada*, 242.

147 *Colonial Advocate*, 1 May 1828, 1.

148 Upper Canada, Journals of the House of Assembly, 10th parliament, 2d session, app. public accounts, 222.

149 H.G.J. Aitken, "The Family Compact and the Welland Canal Company," in *Historical Essays on Upper Canada*, 155.

150 Barnett, "Silas Fletcher, Instigator of the Upper Canadian Rebellion," 7–11.

151 Craig, *Upper Canada*, 48.

152 Read, *The Rising in Western Upper Canada, 1837–8*, 55.

153 NA, RG 19, E5 (a), Board of Claims, Finlay Malcolm, Sr, claim 442; Finlay, Jr, claims 1286, 445; John, claims 443,444.

154 Read, *The Rising in Western Upper Canada, 1837–8*, 174; The average age of the rebels was 30.2 years.

155 "Allan Napier MacNab," *Dictionary of Canadian Biography*, 9:522.

156 Burroughs, "Tackling Army Desertion in British North America," 58.

157 *The Arthur Papers*, Arthur to Love, 18 April 1840, 3:39; Arthur to Thomson, 12 May 1840, 3:46.

158 *The Arthur Papers*, Arthur to Jackson, 18 August 1840, 3:111.

159 *Kingston Chronicle & Gazette*, 1 August 1840, 2.

160 *The Arthur Papers*, Arthur to Jackson, 18 August 1840, 3:111.

CHAPTER 9 "A Greater Degree of Patriotism"

1 *Explanation of the Proceedings*, app. 3, 3.

2 Richardson, "The Mystery of the Medals," 133.

3 *Explanation of the Proceedings*, app. 3, 35.

4 Upper Canada, Journals, 11th parliament, 2d session, Medal Committee Report, app., 130.

5 "John Strachan," *Dictionary of Canadian Biography* 9:761.

6 *The Arthur Papers*, Arthur to Armstrong, 2:410.

7 Ireland, "John H. Dunn and the Bankers," 84; Craig, *Upper Canada*, 272–5.

8 AO, Strachan Papers, "Report of the Select Committee on ... Certain Medals," 33.

9 Ibid., 39, 51.

10 *Explanation of the Proceedings*, 15–16.

11 Roberton, *The Fighting Bishop*, 28.

12 "William Allan," *Dictionary of Canadian Biography* 8:5.

13 Robinson, *The Life of John Beverley Robinson*, 410.

14 Craig, "The Loyal and Patriotic Society," 45.

15 Canada, *Statement Showing the Name*, iii.

16 AO, Miscellaneous Collection, no. 26, box 1 (1875), list of veterans, MU2095.

17 Gidney, "Upper Canadian Public Opinion," 48–59.

18 Campbell, *Travels in the Interior*, 186.

19 *Canadian Letters*, 41.

20 Hounson, *Toronto*, 17.

21 Muir, "The Last Canadian Duel," 24.

22 *Upper Canada Gazette*, 25 September 1817, 3.

23 H.P. Gundy, "Hugh Thomson: Editor and Politician," in *To Preserve and Defend*, 219; Romney, *Mr Attorney*, 154, 204.

24 Brymer, *Report on Canadian Archives*, xviii.
25 Richardson, *War of 1812*, 1. Although Richardson was supposed to complete two more books, on the centre and left divisions, respectively, he considered the $250 fee sufficient payment for only one volume and refused to honour the terms of the original contract; Beasley, *The Canadian Don Quixote*, 133–5.
26 Canada, Legislative Assembly, 5th parliament, 3d session, 1857, app. 60.
27 AO, Merritt Papers, package 2, John Clark to unknown, October 1857, MS 74.

APPENDIX C

1 NA, RG 19, E5, (a), Board of Claims, vol. 3726, files 1–6; CO 42/365, Clarke to Maitland, 6 March, 1820, 45.
2 Ibid., vol. 3728.
3 NA, CO42/369, Galt to unkown, 12 December 1822, 127–30.
4 NA, RG 19, E5 (a), Board of Claims, vol. 3729, file 6; file 7, 2–6.
5 Upper Canada, Journal of the House of Assembly, 9th parliament, Robinson report, 19 March 1828, 111. To uncover the sterling value of the computer-generated total, the result was multiplied by 0.9 (195,980 x 0.9 = £176,382 sterling).
6 NA, RG 19, E5 (a), Board of Claims, vol. 3737, file 3.

Bibliography

MANUSCRIPT SOURCES

ARCHIVES OF ONTARIO (AO)

Percy Band Collection
Black, Charles. "Register of Persons Connected with High Treason during the War of 1812–14 with U.S.A." 1926
Merritt Family Papers
Military Records Collection, 1812, no. 10, Lincoln Militia Casualty Lists, 1812–14
Military Records Collection, Miscellaneous
Miscellaneous Collection, Number 26, box 1 (1875)
Captain James Mustard Papers
Abraham Nelles Papers
Robert Nelles Papers
Eli Playter Diary
Record Group 4, Attorney-General's Correspondence, 1814
Record Group 22, series 26
Richardson Family Papers
Samuel Street Papers
Strachan Papers
Isaac Wilson Diary

FORT YORK

Account Book of the Garrison of York, 3 volumes
Domestic Training Manual

HAMILTON PUBLIC LIBRARY (HPL)

Jones, Frank. "The Militia: The Formative Years, 1793–1846." Paper read at the Head-of-the-Lake Historical Society, 1954
Special Collections. "Estimate of Sums Wanted," 25 September–24 October 1812

METROPOLITAN TORONTO LIBRARY (MTL)

Baldwin Papers. Metropolitan Toronto Library
Breakenridge, M.W. "Some Account of the Settlement of Upper Canada of Robert Baldwin." 1859
Jarvis Papers
Alexander Wood Business Book, 1810–12
Alexander Wood Papers

NATIONAL ARCHIVES CANADA (NA)

Great Britain. Colonial Office, 42 series
Manuscript Group 19 A39, Duncan Clark Papers
Manuscript Group 23 HI4, W.D. Powell Papers
Manuscript Group 24 J48, J.W. Whittaker Papers
Record Group 1, E3, Submissions to the Executive Council on State Matters
Record Group 5, A1, Upper Canada Sundries
Record Group 5, B26, Upper Canada Returns of Population and Assessment
Record Group 8, C Series, British Military Documents
Record Group 9, Upper Canada Militia
Record Group 19 E5 (a), Board of Claims for War Losses
United States National Archives, War of 1812 Papers, "U.S. Marshals' Returns of Enemy Aliens and Prisoners of War of 1812–15"

QUEEN'S UNIVERSITY ARCHIVES (QA)

Stone Papers

NEWSPAPERS

Canadian Emigrant and Western District Advertiser
Colonial Advocate
Hamilton Spectator
Kingston Chronicle
Kingston Chronicle & Gazette
Kingston Gazette

Niagara Gleaner
Niagara Spectator
Upper Canada Gazette
Western Mercury
York Gazette

SECONDARY SOURCES

After Tippecanoe: Some Aspects of the War of 1812. Edited by Philip Mason. Toronto: Ryerson Press, 1963
Akenson, Donald. *The Irish in Ontario: A Study in Rural History.* Montreal and Kingston: McGill-Queen's University Press, 1984
Albion's Fatal Tree: Crime and Society in Eighteenth-Century England. Edited by Douglas Hay et al. New York: Pantheon, 1975
Altman, P.L., and D.S. Dittmer. *Metabolism.* Bethune, 1968
Anderson, Benedict. *Imagined Communities: Reflections on the Origins and Spread of Nationalism.* London: Verso, 1983
Approaches to Canadian Economic History. Edited by W.T. Easterbrook and W.H. Watkins. Toronto: McClelland and Stewart, 1967
Armstrong, F.H. *Handbook of Upper Canadian Chronology.* Revised edition. Toronto: Dundurn Press, 1985
The Arthur Papers: Being the Papers of Sir George Arthur. 3 volumes. Edited by Charles Sanderson. Toronto: University of Toronto Press, 1961
Auchinleck, Gilbert. *A History of the War between Great Britain and the United States of America during the Years 1812, 1813 and 1814.* Toronto 1864
The Bank of Upper Canada: A Collection of Documents. Edited by Peter Baskerville. Toronto: Champlain Society; Carleton University Press, 1987
Barnett, John. "Silas Fletcher, Instigator of the Upper Canadian Rebellion." *Ontario History,* 41 (1949): 7–11
Beasley, David. *The Canadian Don Quioxte: The Life and Works of Major John Richardson, Canada's First Novelist,* Erin: Porcupine's Quill, 1977
Beer, Donald. *Sir Allan Napier MacNab.* Hamilton: W.L. Griffin, 1984
Bell, David V.J. "The Loyalist Tradition in Canada." *Journal of Canadian Studies,* 5 (1970): 22–33
Benn, Carl. *The Battle of York.* Belleville: Mika Publishing, 1984
Berger, Carl. *The Sense of Power: Studies in the Ideas of Canadian Imperialism.* Toronto: University of Toronto Press, 1970
Berton, Pierre. *The Invasion of Canada, 1812–13.* Toronto: McClelland and Stewart, 1980
– *Flames across the Border, 1814.* Toronto: McClelland and Stewart, 1981
Bethune, A.N. *Memoir of the Right Reverend John Strachan, First Bishop of Toronto.* Toronto: Henry Russell, 1870
Bigelow, Jacob. *The War of the Gulls: An Historical Romance.* New York 1812

Bothwell, Robert. *A Short History of Ontario*. Edmonton: Hurtig, 1986

Bouchette, Joseph. *A Topographical Description of the Province of Lower Canada with Remarks upon Upper Canada*. London: W. Faden, 1815

– *The British Dominions in North America*. 2 volumes. London: Longman, 1832

Bowler, Reginald Arthur. "Propaganda in Upper Canada: A Study of the Propaganda Directed at the People of Upper Canada during the War of 1812." MA thesis, Queen's University, 1964

Bowsfield, Hartwell. "Upper Canada in the 1820s: The Development of a Political Consciousness." PhD dissertation, University of Toronto, 1976

Bret-James, Anthony. *Life in Wellington's Army*. London: George Allen and Unwin, 1972

Brett, Albert Sidney. *The Wars of Napoleon*. Wayne: Avery Publishing, 1985

Briggs, G.M. and D.M. Calloway. *Nutrition and Physical Fitness*. Toronto: W.B. Saunders, 1979

Brode, Patrick. *Sir John Beverley Robinson: Bone and Sinew of the Compact*. Toronto: University of Toronto Press, 1984

Brymer, Douglas. *Report on Canadian Archives*, Ottawa: S.E. Dawson, 1898

Burns, John. *True Patriotism: A Sermon Preached in the Presbyterian Church in Stamford, Upper Canada, on the 3d Day of June, 1814, A Provincial Thanksgiving*. Montreal: Mower, 1814

Burns, R.J. "God's Chosen People: The Origins of Toronto Society, 1793–1818." Canadian Historical Association, *Historical Papers*, 1973, 213–28

Burpee, Laurence. "Influence of the War of 1812 upon the Settlement of the Canadian West." *Ontario Historical Society Papers and Records*, 12 (1914): 114–20

Burroughs, Peter. "Tackling Army Desertion in British North America." *Canadian Historical Review*, 61 (1980): 28–68

Burton, Benjamin. *Human Nutrition: A Textbook of Nutrition in Health and Disease*. New York: McGraw Hill, 1976

Campbell, P. *Travels in the Interior Inhabited Parts of North America in the Years 1791 and 1792*. Edinburgh 1793. Reprint edition. Toronto: Champlain Society, 1937

Canada. Census, 1870–1

Canada. Journals of the Legislative Assembly

Canada. *Public Archives of Canada Annual Reports*

Canada. *Statement Showing the Name, Age, and Residence of Militiamen of 1812–15 … and Rank … in Which They Served*. Ottawa: Maclean Roger, 1876

Canadian Letters: Description of a Tour Thro' the Provinces of Lower and Upper Canada, In the Course of the Years 1792 and '93. In "Canadian Antiquarian and Numismatic Journal," July-October 1912. Reprint edition. Montreal: C.A. Marchand, 1912

Cartwright, C.E. *Life and Letters of the Hon. Richard Cartwright*. Toronto: Belford, 1876

Chambers. E.J. *The Canadian Militia: A History of the Origin and Development of the Force*. Montreal: L.M. Frescoe, 1907

Charlton, J.E. *1971 Standard Catalogue of Canadian Coins, Tokens and Paper Money*. Port Carling: Charlton, 1971

Christie, Robert. *The Military and Naval Operations in the Canada's during the Late War ... until the Year 1815*. Quebec 1815

Clark, Colin, and Margaret Haswell. *The Economics of Subsistence Agriculture*. Toronto: Macmillan, 1967

Clarke, C.K. *A History of Toronto General Hospital*. Toronto: William Briggs, 1913

Coffin, William. *1812; The War and Its Moral: Canadian Chronicle*. Montreal: Lovell, 1864

Cole, W.H. "The Local History of the Town of Brockville." *Ontario Historical Society Papers and Records*, 12 (1914): 33–41

Coleman, Thelma. *The Canada Company*. Stratford: Cumming Publishers, 1978

Coles, H.L. *The War of 1812*. Chicago: University of Chicago Press, 1965

Colquhoun, A.H.U. "The Career of Joseph Willcocks." *Canadian Historical Review*, 7 (1967): 287–93

Conant, Thomas. *Upper Canada Sketches*. Toronto: William Briggs, 1898

– *Life in Canada*. Toronto: William Briggs, 1903

The Constitutional History of Canada, 1791–1818. Edited by A.G. Doughty and D.A. McArthur. Ottawa: King's Printer, 1914

The Correspondence of Lieut. Governor John Graves Simcoe, with allied documents relating to his administration of the government of Upper Canada. Edited by E.A. Cruikshank. 5 volumes. Toronto: Ontario Historical Society, 1923

Craig, G.M. "The American Impact on the Upper Canadian Reform Movement before 1837." *Canadian Historical Review*, 29 (1948): 333–52

– *Upper Canada: The Formative Years 1784–1841*. Toronto: McClelland and Stewart, 1963

Craig, Hamilton. "The Loyal and Patriotic Society of Upper Canada and Its Still-Born Child – The Upper Canada Preserved Medal." *Ontario History*, 52 (1960): 31–52

Cruikshank, E.A. *The Battle of Lundy's Lane 25th July 1814: A Historical Study*. Welland: Tribune, 1893

– "A Country Merchant in Upper Canada, 1800–1812." *Ontario Historical Society Papers and Records*, 25 (1928): 145–90

– *The Fight in the Beechwoods: A Study in Canadian History*. Welland: W.T. Sawl and Company, 1895

– "John Beverley Robinson and the Trials for Treason in 1814." *Ontario Historical Society Papers and Records*, 25 (1929): 191–219

– *A Memoir of the Honourable James Kerby, His Life in Letters*. Welland: Historical Society, 1931

- "The Militia of the Eastern District – Records of the Services of the Canadian Regiments in the War of 1812." Toronto: Canadiana House Reprints, 1968
- "The News of Niagara a Century Ago." *Ontario Historical Society Papers and Records*, 23 (1926): 45–64
- *The Origin and Offical History of the Thirteenth Battalion of Infantry and a Desciption of the Early Militia of the Niagara Peninsula in the War of 1812 and the Rebellion of 1837*. Hamilton: L.E.L. Ruddy, 1899
- "Postwar Discontent at Niagara." *Ontario Historical Society Papers and Records*, 29 (1933): 14–46
- "Records of the Services of Canadian Regiments in the War of 1812 – The Glengarry Light Infantry." Toronto: Canadiana House Reprints, 1968
- "A Sketch of the Public Life and Services of Robert Nichol." *Ontario Historical Society Papers and Records*, 19 (1922): 6–79
Darling, E.H. "John Darling of St. Johns U.C., A Pioneer Industrialist and His Day Book, 1768–1825." *Ontario History*, 40 (1948): 53–63
The Defended Border: Upper Canada and the War of 1812. Edited by Morris Zaslow. Toronto: Macmillan, 1964
Demos, John. *A Little Commonwealth: Family Life in Plymouth Colony*. New York: Oxford University Press, 1970
- *Entertaining Satan: Witchcraft and the Culture of New England*. New York: Oxford University Press, 1982
Dent, John Charles. *The Story of the Canadian Rebellion*. Toronto: Blackett Robinson, 1885
Dictionary of Canadian Biography, volumes 5–8 (1800–70). Edited by Francess G. Halpenny. Toronto: University of Toronto Press, 1977–88
Divine, Robert A., et al. *America Past and Present*. New York: Harper Collins, 1991
Documentary History of the Campaign on the Niagara Frontier. 9 volumes. Edited by E.A. Cruikshank. Welland: Lundy's Lane Historical Society, 1902–8
Documents Relating to the Constitutional History of Canada, 1759–1791. Edited by Adam Shortt and A.G. Doughty. Ottawa: King's Printer, 1918
Documents Relating to the Invasion of Canada and the Surrender of Detroit, 1812. Edited by E.A. Cruikshank. Ottawa: Government Printing, 1912
Dorland, Arthur. *The Quakers in Canada: A History*. Toronto: Ryerson Press, 1968
Douglas, John. *Medical Topography of Upper Canada*. London: Burgess and Hill, 1819. Reprint edition. Canton: Science History Publications, 1985
Douglas, Thomas. *Lord Selkirk's Diary 1803–1804*. Edited by P.C.T. White. Toronto: Champlain Society, 1958
Dunham, Aileen. *Political Unrest in Upper Canada, 1815–1836*. Toronto: McClelland and Stewart, 1963
Dunlop, William. *Recollections of the War of 1812*. Toronto: Historical Publishing, 1908

Ecksteins, Modris. *Rites of Spring: The Great War and the Birth of the Modern Age*. Boston: Houghton Mifflin, 1989

Edgar, Matilda Ridout. *Ten Years of Upper Canada in Peace and War, 1805–1815*. Toronto: William Briggs, 1890

Eleven Exiles: Accounts of Loyalists of the American Revolution. Edited by John Grant. Toronto: Dundurn Press, 1982

Engels, Donald. *Alexander the Great and the Logistics of the Macedonian Army*. London: University of Los Angeles, 1978

Ermatinger, C.O. *The Talbot Regime or the First Half of the Talbot Settlement*. St Thomas: Municipal World, 1904

Errington, Jane. "Friends and Foes: The Kingston Elite and the War of 1812 – A Case Study in Ambivalence." *Journal of Canadian Studies*, 20 (1985): 58–79

– *Greater Kingston: Historic Past and Progressive Future*. Burlington: Windsor Press, 1988

– *The Lion, the Eagle, and Upper Canada: A Developing Colonial Ideology*. Montreal and Kingston: McGill-Queen's University Press, 1987

Explanation of the Proceedings of the Loyal and Patriotic Society of Upper Canada. Toronto: Stanton, 1841

Finlay, J.L., and D.N. Sprague. *The Structure of Canadian History*. Scarborough: Prentice Hall, 1979

Firth, Edith. "The Administration of Peter Russell, 1796–1799." *Ontario History*, 48 (1956): 163–81

– "Alexander Wood, Merchant of York." *York Pioneer and Historical Society* (1958): 5–28

Fitzgibbon, Mary Agnes. *A Veteran of 1812: The Life of James Fitzgibbon*. Toronto: William Briggs, 1894

Fleming, Roy. "Negro Slaves with the United Empire Loyalists in Upper Canada." *Ontario History*, 45 (1953): 27–30

Francis, R.D., et al. *Origins: Canadian History to Confederation*. Toronto: Holt, Rinehart, and Winston, 1988

Fraser, R.L. "Like Eden in Her Summer Dress: Gentry Economy and Society, Upper Canada, 1812–1840." PhD dissertation, University of Toronto, 1979

Fryer, Mary Beacock. *King's Men: The Soldier Founders of Ontario*. Toronto: Dundurn Press, 1980

Galt, John. *The Autobiography of John Galt*. 2 volumes. London: Cochrane & McCrone, 1833

Garland, M.A., and J.J. Talman. "Pioneer Drinking Habits and the Rise of Temperance Agitation in Upper Canada Prior to 1840." *Ontario Historical Society Papers and Records*, 27 (1931): 341–64

Gates, Lilian F. *Land Policies of Upper Canada*. Toronto: University of Toronto Press, 1968

Gidney, R.D. "Upper Canadian Public Opinion and Common School

Improvements in the 1830s." *Histoire sociale/Social History*, 5 (1972): 48–59

Glazebrook, G.P. de T. *Life in Ontario: A Social History*. Toronto: University of Toronto Press, 1968

Goldie, John. *Diary of a Journey through Upper Canada and Some of the New England States, 1819.* [privately published]

Gourlay, Robert. *General Introduction to Statistical Account*. London: Simpkin and Marshall, 1822. Reprint edition. New York: Johnson, 1966

– *Statistical Account of Upper Canada: Compiled with a View to a Grand System of Emigration*. 2 volumes. London: Simpkin and Marshall, 1822. Reprint edition. New York: Johnson, 1966

Graves, Donald E. "Joseph Willcocks and the Canadian Volunteers: An Account of Political Disaffection in Upper Canada during the War of 1812." MA thesis, Carleton University, 1982

– "The Best Means of Suppressing the Growing Evil: British Military Commanders and Martial Law." Paper presented at Acadia University, April 1991

Gray, Hugh. *Letters from Canada Written during a Residence There in the Years 1806, 1807, and 1808.* London: Longman, Hurst, Rees, and Orne, 1809. Reprint edition. Toronto: Coles, 1971

Gray, Leslie. "From Bethlehem to Fairfield – 1798 – Part Two." *Ontario History*, 48 (1954): 37–61

Guest, Harry. "Upper Canada's First Political Party." *Ontario History*, 54 (1962): 275–96

Guitard, Michelle. *The Militia of the Battle of Chateauguay: A Social History*. Ottawa: Parks Canada, 1983

Hamil, Fred Coyne. "Colonel Talbot's Principality." *Ontario History*, 44 (1954): 183–92

Hansen, Marcus. *The Mingling of the Canadian and American Peoples*. 2 volumes. New York: Russell & Russell, 1940

Harkness, John Graham. *Stormont, Dundas, and Glengarry: A History 1784–1945.* Oshawa: Mundy Goodfellow, 1946

Harper, J.M. *The Annals of War: In Commemoration of the "Century of Peace.* Toronto: Musson, 1914

Havran, Martin J. "Windsor – Its First Hundred Years." *Ontario History*, 46 (1954): 179–86

Hayes, C.J.H. *The Historical Evolution of Modern Nationalism*. New York: Russell & Russell, 1931

Hein, Edward Bernard. "The Niagara Frontier and the War of 1812." PhD dissertation, University of Ottawa, 1949

Henderson, J.L.H. *John Strachan: Documents and Opinions*. Toronto: McClelland and Stewart, 1969

Heriot, George. *Travels through the Canadas*. London: Richard Phillips, 1807. Reprinted Toronto: Coles, 1971

Hickey, Donald R. *The War of 1812: A Forgotten Conflict*. Chicago: University of Illinois Press, 1989

Historical Essays on Upper Canada. Edited by J.K. Johnson. Toronto: McClelland and Stewart, 1975

Historical Essays on Upper Canada: New Perspectives. Edited by J.K. Johnson. Ottawa: Carleton University Press, 1989

Hitsman, J. Mackay. *The Incredible War of 1812: A Military History*. Toronto: University of Toronto Press, 1965

– *Safeguarding Canada, 1763–1871*. Toronto: University of Toronto, 1968

Hopkins, J.C. "The War of 1812–15." *Ontario Historical Society Papers and Records*, 12 (1914): 42–57

Hounson, Eric Wilfrid. *Toronto in 1810*. Toronto: Ryerson Press, 1970

Houston, C.J., and W.J. Smyth. *The Sash Canada Wore: A Historical Geography of the Orange Order in Canada*. Toronto: University of Toronto Press, 1980

Howison, John. *Sketches of Upper Canada*. Edinburgh: Oliver and Boyd, 1821

Hyatt, A.M.J. "The Defence of Upper Canada in 1812." MA thesis, Carleton University, 1961

Ireland, John. "John H. Dunn and the Bankers." *Ontario History*, 62 (1970): 83–100

Irving, L.H. *Officers of the British Forces in Canada during the War of 1812–15*. Welland: Tribune Print, 1908

Jarvis, Eric. "Military Land Granting in Upper Canada following the War of 1812." *Ontario History*, 67 (1975): 121–34

The John Askin Papers. 2 volumes. Edited by M.M. Quaife. Detroit: Library Commission, 1928

Johnson, J.K. *Becoming Prominent: Regional Leadership in Upper Canada, 1791–1841*. Montreal and Kingston: McGill-Queen's University Press, 1989

Johnson, Leo. "The Mississauga – Lake Ontario Land Surrender of 1805." *Ontario History*, 83 (1990): 233–53

Jones, Robert L. *History of Agriculture in Ontario 1613–1880*. Toronto: University of Toronto Press, 1946

Keegan, John. *The Face of Battle*. London: Jonathan Cope, 1976

Kilbourn, William. *The Firebrand: William Lyon Mackenzie and the Rebellion in Upper Canada*. Toronto: Clark, Irwin, 1956

Killan, Gerald. "Preserving Ontario's Heritage: A History of the Ontario Historical Society." PhD dissertation, McMaster University, 1973

La Rochefoucault-Liancourt, François. *Travels in Canada 1795* in *Ontario Bureau of the Archives Report*, 1916

Landon, Fred. "The Evolution of Local Government in Ontario." *Ontario History*, 42 (1950): 1–5

Leavitt, T.W. *History of Leeds and Grenville*. Brockville: Recorder Press, 1879

Leibbrandt, Gottlieb. *Little Paradise: The Saga of the German Canadians of Waterloo County, Ontario 1800–1975*. Kitchener: Allprint, 1980

Lord Selkirk's Diary, 1803–1804: A Journal of His Travels in British North America and the Northern United States. Edited by P.T.C. White. Toronto: Champlain Society, 1958

Lossing, Benson J. *The Pictorial Field-Book of the War of 1812.* New York: Benchmark Publishing, 1970

Loyalist Narratives from Upper Canada. Edited by James Talman. Toronto: Champlain Society, 1946

Lucas, C.P. *The Candian War of 1812.* Oxford: Clarendon, 1906.

Macewen, William. "Excerpts from the Letters from Lieutenant and Adjutant William Macewen to His Wife, Canada, 1813–14"

MacGillivray, Royce. *The Mind of Ontario.* Belleville: Mika, 1985

Machar, Agnes. *The Story of Old Kingston.* Toronto: Musson Book, 1908

Magill, M.L. "William Allan and the War of 1812." *Ontario History*, 64 (1972): 132–41

Mahant, E.E. and G.S. Mount, *An Introduction to Canadian-American Relations.* Toronto: Methuen, 1984

Mann, James. *Medical Sketches of the Campaigns of 1812, 13, 14.* Dedham 1816

Manitoba Essays. Toronto: Macmillan, 1937

Matthews, W.T. "By and for the Large Propertied Interests: The Dynamics of Local Government in Six Upper Canadian Towns during the Era of Commercial Capitalism, 1832–1860." PhD dissertation, McMaster University, 1985

McCalla, Douglas. "The 'Loyalist' Economy of Upper Canada, 1784–1806." *Histoire sociale/Social History*, 16 (1983): 279–304

McConnell, Jennie. "The Effect of the War of 1812 on Canada." Women's Canadian Historical Society of Ottawa, Transactions, 1 (1901): 177–188

McKee, Christopher, "The Pathology of a Profession: Death in the United States Officer Corps, 1797–1815." *War & Society*, 3 (1985): 1–25

McKenzie, Ruth. *Laura Secord: The Legend and the Lady.* Toronto: McClelland and Stewart, 1971

McLeod, Donald. *A Brief Review of the Settlement of Upper Canada.* Mika: Belleville, 1972

McNaught, Kenneth. *The Pelican History of Canada.* Toronto: Penguin, 1976

Mecredy, Stephen. "Some Military Aspects of Kingston's Development during the War of 1812." MA thesis, Queen's University, 1982

Melish, John. *Travels through the United States of America in the Years 1806 & 1807, and 1809, 1810, & 1811.* London: George Cowie 1818. Reprint edition. New York: Johnson, 1970

Milani, Lois Darroch. *Robert Gourlay, Gadfly.* Toronto: Ampersand Press, 1971

Military History and the Military Profession. Edited by David A. Charters. Westport, Conn.: Praeger, 1992

Miller, Geneviève. *William Beaumont's Formative Years: Two Early Notebooks*. New York: Henry Schuman, 1946

Miller, Orlo. "The Notorious Ebeneezer Allan." *Western Historical Notes*, 5 (1947): 76–82

Mills, David. *The Idea of Loyalty in Upper Canada 1784–1850*. Montreal and Kingston: McGill-Queen's University Press, 1988

Moir, J.S. "Early Methodism in the Niagara Peninsula." *Ontario History*, 42 (1951): 51–8

Morden, J.C. *Historical Monuments and Observatories of Lundy's Lane and Queenston Heights*. Toronto: Lundy's Lane Historical Society, 1929

Morgan, Elizabeth M. "Joel Stone: Connecticut Loyalist, 1749–1833." MA thesis, York University, 1980

Morgan, Henry James. *The Canadian Men and Women of the Time*. Toronto: William Briggs, 1898

Morgan, J.C. "The Emigrant's Notebook." *Kingston! Oh Kingston!* Edited by A.B. Smith. Kingston: Brown & Martin, 1987

Muir, Elizabeth Gillan. *Petticoats in the Pulpit: The Story of Early Nineteenth-Century Methodist Women Preachers in Upper Canada*. Toronto: United Church, 1991

Muir, Major R.C. "The Last Canadian Duel." *Brant Historical Society Papers and Records* (1930): 24–7

Murray, J. "A Recovered Letter: W.W. Baldwin to C.B. Wyatt, 6th April 1813." *Ontario Historical Society Papers and Records* 35 (1938): 48–55

Neufeld, E.P. *Money and Banking in Canada*. Toronto: McClelland and Stewart, 1964

Norrie, Kenneth, and Douglas Owram. *A History of the Canadian Economy*. Toronto: Harcourt, Brace, Jovanovich, 1991

Nutrient Value of Some Common Foods. Revised edition. Ottawa: Health and Welfare, 1987

Nutrition and Malnutrition: Identification and Measurement. Edited by A.F. Roche and Frank Falkner. New York: Plenum Press, 1974

[An Ohio Volunteer] "The Capitulation, or A history of the Expedition conducted by William Hull, Brigadier-General of the North-Western Army." in *War on the Detroit*, edited by M.M. Quaife. Chicago: Lakeside, 1940, 179–320

Ontario. Bureau of the Archives, *Report*. Toronto 1913–14

Osborne, Brian, and Donald Swainson. *Kingston: Building on the Past*. Westport: Butternut Press, 1988

"Our First Legislative Assembly 1792." *Ontario History*, 46 (1954): 1–2

Patterson, E.P. *The Canadian Indian: A History since 1850*. Don Mills: Collier-MacMillan, 1972

Patterson, Graeme. "Whiggery, Nationality, and the Upper Canadian

Reform Tradition." *Canadian Historical Review* 56 (1975): 25–44

Petersen, William and Renée. *Dictionary of Demography*. 2 volumes. New York: Greenwood, 1986

Porter, Stephen. "The Fire-raid in the English Civil War." *War & Society*, 2 (1984): 27–40

– "Property Destruction in the English Civil War." *History Today*, 36 (1986): 36–41

Powell, W. Drummer. "A letter ... regarding the appointment of Alexander Wood as a Commissioner for the Investigation of claims." York 1831

Profiles of a Province. Edited by Edith Firth. Toronto: Ontario Historical Society, 1967

Quealy, Francis Michael. "The Administration of Sir Peregrine Maitland: Lieutenant Governor of Upper Canada." PhD dissertation, University of Toronto, 1968

Rea, J.E. *Bishop Alexander Macdonell and the Politics of Upper Canada*. Toronto: Ontario Historical Society, 1974

Read, Colin. *The Rising in Western Upper Canada, 1837–8: The Duncombe Revolt and After*. Toronto: University of Toronto Press, 1982

Recollections of Rifleman Harris. Edited by Christopher Hibbert. London: Archon Books, 1970

Recollection of the War of 1812: Three Eyewitness Accounts. Edited by John Gellner. Toronto: Baxter, 1964

Redish, Angela. "Why Was Specie Scarce in Colonial Economies?" *Journal of Economic History*, 44 (1984): 713–28

The Report of the Loyal and Patriotic Society of Upper Canada. Montreal: William Gray, 1817

Richards, Elva M. "The Jones of Brockville and the Family Compact." *Ontario History*, 60 (1960): 169–84

Richardson, James H. "The Mystery of the Medals." *University of Toronto Monthly* (1902): 130–2

Richardson, John. *Eight Years in Canada*. Montreal: Cunningham, 1847. Reprint edition. New York: Johnson Reprint, 1967

– *Richardson's War of 1812*. Toronto: Historical Publishing, 1902

– *War of 1812 Containing ... the Right Division of the Canadian Army*. Brockville 1842

– *Westbrook the Outlaw; Or the Avenging Wolf*. Montreal: Grant Woolmer, 1973

Richardson, John. "The Letters of Veritas ... Narrative of the Military Administration of Sir George Prevost." Montreal: W. Gray, 1815

Riddell, W.R. "The Ancaster 'Bloody Assize' of 1814." *Ontario Historical Society Papers and Records*, 20 (1923)

– "An Echo of the War of 1812." *Ontario Historical Society Papers and Records*, 23 (1926): 434–49

– "Joseph Willcocks: Sheriff, Member of Parliament, and Traitor." *Ontario Historical Society Papers and Records*, 24 (1928): 475–499
– "Robert Fleming Gourlay." *Ontario Historical Society Papers and Records*, 14 (1916): 5–133
Rives, W.R., and W.J. Serow. *Introduction to Applied Demography: Data Sources and Estimation Techniques*. Beverly Hills: Sage, 1984
Roberton, Thomas. *The Fighting Bishop: John Strachan, the First Bishop of Toronto*. Ottawa: Graphic Publishers, 1926
Robertson, H.H. "The Gore District Militia ... with the Lists of Officers." Hamilton: Griffin and Kidner, 1904
Robinson, C.W. *The Life of John Beverley Robinson*. Toronto: Morang & Company, 1904
Robinson, Corrine. *Normal and Theraputic Nutrition*. New York: Macmillan, 1977
Rogers, R.L. *History of the Lincoln and Welland Regiment*. Ottawa: R.L. Rogers, 1954
Romney, Paul. *Mr Attorney: The Attorney General for Ontario in Court, Cabinet, and Legislature 1791–1899*. Toronto: University of Toronto Press, 1986
– "The Spanish Freeholder Imbroglio of 1824: Inter-Elite and Intra-Elite Rivalry in Upper Canada." *Ontario History*, 76 (1984): 32–45
Royster, Charles. *A Revolutionary People at War: The Continental Army and American Character, 1775–83*. Chapel Hill: University of North Carolina Press, 1983
Russell, Peter A. *Attitudes to Social Structure and Mobility in Upper Canada 1815–1840*. Queenston: Edwin Mellen Press, 1990
– "Wage Labour Rates in Upper Canada 1818–1840." *Histoire Sociale/Social History*, 16 (1983): 61–80
Ryerson, Egerton. *The Loyalists of America and Their Times: From 1620 to 1816*. Second edition. 2 volumes. Toronto: William Briggs, 1880
Salisbury, Neal. *Manitou and Providence: Indians, Europeans, and the Making of New England 1500–1643*. New York: Oxford University Press, 1982
Sandham, Alfred. *Coins, Tokens and Medals of the Dominion of Canada*. Winnipeg: Canadian Numismatic Publishing, 1869
Scott, Duncan Campbell. *John Graves Simcoe: The Makers of Canada Series*, volume 4. Toronto: Oxford University Press, 1926
Select British Documents of the Canadian War of 1812. Edited by William Wood. Toronto: Champlain Society, 1923
Sheehan, Bernard. *Savagism and Civility: Indians and Englishmen in Colonial Virginia*. London: Cambridge University Press, 1980
– *Seeds of Extinction: Jeffersonian Philanthropy and the American Indian*. Chapel Hill: University of North Carolina Press, 1973
Sheppard, George. "Deeds Speak: Militiamen, Medals and the Invented Traditions of 1812." *Ontario History*, 83 (1990): 207–32

Shortt, Adam. *Adam Shortt's History of Canadian Currency and Banking, 1600–1880.* Toronto: Canadian Bankers, 1986

Showalter, Denis E. "Even Generals Wet Their Pants: The First Three Weeks in East Prussia, August 1914." *War & Society,* 2 (1984): 61–86

Sider, Morris. "The Early Years of the Tunkers in Upper Canada." *Ontario History,* 51 (1959): 121–9

Smith, Alison. "John Strachan and Early Upper Canada, 1799–1814." *Ontario History,* 52 (1950): 159–73

Smith, Donald B. "The Dispossession of the Mississauga Indians: A Missing Chapter in the Early History of Upper Canada." *Ontario History,* 72 (1980): 67–87

– "The Mississauga, Peter Jones, and the White Man: The Algonkians Adjustment to the Europeans on the North Shore of Lake Ontario to 1860." PhD dissertation, University of Toronto, 1975

Smith, Michael. *A Geographical View of the Province of Upper Canada and Promiscuous Remarks on the Government.* Second edition. Trenton: Moore & Lake, 1813

Snake Hill: An Investigation of a Military Cemetery from the War of 1812. Edited by Susan Pfeiffer and Ronald F. Williamson. Toronto: Dundurn, 1991

Spragge, G.W. "Dr. Strachan's Motives for Becoming a Legislative Councillor." *Canadian Historical Review,* 19 (1938): 397–402

– *The John Strachan Letterbook: 1812–1834.* Toronto: Ontario Historical Society, 1946

Spragge, Shirley Campbell. "Organizing the Wilderness: A Study of A Loyalist Settlement Augusta Township, Grenville County, 1784–1820." PhD dissertation, Queen's University, 1986

Stacey, C.P. "Upper Canada at War 1814: Captain Armstrong Reports." *Ontario History,* 48 (1956): 37–42

– "The War of 1812 in Canadian History." *Ontario History,* 50 (1958): 153–9

Stagg, J.C.A. "Enlisted Men in the United States Army, 1812–1815: A Preliminary Survey." *William & Mary Quarterly,* 43 (1986): 621–34

Stanley, G.F.G. *Canada's Soldiers: The Military History of an Unmilitary People.* Third edition. Toronto: Macmillan, 1983

– "The Indians in the War of 1812." *Canadian Historical Review,* 31 (1950): 145–65

– "The Significance of Six Nations Participation in the War of 1812." *Ontario History,* 55 (1963): 213–31

– *The War of 1812: Land Operations.* Toronto: Macmillan, 1983

Steppler, G.A. "A Duty Troublesome beyond Measure: Logistical Considerations in the Canadian War of 1812." MA thesis, McGill University, 1974

Stevenson, James. "The Circulation of Army Bills with Some Remarks upon the War of 1812." *Literary and Historical Society of Quebec Transactions,* 21 (1891–2): 1–79

Stewart, Walter. *True Blue: The Loyalist Legend.* Toronto: Collins, 1985

Stigler, Stephen. *The History of Statistics: The Measurement of Uncertainty before 1900.* Cambridge: Belknap Press, 1986

Strachan, James. *A Visit to the Province of Upper Canada in 1819.* Aberdeen: D. Chalmers, 1820. Reprint edition. Toronto: S.R. Publishers, 1968

Strachan, John. "A Sermon Preached at York, On the Third of June, Being the Day Appointed for a General Thanksgiving." Montreal: William Gray, 1814

Stuart, James. "Refutation of Aspersions on Stuarts Three Years in North America." London 1834

Surtees, Robert. "Indian Land Cessions in Ontario 1763–1862: The Evolution of a System." PhD dissertation, Carleton University, 1983

Swainson, Donald. "Chronicling Kingston: An Interpretation." *Ontario History*, 74 (1982): 302–33

Talbot, E.A. *Five Years' Residence in the Canadas ... 1823.* 2 volumes. London: Longman Hurst, 1824. Reprint edition. New York: Johnson Reprint, 1968

Talman, James. "Life in the Pioneer Districts of Upper Canada 1815–40." PhD dissertation, University of Toronto, 1930

Tanner, Helen. *Atlas of Great Lakes Indian History.* Norman: University of Oklahoma Press, 1987

Timothy, H.B. *The Galts: A Canadian Odyssey.* Toronto: McClelland and Stewart, 1977

Tindall, G.B. *America: A Narrative History.* 2 volumes. New York: W.W. Norton, 1984

To Preserve and Defend: Essays on Kingston in the Nineteenth Century. Edited by G. Tulchinsky. Montreal and Kingston: McGill Queen's University Press, 1976

Town of York, 1793–1815. Edited by Edith Firth. Toronto: Champlain Society, 1962

Turner, Wesley. *The War of 1812: The War That Both Sides Won.* Toronto: Dundurn, 1990

Upper Canada. Journals of the House of Assembly, 1825–41

Upper Canada. Journals of the Legislative Assembly, 1805–24. In *Ontario Bureau of the Archives Reports*, 1911–14

Upper Canada. "Report of the Select Committee on ... Certain Medals." Toronto: W.J. Coates, 1840

Upper Canada. "Seventh Report from Select Committe of House of Assembly on Grievances." 1835

Upper Canada. *Statutes of the Province of Upper Canada.* 1841

The Valley of the Six Nations: A Collection of Documents on the Indian Lands on the Grand River. Edited by C.M. Johnston. Toronto: University of Toronto Press, 1964

Van Creveld, Martin. *Supplying War: Logistics from Wallenstein to Patton.* New York: Cambridge Press, 1977

Vaughn, C.L. "The Bank of Upper Canada in Politics, 1817–1840." *Ontario History*, 60 (1968): 185–204

Verchères de Boucherville, Thomas. "The Chronicles of Thomas Verchères de Boucherville." in *War on the Detroit*. Edited by M.M. Quaife. Chicago: Lakeside: 1940, 3–178

Walden, Keith. "Isaac Brock: Man and Myth – A Study of the Militia Myth of the War of 1812 in Upper Canada, 1812–1912." MA thesis, Queen's University, 1971

Wallace, Malcolm. "Pioneers of the Scotch Settlement on the Shore of Lake St. Clair." *Ontario History*, 41 (1949): 173–200

Wallace, W.S. *The Periodical Literature of Upper Canada*. Canadian Historical Review reprint, 1931

War along the Niagara: Essays on the War of 1812 and Its Legacy. Edited by R. Arthur Bowler. Youngstown, New York: Old Fort Niagara Association, 1991

War on the Great Lakes: Essays Commemorating the 175th Anniversary of the Battle of Lake Erie. Edited by W.J. Welsh and D.C. Skaggs. Kent, Ohio: Kent State University Press, 1991

Watson, O.K. "Moraviantown." *Ontario History*, 28 (1932): 125–31

Webb, R.K. *Modern England from the Eighteenth Century to the Present*. Second edition. New York: Harper and Row, 1980

Weekes, William. "The War of 1812: Civil Authority and Martial Law in Upper Canada." *Ontario History*, 48 (1956): 147–62

Weld, Isaac. *Travels through the United States of North America and the Provinces of Upper & Lower Canada during the Years 1795, 1796 & 1797*. Fourth edition. 2 volumes. London: Stockdale, 1807

Williams, Jack. *Merritt: A Canadian before His Time*. St Catharines: Stonehouse Publications, 1985

Williams, Samuel. *Sketches of the War ... and Biographical Notices of Distinguished Military and Naval Commanders*. Rutland: Fay and Davison, 1815

Wilson, Allan. *The Clergy Reserves of Upper Canada*. Toronto: University of Toronto Press, 1968

Wilson, Bruce G. *The Enterprises of Robert Hamilton: A Study of Wealth and Influence in Early Upper Canada 1776–1812*. Ottawa: Carleton University Press, 1983

– "The Struggle for Wealth and Power at Fort Niagara, 1775–1783." *Ontario History* 68 (1976): 137–52

Winks, Robin W. *The Blacks in Canada: A History*. Montreal and Kingston: McGill-Queen's University Press, 1971

Wise, S.F., and R.G. Brown. *Canada Views the United States: Nineteenth-Century Political Attitudes*. Seattle: University of Washington Press, 1967

Wood, William. *The War with the United States*. Toronto: Glasgow Brook, 1920

Wyatt-Brown, Bertram. *Southern Honor: Ethics and Behavior in the Old South*. New York: Oxford University Press, 1982

Index